W9-BKG-375

The Newly Independent States of Eurasia

Handbook of Former Soviet Republics

Second Edition

by
Stephen K. Batalden
and
Sandra L. Batalden

ORYX
1997

WINGATE UNIVERSITY LIBRARY

Ethel K. Smith Library
Wingate University
Wingate, North Carolina 28174

In Honor Of
Christopher R. Stinson
Given By
John and Leslie Stinson

The rare Arabian oryx is believed to have inspired the myth of the unicorn. This desert antelope became virtually extinct in the early 1960s. At that time several groups of international conservationists arranged to have 9 animals sent to the Phoenix Zoo to be the nucleus of a captive breeding herd. Today the oryx population is over 1,000, and over 500 have been returned to the Middle East.

© 1997 by The Oryx Press
4041 North Central at Indian School Road
Phoenix, Arizona 85012-3397

Maps prepared by Thomas C. Brennan and Lisa Harner.

All rights reserved. No part of this publication may be reproduced or transmitted in any form or by any means, electronic or mechanical, including photocopying, recording, or by any information storage and retrieval system, without permission in writing from The Oryx Press.

Published simultaneously in Canada
Printed and bound in the United States of America

∞ The paper used in this publication meets the minimum requirements of the American National Standard for Information Sciences—Permanence of Paper for Printed Library Materials, ANSI Z39.48-1984.

Library of Congress Cataloging-in-Publication Data

Batalden, Stephen K.
    The newly independent states of Eurasia : handbook of former
Soviet republics / by Stephen K. Batalden and Sandra L. Batalden. —
2nd ed.
        p. cm.
    Includes bibliographical references and index.
    ISBN 0-89774-940-5 (pbk. : alk. paper)
    1. Former Soviet republics—Handbooks, manuals, etc.
I. Batalden, Sandra L. II. Title.
DK17.B34 1997   97-3893
947.086—dc21   CIP

To Peder and Karl

CONTENTS

LIST OF MAPS

PREFACE

Until its collapse in 1991, the Soviet Union was a world superpower, incorporating within its borders much of the landmass of Europe and Asia—modern Eurasia. Most observers of the Soviet state, conditioned to view it as a monolithic great power, have found it difficult to comprehend the rapid disintegration of this once mighty empire. Yet, all 15 former Soviet republics, responding to events in Eastern Europe and the abortive August 1991 coup d'état in Moscow, have established their independence. In asserting sovereignty, these newly independent states of Eurasia have become the legitimate successors to the Union of Soviet Socialist Republics (USSR).

For specialists, policy makers, and citizens alike, the formation of these independent states now requires a far greater understanding of the regional and ethnic diversity of Eurasia. In the era of the Cold War, regional and international events tended to be interpreted within the framework of a simple, bipolar view of the world—there was the Soviet Union along with its allies, and there was "the West." The breakup of the Soviet Union has undermined such a view, necessitating a reconsideration of the lands and peoples of that region. In this rethinking, the newly independent states of Eurasia must be understood in terms of their own historical, geopolitical, economic, and environmental significance, quite apart from their identification with the former Soviet Union. This handbook seeks to help in such rethinking, by addressing the regional and ethnic diversity of the Eurasian states while also examining elements of continuity that inevitably link these states with their Soviet past.

Continuity and Change

Distinct Histories and Cultures Two basic assumptions have guided the preparation of this handbook. The first, often obscured by both Soviet and Western Cold War rhetoric, is that despite centuries of tsarist and Soviet imperial domination, the non-Russian subject nations of the former USSR have not only managed to endure, but have preserved their unique histories and cultures. Russian (including Muscovite, Imperial, and Soviet) rule over its Eurasian empire dates from the fifteenth century, with most areas added between the sixteenth and nineteenth centuries. Yet many of the peoples who were drawn into that empire claim historical roots in a more distant past, well before the onset of Russian rule. Shortly after the attempted 1991 Moscow coup, one historian compared the failing Soviet Union to the surface of an aged and unserviceable linoleum floor: worn-out areas in the linoleum exposed the underlying and much older wooden floorboards (see Edward L. Keenan, "Rethinking the U.S.S.R., Now That It's Over," *New York Times*, 8 September 1991, E3). The first assumption of this handbook is that the histories and cultures of the various peoples of the former Soviet Union—Russian and non-Russian—are important in their own right. One of the central tasks of this volume is to present the histories of these diverse peoples—to uncover the wooden floorboards.

Enduring Soviet Legacy The second assumption of this handbook may appear, on the surface, to be in conflict with the first: this volume recognizes the ongoing significance of Soviet rule for Eurasia. Politically, many of the new states continue to operate with the legacy of Communist Party rule. Many former Communist Party leaders have continued to serve as state presidents, such as Eduard Shevardnadze of Georgia, Nursultan Nazarbaev of Kazakhstan, and Boris Yeltsin of Russia. Although they have abandoned formal Party affiliations, the reality is that, behind the rule of these leaders, Communist Party–appointed officialdom, or nomenklatura, has remained remarkably secure at virtually all levels of the new state bureaucracies. The efforts of conservative Belarusian political leadership in 1996 to reinforce old linkages with Russia are an especially dramatic example of the political significance of this continuing Soviet legacy.

In much of Central Asia and Transcaucasia, as well as in other European republics, the continuity in political leadership has likewise been accompanied by a retreat from an initial movement toward democratization. Aided by security police, oftentimes holdovers from the preceding regime, many of the newly independent states have sought to limit the influence of informal political groups.

The economic realities of post-Soviet life exemplify the tension between a newly secured independence and the continuing Soviet legacy. Since the publication of the first edition of this volume in 1993, all of the former Soviet republics have begun to circulate their own currencies. The so-called "ruble zone," a region that extended beyond the Russian Federation where in the early 1990s the Russian ruble continued to be a viable currency, has virtually ceased to exist. Similarly, although the international trade of the newly independent states was initially dominated by old commercial ties with Russia, the foreign trade figures of most of these states now show the percentage of commerce with Russia to have dropped dramatically. Still, the newly independent states continue to confront the Soviet legacy of centralized planning, whether this be in the complicated process of property de-nationalization, in the continued subsidization of large state-run enterprises, or in legislation controlling foreign investment. For example, in the old Soviet model, central economic planning encouraged such problematic agricultural practices as the development of a cotton monoculture in the republics of Central Asia. This centralized marketing and distribution system for cotton linked outlying republics to Moscow like spokes on a wheel. Despite the development of private business, agricultural cooperatives, freer markets, and independence from Moscow-centralized planning, the old Soviet infrastructure continues to function, as in the ongoing cotton monoculture of Central Asia that links, even if less forcefully, the economies of the non-Russian republics of Eurasia to the Russian Federation.

As in economic life, so also in environmental affairs, there are undeniable elements of continuity. The newly independent states have inherited serious environmental and ecological problems from the Soviet era. Simply put, environmental disasters such as the Chernobyl nuclear explosion near the Ukrainian-Belarusian border and the drying up of the Aral Sea in Central Asia have resulted from Soviet industrial and agricultural policies. The magnitude of these problems, however, defies solution at the level of any single state, for like the health problems they have caused, these larger ecological crises require regional, interstate co-operation (see Murray Feshbach and Alfred Friendly Jr., *Ecocide in the USSR,* New York: Basic Books, 1992).

Ironically, the breakup of the Soviet Union has tended to undermine the kinds of interrepublican efforts needed to address major health and environmental problems. In the case of the vanishing Aral Sea, any long-term solution requires cooperation between the states where the richest water resources are located (Kyrgyzstan and Tajikistan) and the states most heavily dependent upon those water resources (Uzbekistan, Turkmenistan, and Kazakhstan). Under the administration of the first and only Soviet minister of the environment (Nikolai Vorontsov, a research biologist sensitive to ecological problems) both short- and long-term plans were devised for solving interrepublican environmental issues, but these plans now await the inevitably slow development of interstate cooperation, without central planning and authority. The Soviet Union offered mechanisms, however undemocratic, for resolving interrepublican conflict.

The legacy of Soviet rule is also reflected in the structure of this volume. The book uses the republics that formerly constituted the Soviet Union—now the newly independent states of Eurasia—for the basic chapter structure. In using these old republican divisions, we recognize the contemporary importance of borders that, at the onset of Soviet rule, were often assigned arbitrarily. Often, these borders reflected lines of genuine national and cultural division, although sometimes, as in Central Asia, Soviet establishment of a republic's borders rewarded certain national and regional "winners," at the expense of other, often minority, interests. Such Soviet decision making, although now subject to reexamination, has nevertheless determined the course of political and national leadership.

The Baltic Republics For several reasons, the three Baltic republics—Lithuania, Latvia, and Estonia—have been excluded from the volume. These Baltic republics, even after the imposition of Russian imperial rule in the eighteenth century, drew more upon their traditional ties to a dominant German culture, and their history has not been an integral part of wider Russian, Eurasian patterns. Each has a legacy of independence in the interwar period before Soviet occupation, and each was annexed to the Soviet Union under secret terms of the Nazi-Soviet Pact of 1939. Despite heavy Russian migration into Latvia and Estonia after World War II, the Baltic republics remained significantly apart from the rest of Soviet society. The Baltic states also broke away from the USSR before its ultimate dissolution: by August 1991, four months prior to the demise of the Soviet Union, they had already established their independence. Finally, it is symbolic of their separateness that the Baltic states are the only former Soviet republics never to have joined the Commonwealth of Independent States (CIS), a loose confederation established in late December 1991 to coordinate interrepublican policies in the wake of the fall of the Soviet Union.

New Challenges from Ethnic Minorities The newly independent states of Eurasia, heirs to the system of Soviet republics, now face new and potent challenges to their own authority from ethnic groups dissatisfied with minority status. The violence in Chechnya (Checheniia), the conflict over the Trans-Dniester region in Moldova, the Armenian-Azerbaijan struggle over Nagorno-Karabakh, and the Abkhazian impasse in Georgia all demonstrate the destabilization that can arise when these old Soviet republican borders are challenged by minorities seeking revisionist ethnic justice. As in dismembered Yugoslavia, the forces of republican independence in Eurasia, when aided by political demagoguery and unmet ethnic concerns, can occasion enormous international violence and territorial conflict. This handbook seeks to foster understanding of such potential conflicts by examining the roots of national and republican independence in Eurasia alongside the enduring legacy of a Soviet past.

As recently as a decade ago, the reading public was largely unaware of the power of the internal forces at work in such disparate parts of the former Soviet world as Kazakhstan, Uzbekistan, Belarus, and Georgia. Today, foreign embassies are housed in these independent states, and the peoples of these lands command attention as much for their own rich history as for the products they now wish to introduce on the world market. This handbook, intended for a broad audience of scholars, policy makers, and informed citizens, builds upon two generations of Western scholarship on the ethnography and history of Russian and non-Russian peoples of the former Soviet Union to provide a basic reference guide to the lands and peoples of Eurasia.

Organization of This Volume

Parts The handbook is divided into four major parts: Part One for the Russian Federation, Part Two for the non-Russian republics in Europe, Part Three for Transcaucasia, and Part Four for Central Asia. Each part is introduced by a narrative section, a list of suggestions for additional reading, and a map of the region.

Chapters The Russian Federation, much larger in size and population than other parts of Eurasia, has been divided into two chapters—one on European Russia, the other on Asian Russia (Siberia and the Russian Far East). This division corresponds to the natural east-west divide created by the Ural mountain range. In addition to the two sections addressing the Russian Federation, there are three chapters dealing with the other European republics (Belarus, Moldova, and Ukraine), three chapters dealing with Transcaucasia (Armenia, Azerbaijan, and Georgia), and five chapters dealing with Central Asia (Kazakhstan, Kyrgyzstan, Tajikistan, Turkmenistan, and Uzbekistan). These chapter divisions correspond to 12 of the former 15 "union republics" of the USSR. As explained above, descriptions of the three Baltic states—Estonia, Latvia, and Lithuania—are not included in this volume.

Statistical Profiles Because this handbook is intended to serve as a general reference work, each chapter opens with a statistical profile of the featured republic, highlighting major demographic, governmental, educational, socioeconomic, and physical data. The first edition of this volume drew its statistical data largely from the 1989 Soviet census and related government documentation published in the former Soviet Union or abroad. However, because of the very substantial population migrations that have been occurring in and between the former Soviet republics, the 1989 census data is becoming outdated. In the case of the Central Asian republics, for example, the census statistics do not reflect the very substantial post-1989 outward migration of Slavs (Russians, Ukrainians, and Belarusians) from the area. To compensate for such rapid changes in demographic and socioeconomic statistics, this second edition has utilized the CIS demographic and socioeconomic data provided in the *Demograficheskii ezhegodnik 1995 (Demographic Yearbook 1995)*, published by the statistical offices of the Russian Federation. These CIS statistics have been augmented with data from the on-line "CIA World Factbook" and the 1996 edition of the *Europa World Yearbook*.

Description, History, and Contemporary Issues Following each chapter's statistical profile is a comprehensive, analytical discussion of the republic, divided into two sections. The first section—a history and description of the republic—includes subsections devoted to topography, ethnogenesis or the origins of the dominant ethnic group(s) of the republic, and the history of the territory, including its incorporation into the Russian Empire and its recent Soviet experience.

Alongside the republic's political history, there is a description of the major self-governed, or autonomous, regions within each republic. Twentieth-century Communist Party leadership is identified, as are the circumstances leading to declarations of sovereignty in the recent period.

The second section of each chapter narrative examines issues currently being faced by each newly independent state. This section builds on the prior narrative, but is structured in such a way as to allow readers to move directly to the consideration of contemporary issues. It examines a variety of topics, such as political and ethnic conflict, economic restructuring, environmental/ecological affairs, and cultural and intellectual developments. The contemporary issues section for each chapter has been completely rewritten for this second edition, reflecting the rapid changes underway in Eurasia.

Glossary and Index A glossary is provided at the end of the volume to explain terms that may be unfamiliar. A comprehensive index enables a reader to locate all references to a topic and is especially useful for finding information on issues that have affected several regions or states.

Spellings We have incorporated all of the major name changes of the post-Soviet period (e.g., St. Petersburg, not Leningrad; Nizhnii Novgorod, not Gorky; Semey, not Semipalatinsk). Often we have provided the old name in parentheses. Many of the cities of the non-Russian republics now bear a spelling different from that used during the Soviet period (Qŭqon, not Kokand; Almaty, not Alma-Ata). Such spelling changes reflect abandonment of Russified place names in non-Russian areas. We have tried to incorporate these spelling changes for all non-Russian names, using the transliteration employed by the National Geographic Society in its standardized map, "Russia and the Newly Independent Nations of the Former Soviet Union" (1993). In some cases the more familiar Russian transliteration is offered in parentheses. For Russian place names, we have followed a modified Library of Congress transliteration system, with the exception of cities commonly known by Anglicized spellings (e.g., Moscow).

Acknowledgments

As in the first edition, it is a pleasure to acknowledge the help of others in the preparation of this revised handbook. The second edition has benefitted greatly from the professional editorial expertise of Elizabeth Welsh. Dmitry Tartakovsky, a graduate assistant in the Arizona State University History Department, has contributed significantly to the revision of the statistical profile sections. His work adds to that of Jonathan Haring and Dylan Zoller, acknowledged in the first edition. We continue to benefit from the advice of other colleagues who have been generous in their evaluation of separate sections of the volume.

Sandra L. Batalden
Stephen K. Batalden
Skopje, Macedonia
February 1997

INTRODUCTORY REMARKS

Sergei A. Arutiunov

Many voices in the late 1960s and early 1970s had begun to predict the imminent and unavoidable collapse of the Soviet empire. Soviet dissidents, some open and outspoken, others silent and hidden, were sure this collapse would come quite soon. Still, it caught most people in the West—and not only in the West—surprisingly unprepared.

How well I recall those compelling "Moscow kitchen sessions" of the 1970s and early 1980s, when we discussed within a close circle of friends and colleagues possible scenarios for such a collapse. Our projections concerning the basic events and their sequence proved amazingly accurate, but we were utterly wrong on the timing. We predicted that a "Gorbachev"—one of our generation, born in the early 1930s—would become general secretary of the Communist Party around 1992. (Gorbachev himself was little known in the 1970s, and unforeseen as the one likely to pull the trigger leading to collapse.) In such a scenario, conflicts would develop in the late 1990s—we thought a crisis in the Farghona Valley in Central Asia would precede the Karabakh conflict in Transcaucasia. The secession of the Baltic republics would be followed by the break-up of the entire Kremlin axis in the early 2000s.

In fact, all this happened at least 10 years earlier than anticipated, even by those inside the system who were better informed about the latent volcanic activity present in Soviet society. Our Western colleagues, meanwhile, seemed to think that the stagnation of the Soviet imperial system would simply continue for an indeterminate period of time.

Soviet anthropologists by the late 1950s and early 1960s already had recognized the growing interethnic tensions in their society. These tensions, while well known to specialists, were never allowed to be published openly. Our "top-secret" classified reports submitted to the Communist Party Central Committee after each season's fieldwork were received grudgingly. We were often told from the top that we exaggerated the miserable conditions of the minorities of the far north, and so on. It was astonishing to what extent wishful thinking had become the basic modus operandi among the Party's top brass during the Brezhnev era (1964–82).

Perhaps only Iurii Andropov (Communist Party general secretary, 1982–84) really knew and understood the true scale of the threat to the Soviet establishment. His reign was too short, however, and his methods, oriented toward police repression, could not alter the actual course of events. Nevertheless, Andropov appears to have been very instrumental—perhaps unwillingly and unknowingly—in the education of Mikhail Gorbachev, instructing him in dealing with arch-conservative Brezhnevites.

One of the hallmarks of official Communist ideology was the notion of a new, historic, "*Soviet* people." According to such ideology, all nations of the USSR would tend toward "mutual rapprochement" and eventual merger. Professional anthropologists in the Soviet Union never took seriously this wishful thinking. It was unacceptable, however, to emphasize openly the differences between the constituent nations of the USSR—differences that in Central Asia, for example, seem actually to have been created deliberately by the Soviet regime to supplant the initial, rather undifferentiated ethnic situation. These ethnic differences, the development of which was powerfully triggered by official "nation building" (*natsionalnoe stroitelstvo*) of the 1920s and 1930s, continued to grow. There had been, of course, a short period in the 1920s of "proletarian internationalism," a movement quite naturally proletarian since those who possessed nothing had little to quarrel about. Eventually, after World War II, the standard of living improved, especially during the years of Nikita Khrushchev (Communist Party general secretary, 1953–64). But this improvement occurred with a very different tempo in each region—rapidly in Georgia, Armenia, and the Baltic republics, and very slowly in Central Asia. In fact, this differentiation yielded not a mutual rapprochement of Soviet nations but, on the contrary, a process of mutual alienation and separation.

Soviet statistics and popular literature, based upon the same wishful thinking, tended to exaggerate the level of literacy among the peoples of the far north and of Central Asia. Official propaganda grossly overstated the proficiency and use of Russian as a second language. And, it fabricated the demise of religious practices and the spread of atheism. I must confess that the authentic preservation, despite terrible persecution, of shamanistic and animistic "pagan" traditions, not only among people of Siberia but also in the middle Volga basin, was never fully understood even by those anthropologists who, facing incredible difficulties, tried to study such phenomena professionally. Similarly, they failed to comprehend the practical functioning of the norms of *adat* (customary law) and *sharia* (Islamic law) among peoples of Central Asia and the Caucasus.

Thus, it is not surprising that for most people outside the USSR, the Soviet Union was basically "Russia." The cultural and social differences between the constituent nations of that union seemed to be obsolete, irrelevant, and largely nonexistent. Clearly, that misperception yielded serious shortcomings in Western understanding and public opinion.

Today, more than ever, people in America and Europe need to overcome such misperceptions. Increasingly they need to deal not with some loosely defined "Soviet Russia," or Moscow, but directly with Ukrainians, Georgians, Uzbeks, and Kyrgyz—also perhaps very soon with Tatars, Iakuts, Tuvinians, and Chechens. In such a context, this important, insightful work of the Bataldens, filled with accurate, useful, and up-to-date information, will prove particularly valuable.

These remarks were written in July 1993 as a foreword to the first edition. Arutiunov is Chair of the Department of Caucasian Studies, Institute of Ethnology and Anthropology (Moscow), and a Corresponding Member of the Russian Academy of Sciences.

PART ONE

THE RUSSIAN FEDERATION

INTRODUCTION

The Russian Federation, formerly the Russian Soviet Federated Socialist Republic (RSFSR) of the Union of Soviet Socialist Republics (USSR), is today the world's largest country. Even after declaring sovereignty and separating from the other 14 union republics with which it was previously joined, the Russian Federation remains almost twice the size of the United States. The new Russia continues to be a country of rich natural resources and great ethnic diversity. Originally the home of the Great Russians, an East Slavic people who dwelt in the wintry and forested lands around Moscow, Russia now encompasses a landmass covering more than 6.5 million square miles, or approximately three-fourths of the old Soviet Union. Russia's immense territory was accumulated over many centuries, first by a series of autocratic, often despotic, tsars, and later by Communist Party rulers. It continues to be the home of dozens of distinct ethnic groups that speak non-Russian languages and observe varied cultural traditions. The territory comprised by the Russian Federation consists of two major regions that are separated by the Ural Mountains: the lands of western or European Russia, and the lands of eastern or Asiatic Russia. Part One has been subdivided to reflect this natural geographic division of Russia.

In 1991, the RSFSR declared its independence from the Soviet Union, renaming itself the Russian Federation *(Rossiiskaia Federatsiia)*. Although it is commonly called simply "Russia," the official term, "Russian Federation," more accurately reflects the regional and ethnic diversity of this vast Eurasian country. The Russian Federation, like the United States, is a multi-ethnic country. Unlike the United States, where only Native Americans can claim indigenous territorial holdings, the constituent ethnic groups of the Russian Federation are invariably identified with ancient ethnic homelands. While ethnic Russian population has settled in most of the non-Russian homelands of

the country, even in the far reaches of Siberia, it is the sense of ancient territorial rights that today occasionally gives rise to conflict between Russian and non-Russian populations. The issue of ethnic diversity is critical for understanding not only the Russian Federation, but also the other newly independent states of Eurasia. Today, the minority status of ethnic Russians living outside Russia in the so-called "near abroad" remains a sensitive issue within the Russian Federation.

The Russian Federation is a constitutional democracy. Initially functioning under the old RSFSR constitution after declaring independence from the USSR, the Russian Federation adopted by referendum in December 1993 a new constitution providing for a division of powers. While it gives broad executive privileges to an elected president, the constitution also provides for an independent judiciary and two legislative chambers—the Russian Duma (or Parliament), and the Federation Council, composed of representatives from various regions and republics within the federation. For the first time since the beginning of Soviet rule, Russia has also reintroduced trial by jury.

The transition from Soviet to Russian rule has not been easy for the new Russian Federation. Although Russia declared its sovereignty in 1990, the collapse of the Soviet Union came more rapidly than anticipated, hastened in August 1991 by an attempted coup d'état directed against Soviet president Mikhail Gorbachev. Although he survived the coup, those who had fashioned his overthrow helped to discredit the Soviet system and, along with it, Gorbachev, as the architect of *perestroika* (see Glossary). The foremost beneficiary of this collapse was Boris Yeltsin, who had just been elected president of the Russian Soviet republic. A former Communist Party leader from the Ural region of Sverdlovsk (now Ekaterinburg), Yeltsin broke decisively with Mikhail Gorbachev during 1990 and 1991. By focusing his leadership upon the Russian republic, and not on the transformation of old Soviet institutions, Yeltsin effectively bridged the collapse of Soviet authority and the beginnings of the newly independent Russian Federation. The two chapters that follow document the history and contemporary issues confronting this new Russian Federation.

Bibliography

Anderson, John. *Religion, State and Politics in the Soviet Union and Successor States, 1953–1993.* New York: Cambridge University Press, 1994.

Batalden, Stephen K., ed. *Seeking God: The Recovery of Religious Identity in Orthodox Russia, Ukraine, and Georgia.* DeKalb: Northern Illinois University Press, 1993.

Bobrick, Benson. *East of the Sun: The Epic Conquest and Tragic History of Siberia.* New York: Poseidon Press, 1992.

Bradshaw, Michael J., ed. *The Soviet Union: A New Regional Geography?* London: Belhaven Press, 1991.

Bremmer, Ian, and Ray Taras, eds. *Nations and Politics in the Soviet Successor States.* New York: Cambridge University Press, 1993.

Bugajski, Janusz. *Ethnic Politics in Eastern Europe: A Guide to Nationality Policies, Organizations and Parties.* Armonk, NY: M.E. Sharpe, 1994.

Cambridge Encyclopedia of Russia and the Former Soviet Union. Cambridge, England: Cambridge University Press, 1993.

Carrère d'Encausse, Hélène. *The End of the Soviet Empire: The Triumph of the Nations.* New York: Basic Books, 1993.

Chan, Adrian. *Teaching About the Soviet Successor States: A Teacher's Guide and Resource for History and Social Science.* Stanford: American Association for the Advancement of Slavic Studies, 1993.

Collins, David Norman. *Siberia and the Soviet Far East.* Oxford, England: Clio Press, 1991.

Conquest, Robert, ed. *The Last Empire: Nationality and the Soviet Future.* Stanford: Hoover Institution Press, 1986.

Current Digest of the Post-Soviet Press. Columbus, Ohio: Current Digest of the Post-Soviet Press. Published weekly since 1949.

Dewdney, J. C. *USSR in Maps.* New York: Holmes & Meier Publishers, Inc., 1982.

Diuk, Nadia, and Adrian Karatnycky. *The Hidden Nations: The People Challenge the Soviet Union.* New York: William Morrow and Company, Inc., 1990.

Ellis, Jane. *The Russian Orthodox Church: A Contemporary History.* Bloomington: Indiana University Press, 1986.

Fainsod, Merle. *How Russia Is Ruled.* Cambridge: Harvard University Press, 1953. (See also the edition revised by Jerry F. Hough, *How the Soviet Union Is Governed,* Harvard University Press, 1979.)

Feshbach, Murray, and Alfred Friendly Jr. *Ecocide in the USSR: Health and Nature under Siege.* New York: Basic Books, 1992.

Forsyth, James. *A History of the Peoples of Siberia: Russia's North Asian Colony, 1581–1990.* Cambridge, England: Cambridge University Press, 1992.

Hajda, Lubomyr, and Mark Beissinger, eds. *The Nationalities Factor in Soviet Politics and Society.* Boulder, CO: Westview Press, 1990.

Horak, Stephan M., ed. *Guide to the Study of the Soviet Nationalities: Non-Russian Peoples of the USSR.* Littleton, CO: Libraries Unlimited, Inc., 1982.

Horak, Stephen M. *Russia, the USSR, and Eastern Europe: A Bibliographic Guide to English Language Publications, 1981–85.* Littleton, CO: Libraries Unlimited, 1987.

Hosking, Geoffrey. *The Awakening of the Soviet Union.* Cambridge: Harvard University Press, 1990.

Kaiser, Robert J. *The Geography of Nationalism in Russia and the USSR.* Princeton: Princeton University Press, 1994.

Katz, Zev, ed. *Handbook of Major Soviet Nationalities.* New York: The Free Press, 1975.

Kort, Michael. *Russia.* New York: Facts on File, 1995.

Lincoln, W. Bruce. *The Conquest of a Continent: Siberia and the Russians.* New York, Random House, 1994.

Lydolph, Paul E. *Geography of the USSR.* 5th ed. Elkhart Lake, WI: Misty Valley Publishing, 1990.

Mandelstam Balzer, Margerie, ed. *Shamanism: Soviet Studies of Traditional Religion in Siberia and Central Asia.* Armonk, NY: M.E. Sharpe, 1990.

Marks, Steven G. *Road to Power: The Trans-Siberian Railroad and the Colonization of Asian Russia, 1850–1917.* Ithaca, NY: Cornell University Press, 1991.

Matlock, Jack E. Jr. *Autopsy of an Empire: The American Ambassador's Account of the Collapse of the Soviet Union.* New York: Random House, 1996.

Miller-Gulland, Robin, with Nikolai Dejevsky. *Atlas of Russia and the Soviet Union.* Oxford, England: Phaidon, 1989.

Modern Encyclopedia of Russian and Soviet History. 53 vols. Gulf Breeze, FL: Academic International Press, 1975–1990.

Motyl, Alexander J. *The Post-Soviet Nations: Perspectives on the Demise of the USSR.* New York: Columbia University Press, 1995.

Nahaylo, Bohdan, and Victor Swoboda. *Soviet Disunion: A History of the Nationalities Problem in the USSR.* New York: The Free Press, 1990.

Nationalities Papers, 1972–. Quarterly. Abingdon, UK: Carfax Publishing Co.

RFE/RL [Radio Free Europe/Radio Liberty] *Research Report.* Munich: Board of Foreign Broadcasting. *RFE/RL Research Report* was formerly published under the title, *Report on the USSR* (1989–91), and prior to 1989 under the title, *Radio Liberty Research Bulletin Weekly.* See also *Transition.*

Riasanovsky, Nicholas V. *A History of Russia.* 5th ed. New York: Oxford University Press, 1993.

Rorlich, Azade-Ayse. *The Volga Tatars: A Profile in National Resilience.* Stanford: Hoover Institution Press, 1986.

Shabad, Theodore. *Geography of the USSR: A Regional Survey.* New York: Columbia University Press, 1951.

Slezkine, Yuri. *Arctic Mirrors: Russia and the Small Peoples of the North.* Ithaca: Cornell University Press, 1994.

Smith, Graham, ed. *The Nationalities Question in the Soviet Union.* New York: Longman, 1991.

Solzhenitsyn, Aleksandr. *The Gulag Archipelago.* 3 vols. New York: Harper & Row, 1976.

———. *The Russian Question: At the End of the Twentieth Century.* New York: Pantheon, 1994.

Stewart, John Massey, ed. *The Soviet Environment: Problems, Policies, and Politics.* Cambridge, England: Cambridge University Press, 1992.

Thompson, Anthony, ed. *Russia/U.S.S.R.: A Selective Annotated Bibliography of Books in English.* Santa Barbara: Clio Press, 1979.

Transition: Events and Issues in the Former Soviet Union and East-Central and Southeastern Europe, 1995–. Prague: Open Media Research Institute, 1995. This biweekly journal continues the coverage of *RFE/RL Research Report.*

Vaillant, Janet, and John Richards. *From Russia to USSR and Beyond: A Narrative and Documentary History.* New York: Longman, 1993. Distributed by Addison Wesley.

Vakhtin, Nikolai B. *Native Peoples of the Russian Far North.* London: Minority Rights Group, 1992.

Wixman, Ronald. *The Peoples of the USSR: An Ethnographic Handbook.* Armonk, NY: M.E. Sharpe, 1984.

Wolfson, Ze'ev. *The Geography of Survival: Ecology in the Post-Soviet Era.* Armonk, NY: M.E. Sharpe, 1994.

Wood, Alan, and R. A. French, eds. *The Development of Siberia: People and Resources.* London: Macmillan, in association with the School of Slavonic and East European Studies, University of London, 1989.

Wood, Alan, ed. *The History of Siberia: From Russian Conquest to Revolution.* London: Routledge, 1991.

Russian Federation

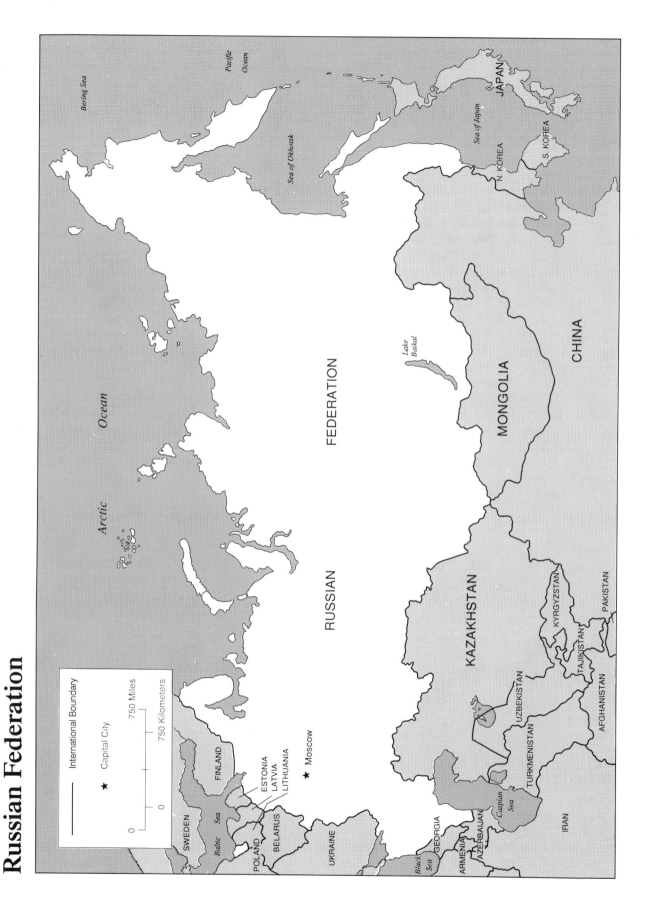

THE RUSSIAN FEDERATION

Statistical Profile

Demography

Population: 148,306,000

Ethnic population (1989 census)

Russian	81.5%
Tatar	3.8%
Ukrainian	3.0%
Chuvash	1.2%
Bashkort	0.9%
Belarusian	0.8%
Mordvinian	0.7%
Chechen	0.6%
German	0.6%
Udmurt	0.5%
Mari	0.4%
Kazakh	0.4%
Avar	0.4%
Jewish	0.4%
Armenian	0.4%
Buriat	0.3%
Ossetian	0.3%
Kabard	0.3%
Dargin	0.2%
Komi	0.2%
Azerbaijani	0.2%
Kumyk	0.2%
Lezghin	0.2%
Ingush	0.1%
Tuvinian	0.1%
Moldovan	0.1%
Kalmyk	0.1%
Roma	0.1%
Karachai	0.1%
Komi-Permiak	0.1%
Karelian	0.1%
Adygei	0.1%
Korean	0.1%
Lak	0.1%
Polish	0.1%
Other	1.1%

Major urban centers and populations

Moscow	8,746,700
St. Petersburg	4,436,700
Novosibirsk	1,441,900
Nizhnii Novgorod (Gorky)	1,440,600
Ekaterinburg (Sverdlovsk)	1,370,700
Samara (Kuibyshev)	1,239,200
Omsk	1,168,600
Cheliabinsk	1,143,000
Kazan	1,104,000
Perm	1,098,600
Ufa	1,097,200
Rostov na Donu	1,027,100
Volgograd (Stalingrad)	1,006,100
Krasnoiarsk	925,000
Saratov	909,300
Voronezh	902,200
Togliatti	665,700
Simbirsk (Ulianovsk)	656,400
Izhevsk	650,700
Vladivostok	647,800
Irkutsk	637,000
Iaroslavl	636,900
Krasnodar	634,500
Khabarovsk	614,600
Barnaul	606,200
Novokuznetsk	600,200
Orenburg	556,500
Penza	552,300
Tula	541,400
Riazan	528,500
Kemerovo	520,600
Naberezhnye Chelny	514,400
Astrakhan	512,200
Tomsk	504,700

Historic religious traditions

Christianity	88.8%
Islam	7.3%

Languages: Russian, many others

Population by age

Age	Total	Males	Females
0–14	22%	11.2%	10.8%
15–64	66%	32.8%	33.2%
65 and over	12%	3.6%	8.4%

Male/Female ratio: 47.6% male/52.4% female

Rural/Urban population
27.0% rural/73.0% urban

Annual population growth rate: 0.0%

Population density: 22.5 persons per sq mi

Government

Official name
Rossiiskaia Federatsiia (Russian Federation)

Capital: Moscow

Date of sovereignty declaration: 11 June 1990

Date of independence declaration
24 August 1991

Voting age: 18

Internal republics	Capitals
Republic of Adygeia	Maikop
Republic of Altai	Gorno-Altaisk
Republic of Bashkortostan	Ufa
Republic of Buriatiia	Ulan-Ude
Republic of Checheniia (Chechnya)	Groznyi
Republic of Chuvashiia	Cheboksary
Republic of Dagestan	Makhachkala
Republic of Ingushetiia	Nazran
Republic of Kabardino-Balkariia	Nalchik
Republic of Kalmykiia	Elista
Republic of Karachai-Cherkessiia	Cherkessk
Republic of Kareliia	Petrozavodsk
Republic of Khakassiia	Abakan
Republic of Komi	Syktyvkar
Republic of Marii-El	Ioshkar Ola
Republic of Mordviniia	Saransk
Republic of North Ossetiia	Vladikavkaz
Sakha (Iakut) Republic	Iakutsk
Republic of Tatarstan	Kazan
Republic of Tuva	Kyzyl
Republic of Udmurtiia	Izhevsk

Education

Literacy (age 15 and over who can read and write)

total population	98%
male	100%
female	97%

Level of education for persons over 15

completed higher education	11.3%
completed secondary education	48.3%
incomplete secondary education	21.0%

Number of higher education institutions: 514

Higher education enrollment: 4,587,000 students

Selected institutions of higher education (and enrollment)

Moscow

Polytechnic Institute	43,000
Timiriazev Academy of Agriculture	31,000
Commercial Institute	30,000
Lomonosov State University	28,000
State Open University	22,000
Institute of Railway Engineers	16,500
Bauman State Technical Institute	15,000
Plekhanov Institute of National Economy	15,000
Technical University of Communication and Informatics	14,000
Pirogov State Medical Institute	7,000
Russian Peoples' Friendship University	6,700
State Institute of International Relations	3,000
Architectural Institute	2,000
State Institute of Cinematography	1,600
Tchaikovsky State Music Conservatory	900

St. Petersburg

State University	16,600
State Technical University	16,000
University of Economics and Finance	12,000
Electrical Engineering Institute	10,000
Civil Engineering Institute	10,000
Agricultural Institute	10,000
Forestry Academy	9,000
Repin Institute of Painting, Sculpture, and Architecture	1,400
Rimskii-Korsakov State Music Conservatory	1,000
Orthodox Theological Academy and Seminary	600

Arkhangelsk

Kuibyshev Forestry Technical Institute	5,500

Barnaul

Altai Agricultural Institute	7,000
State University	6,000

Cheliabinsk

Institute of Agricultural Mechanization and Electrification	4,500
State University	4,100

Cheboksary

Chuvash State University	10,600

Ekaterinburg (Sverdlovsk)

Law Institute	8,500
Urals Electromechanical Institute of Railway Engineering	7,500
Institute of National Economy	7,500
Gorkii State University of the Urals	7,000
Urals Forestry Technical Institute	6,400
Vakhrushev Mining Institute	6,000

Elista

Kalmyk State University	5,000

Groznyi

Petroleum Institute	6,400
Chechen State University	5,600

Iakutsk

State University	8,700

Iaroslavl
State University 4,000

Ioshkar Ola
Mari State University 3,600

Irkutsk
State Technical University 13,000
State University 7,000

Ivanovo
State University 5,000

Izhevsk
Udmurt State University 11,000

Kaliningrad
Technical Institute for the Fishing Industry
and Economics 7,300
State University 6,000

Kazan
State University 7,500
Civil Engineering Institute 6,200

Kemerovo
State University 6,500

Khabarovsk
Institute of Railway Engineers 7,000

Krasnodar
Kuban State University 10,500

Makhachkala
Dagestan State University 9,000

Nalchik
Kabardino-Balkariia State University 9,000

Nizhnii Novgorod
State Technical University 12,300
Lobachevskii State University 9,500

Novosibirsk
State Technical University 11,900
State University 3,700

Omsk
State Technical University 6,200
Institute of Railway Engineers 5,500
State University 3,650

Orenburg
Polytechnic Institute 5,700

Perm
State Technical University 12,000

Petrozavodsk
State University 6,100

Rostov na Donu
State University 9,600
Institute of National Economy 6,000

Samara
Aviation Institute 9,000
Agricultural Institute 7,900

Saransk
Ogarev Mordvinian State University 16,600

Saratov
State Technical University 13,000
Chernyshevskii State University 9,800

Syktyvkar
State University 3,000

Tiumen
State University 6,000

Tomsk
Polytechnic University 12,000
State University 10,000
Civil Engineering Institute 6,600

Ufa
Bashkort State University 8,300

Ulan-Ude
Buriat Agricultural Institute 5,000

Vladikavkaz
North Ossetian Khetagurov State University 7,600
North Caucasian State University of
Technology 5,000

Vladivostok
Far Eastern State University 10,000
Far Eastern State Technical University 8,500

Volgograd
Polytechnic Institute 11,500
Civil Engineering Institute 7,300
State University 6,000

Voronezh
State University 12,000
Technical Institute 7,700
Forestry Institute 6,000

Socioeconomic Indicators

Annual birth rate: 9.5 births/1,000 population

Fertility rate: 1.8 children/woman

Infant mortality: 18.6 deaths/1,000 live births

Average life expectancy
62.2 years (males 58.9, females 65.1)

Annual death rate: 15.7 deaths/1,000 population

Average family size: 3.2

Annual consumption of electrical energy
5,800 kWh/person

Hospital beds per 10,000 persons: 137.5

Physical Features

Area: 6,592,812 sq mi

Land use

forests	45%
cultivated	8%
pasture	4%

Highest elevation: 18,510 ft (Mt. Elbrus)

Economic Production

Estimated per capita GNP: $2,650 (1994)

Agricultural output

potatoes, sugar beets, grain, flax, tobacco, dairy products, livestock, vegetables, fruits

Natural resources

oil and natural gas, coal, gold, tin, copper, iron, mica, lead, manganese, diamonds, rock salt, asbestos, graphite, aluminum, uranium, timber

Industrial output

energy production, machinery, petroleum, metallurgy, forest products, motor vehicles, aerospace industry, chemicals, ship building, rail transportation equipment, construction building and trades, electronics and communications

Currency: Russian ruble, 1 ruble = 100 kopeks

Communications

Length of rail lines: 53,100 mi

Length of highways: 342,800 mi

Pipelines

crude oil	30,000 mi
natural gas	87,500 mi

Telephones: 162.8 per 1,000 persons

Sources *Narodnoe khoziaistvo SSSR v 1990g.* (Moscow, 1991); *Naselenie SSSR* (Moscow, 1989); Matthew J. Sagers, "News Notes: Iron and Steel," *Soviet Geography* 30 (May 1989): 397–434; Lee Schwartz, "USSR Nationality Redistribution by Republic, 1979–1989: From Published Results of the 1989 All-Union Census," *Soviet Geography* 32 (April 1991): 209–48; *World of Learning,* 46th ed. (London, 1996); "Russia . . ." (National Geographic Society Map, 1993); *Europa World Yearbook, 1996* (London, 1996); *Demograficheskii ezhegodnik 1995* (Moscow, 1995); *Demograficheskii ezhegodnik rossiiskoi federatsii, 1993* (Moscow, 1994); "CIA World Factbook, 1995" (http://www.odci.gov/cia/publications/95fact/rs.html).

THE RUSSIAN FEDERATION: EUROPEAN RUSSIA

History and Description

Physical Description

Borders Despite the Eurasian character of Russian civilization, the center of Russian cultural and political life has always been in Europe. European Russia, the eastern half of the European continent, is bordered on the north by the Arctic Ocean; more precisely, by three seas of the Arctic—the Kara, the Barents, and the White. At its northwesternmost corner, the Russian boundary touches Norway and then traces southward along the Finnish-Russian frontier to the Gulf of Finland at the extreme eastern edge of the Baltic Sea. The Russian border continues southward from the Baltic along the frontiers of Estonia, Latvia, Belarus, and Ukraine, all former republics of the Soviet Union. Southeast of Ukraine, Russian lands encompass the eastern shoreline of the Sea of Azov and the Black Sea. Approaching Transcaucasia, European Russia includes the northern slopes of the Caucasus Mountains. The Caucasus range provides a formidable natural barrier between Russia and the former Soviet republics of Georgia and Azerbaijan to the south. From the Caucasian boundary with Azerbaijan, Russian lands extend north along the western shore of the Caspian Sea as far as the territory of the newly independent state of Kazakhstan, another former Soviet republic. The Kazakh-Russian boundary then follows a crooked path from the Caspian Sea toward the Ural Mountains. The Urals, as they stretch northward to the Arctic Ocean, form a geographical divide between European Russia to the west and Asian Russia to the east.

A geographically separate area that is also part of the Russian Federation is Kaliningrad, located along the Baltic Sea between Poland and Lithuania. Kaliningrad (formerly part of East Prussia) is primarily an agricultural area, similar in size to Connecticut. Its capital, also called Kaliningrad, is a naval port with fishing and shipbuilding industries.

Topography European Russia is essentially a lowland area dominated by the East European Plain, occasionally referred to as the Russian Plain. Nowhere on this plain does the topography reach any significant altitude, although the vast territory is distinguished by a number of upland regions. The most important of these is the area beginning near the Belarusian-Russian border. Known as the Valdai Hills, this area gives rise to such important Russian rivers as the Volga, the Dnieper, and the Western Dvina. Aside from a series of uplands separating river valleys in the southern part of the East European Plain, Russian lands increase in altitude only as they approach the country's mountainous borders in the south and the Ural Mountains to the east.

Vegetation and Soil Types The lands of European Russia are made up of seven basic vegetation and soil zones running in more-or-less horizontal bands across the width of the country. In the far north, the arctic tundra prevails, a landscape in which extremes of cold create an inhospitable soil type known as permafrost, although moss, lichen, and berries can be found there (see page 29 for a more complete description of arctic tundra). South of the tundra lies the vast coniferous forest zone, the taiga. A landscape most often thought of as "Russian," the taiga's extensive pine and birch forests at one time covered almost all historic Russian lands. A transitional zone of mixed forest called the wooded steppe leads to the black earth *(chernozem)* area that supports much of European Russia's agricultural output. This zone, composed of rich, dark soil, is

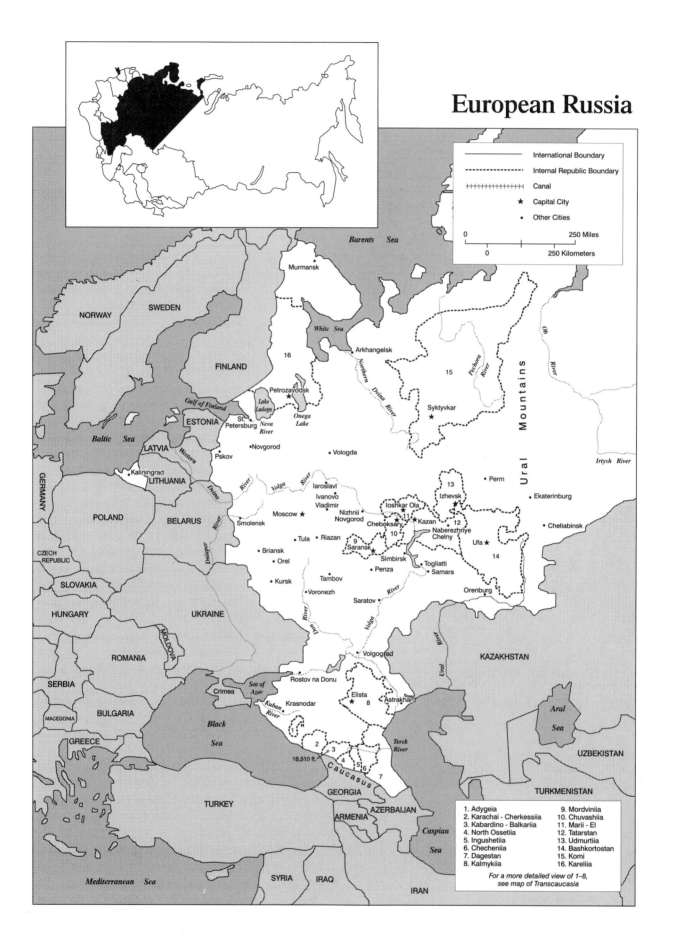

European Russia

International Boundary
Internal Republic Boundary
Canal
★ Capital City
• Other Cities

0   250 Miles
0   250 Kilometers

Barents Sea

Murmansk

White Sea

NORWAY
SWEDEN
FINLAND

16

Arkhangelsk

15

Pechora River

Ural Mountains

Ob River

Petrozavodsk ★

Lake Ladoga
Onega Lake

Northern Dvina River

Syktyvkar ★

Irtysh River

Gulf of Finland
ESTONIA
St. Petersburg
Neva River

Novgorod •

• Vologda

Baltic Sea

LATVIA
Western Dvina River
Pskov •

Kaliningrad •
LITHUANIA

GERMANY

POLAND

BELARUS

Dnieper River

Smolensk •

• Perm

13
Izhevsk ★
• Ekaterinburg

• Cheliabinsk

Ioshkar Ola ★
Kazan ★
11
12
Naberezhnye Chelny
Ufa ★

14

Volga River
Iaroslavl
Ivanovo
Vladimir
Nizhnii Novgorod
Cheboksary ★
10

Moscow ★

• Tula   • Riazan
9
Saransk ★
Simbirsk •
• Togliatti
• Samara

CZECH REPUBLIC
SLOVAKIA
HUNGARY

• Briansk
• Orel

• Kursk

Tambov •

• Penza

UKRAINE

• Voronezh

Saratov •

Volga River

Orenburg •

Don River

KAZAKHSTAN

ROMANIA
MOLDOVA

Ural River

SERBIA
BULGARIA
MACEDONIA

Volgograd •

Rostov na Donu •

Sea of Azov
Crimea

Krasnodar •
Kuban River

Elista ★
8
Astrakhan •

Terek River

Aral Sea

GREECE

Black Sea

2
3
18,510 ft.
4
5
6
Caucasus
7

UZBEKISTAN

Caspian Sea

TURKEY

GEORGIA

AZERBAIJAN

ARMENIA

TURKMENISTAN

Mediterranean Sea

SYRIA   IRAQ

IRAN

1. Adygeia
2. Karachai - Cherkessiia
3. Kabardino - Balkariia
4. North Ossetiia
5. Ingushetiia
6. Checheniia
7. Dagestan
8. Kalmykiia

9. Mordviniia
10. Chuvashiia
11. Marii - El
12. Tatarstan
13. Udmurtiia
14. Bashkortostan
15. Komi
16. Kareliia

*For a more detailed view of 1–8,
see map of Transcaucasia*

the true steppe, lands once thickly covered by grasses but now almost entirely under cultivation. The progressively drier climate of the south eventually becomes the semi-desert north of the Caspian Sea. A true desert zone can be found in Central Asian lands located beyond the borders of European Russia. Finally, a mountainous zone exists along the northern slopes of the Caucasus in the south.

Rivers The river systems of European Russia have long been essential to the economic and political development of the Russian state. The early availability of short portages between rivers led to the construction of canals, and eventually to a network of water passages that linked the lowland areas of historic Russia—from the northern waters of the Baltic and Arctic seas to the shores of the Caspian and Black seas far to the south. The Volga River, celebrated in Russian music and literature, may be the best-known waterway in this network, but because the Volga empties into the landlocked Caspian Sea, its importance would be diminished without the canals that link it to internationally accessible waterways. Other major Russian rivers draining into the somewhat salty Caspian, the world's largest inland sea, are the Ural and the Terek rivers. In the south of Russia, the Don and Kuban rivers feed into the Sea of Azov and thence into the Black Sea. In northern European Russia, the Neva and the Western Dvina rivers empty into the Baltic Sea, while the Northern Dvina and the Pechora rivers drain into the Arctic. In northwestern Russia, especially in formerly glaciated areas, there are many freshwater lakes, the largest being Lake Ladoga near St. Petersburg, and Onega Lake to the northeast of Ladoga.

Climate The climate of European Russian is clearly continental and, therefore, subject to extremes of heat and cold. Although located far from any oceans, the vast and very open stretches of the East European Plain receive a limited flow of warm air from the Atlantic via the Baltic Sea, serving to balance the frigid polar air masses that also visit the area. Rainfall averages are greatest in the more westerly parts of European Russia, gradually decreasing to the east and south.

Cities Although it has become a land of large cities, two metropolitan areas overshadow all other urban centers in European Russia. Moscow (approximately nine million residents) and St. Petersburg (over five million) dwarf all of the country's remaining cities. Many other urban centers of European Russia reflect historic administrative and economic regions. Associated with the industrialized area around Moscow are the nearby cities of Iaroslavl, Ivanovo, Vladimir, Tula, Smolensk, and Briansk. To the south of this area, the central black earth region accommodates the large cities of Orel, Tambov, Voronezh, and Kursk. European Russia's northern cities of Murmansk, Vologda, and Arkhangelsk, and its historic centers of Novgorod, St. Petersburg, and Pskov have all become industrialized in the modern period. Nizhnii Novgorod (Gorky), Kazan, Saratov, Samara (Kuibyshev), Volgograd, and Astrakhan are some of the large cities along the Volga. The metropolitan center of Rostov na Donu (Rostov on the Don) in the south rests on the Don River, while Ekaterinburg (Sverdlovsk) and Cheliabinsk are mining centers located in the Urals. Although the Volga cities are among the oldest of historic Russia, the large industrial cities on the Don and in the Urals now approximate in size these early river centers.

Agriculture Apart from the black earth area, agricultural activity is not ideally suited to the lands of European Russia. Much of the region is covered by forests and swamps. The fact that most of its landmass is located at a very northerly latitude (north of the Canada–United States border) in an area subject to severe weather extremes has resulted in just a small percentage of the land being truly arable. The area most suitable for planting lies between the inhospitable cold of the north and the arid heat of the south. The best arable land is found in the Volga region, the northern part of the Caucasus, and the area to the west of the Urals.

The highest-yielding grain crops of European Russia are wheat, barley, oats, and rye. These are supplemented by potatoes and traditional vegetable crops such as beets, cabbage, peas, carrots, onions, cucumbers, and tomatoes. Fruits that do well are apples, pears, and plums. In the last two decades, Russians have been sowing much of their arable land with fodder crops to support livestock raising. The planting of such feed crops has led to shortages of wheat. After years of being a wheat exporter, Russia has, in the past 25 years, become dependent on other countries for its most staple food grain.

Ethnic Regions

On the edges of European Russia, many so-called "autonomous" regions were established long ago as national homelands for peoples whose ethnic and religious backgrounds were different from those of the dominant Russian population. The Soviet authorities created most of these regions in the 1920s to provide territorial bases for specific nationalities within the confines of the larger Russian republic. Administratively, each autonomous region was designated either as a republic, oblast, or okrug. Autonomous republics

Russia's Internal Republics: A Population Breakdown
Population in Absolute Figures and in Percentages of Titular Nationality and Russians

Adygeia: 432,000
Adygei 22.1%
Russian 68.0%

Altai: 191,000
Altai 31.0%
Russian 60.4%

Bashkortostan: 3,943,000
Bashkort 21.9%
Russian 39.3%
Tatar 28.4%

Buriatiia: 1,038,000
Buriat 24.0%
Russian 69.9%

Checheno-Ingushetiia: 1,270,000
Chechen 57.8%
Ingush 12.9%
Russian 23.1%

Chuvashiia: 1,338,000
Chuvash 67.8%
Russian 26.7%

Dagestan: 1,802,000
Dagestani 80.2%
Russian 9.2%

Kalmykiia: 323,000
Kalmyk 45.4%
Russian 37.7%

Karachai-Cherkessiia: 415,000
Karachai 31.2%
Cherkess 9.7%
Russian 42.4%

Karbardino-Balkariia: 754,000
Kabard 48.2%
Balkar 9.4%
Russian 31.9%

Kareliia: 790,000
Karelian 10.0%
Russian 73.6%

Khakassiia: 567,000
Khakass 11.1%
Russian 79.5%

Komi: 1,251,000
Komi 23.3%
Russian 57.7%

Marii-El: 749,000
Mari 43.3%
Russian 47.5%

Mordviniia: 964,000
Mordvin 32.5%
Russian 60.8%

North Ossetiia: 632,000
Ossetian 53.0%
Russian 29.9%

Sakha (Iakutiia): 1,094,000
Iakut 33.4%
Russian 50.3%

Tatarstan: 3,642,000
Tatar 48.5%
Russian 43.3%

Tuva: 309,000
Tuvinian 64.3%
Russian 32.0%

Udmurtiia: 1,606,000
Udmurt 30.9%
Russian 58.9%

Note There are no separate data for Checheniia and Ingushetiia, since Checheno-Ingushetiia was officially separated into two republics only in 1992.

Source *RFE/RL Research Report*, 2, no. 20, 14 May 1993, 38.

ranked directly beneath union republics in the USSR, their "autonomous" standing due to the fact that their nationality group was not considered sufficiently large or powerful to merit full union republic status. Autonomous oblasts were set aside for nationalities with relatively small populations that lived in remote areas. Autonomous okrugs were designated for yet smaller nationalities and were often located on large tracts of undeveloped land inhabited by relatively few people. In the aftermath of the breakup of the Soviet Union, however, virtually all of these autonomous regions declared their sovereignty, often accompanying such declarations with a change of name to reflect their new status. However, these declarations of sovereignty should not be confused with the declarations of independence made by the former union republics, which have achieved international status as independent states.

Responding to the declarations of sovereignty proclaimed by most of these ethnic regions, the sixth session of the Congress of People's Deputies of the Russian Federation adopted in April 1992 a constitutional amendment recognizing their unique status and deleting the word "autonomous" before the word "republic" in their names. What had been an "autonomous republic" in the RSFSR became simply a "republic" within the newly independent Russian Federation. The legislation also identified four former autonomous oblasts (Adygeia, Altai, Karachai-Cherkessiia, and Khakassiia) as republics, though no changes were made in the labeling of autonomous okrugs. Thus, the Russian Federation is now home to 21 internal republics, 16 in European Russia and 5 in Siberia and the Russian Far East (see page 14).

European Russia's internal republics tend to be located on the outskirts of the lands considered as historic Russia (see map on page 12). In the northwest, for example, between Finland and the White Sea, lies the Republic of Kareliia. The Karelians are an Eastern Orthodox, Finnic-speaking people. Farther north, along the shore of the Barents Sea, live the Nenets, a Samoyedic group that follows a combination of Eastern Orthodox and shamanistic religious practices. To the south of the Nenets are the Komi and Udmurt republics, both ethnically Finnic regions. Far to the east of Moscow lie two other regions of ethnically Finnic population—the Republic of Marii-El (Mari), whose people practice shamanism with admixtures of Islam and Eastern Orthodoxy; and the Republic of Mordviniia, inhabited by a traditionally Eastern Orthodox population. Adjoining Mordviniia and Marii-El is the Chuvash republic, home to a Turkic-speaking people who adopted Eastern Orthodox Christianity in the modern period.

Farther to the east and south, between the Volga River and the Ural Mountains, there are regions inhabited by primarily Turkic populations, traditionally Islamic in their culture. The Republic of Tatarstan, centered in Kazan, is the homeland of the predominantly Sunni Muslim Volga Tatars. Adjacent to Tatarstan is the Republic of Bashkortostan (Bashkiriia), traditional homeland of the Turkic, Sunni Muslim Bashkorts. Farther to the south, the Republic of Kalmykiia is populated by descendants of the Mongols who traditionally followed Buddhist religious practices.

Yet farther south, along the northern slopes of the Caucasus Mountains, the plethora of local ethnic groups resulted in the establishment of seven autonomous regions, some of them originally representing more than one ethnic group per administrative unit. The Kabardino-Balkar republic is named for the Sunni Muslim Kabard people who speak a Circassian language. The Republic of North Ossetiia, which borders modern Georgia (see page 93), is inhabited primarily by Ossetians whose language is related to modern Iranian. Many of the North Ossetians converted to Eastern Orthodoxy in the modern period. Also in the Caucasus, the Chechen republic (formerly part of the Chechen-Ingush Autonomous Oblast, subsequently the Chechen-Ingush Republic) has been recognized since mid-1992 as a separate republic. The Chechen people (see page 27) are traditionally Sunni Muslims who speak a Caucasian language. The Ingush of the newly separate Ingush republic also speak a Caucasian language. They also are Sunni Muslims.

Inhabiting the Republic of Dagestan, an area adjacent to the Caspian Sea, are the Dagestani people, an indigenous Sunni Muslim group that speaks yet another Caucasian language. The Chechen, Ingush, and Dagestani people are among the dozen or more separate north Caucasian nationalities, each of which speaks a distinct language within the family of Caucasian languages. In addition to these indigenous Caucasian nationals, the region is also home to the Republic of Adygeia and the Republic of Karachai-Cherkessiia. The Adygei, representing an ethnic group formed by the unification of as many as 10 Circassian tribes, are Sunni Muslim. The peoples of Karachai-Cherkessiia are divided between the Karachai, who speak a Turkic language, and the Cherkess, whose speech derives from the Circassian branch of the Caucasian language family. Both the Karachai and the Cherkess are also Sunni Muslim by religious tradition.

Although the removal of the word "autonomous" before the title of republic reflects the greater measure of sovereignty assumed by many of these regions, the Russian government considers them, along with autonomous okrugs, integral parts of the Russian Federation. In many places, for example, Kazan, the capital city of Tatarstan, there continues to be a large ethnic Russian population in the urban centers of these "republics within a republic." Indeed, the majority population of these ethnic republics is sometimes Russian, leaving the titular nationality in the minority.

Defining Russia's Past

Statist View The Great Russians (or, simply, Russians) are the largest of the East Slavic nations. They became the dominant nationality within the Muscovite, Imperial, and Soviet Russian empires. As Russia expanded territorially, it imposed its institutions, language, and culture upon the multinational landscape of Eurasia. Because of the sheer power of this Russian imperium, it is tempting to define Russia's past exclusively in terms of the political and legal changes that marked each stage of its empire.

According to this view, the Great Russians were the inheritors of the early Kievan Rus grand princedom, a state that united Eastern Slavic tribes from the ninth to the thirteenth centuries. When that Kievan political structure was destroyed by the Mongol invasions of the Golden Horde in the mid-thirteenth century, new centers of Eastern Slavic, Russian civilization arose on the Volga River tributaries of the north. By the fifteenth century, one such settlement, the city of Moscow, became an independent center of power. In defeating the Mongols in the fifteenth and sixteenth centuries, the ruling tsars of Muscovy (the Muscovite Empire based in Moscow) established an independent Russian state that eventually stretched from Poland (the Polish-Lithuanian Commonwealth) in the west all the way to the Pacific Ocean in the east.

According to this "statist" view, political, legal, and institutional changes once again transformed the Muscovite state in the seventeenth and eighteenth centuries, first during the crisis of succession known as the Time of Troubles (1598–1613), and then definitively during the reforms of the Romanov tsar, Peter the Great (1682–1725). The result of Peter's reforms was the creation of an early modern bureaucratic state that came to be known as the Russian Empire (*Vserossiiskaia Imperiia*; literally, the All-Russian Empire). Until the fall of the Romanov dynasty and the collapse of that state in the Revolution of 1917, the Russian Empire maintained effective bureaucratic and military control over its expanding territories. The 1917 Bolshevik-led revolution launched the modern Soviet state.

While the earliest Soviet constitution of 1918 proclaimed the new revolutionary state to be federalist, this federalism was not clarified until December 1922 when the four republics under Bolshevik control—Russia, Ukraine, Belorussia (now Belarus), and Transcaucasia—united to form the Union of Soviet Socialist Republics (USSR). Throughout the 1920s, the identity of the constituent republics of the USSR continued to change. For example, in 1922, when the Red Army assumed control of Vladivostok, the Far Eastern Republic was dissolved and became a part of the Russian Soviet Federated Socialist Republic (RSFSR). Not until 1924 were the five Central Asian republics established. The integration of outlying republics into the new Soviet empire awaited in each case the successful advance of the Red Army, a key force engineering Bolshevik triumphs in the aftermath of the Revolutions of 1917.

As in the case of earlier political and institutional transformations, from Kievan Rus to the twentieth century, statist historians can find in the 1917 Bolshe-

vik Revolution and the ensuing Civil War yet another new stage in Russian history in which political, institutional, and military forces have continued to determine the course of Russia's past.

Marxist View Marxist historians, on the other hand, see the political evolution of Russia as secondary to fundamental, underlying economic forces. In such a view, the defining feature of Russian history has been the "feudal" nature of agrarian economic relations that prevailed for virtually a millennium, from the ninth to the nineteenth centuries. According to the Marxist perspective, this feudalism existed in Russia at least until the emancipation of Russian serfs in 1861. (Vladimir Lenin, the Russian revolutionary leader, considered Russia to be a feudal, agrarian state even into the twentieth century.) Until the 1980s, Soviet historians rigidly divided Russian history into three periods—a period of feudalism (ninth century to 1861), a period of capitalism (1861–1917), and a period of socialism (1917 to the present). Such periodization was also reflected in the structural organization of academic departments of history in the Soviet Union. Underlying this definition of Russia's past was the assumption that the most important cause of change in Russian history was economic conflict. Such conflict, in this view, determined the control and organization of economic production.

Intellectual and Cultural View Others have defined Russia's past in terms of major intellectual and cultural changes shaping the world view of the Russian people and their leaders. Accordingly, for some, the most significant event in early Russian history was the baptism of Kievan Grand Prince Vladimir into Byzantine-rite, Eastern Orthodox Christianity in A.D. 988. The Christianization of pagan Russia became, in this view, a defining process in Russian culture. By the sixteenth century, however, Russian religious life was no longer controlled by the ecclesiastical institutions of Byzantium. Russia's independent authority in the Eastern Orthodox world was recognized by the creation in 1588 of the office of the autocephalous (self-ruled) Moscow Patriarchate. The subsequent religious schism of the seventeenth century and the subordination of church to state in the administration of Peter the Great paved the way, in this view, for Russia's secularization. For writers such as Aleksandr Solzhenitsyn, official Soviet atheism was but a culmination of this process of secularization or "perversion" of Russia's earlier "moral foundation":

> For a thousand years Russia lived with an authoritarian order—and at the beginning of the twentieth century both the physical and spiritual health of her people

were still intact. . . . that authoritarian order possessed a strong moral foundation . . . not the ideology of universal violence, but Christian Orthodoxy, the ancient, seven-centuries-old Orthodoxy of Sergei Radonezhsky and Nil Sorsky, before it was battered by Patriarch Nikon and bureaucratized by Peter the Great. . . . Once this moral principle was perverted and weakened, the authoritarian order, despite the apparent external successes of the state, gradually went into a decline and eventually perished. (Aleksandr Solzhenitsyn, *Letter to the Soviet Leaders*, trans. by Hilary Sternberg, New York: Harper and Row, 1974, 52)

Twentieth-Century Events

By whatever means Russia's past is defined—be it in terms of state power, economic production, cultural inheritance, or some other organizing principle—the twentieth century has surely been its most revolutionary and fateful epoch. From the turbulent events of the 1917 Revolutions and subsequent Civil War to the agricultural collectivization, industrialization, and purges of the 1930s, the Soviet experiment brought lofty utopian goals to the modernization of Russian society, but at an unprecedented price in human suffering. As many as one million land-owning peasants *(kulaks)*, not counting their families, were either killed in the process of collectivization or were sent to labor camps in the expanding gulag of Soviet Asia (see page 36 for a more complete description of the gulag). In the forced industrialization of the country, dramatic increases in production were accomplished in heavy industry, but the very people who were forced to work harder were confronted with shortages of basic consumer goods and widespread rationing. The great purge (arrests followed by imprisonment or execution) of the 1930s further filled the labor camps of the gulag, as the Communist Party began to consume its own. Reaching a crescendo of violence in the period after 1936, the purge affected all Party and government offices, including the army. The purges also exacted a heavy toll from the Russian technical and academic intelligentsia.

Stalin Behind both the collectivization and industrialization policies, as well as the purges, stood Joseph Stalin (1879–1953). Born and raised in the Georgian town of Gori as Josef Dzhugashvili, he later joined the Russian Social Democratic Workers' Party, aligning himself with its Bolshevik wing after 1903. Assuming the name of Stalin, he rose within Party ranks, and after the Bolshevik Revolution took the post of commissar for national minorities. In 1922, Stalin se-

cured for himself the post of Communist Party general secretary. Using his leadership in Party affairs, Stalin gradually eliminated potential rivals as he built an increasingly loyal Party machine. By 1928, the onset of the first Five Year Plan for industrialization, Stalin was in complete personal control of Party and governmental affairs—a control he maintained until his death in 1953.

World War II Of all the tragedies of Stalinism, none was more fateful than the losses sustained in World War II. The Soviet Union initially sought to avoid confrontation with German armies by signing the Nazi-Soviet Pact of 1939—an agreement that divided Eastern Europe between German and Soviet spheres. While the Soviet Union was able to use the pact to secure additional territorial gains at the expense of Polish and Baltic lands, Stalin was left unprepared militarily for Germany's invasion of Russia in June 1941. The Red Army suffered catastrophic losses in the early months of fighting. Countless civilians also perished, either in the fighting itself, in German camps, or from starvation (as in the besieged city of Leningrad, now St. Petersburg). In the case of Soviet Jews, Gypsies, Communists, and members of certain other groups, the Germans carried out both forcible exterminations and mass killings.

The Red Army eventually held along the lower Volga against the invading German forces at the prolonged Battle of Stalingrad (now Volgograd), and the subsequent rout of the German Army in 1943–44 served as a turning point in World War II. Appealing for patriotic support, even making concessions to the Russian Orthodox Church, Stalin in the end managed to preserve the Soviet regime, but the cost in human life was unprecedented. As many as 27 million people died in the Soviet Union in World War II, at least half of them civilians. (See Nicholas Riasanovsky, *A History of Russia*, 5th ed., 528. Riasanovsky has altered his assessment of war losses from 20 to 27 million in the fifth edition of his standard text, a reflection of new demographic evidence.) In effect, World War II yielded a biological revolution in the Soviet Union, for an entire generation of males was lost in the war effort. Despite these losses, World War II continued to be emphasized by postwar leaders who used the defeat of fascism to justify and legitimize Soviet rule.

Post-Stalin Era Stalin's death in 1953, while it did not prove the final end of Stalinism, nevertheless opened up prospects for liberalization under the reformist leadership of Party General Secretary Nikita Khrushchev. Khrushchev's 1956 speech to the Twentieth Congress of the Communist Party publicly exposed the evils of Stalinism and the purges. While Khrushchev's liberalization measures did not extend to religious communities, several of which suffered even worse persecution in the Khrushchev era than they had in the aftermath of World War II, the "thaw" could be felt in other areas of Russian culture where censorship in literature and the arts was relaxed.

In 1964, Nikita Khrushchev was relieved of his position in both the Communist Party and the government, and his post as general secretary of the Party was assumed by Leonid Brezhnev. While Brezhnev's leadership came to be associated with a period of détente with the West in the 1970s, the formal relaxation of tensions between the Cold War superpowers was matched by a strengthening of Soviet military power. The costs of such a military build-up eventually came to be felt in economic shortages that had become increasingly difficult to hide from consumers by the time of Brezhnev's death in 1982. Within three years, following the brief tenure of Communist Party leaders Iurii Andropov and Konstantin Chernenko, Party authorities were prepared to turn to an energetic new leader, the future architect of *perestroika* (restructuring), Mikhail Sergeevich Gorbachev.

Starting with his 1985 directives against alcoholism and lost worker productivity, Gorbachev presented a new and much more vigorous style of Russian leadership. His goal was to restructure social, political, and economic life in such a way as to modernize the flagging Soviet economy. In spite of his focus upon domestic restructuring, however, he was forced to deal with one international crisis after another—including the Chernobyl nuclear power plant disaster of 1986, the withdrawal of Soviet military forces from Afghanistan, and the dismemberment in 1989 of the once-solid Soviet bloc in Eastern Europe. Gorbachev found that he was ultimately unable to maintain the commanding political authority of the Communist Party in the reform process. Moreover, he faced the new challenge of autonomy movements within the union republics, most notably from within the Russian republic.

Yeltsin versus Gorbachev According to the traditional Soviet exercise of power, political leaders of the 15 union republics were to be unfailingly loyal to the directives of the Moscow center. There was opportunity for flexibility on certain local issues, but republican leadership did not routinely challenge the central institutions of the Communist Party of the Soviet Union. Nevertheless, in the person of the maverick populist and Communist Party leader Boris Yeltsin, a remarkably independent executive authority came to be associated with the unprecedented drive in 1990–91 for the autonomy of the Russian republic (RSFSR)

within the wider Soviet Union.

Boris Yeltsin's political ascendancy came to be linked with the Russian republic following his conflict with the reforming Soviet president Mikhail Gorbachev. After having risen from his post as head of the Communist Party of Sverdlovsk (Ekaterinburg) to head the Moscow Party organization, Boris Yeltsin was summarily dismissed from the Moscow post in November 1987. As an outspoken advocate of more rapid economic reform and democratization, and as an opponent of political cronyism, Yeltsin had by the end of 1987 established a reputation as a popular politician. In his ongoing policy disputes with Gorbachev, Yeltsin tied his own political fortunes to two strategies—winning electoral support and, somewhat later, gaining autonomy and eventual independence for the Russian republic.

Yeltsin's personal popularity came to be measured in a series of stunning electoral triumphs, first in the March 1989 elections to the Soviet Parliament, the All-Union Congress of People's Deputies. An effective campaigner, Yeltsin won a 90 percent electoral majority. Later, on the republic level, Yeltsin added to his 1989 victory by being elected a deputy to the Russian Congress of People's Deputies in March 1990. His majority was more than 80 percent. Yeltsin followed these electoral successes by seeking the office of president of the Soviet Russian republic (RSFSR). This new republican presidency, established by Gorbachev, was to be chosen by ballot of the deputies of the Russian republic's Congress of People's Deputies. In the May 1990 balloting, Yeltsin secured 535 votes, barely more than the 50 percent needed for election. In winning the office, however, Yeltsin scored a major electoral triumph over Gorbachev's own hand-picked candidate, Aleksandr Vlasov, who received 467 votes. Adding yet further to his public mandate, Yeltsin called for popular election of the Russian president, ran for the office, and won a landslide election in June 1991.

What Yeltsin had accomplished in little more than three years was to focus public debate upon the slow pace and relative ineffectiveness of Gorbachev's domestic reforms, while at the same time using republican offices as the springboard for his own political ascendancy. In mid-1991, Yeltsin was in the unchallenged position of being the only popularly elected president of a Soviet republic, the RSFSR.

Along the way, Yeltsin had built considerable momentum for Russian republican autonomy. In a landmark measure approved by 544 members of the Russian Congress of People's Deputies in June 1990, The Russian republic asserted its right to veto any federal Soviet law affecting Russian territory. While the constitutional standing of such a measure was dubious, the clear message was that of support for Yeltsin's political drive toward Russian republican sovereignty. Symbolic of Yeltsin's commitment to republican—as opposed to all-union or Soviet—institutions was his resignation from the Soviet Communist Party in July 1990.

The August 1991 Coup Attempt By distancing himself from Soviet Communist Party organizations, Russian president Boris Yeltsin was in a unique position to bring his own leadership and that of Russian parliamentary institutions to bear against an attempted coup d'état. That coup attempt was launched on the 19th of August, 1991, by leading Communist Party figures from within Gorbachev's own appointed Council of Ministers. While President Gorbachev was vacationing in the Crimea, these ministerial-level appointees, led by Soviet Defense Minister Dmitrii Iazov (who later committed suicide), sought to seize control of governmental and communications bureaus. If successful, the coup would have reinstated firm, Soviet Communist Party leadership, undermining Yeltsin's drive toward Russian republican autonomy. In the pivotal showdown with the coup plotters, Yeltsin stood atop army tanks in front of the Russian parliament building, calling for popular resistance to the coup. Four days after the coup's launching, Yeltsin and his advisors within the Russian republic had managed to defuse it. Soviet military authorities refused to shoot at the throngs of Russians gathered around the parliament building. Gorbachev returned from the Crimea, but he had been politically damaged by a coup that had been launched by his own conservative Communist Party appointees.

In the months that followed, power devolved to leadership in the Soviet republics as the Union of Soviet Socialist Republics effectively collapsed. By December 1991, after several unsuccessful attempts to forge a new union treaty, the Soviet Union ceased to exist, and power passed to the 15 former union republics. The radical transformation of Russian life that ensued has yet to play itself out.

European Russia: Contemporary Issues

President Boris Yeltsin and the Limits of Democratization in Russia

The failure of the August 1991 coup demonstrated the degree to which political power in the USSR had, in the six short years of Mikhail Gorbachev's tenure, shifted away from the Communist Party and into the hands of an elected Russian Parliament headed by an elected Russian president. In a crucial showdown between discredited hard-line Soviet Communist coup plotters and new Russian president Boris Yeltsin, the armed forces—a traditional source of support for Communist leaders—refused to back the coup. By the time the plotters released Gorbachev from house arrest in the Crimea and he returned to Moscow, his authority (as well as that of the Soviet Union) was already crippled. By the end of August, most Soviet republics, including the Russian republic, had declared their independence from the USSR. In December 1991, the Soviet Union ceased to exist, and the Communist Party was outlawed (a measure partially reversed by the courts in 1992). Gorbachev no longer had any power, and the Soviet Parliament was effectively supplanted in Russia by its republican counterpart, the Russian Parliament, or Congress of People's Deputies. Although a new Commonwealth of Independent States (CIS) was launched in December 1991 by Russia, Ukraine, and Belarus, the politics of republican sovereignty, not those of the interrepublican CIS, would come to dominate most policymaking in the post-Soviet era.

Yeltsin and the Russian Parliament

Although the prospects for political restructuring and democratization looked bright in the aftermath of August 1991, the new Russian Federation soon became mired in conflicts that pitted the enhanced executive authority of its president, Boris Yeltsin, against a willful Russian Parliament and increasingly strident calls for regional autonomy. Complicating this picture was the uncertain health of President Yeltsin and the rapid turnover amongst his closest advisors. Initially, Yeltsin overshadowed a deferential Russian Parliament, which in November 1991 even granted Yeltsin special powers to undertake radical economic reform in Russia. A series of far-reaching measures, including sweeping price deregulation, ensued in January 1992. The personal authority of Boris Yeltsin, reinforced by support from the Democratic Russia movement that had brought him to power in 1990, seemed destined to sustain the momentum for political and economic reform. Had parliamentary elections been called in late 1991 or early 1992, Yeltsin's supporters would likely have swept to overwhelming victory.

By the end of 1992, however, the process of political and economic reform had come under significant challenge from a Parliament that had begun to reflect the public's uneasiness over price deregulation and rising unemployment. Using what it claimed to be rightful legislative authority, the Russian Parliament sought to limit President Yeltsin's power. Yeltsin loyalists argued with some justification that the Russian Parliament had been elected in 1990 when the Communist Party still affected the outcome of elections. In this view, Parliament's conservative brake on reform was a reflection of its ties to old politics and the apparatus of the Party-appointed nomenklatura. In fact, former Communist and right-wing nationalist deputies had coalesced into a strong opposition to an ever-more-dispirited Yeltsin alliance. Responding to the challenges to his executive power, Boris Yeltsin sought to reach beyond the Russian Parliament by seeking a direct mandate from the people. To do this, he scheduled a public referendum for April 1993. The referendum specifically asked the electorate to pass judgment on Yeltsin's presidency and the Russian Parliament. The April referendum effectively endorsed presidential leadership, while demonstrating widespread popular opposition to the machinations of Parliament. In the absence of a new post-Soviet constitution, however, the office of the Russian presidency remained the subject of controversy.

The challenge to Yeltsin's power was not, however, the simple result of a defiant Parliament. The "shock therapy" of sudden price deregulation, tightened money supply, and privatization of state enterprises posed a threat to large, unprivatized state industries, with consequent public concern over rising unemployment. By mid-1992, an industrial lobby had organized itself into a group known as Civic Union, and this union declared its opposition not only to radical economic reform, but more generally to Yeltsin's political leadership. In a symbolic victory over the Yeltsin reform agenda, the Russian Parliament in December 1992, led by its chair Ruslan Khasbulatov from the Republic of Checheniia, established the right to approve or reject four key presidential cabinet appointments. The subsequent parliamentary rejection of Egor Gaidar, Yeltsin's original architect of radical economic reform, and his replacement by the Civic Union favorite Viktor Chernomyrdin signaled how powerful the Russian Parliament had become.

The conflict came to a head in September 1993 when Yeltsin dissolved Parliament. Despite the fact that the president was expressly forbidden to undertake such action under the outdated Soviet constitution, Western observers tended to support the move as an effort to overcome obstructionist elements in a Russian Parliament that had been put in office before the end of the Soviet Union. In the subsequent holdout by parliamentary leaders in the Russian "White House," the parliamentary building, Yeltsin called in military troops to fire upon the parliamentary resisters. By October 1993, Yeltsin's moves had succeeded, but only after extra-legal measures that dramatized the inability of executive and legislative leaders to reach a compromise by democratic means. Thus, in the fall of 1993, Russia functioned without a parliament and without an independent judiciary.

The Russian Constitution of 1993 and Increased Executive Authority

Since the political crisis of fall 1993, several major developments have served to test the viability of reform in Russia. The first of these was the election of December 1993. Seeking to restore legitimacy to the political process, President Yeltsin placed before the electorate—at the same time that elections were held for deputies to the Russian Parliament—a referendum on a new constitution. The new Russian constitution, which granted broad executive authority to the Russian president, was approved by approximately 60 percent of those voting (only slightly more than 50 percent of those eligible voted). Alongside this somewhat unenthusiastic endorsement of the new constitution, the electorate voted into office a parliament in which the reformist and pro-government forces were outpolled by resurgent Communist and agrarian deputies on the left and extreme nationalists on the right. The balloting by party affiliation yielded the largest vote totals for Vladimir Zhirinovsky's right-wing party, the misnamed Liberal Democratic Party (it received 23 percent of the vote).

In a subsequent round of parliamentary elections held in December 1995, Russia's Communist and right-wing nationalist parties further consolidated their positions at the expense of centrist and reform candidates. In the 1995 balloting, the Communist Party emerged as the largest single bloc in the Russian Parliament, receiving more than twice the vote total (22.3 percent) of its nearest rival, Zhirinovsky's nationalist party. Both the 1993 and 1995 parliamentary elections documented the strength of the political opposition to the Yeltsin government.

The Russian constitution adopted by referendum in 1993 became, in its own right, a key factor in political stabilization, making it possible for the president—despite the strength of the parliamentary opposition to the Yeltsin government—to exercise broad executive authority in the day-to-day management of the affairs of the Russian Federation. This stability came at the expense, however, of a balance of powers between executive, legislative, and judicial authority. Not only does the Russian president now have the authority to dissolve parliament (newly named the Russian Duma) and to veto parliamentary legislation, but also the right to change the authority given to local and regional governments. The most glaring example of executive authority is the power vested in the presidency to arbitrate conflicts between federal and regional institutions (such authority was previously vested in a constitutional court). Any regional or republican-level legislation that the president determines to be in conflict with the constitution, federal laws, or international treaties can be suspended, and such suspensions are also declared not subject to appeal. In short, the Russian presidency in the 1993 constitution came to assume broadly expanded executive, judicial, and legislative authority.

The Drive for Regional Self-Governance

Russia's local regions, including the formerly autonomous republics and oblasts of the RSFSR, have played an important role in the transformation of Russian politics. The 1993 Russian constitution created a Federation Council with the authority to review legislation passed by the Russian Parliament or Duma. The Federation Council is meant to represent all of Russia's 89 regions and internal republics. Although this assembly of regional representatives has become a largely hollow institution, the drive for local, regional, and republican authority within the Russian Federation remains one of the most lively issues in post-Soviet politics. Most notably, rebel forces fighting for independence in the north Caucasus Republic of Checheniia (Chechnya) have tested the capacity of the Russian Federation to maintain its far-flung holdings, particularly in non-Russian regions distant from Moscow. On the other hand, political leadership in some Russian regions, such as Nizhnii Novgorod, has effectively introduced local self-government and political reform. Boris Nemtsov, the provincial governor in the city of Nizhnii Novgorod (Gorky), is notable in this connection. He has developed a reputation for avoiding the cronyism that has traditionally characterized local government. His election and the election of other local governors in 1995 and 1996 advanced the prospects for political reform. Although the Russian constitution has given the president wide latitude to reimpose Moscow-based authority in the regions, some of the most innovative governmental reform has come from those locales where self-government has been permitted.

Given the new political power of the Russian presidency, the personal fortunes of Russian President Boris Yeltsin have naturally assumed paramount importance in advancing the process of political reform. In June and July of 1996, Yeltsin faced two rounds of presidential elections, the first Russian presidential balloting in the post-Soviet era. In the wake of the electoral strength the Communist Party exhibited in the December 1995 parliamentary elections, Yeltsin supporters had particular reason to fear the popularity of Gennadii Zyuganov, candidate of the revived Communist Party. Zyuganov appealed to several disaffected elements of the population; notably, pensioners suffering from inflationary pressures on the ruble and Russian nationals in outlying republics where non-Russians were assuming greater local authority. In the end, Yeltsin's anti-Communist campaign message, a tactic designed to make Zyuganov appear wedded to the past, was successful. Joining forces in the second round of the election with the popular Russian military officer Aleksandr Lebed, a candidate who placed third in the first round, Yeltsin (with 53.7 percent of the vote) defeated Zyuganov in a major setback for the Communist Party.

The personal fortunes of President Yeltsin, however, were equally threatened in 1996 by his deteriorating physical health. After a grueling electoral battle that taxed an already serious cardiac condition, Boris Yeltsin announced to the public in September 1996 that he would undergo open-heart surgery. In the ongoing struggle for ascendancy among Yeltsin's close advisors, Prime Minister Viktor Chernomyrdin was chosen to serve while the president was incapacitated. In the years following the collapse of the Soviet Union, Yeltsin had managed to overcome parliamentary opposition while putting in place a new Russian constitution that granted broad executive authority. The immediate question facing citizens of Russia was no longer just the uncertainty of political democratization, but the very survival of their president.

Economic Restructuring and Privatization

Price Deregulation and Monetary Control If 1991 marked the major turning point in Russia's political transformation—including the August coup and the collapse of the Soviet Union—then 1992 marked the dramatic restructuring of the Russian economy. Effective January 1992, broad measures eliminating price controls—except on basic energy and food commodities—were introduced throughout the Russian economy in an effort to establish real market prices for Russian goods. Not only did this set off a wave of price increases in the Russian Federation, but the ripple effect of the deregulation affected virtually every newly independent state of the former Soviet Union, forcing economic accommodation throughout Eurasia.

"Shock therapy," a term used to describe similar radical economic reforms launched in Eastern Europe, included a tight monetary policy and carefully monitored wage increases designed to avoid excessive inflationary pressure. While some of the inspiration for the reforms came from Western economic consultants, the Russian architect of these radical economic measures was President Boris Yeltsin's initial economic advisor, Egor Gaidar.

Privatization Accompanying price deregulation and monetary controls, a plan for the privatization of some state property and industrial assets was put into place. In 1992, for example, it became possible for individuals to buy, or "privatize," their state-owned apartments. In the high-demand urban markets of Moscow and St. Petersburg, however, brokers emerged on the scene offering financial inducements and more spacious apartment units outside the city core to cramped inner-city communal apartment dwellers. The incentive for such brokers was that office space in prime areas, such as central Moscow, had skyrocketed in value to as much as $1,000 per square meter (see "In Moscow, Privatization Brings Real Estate Boom," *New York Times*, 28 February 1993). The conversion of crudely divided communal living spaces into spacious offices and multiroom apartments constituted one of the many curious post-Soviet reversals in which once-elegant, prerevolutionary, nineteenth-century buildings were restored in what might be called the "regentrification" of prime Moscow and St. Petersburg property—returning it to its previously elite standard. Most Russian cities, less accessible to international investment and foreign commerce, failed to experience the scale of property privatization and gentrification underway in Moscow and St. Petersburg.

Privatization also came to affect the service sector and some manufacturing activity. Although the difference between state-owned and private enterprises was often blurred, three types of nonstate enterprises emerged—joint stock companies, cooperatives, and small private businesses. Privatization proceeded very slowly. By late 1992, only about 5 percent of industrial, small trade, and service establishments had been privatized (see Erik Whitlock, "New Russian Government to Continue Economic Reform?" *RFE/RL Re-*

search Report, 15 January 1993, 23–24). Equally slow was the implementation of a system of vouchers, by which every Russian citizen was granted a certificate worth 10,000 rubles ($35 at the official exchange rate when first issued in October 1992—a figure then in excess of one month's average wages) for the purchase of government assets being offered for privatization. Not until the vouchers had been distributed did the auctioning of state enterprises begin to gather steam in late 1992 and early 1993. Then, the presence of vouchers on the market without adequate opportunities for investment not only added to inflationary pressures, but also led many Russians to sell off their vouchers for cash (see Steven Erlanger, "Russia's Big Sell-Off of Companies Gains Speed," *New York Times*, 25 February 1993).

Despite such problems and the traumatic changes in employment accompanying privatization, by the mid-1990s the success of the privatization effort began to be felt clearly in increased production. Today, more than half of the Russian gross domestic product is being generated from newly established or privatized agricultural and industrial enterprises. Well over two-thirds of retail sales are coming from privatized outlets. Even the banking industry, long a protected zone of state control, has become increasingly privatized. Despite some adjustment problems in 1995 when the Central Bank, the leading government financial institution, began to limit the volume of credit to commercial banks, thereby affecting their speculative profits, banks have begun to invest significantly in Russia's privatization.

Crime Privatization and economic restructuring have also been accompanied by a rise in crime, including organized crime (see Penny Morvant, "Corruption Hampers War on Crime in Russia," *Transition* 2, no. 5, 8 March 1996, 23–27). In the five-year period from 1990 to 1995, the number of murders in Russia increased more than 100 percent. Robbery and thefts rose by more than 75 percent. Bribery went up 90 percent. Drug-related crimes increased 250 percent. Worst of all, some of the new financial elite who have benefited most from privatization have done so by forging mafia-linked private security and insurance protection rings. The rise of organized crime has been aided by elements of the old internal security apparatus, the KGB, and related elite forces (see Vladimir Zhdanov and James Hughes, "Russia's 'Alpha Group' Changes with the Times," *Transition* 2, no. 5, 8 March 1996, 28–31; also, Jack F. Matlock, "Russia: The Power of the Mob," *New York Review of Books*, 13 July 1995, 12–15). Accompanying the rise of criminal violence has been the debilitating loss of state revenue arising from corporate and regional tax evasion. Not surprisingly, the issue of corruption and organized crime became a part of the 1996 presidential elections, with the candidate Aleksandr Lebed gaining considerable support with his appeal for a more concerted government crackdown on crime and corruption.

Standard of Living For the Moscow citizen, whose modest standard of living still exceeds by far the level of someone living in a remote part of the Russian Federation, the publicized exploits of the newly wealthy elite can only breed cynicism. The minimum subsistence-level salary for a Moscow resident is the equivalent of about $125 per month. Although the average Muscovite continues to spend very little for housing—often only the equivalent of $30 for utilities in an otherwise rent-subsidized apartment—more than $80 per month is needed for food. Spending patterns in which food takes up the vast majority of the monthly wage are in stark contrast to those of Western Europe or the United States.

Current Challenges

Sustaining Economic Production The future of economic restructuring and privatization in contemporary Russia will be determined by success or failure on at least three basic fronts. First, there is the problem of sustaining economic production in a period of major employment dislocation. Production figures for the Russian economy plummeted in 1992. In the depression of the early 1990s, some industrial sectors suffered production declines of more than 20 percent. Much of this loss of productivity reflected the lack of market demand for goods produced in the traditional state-run military and heavy industry sectors. Nevertheless, continued declines in production can only mean serious unemployment and/or continued inflationary pressure upon the government in the form of monetary subsidies for outmoded industries. In effect, the dramatic drop in production figures points to the dilemma of market-oriented restructuring. Shock therapists argue that restructuring should be implemented with greater firmness, while directors of large state enterprises have argued that restructuring should not be allowed to undermine previously productive enterprises before new productive sectors have been established.

Stabilizing Economic Policy Second, the Russian Parliament's early ouster of Egor Gaidar as chief economic advisor and his replacement by prime minister Viktor Chernomyrdin has introduced uncertainty regarding long-term economic policy leadership within the Russian government. Both foreign investment and domestic markets suffer from economic policies that are wildly fluctuating. This uncertainty can also affect the process of privatization, inasmuch as many privatizing enterprises are faced with substantial indebtedness and need to know what government policies will be with respect to issues such as price regulation, credit guarantees, and debt forgiveness. Although Chernomyrdin has carried forward most of the policies of his predecessors and has sought to conform to guidelines set forth by international creditors, such as the International Monetary Fund, the uneasiness amongst international investors during the presidential elections of 1996 reflects the wider concern for continuity in Russian economic leadership.

Increasing Foreign Investment Finally, although the Russian Federation possesses ample natural resources and a remarkably well-trained, literate work force, the process of economic restructuring requires far greater international investment than has been made as yet. Such investment is needed not only for the success of restructuring, but also for continued political stability. Despite Russia's membership in the International Monetary Fund and the stated willingness of creditor nations to assist the Russian economy, the legal barriers to investment and the short-term profitability of Russian enterprises continue to limit the attractiveness of investment in the Russian economy.

Problems of Cold War Demobilization

Expense Added to the problems of economic restructuring has been the drain of a costly military defense budget geared to old, Cold War, realities. At the time of its collapse in 1991, the Soviet Union had four million troops in uniform—the world's largest armed force. (The United States, by comparison, had a combined military force of approximately two million.) More than 500,000 of these Soviet troops were stationed in Eastern Europe under Warsaw Pact auspices, and the gradual return of those units following the 1989 revolutions added untold financial burdens (such as housing costs) to the Russian economy. In addition, the Russian Federation, unlike its former CIS nuclear partners (Kazakhstan, Ukraine, and Belarus), continues to maintain nuclear weapons bases, the guarding and decommissioning of which under international agreements has required further spending. In short, the legacy of the Cold War continues to drain Russia's already overtaxed budget.

Military Command Structure Perhaps the most complicated problem facing the military is to clarify the command structure of the armed forces. Following the August 1991 coup attempt, Boris Yeltsin, then president of the Russian republic, secured the appointment of a new Soviet defense minister, Evgenii Shaposhnikov. Upon the demise of the Soviet Union in December 1991, the Soviet defense ministry effectively came to be identified as the headquarters of the central military command of the newly established Commonwealth of Independent States. Even though the Soviet Union had split up into sovereign republics, the military command structure was still based on a unified Soviet organizational pattern. The new civilian political realities were simply not reflected in the military. For a time in early 1992, this awkward situation could only be overcome through the personal intermediation of Russian President Yeltsin and CIS armed forces head Shaposhnikov. Today, there is no longer an integrated CIS command; rather, each new state has its own military force, with bilateral military agreements covering special cases of joint command (for example, the joint Russian-Ukrainian Black Sea naval fleet; see page 84).

Nuclear Weapons Three problems forced a further clarification of civil-military relations in Russia. First was the obvious need to develop a post-Soviet policy on nuclear weapons. In the initial talks among CIS leaders at the end of 1991, an agreement was made that all nuclear weapons not on Russian soil should either be transferred to the Russian Federation or destroyed. In the meantime, the CIS military command structure remained nominally in control of the various nuclear arsenals of the USSR. There followed in 1992 a transfer of all tactical nuclear weapons to Russia from the other former Soviet republics that housed such armaments: Ukraine, Belarus, and Kazakhstan. When the question of moving the larger, strategic nuclear weapons was considered in mid-1992, Ukraine and Kazakhstan pulled back from their initial commitment to destroy these arsenals or transfer them to Russia. Under international pressure, however, they agreed to abide by their original position, and Russia became the sole custodian of nuclear weapons in Eurasia.

Related to the oversight of nuclear weapons has been the problem of security for Russia's nuclear weapons, as well as for its nuclear weapons–grade plutonium and enriched uranium. Between 40 and 50 nuclear sites remain on Russian soil, few of them with the kinds of safeguards that would prevent nuclear smuggling or terrorist attack. In one well-publicized instance, Iranian smugglers sought to purchase weapons-grade nuclear materials from Kazakhstan. United States President Clinton included the nuclear security issue in informal talks with President Yeltsin held in Russia in April 1996. Although there have been pilot programs underwritten by the U.S. government in which American laboratories have worked directly with Russian institutes to develop nuclear security systems, there has been neither the level of financial support nor the sense of urgency needed to carry forward a comprehensive program for nuclear security. Russian missile sites are all under military protection, but that is not true for the sites currently producing nuclear weapons–grade materials (see Michael R. Gordon, "Russia Struggles in Long Race to Prevent an Atomic Theft," *New York Times*, 20 April 1996, 1, 4).

Independent Armed Forces A second major issue to confront the CIS military command was the establishment of independent republican armed forces in several of the new states. Again, Ukrainian initiatives forced the issue, for at the end of 1991, more than half a million former Soviet troops were still being housed on Ukrainian soil. From the perspective of Ukrainian sovereignty, there was an urgent need to clarify the lines of authority between the Ukrainian civilian government and these CIS troops. In early January 1992, Ukraine announced that all forces on Ukrainian soil would henceforth be directly under the authority of the Ukrainian defense minister. This announcement was followed by measures calling for an oath of allegiance to Ukraine by all those former Soviet troops intending to continue their military service in Ukraine. Although some troops deserted and others sought reassignment, more than half of the forces in Ukraine took the oath of allegiance by the end of January 1992. (On the question of the Black Sea fleet, see page 84.)

Meanwhile, most other former Soviet republics moved to create their own national armies. The Russian decision in May 1992 to establish its own independent Russian army ended any thought that CIS military forces would be able to maintain a unified command structure throughout the territories of the former Soviet Union. Despite continuing CIS coordination on critical military deployments, such as those of Russian forces in Tajikistan or joint Russian-Ukrainian control over the Black Sea naval fleet, negotiations over military placement are increasingly the result of bilateral agreements.

Troops outside the Russian Federation The third major military issue confronting Russia was precisely how to deploy those former Soviet troops that continued to be stationed outside the borders of the Russian Federation. President Yeltsin has faced increasing pressure from Russian nationalists to maintain the presence of Russian forces in the "near abroad," if for no other reason than to protect Russian nationals who remain in residence there. In Moldova, the withdrawal of Russian forces from the Trans-Dniester region has been the subject of a formal agreement (see page 68). In Georgia, Russian troops have been deployed in the breakaway republic of Abkhazia. In Central Asia, particularly in the volatile Republic of Tajikistan, Russian forces have been sent to protect the Tajik government from insurgents. Although the costs of such military deployment have led to disgruntled comments from President Yeltsin and others, there seems to be little support for recalling all troops at a time when Russia is cultivating for itself an expanded role as arbiter and "peacemaker" with its new European, Central Asian, and Transcaucasian neighbors. For now, President Yeltsin has indicated that these ongoing deployments of Russian troops are meant simply to quell interethnic fighting, and that the assignments are subject to bilateral interrepublican agreements. At the same time, Yeltsin must contend with those Russian military and ultranationalist leaders who cling to the fading hope that Russian forces will be able to secure military reintegration of the Commonwealth of Independent States.

Intelligence Agencies Not all the problems confronting Russian Cold War demobilization are confined to the fate of former Soviet armed forces. There is no institution more symbolic of the Cold War than the vaunted KGB (*Komitet gosudarstvennoi bezopasnosti*, the Committee of State Security). As one commentator put it, "Where has the KGB gone?" (Victor Yasmann, *RFE/RL Research Report*, 8 January 1993, 17–20). A search for the KGB in contemporary Russia reveals both significant changes and some continuity in this former Cold War security agency.

To begin with, the name of the agency has changed. Although Russian citizens still refer to it as the KGB, the legal successor to this agency in the Russian Federation is the Federal Security Service (FSB). Officially, the size of the agency has remained about the same—the service reported in September 1992 that it had 135,000 officers, a slight drop from its pre-August 1991 officer-level figures. The law on security passed by the Russian Supreme Soviet in March 1992 also extended to other agencies the right to gather intelligence. These other agencies include the Foreign Intelligence Service, the armed forces, and the Ministry of Internal Affairs. The relationship between Russia's FSB and former Soviet KGB offices and KGB personnel in other newly independent states remains unclear. The Russian need for intelligence on other republics continues, especially in connection with

problems of political instability. Former KGB officers working in such republics may well have been retained because of their experience. Yet, the nature of the links between the intelligence personnel of Russia and the other newly independent states is rarely examined in the public media.

What has been openly discussed is the expansion of intelligence-gathering capabilities to include agencies and tasks previously not part of the KGB. Political leaders in Russia have been remarkably candid about the new tasks that they envision for the intelligence community. When Egor Gaidar was acting prime minister, he authorized creation of a Commission for Combating Corruption and for Financial Control, a government effort to use intelligence officers to identify schemes involving illegal foreign trade and commerce, as well as other forms of corruption. While the old KGB played an occasional role in anticorruption campaigns, such efforts invariably focused upon the widespread official corruption amongst Soviet government and Party personnel.

There is the sense that, while maintaining the old components of internal and foreign security forces, the new Russian Federation is involved in a modest effort to redirect the focus of intelligence gathering. Such a change is reflected in the pronouncements of Evgenii Primakov, former director of the Russian Foreign Intelligence Service and current minister of foreign affairs. Primakov has called for collaboration with Western intelligence agencies in attacking problems of nuclear proliferation, international terrorism, and drug trafficking.

On the other hand, despite the sensational articles published in Russian newspapers and the revelations offered from KGB archives, the details of most former KGB operations have remained secret, as have the estimates of the number of paid informers in Russia, a figure that is assumed to be in the millions. KGB records documenting abuses in the gathering of Soviet domestic intelligence have also been largely inaccessible. It appears as though new assignments have been delegated to the Federal Security Service and other intelligence agencies without any systematic effort to root out the intelligence abuses of the Soviet period. The KGB was powerless to halt the collapse of the Soviet Union, and it is no doubt also incapable of directing the course of Russian domestic politics in the present. Nevertheless, the failure to undertake major reform in the intelligence field, much less to limit the corruption and influence of former KGB officers, suggests the difficulty in demobilizing well-entrenched Cold War institutions.

"Self" and "Other" in Post-Soviet Russia: The Struggle for Identity

Russian Identity Russia today struggles with the legacy of its own imperial past. As the diverse peoples of the Russian Federation seek to recover for themselves lost identities or fashion new identities in a post-Soviet era, they do so under the common impact of lost empire. For ethnic Russians, the loss of empire has left millions of their fellow nationals scattered throughout the other Eurasian republics, the "near abroad." Ultranationalist Russians, unable to accept this loss of empire, have called for its reestablishment. Western observers were shocked to hear the right-wing polemicist Vladimir Zhirinovsky call for the recovery even of Russian Alaska. Yet, while Zhirinovsky's extremism has tended to discredit him before a Russian audience tired of his antics in the Russian Parliament, the message of restored imperial borders still carries for some a certain allure. The Russian writer Aleksandr Solzhenitsyn, who returned to Russia in 1995 after more than 20 years of exile in the West, has proposed the restoration of a Slavic empire incorporating the republics of Ukraine, Belarus, Russia, and part of Kazakhstan (*The Russian Question: At the End of the Twentieth Century,* New York: Pantheon, 1994).

The dilemma for Russian nationalists and, more broadly, for Russian identity is that there are many citizens—particularly non-Russians whose ancient homelands remain within the borders of the new Russian Federation—who continue to see Russia as an imperial power. Among these non-Russians, referred to as *inorodtsy* (alien-born) in the nineteenth century, are those who seek sovereignty for their homelands. Declarations of sovereignty from these republics within the Russian Federation have challenged Russian integrity, requiring new definitions of the relationship between center and periphery, between "self" and "other."

Russia and Tatarstan The Republic of Tatarstan, the former Tatar Autonomous Republic of the Soviet Union, is situated on the northern Volga. Its capital, Kazan, is a city of mixed Russian and Volga Tatar population. The Volga Tatars, Islamic by religious tradition, speak a Turkic language. In March 1992, the local Volga Tatar leadership confronted Russian authorities with what was, in essence, a threat to the unity of the Russian Federation: a referendum asking the people of the Tatar republic, both Russian and Tatar, whether they wanted Tatarstan to be "a sovereign state and a subject of international law whose relations with the Russian Federation and other republics and states are based on equal treaties" (see Steven Erlanger, "Tatar

Area in Russia Votes on Sovereignty Today," *New York Times,* 21 March 1992). In the voting, 61.4 percent of the voters approved the referendum on sovereignty. Despite the fact that the chair of the Tatar Supreme Soviet, Farid Mukhamadshin, assured Russian leaders that the referendum did not imply any intention on the part of Tatarstan to secede from the Russian Federation, the message was clear: the Volga or Kazan Tatars—as well as other groups in European Russia, Siberia, and the Russian Far East—wish to be treated as sovereign units within a confederated Russia.

The political situation in Tatarstan, as in other national homelands within the Russian Federation, is complicated. The prevailing leadership is made up of former Communist Party figures who have, on the issue of national sovereignty, sought to retain their power by making common cause with Tatar nationalists. Thus, the issue behind the Tatar referendum was not just that of political self-rule, but a subtle jockeying for power among rival Tatar politicians. In the end, the referendum vote confirmed Tatarstan's sovereignty, even though it remains a turbulent part of the Russian Federation.

President Yeltsin's unwillingness to use force to stop the 1992 Tatarstan referendum reflected a new caution on his part. His caution ultimately made possible in February 1994 a formal treaty between the Republic of Tatarstan and the Russian Federation in which Tatarstan republican authorities were granted the following: (1) the right to determine citizenship within the Republic of Tatarstan; (2) the right to conduct independent foreign policy and trade negotiations; (3) the right to exempt citizens of Tatarstan from Russian military service; (4) the right to establish a budget and tax system; and (5) the right to administer its own natural resources. In return, Moscow authorities would continue to receive taxes from Tatarstan and would secure a separate agreement on control over oil production in the region (see Elizabeth Teague, "Russia and Tatarstan Sign Power-Sharing Treaty," *RFE/RL Research Report* 3, no. 14, 8 April 1994, 19–27).

1992 Federal Treaty Well before the Russian-Tatarstan agreement, President Yeltsin had signaled his desire to maintain normal Russian relations with the other internal republics of the Russian Federation. In March 1992, he signed a federal treaty with those subunits of the Federation, saying at the time, "there is a particularly strong understanding that only together will we be able to overcome our difficulties and turn our common homeland of Russia into a free, democratic and prosperous state" (Steven Erlanger, "Most Pieces of Russia Agree to Coalesce, for Now," *New York Times,* 1 April 1992). The treaty offered greater political and economic independence to the local regions, especially over their considerable natural resources. The Tatarstan, Chechen, and Ingush republics were the only participants not to sign the treaty, but 80 governmental leaders of local republics, oblasts, and other regions agreed to the terms of the compact. Unexpectedly, even the leader of the Republic of Bashkortostan signed onto the pact. While the Russian constitution of 1993 supersedes the 1992 federal treaty, the lesson for President Yeltsin in the federal treaty of 1992 and the separate Tatarstan treaty of 1994 ought to have been that the integrity of the Russian Federation is best maintained by negotiated agreement, rather than by the use of armed force.

War in Chechnya The benefits of military restraint have clearly been forgotten in the most divisive and tragic conflict of the Yeltsin administration—the war in Checheniia. Labeled "Chechnya" by Russian and Western media, this north Caucasian republic was linked with Ingushetiia in the Soviet period, forming the Autonomous Republic of Checheno-Ingushetiia. The entity was divided into separate Chechen and Ingush republics in 1992. Chechens refer to Checheniia or Chechnya as the independent Chechen republic of "Ichkeriya." The Chechen people are descended from mountainous tribes of the Caucasus, who fiercely protected their autonomy in the tsarist period when confronted with Russian imperial takeover. The protracted, 50-year war between Chechens and the Russian Empire in the nineteenth century, often referred to as the Great Caucasian War, shares much in common with the recent fighting in the north Caucasus. Then, as now, Chechen tribal leaders set aside their own differences to confront the alien "other," the Russian Empire. Resisting incorporation into that empire, the Chechens were never subjected to Russian serfdom. Despite Russian settlement in their capital, Groznyi, the Chechens remained remarkably unaffected by the imposition of Russian and Soviet bureaucratic government in the area. Although Russians built rail lines through Checheniia to carry their oil products from Baku and the Caspian oil fields, the self-sufficient Chechen mountain communities of the nineteenth century were never effectively Russified.

The latest round of mindless Russian-Chechen fighting dates from the return to Checheniia in 1991 of the Soviet military officer General Dzhokhar Dudaev, a Chechen. Like nineteenth-century Chechen tribal leaders who watched for opportunities to capitalize upon Russian weakness, General Dudaev assumed the presidency of Checheniia and declared the republic independent. In the fractious world of Caucasian mountain politics, Dudaev was not alone in his claims to power. By 1994, Russian authorities had identified a Chechen opposition to Dudaev, one that Moscow would use as a critical foundation for their increasingly deep involvement in local Chechen affairs. That Chechen opposition, backed by Russian tank drivers posing as Chechens, attacked the Chechen capital of Groznyi in late 1994, but failed to take the city. By December 1994, Russian troops had entered Checheniia, though in the bloody fighting that followed, they failed to take control of Groznyi until well into the spring of 1995.

General Dudaev, who reportedly died in battle in 1996, successfully presented himself as another in the long line of glorious Chechen fighters who sought to protect the independence of Chechen mountain communities (even though those communities may no longer have been truly self-sustaining). President Yeltsin, hesitant before 1994 to involve Russian troops in the north Caucasus, ultimately committed such troops in order to defend the sovereign territory of the Russian Federation. Not to challenge the independence claims of the rebel Dudaev might have sent the wrong signals to other potentially separatist republics, such as Tatarstan or Bashkortostan. In the protracted fighting that followed, the effective stand of Dudaev's Chechen rebels revealed fundamental problems within the Russian military. In 1995, embarrassed by Chechen seizure of hostages across the border in the south Russian town of Budennovsk, the Yeltsin government sought on several occasions to negotiate a cease-fire. War casualties numbering in the tens of thousands had turned Russian public opinion decidedly against the war effort.

Sensing that widespread public opposition to the Chechen fighting might affect his reelection prospects, President Yeltsin sought to distance himself from the crisis while calling for its peaceful resolution. After the presidential elections in mid-1996, Yeltsin turned to his newly appointed national security advisor, Russian military officer and presidential candidate Aleksandr Lebed, to negotiate a settlement with the Chechen rebels. Lebed had earlier negotiated the withdrawal of Russian troops from the Trans-Dniester region (see page 68). In late August 1996, Lebed announced the terms of a cease-fire that called for the withdrawal of Russian forces. Because the agreement postponed resolution of the question involving Chechen independence, the Lebed pact met with a mixed reception in Moscow. Prime Minister Chernomyrdin, who was also wary of the ascendant position of Lebed in the Yeltsin administration, remarked, "the agreements signed by Lebed cause some concern, but on the whole we consider them right"

(Michael R. Gordon, "Chechnya Toll Is Far Higher, 80,000 Dead, Lebed Asserts," *New York Times*, 4 September 1996, 3). Although the Russian government announced the completion of its military withdrawal from Checheniia in January 1997, sporadic outbreaks of violence, such as the killing of Red Cross volunteers in Groznyi in December 1996, reflect the ongoing instability of the region. In internationally monitored presidential elections of January 1997, Aslan Maskhadov was elected president of the Chechen republic. Born in Kazakhstan where his family had been exiled from the Caucasus by Stalin, Maskhadov rose within the ranks of the Soviet Red Army before returning to Checheniia in 1991 to become commander-in-chief of Chechen rebel forces during the war. Alongside his avowed commitment to Chechen independence, the new president has indicated a desire to maintain economic and political ties with Moscow. Whatever the outcome of ongoing Chechen-Russian negotiations may be, the wider significance of the war in Checheniia (Chechnya) cannot be lost upon a Russian Federation that continues to be plagued with problems in effectively integrating its vast domains.

The Russian Orthodox Church For ethnic Russians, conflict with non-Russians of the Federation begs the equally urgent question of Russian national identity within the new Russian Federation. The rediscovery of Russian national and religious identity, while it has been made possible by greater openness, or *glasnost,* has not come without painful memories of Stalinist crimes. The Russian Orthodox Church has emerged as a key institution in the reawakening of this national and religious consciousness. The Orthodox Church, however, has also suffered from the perception that during the Soviet years it preserved itself by making excessive compromises with state authority (see Stephen Batalden, ed., *Seeking God: The Recovery of Religious Identity in Russia, Ukraine, and Georgia,* DeKalb: Northern Illinois University Press, 1993). The result has been a challenge to Russian Orthodoxy, not only from émigré-based Orthodox groups, but from Protestant sectarian interests, and even from right-wing Russian nationalists who have advanced a more radical, often anti-Semitic, agenda. Struggling with their Soviet Stalinist past, Russians are today refashioning their own religious, as well as national, identity.

THE RUSSIAN FEDERATION:
SIBERIA AND THE RUSSIAN FAR EAST

History and Description

Physical Description

Siberia and the Russian Far East constitute the great land mass stretching east from the Ural Mountains and European Russia all the way to the Pacific Ocean—a distance of approximately 3,000 miles. The term "Siberia" is sometimes used to mean the entire region from the Ural Mountains to the Pacific Ocean, but in this chapter, the Russian distinction between Western Siberia, Eastern Siberia, and the Russian Far East (in Russian, *Dal'nyi Vostok*) is employed for greater precision.

Larger than the entire United States, this vast northern territory comprises essentially the Asian part of the former Russian and Soviet empires. It is bordered by Kazakhstan, China, Mongolia, and North Korea on the south and by the icy waters of the Arctic Ocean in the north.

The name "Siberia" comes from the Tatar Khanate of Sibir. Before Russian conquest in the sixteenth century, the Tatars of Sibir controlled much of the Ob River valley in what we now call Western Siberia.

Western Siberia Western Siberia extends from the edge of the Urals roughly to the Enisei River. The basic geographic feature of this region is the immense flat plain called the Western Siberian Lowland. In the north, this great plain includes tundra, a treeless type of landscape prevalent within the Arctic Circle. Tundra features low vegetation, lichens, mosses, and stunted shrubs. In most of the tundra region, permafrost conditions exist. The moisture below the ground's surface becomes permanently frozen, leaving just a thin layer of soil on top. Thickness of permafrost varies from a depth of more than 3,000 feet along the shores of the Arctic Ocean to a depth of 3 feet along the southern boundary of the permafrost region. Farther south, the permafrost zone evolves into small frozen patches.

Spring floods are common in the Western Siberian Lowland, due in part to overflowing rivers that thaw near their sources in the south before reaching the still-frozen northern points where they empty into the Arctic. Because of poor drainage in this region, large areas of marsh and bog prevail, as well as many shallow lakes. About half of Western Siberia is swamp; indeed, the world's largest swamp, the Vasiugan Swamp, is found here between the Ob and Irtysh rivers.

Interspersed with the marshes and bogs is the taiga, a type of land characterized by a wealth of coniferous forests. Fir, spruce, cedar, larch, and pine cover the taiga, providing vast lumber resources and accommodating an abundance of animal life such as brown bear, elk, and small fur-bearing animals. In all, Siberia possesses the world's largest coniferous forest, an oxygen resource of enormous ecological significance in an age of global warming. Toward the southern border with Kazakhstan and Mongolia, the Siberian terrain becomes drier and better suited to agriculture. The taiga gives way to an area of deciduous forest, a land of wooded steppes conducive to the growth of aspen and birch. Continuing south, the landscape gradually changes to open steppe, a distinctly flat, almost treeless panorama in which grasses predominate. A rich black earth is found here, its grassy mat-like covering revealing underneath a fertile loamy soil prized by Russian peasants who colonized the area in earlier centuries.

Siberia and the Russian Far East

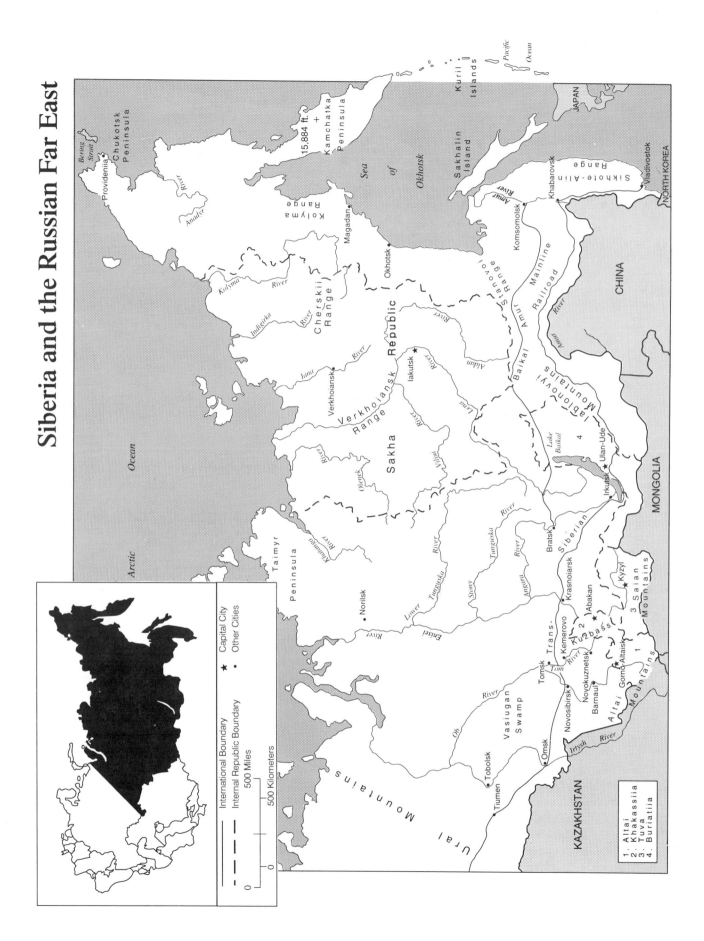

Legend:
- International Boundary
- Internal Republic Boundary
- ★ Capital City
- • Other Cities

Scale: 0 — 500 Miles / 0 — 500 Kilometers

1: Altai
2: Khakassiia
3: Tuva
4: Buriatiia

The major rivers of Western Siberia all flow northward and empty into the Arctic Ocean. Rising in the mountainous border regions shared with China and Mongolia, the Ob River and its main tributary, the Irtysh, cut through the steppe and continue across the taiga and tundra before reaching the frigid Arctic Ocean. The rivers of the Western Siberia region became major transportation routes during Russian colonization, linking the lumber and fur-trading industries to urban markets.

On Western Siberia's southern frontier, the Altai mountain range provides a natural barrier to China. Mount Belukha, on the Kazakh border, is the highest point in this range at 14,783 feet. Two subsidiary ranges extend to the northwest around the heavily industrialized Kuznetsk Basin (Kuzbass).

The Western Siberian region is noted for winters that last as long as seven or eight months, even in the more southerly zones. Average temperatures range from –22°F in the north, to –5°F in the south. The summers are moderate, occasionally quite warm, with temperatures not usually exceeding 55°F in the north and 68°F in the south.

Most farming in Western Siberia takes place in the southern black earth regions shared with northern Kazakhstan. The Virgin Lands program, established there in the 1950s, successfully increased agricultural output for some years (see page 144). Dry farming of spring wheat and corn, plus acreage for fodder and pasturage, are the most common usage of arable land. A greater resource in Western Siberia is the coniferous forest that provides valuable timber and wood products.

By far the greatest wealth of Western Siberia is the rich oil, gas, and coal reserves found in many parts of the region. Coal has long been mined in the Kuznetsk Basin in the area of the Tom River. Oil was found beginning in the 1950s in several parts of Tiumen oblast (particularly in the Vasiugan Swamp). Natural gas has more recently been discovered in the far north, near the mouth of the Ob River and adjacent areas of the Arctic hinterland.

The Trans-Siberian Railroad (5,800 miles) provides the major means of transportation in Western Siberia, with many secondary spurs augmenting the main line. Although river routes supplement the rail link, pipelines have been used extensively to transport oil and gas. Air transport continues to be vital for travel to more remote areas, such as the Arctic coast.

Eastern Siberia Eastern Siberia extends from the Enisei River roughly to the Lena River valley, encompassing most of the Sakha Republic (formerly the Iakut Autonomous Soviet Socialist Republic). This region of Siberia comprises primarily an elevated area called the Central Siberian Upland, augmented by numerous highland regions. Eastern Siberia, like Western Siberia, exhibits a pattern of climate, soil, and vegetation zones that begins with tundra in the frozen north and gradually changes to taiga in the mountainous south. The zone of permafrost in this region extends to the northern border of Mongolia. The taiga zone here is extremely dense because of good drainage.

The Saian mountain system, located west of Lake Baikal along the border with Mongolia, features peaks more than 11,000 feet high. The Iablonovyi Range to the east of Baikal serves to divide rivers flowing to the Arctic from those flowing to the Pacific. Lesser mountain ranges are found to the west and northeast of Lake Baikal. In the far north, mountains on the Taimyr Peninsula along the Arctic Ocean fall within the tundra zone.

The major East Siberian river system, draining into the Arctic Ocean, is made up of the Enisei and its three main tributaries: the Angara, the Stony Tunguska, and the Lower Tunguska. These rivers provide Siberia with an immense potential for hydroelectric energy. The Angara River is the only outlet for Lake Baikal, the world's largest and deepest freshwater lake—approximately 400 miles long, 30 miles wide, and 4,250 feet deep. More than 300 rivers flow into Lake Baikal.

Although little farming is done in Eastern Siberia, some spring wheat is planted in the southern regions. Grazing pastures for cattle, sheep, and goats are extensive, and in the north, reindeer herding is common. The greatest natural wealth of Eastern Siberia may be considered the heavily wooded lands that constitute more than one-third of Russia's forest reserve. The conservation of these forested lands, along with those of Western Siberia, is vitally important to the world's ecological balance. Poorly planned forestry practices during the Soviet period polluted the waters of formerly pristine Lake Baikal with the wastes of wood-products factories. Other natural resources abound in the Eastern Siberian region, most prominently coal. Coal deposits are found in many parts of Siberia, and abundant reserves ensure a supply far into the future. Gold, copper, and iron ore fields are also widespread.

The Russian Far East The Russian Far East region is clearly the largest economic and administrative unit within the Russian Federation. Encompassing more than one-quarter of Russia's territory, this region extends from the Lena River and its tributaries east to the Pacific Ocean, and from the Arctic Ocean south to the Russo-Chinese border. Including the easternmost portion of the Sakha Republic, the Kamchatka Peninsula, the Chukotsk Peninsula, the coast along the Sea of Okhotsk, and Sakhalin Island, the predominant landscape of the Far East is mountainous.

Most of the mountain ranges in the Far East are low in altitude, although they have an alpine appearance because of the northerly latitudes in which they are located. The Stanovoi Range in the southern reaches of the Sakha Republic divides the rivers of the area between those flowing to the Arctic and those extending to the Pacific. To the southeast of the Stanovoi lie smaller ranges. Parallel to the coast is the heavily timbered Sikhote-Alin Range. Across the water, the mountainous island of Sakhalin shows much volcanic activity. North of the Stanovoi Range, steep and rugged mountains cling to the coastline of the Sea of Okhotsk. Still farther north, highland areas are spread out in such a fashion that the entire remainder of the region is basically mountainous. The Verkhoiansk Range east of the valley of the Lena River leads to the Cherskii Range, where the heights are covered with tundra vegetation. From the Chukotsk Peninsula to the Kolyma Range farther south, the mountainous terrain extends onto the volcanic Kamchatka Peninsula. Of the more than 100 volcanoes found on Kamchatka, 20 or more are currently active, the highest being Mt. Kliuchevskaia (15,884 feet). Trailing off the southern tip of Kamchatka are the Kurils, a chain of islands formed by the tips of volcanic mountains.

The river systems of the Russian Far East region are vitally important both as sources of hydroelectric power and as a means of transport. Much has been done to take advantage of the short periods during which navigation is possible on these Siberian rivers before they freeze during the winter months. Two major river systems drain the lands of the Far East. The Amur, second longest river in the Russian Federation, flows toward the Pacific from the region east of Lake Baikal (the Trans-Baikal). The Lena and its Aldan tributary, the third longest river system in Russia, mark the western border of the Far East region and flow toward the Arctic. The Olenek, Kolyma, Indigirka, and Iana rivers also empty into the Arctic. With the exception of the Amur, spring thaws in the headwater areas of these rivers bring widespread flooding to the more northerly river deltas, which remain frozen until much later in the year. One other river in the Far East, the Anadyr on the Chukotsk Peninsula, flows into the Bering Sea.

The climate of the Russian Far East is similar to that of the rest of Siberia and generally exhibits the same arctic to sub-arctic temperature range. In fact, some of the lowest winter temperatures in the world have been noted in northern interior valleys of the Russian Far East, specifically in the Iana river valley at Verkhoiansk where −90°F was once recorded. Although these record low temperatures occur in the interior regions, winter along the Arctic and Pacific coasts can be even harsher because constant strong winds make for a phenomenal wind-chill factor. Winter lasts for 11 months in the Chukotka area, 6 to 8 months in the Amur basin, and 7 to 8 months on Sakhalin Island. Summers are short in the Far East, with a frost-free season of only 45 days in some places. Local topographical conditions and solar radiation cause a marked rise in temperature in May, such that spring passes so quickly it is scarcely recognizable. On the coastal regions of the southeast, the climate is damp and foggy with frequent rain.

The northern zone of the Russian Far East region, like the rest of Siberia, consists of tundra, and most of the soil lies on perennially frozen ground with poor drainage. South of this zone lies more forested tundra, which gradually gives way to coniferous taiga. The taiga belt is relatively large, extending through 20 or more degrees of latitude.

Agriculture has played a minor role in the economy of the Russian Far East. Most of the arable land is used for grazing; crops are limited primarily to grains, soybeans, and sugar beets. Forestry products from the southern part of the region and Sakhalin Island are proving increasingly valuable. Reindeer herding is a common occupation for those who still live on the land. The Far East has also become the most important region in Russia for fishing and the production of fish products, especially along the Amur River and in the Sea of Okhotsk. Furs, once the primary focus of early Russian settlement, still constitute a limited economic resource for the region.

Important natural resources in the Russian Far East region are the largely unexploited reserves of coal, iron ore, oil, and natural gas. Even more significant, however, are rich gold and diamond mines (the latter in the Sakha Republic), valuable sources of foreign currency. The region also holds tin, tungsten, mica, lead, and zinc.

The Trans-Siberian Railroad, built in the 1890s, continues to provide the region's major transportation system. Although the supplementary BAM (Baikal-Amur Mainline), north of the Trans-Siberian, was opened in 1984, it was built at considerable cost in labor and natural resources and has been plagued with problems. River and air transport complement the rail system.

Ethnic Groups of Siberia and the Russian Far East

Although Russians make up by far the largest percentage of the population in Siberia and the Russian Far East (95 percent), dozens of smaller ethnic groups reside within the boundaries of this territory. In very few of the regions or autonomous units, however, do the indigenous peoples make up a majority of the population. The highest percentages of non-Russian population are in the Republic of Tuva, where 64.3 percent of the people are Tuvinian, and in the Sakha Republic where 33.4 percent of the people are Iakut or Sakha. One way of categorizing these non-Russian ethnic groups is on the basis of the language they speak. Four major language groups have been identified amongst Siberian inhabitants: Paleo-Asiatic, Uralic, Altaic, and Indo-European.

Paleo-Asiatic languages are spoken by the indigenous population of northern Siberia and the Russian Far East. Their languages do not appear to be a part of any major language family. Called in Russian the "peoples of the north," these traditionally nomadic tribes hunted, fished, and gathered for a living. Those who bred reindeer followed their herds from place to place. The seminomadic tribes changed their residence twice a year, whereas the sedentary tribes lived in more permanent villages or towns.

Amongst those speaking Paleo-Asiatic languages are several groups who traditionally herded reindeer: the Chukchi (numbering approximately 14,000), the Koriak (8,000), the Eskimos (1,500), and the Iukagirs (800). These tribes all live in the Arctic region from the Kolyma River to the Bering Strait and from the Anadyr River as far south as the central portion of the Kamchatka Peninsula. Other tribal peoples who speak Paleo-Asiatic languages are the Itelmen (1,300) on Kamchatka, the Nivkh (4,400) of Sakhalin Island, and the Lower Amur people, formerly called Giliak.

Uralic languages are spoken by the Samoyedic peoples (Nenets, Selkup, and Nganasan) and the Ugrian peoples (Khanti and Mansi). The Nenets (29,000) live in the Arctic tundra region east of the Ob river valley. The Selkup (3,500) live east of the Nenets near Tomsk; they were formerly known as the Ostiak-Samoyed. The Nganasan (860), whose name means "people," live in the tundra on the Taimyr Peninsula. The Khanti (21,000), in the Ob and Irtysh river valleys, are an Ugrian speaking tribe, as are the seminomadic Mansi (7,500) in the Tiumen oblast.

The Altaic-speaking tribes employ either a Tungusic, Turkic, or Mongolic language. The six main Tungusic tribes are: the nomadic Orok (1,200) on Sakhalin Island, some of whom were resettled on Hokkaido (Japan) alongside 1,500 Ainu after World War II; the nomadic Evenk (27,500), formerly called Tungus, living along the Enisei River; the nomadic Even (12,500) east of the Lena River along the Arctic coast as far as the Sea of Okhotsk and down into the Kamchatka Peninsula; the Negidal; the Nanai; and the

Udegei—the latter three being semisedentary hunters and fishers.

The most populous Turkic-speaking people of Siberia are the Sakha (328,000) of the Sakha Republic, the capital of which is Iakutsk on the Lena River. The Sakha literary language is written in Cyrillic; their religion is syncretic Eastern Orthodox with overtones of shamanism. The reindeer-breeding Dolgan (5,000), who live in the tundra south of the Khatanga River, are also Turkic speaking.

Other Turkic-speaking tribes in the region are the Siberian Tatars living north of Kazakhstan on the southern edge of Western Siberia. Among these tribes are the Shor, the Khakass, the Altai of the Altai-Saian mountain region, the Tuvinian near the Mongolian border, and various groups of Kazakh nomads. The combined population of these primarily nomadic tribes is approximately 175,000.

A Mongolic language is spoken in Siberia by the Buriat people who live around Lake Baikal in the southern part of Eastern Siberia. They make up a large, formerly seminomadic tribe numbering approximately 353,000. The Republic of Buriatiia was an autonomous republic (the Buriat Mongol ASSR) under the Soviet system. The Buriat literary language, earlier rendered in Old Mongolian, is now written in Cyrillic. Although subjected to secularizing pressures under Soviet rule, the Trans-Baikal Buriats maintain their religious ties with Buddhism.

One other indigenous group in Siberia is the Ket tribe living between the Ob and Enisei river valleys. They speak a unique language seemingly unrelated to any other and therefore have attracted the attention of historical linguists. Numbering less than 1,200 people, they, too, have followed the life of seminomadic hunters and fishers.

The Indo-European language group is represented in Siberia and the Russian Far East by Slavs and other European people who settled in this area mainly as colonizers. Russians, Ukrainians, and Belarusians migrated eastward into Siberia as soon as it was incorporated into the Russian Empire in the latter half of the sixteenth century. German-speaking colonists arrived later, in the nineteenth century. The Indo-European, particularly Russian, population currently dominates the urban centers of Siberia and the Russian Far East.

Religions of Siberia and the Russian Far East

Shamanism, an ancient form of belief dating perhaps from the Stone Age, has long been common among the indigenous peoples of Siberia. The word shaman is derived from the Tungusic word *saman* meaning "one who is excited." The Tungusic word is itself drawn from the Sanskrit *Sramana,* meaning "ascetic." Although shamanism varies from tribe to tribe, all its manifestations feature a spirit helper or shaman who mediates between the visible and spiritual worlds. Shamans heal the sick by invoking a trance-like state; they also guide dead souls to the "other world," communicate between the living and dead, perform sacrificial rites to appease angry spirits, and carry out traditional tribal ceremonies.

With the settlement of Siberia by Europeans, the Russian Orthodox Church attempted to convert native peoples to Christianity. Early imperial policy, dating from the reign of Peter the Great in the first quarter of the eighteenth century, required such conversion. The Khanti and Mansi groups moved from their original homelands to avoid converting, but they could not escape for long. While ostensibly adopting Christianity, they continued to practice their shamanistic religion well into the nineteenth century. The Sakha accepted Russian Orthodoxy through bribery and gifts, but they also continued to practice shamanism. Invariably, the conversion process was paralleled by the retention of tribal religious practices.

In addition to Russian Orthodoxy, Buddhism spread north into Siberia from Mongolia. Buriat Mongols in the Lake Baikal region adopted the Buddhist religion in the eighteenth century and, as a result, were the only native Siberians to have a written language before 1917. Nineteenth-century Protestant missionaries from England, along with missionaries from the Russian Orthodox Church, made largely unsuccessful attempts to convert the Buriats to Christianity.

The Siberian Tatars meanwhile had adopted the religion of Islam. With the influx of Russian settlers, however, they began to lose their hunting grounds and traditional ways, eventually becoming quite impoverished. The process of intermarrying with the Christian Orthodox Russians followed, and many Tatars merged into the dominant culture.

In the 1920s, the new Soviet government banned shamanism. The drums and costumes of the shamans were confiscated, and those who opposed the process were prosecuted. Soviet authorities accused the shamans of deceiving and cheating their own people in pursuit of riches. The shamans in general opposed the incursion of Slavic civilization and spoke against the development of schools, deeming them unnecessary to the traditional way of life. As the healers of native families and clans, they also felt displaced by the introduction of modern medical services. In order to defend themselves against Soviet bureaucrats, however, many shamans did learn to read and write. Buddhism was also affected by official Soviet atheism. The number of lamas in the autonomous Republic of Buriatiia declined and Buddhist monasteries were closed. Today, however, aspects of shamanism have survived alongside Russian Orthodoxy, Buddhism, and Islam.

Russian Conquest and Colonization

According to early Russian Siberian narratives, a Cossack mercenary, Ermak Timofeevich, led an army of several hundred Muscovite Russian loyalists against the Khanate of Sibir in the Ob River valley in 1581. By the fall of 1582, Ermak's forces defeated these Tatars and occupied the capital of Sibir (near the present-day city of Tobolsk). This campaign was the opening round in what ultimately became the Russian conquest of north Asia or Siberia. By 1605, Russians had spread as far as the Enisei, Lower and Stony Tunguska, and Angara rivers. By the 1640s, they had reached the Sea of Okhotsk and the Pacific Ocean and soon established power in the Lake Baikal region also. Russia had crossed Siberia and the Far East in about 50 years. The new land was treated as a single province and divided into 19 districts ruled by a military governor.

A policy of building forts near strategic points on the river systems was implemented. Tiumen, Tobolsk, Tomsk, Iakutsk, Okhotsk, and Irkutsk were some of the first forts built at this time. These forts were generally built near native tribes in an attempt to discourage alliances between the indigenous peoples.

By the eighteenth century, Russian adventurers had begun to take an interest in Siberia and the Far East for its vast wealth in furs, iron, gold, silver, and salt; traders and trappers exploited the region for profit. Russian peasants also were encouraged by the government to move to Siberia and work the land. Often accompanying or in advance of Russian settlement, Russian Orthodox missionaries were sent to convert the indigenous population to Christianity. Alongside Russian settlement came bureaucratic control, with local administrative officials maintaining order and collecting tribute from the local population. As small centers of settlement grew, bureaucratic and commercial interests expanded accordingly. During the eighteenth century, mining for copper, lead, silver, and iron ore was carried out in Western Siberia on the eastern slope of the Ural Mountains, as well as in the more southerly Altai mountain range and in the Trans-Baikal area. Despite these efforts to open up the region, Siberian natural resources in the nineteenth century remained relatively unexploited, even as the fur trade became less profitable.

The most ambitious modern effort to integrate the vast lands of Siberia with the European centers of Russian imperial power was the construction of the Trans-Siberian Railroad, begun in 1891 and completed as far as Irkutsk in 1900. By the time of World War I, the Trans-Siberian track reached from Moscow to Vladivostok on the Pacific. The railroad made the vast reaches of Siberia and the Russian Far East more accessible for economic exploitation and launched major Russian and Ukrainian colonization of the region. While the rail line provided transport for Russian troops and thereby strengthened Russian military authority along its southern border, the Trans-Siberian line also led Russia to negotiate special rights of access through Manchuria, rights that ultimately brought Russia into conflict with Japanese imperial power in the Far East (the Russo-Japanese War of 1904–05).

At the end of the nineteenth century, a combination of peasant uprisings and revolutionary movements prompted the tsarist government to encourage increased colonial settlement and migration to Siberia. The consequent colonization, especially after peasants had become legally free to leave their communal holdings, reached an annual high of 750,000 in 1908. Even more dramatic, perhaps, was the fact that by 1910 Siberia had become agriculturally self-sufficient and even produced enough surplus for export. In contrast, the industrial development of Siberia during the tsarist period was minimal, and manufacturing often came to depend upon foreign investment.

In 1912, the Lena gold mine strike, basically a protest of working conditions, took place in Iakutiia (now, Sakha). Government forces brutally crushed the revolt, but not before further labor unrest had spread across Siberia.

Soviet Rule

Following the 1917 October Revolution, Irkutsk and Krasnoiarsk declared their initial loyalty to the new Bolshevik government, a loyalty that was matched in other regions of Siberia in the early months of 1918. Seeking to keep Russia in World War I, however, the Western allies supported the counterrevolutionary forces of the tsarist admiral Aleksandr Kolchak, a prominent leader during the Russian Civil War that followed the 1917 Revolution. Drawing upon a coalition of local citizens, Cossacks, and various anti-Bolshevik groups, Siberia and the Far East soon became a center of counterrevolutionary activity. By June 1918, these forces, led by Admiral Kolchak and what came to be known as his White Army, overthrew the Bolshevik government in Siberia. In the months that followed, however, the White forces came under in-

creasing challenge from both the Red Army and from sporadic guerrilla activity. By 1921, the Bolsheviks had reestablished their power throughout most of Siberia and the Russian Far East.

To make the administration of this large region more manageable, the new Soviet government divided Siberia into political-administrative units roughly based on the distribution of native ethnic groups. Autonomous regions were established for many of these indigenous peoples. These autonomous administrative regions varied in size and prestige, all the way from the autonomous republic (not to be confused with a union republic), to the autonomous oblast (not to be confused with the purely administrative oblast), to the autonomous okrug. Although always subordinate to Moscow, autonomous republics had their own formal constitutions. Since the late 1980s, the importance of these divisions, and of the ethnic homelands they represent, has been reinforced by their own declarations of sovereignty and independence. Of the 21 republics now forming part of the Russian Federation, 5 are in Siberia—Altai, Buriatiia, Khakassiia, Sakha, and Tuva. Declarations of sovereignty have been made not only by all five of these republics, but also by several of the other formerly autonomous oblasts and okrugs.

Occasionally inspired by grandiose engineering plans, Soviet leaders sought to exploit the rich resources of Siberia, frequently without regard to potential environmental damage. In the name of modernization and development, major efforts were launched to explore for mineral deposits, develop local forest and related industries, and otherwise extract the natural resources of the vast Siberian territory. The first Soviet Five Year Plan (1928–32) mandated the construction of giant hydroelectric plants and a number of metallurgical plants, as well. The coal-rich Kuznetsk basin in Western Siberia was developed and iron ore deposits were discovered nearby. In the 1930s, on the lower Amur River, huge industrial complexes and power stations were built, and military installations now dot the Russian Far East. Not all large-scale development plans were carried through to completion. One of the more controversial plans, noted later, called for the massive diversion southward of northerly flowing Siberian rivers for the purpose of irrigating the drier fields and cotton-growing regions of Kazakhstan and Central Asia.

During World War II, industrial plants were converted to military production and to the manufacture of tanks and other products needed for the war. Factories in European Russia were moved to the Urals and to Siberia, remaining there after the war's end. Despite the difficulty of access and the fragile terrain, ambitious efforts were renewed in the postwar period to exploit Siberia's large mineral deposits, hydroelectric potential, forest preserves, and oil and natural gas resources. Dams and power plants harnessed the energy of the region's many rivers, most notably the large plant in Krasnoiarsk. Wood processing factories were built in Bratsk, diamonds were mined in Iakutiia, and agricultural machinery was produced in the Altai province. Squirrels, polar fox, ermine, and sable supplied the fur industry. Oil and natural gas were extracted and shipped via a large pipeline across the Urals to Moscow and Leningrad (St. Petersburg).

During Nikita Khrushchev's leadership in the 1950s and early 1960s, greater investment in agriculture was proposed, and the "virgin lands" of southern Siberia and northern Kazakhstan were marked for grain production. Yields reached their peak in 1956, but totals thereafter declined due to poor cultivation methods, for the farms did not rotate crops or let the land lie fallow.

Plans for a new line to supplement the Trans-Siberian Railroad were mapped in the early 1970s. The BAM (Baikal-Amur Mainline) railway is located well north of Russia's southern boundary, unlike the Trans-Siberian, which runs just 50 miles north of the border with China. Although track-laying for the BAM (2,250 miles) was completed in 1984 from Bratsk to Komsomolsk near the Pacific coast and traversing the permafrost region north of Lake Baikal, the line continues to face major operational problems related to the frozen soil it crosses, as well as to the seven mountain ranges through which it has had to be tunneled.

The Gulag

In addition to the explorers, traders, settlers, and others who gravitated to Siberia and the Russian Far East in ever-increasing numbers during the nineteenth and twentieth centuries, one group of "immigrants" represented, in an entirely different way, the place of Siberia and the Far East in Russian history. These were the prisoners and exiled subjects who were unwilling to go along with the policies of the tsarist or Soviet systems. In the days of the tsars, Siberia was first used as a place of exile for political prisoners. This practice was continued by Stalin, under whose leadership hundreds of thousands of people arbitrarily termed "antisocial" were sent to prison camps located primarily in Siberia. The gulag (a Russian acronym for Chief Administration of Corrective Labor Camps), written about so movingly by Soviet writers, such as Aleksandr Solzhenitsyn in *The Gulag Archipelago*, was a vast system of work camps and prisons housing the innocent victims of Soviet rule. From peasants unwilling to accept collectivization, to political rivals, to writers, religious believers, and returning Soviet prisoners of war—all were swept off to the camps, in some cases for perpetually renewable terms of imprisonment. The gulag supplied endless workers to exploit the economic riches of the tundra and taiga, many of them giving their lives in the process. According to Solzhenitsyn, between 13 and 25 million people perished in the gulag during the Stalinist era.

Organized in the 1930s and run initially by the NKVD, a precursor of the KGB, the center for one area of camps in the Far East was at Magadan on the Sea of Okhotsk. Magadan served as a transit point for prisoners sent to work in the gold mines located in the frigid climate of the Kolyma region. Another Siberian area worked by prisoners was the Taimyr Peninsula north of Norilsk, where thousands labored in another Arctic setting to develop Soviet mining interests.

Siberia and the Russian Far East: Contemporary Issues

Modernization and the Indigenous Peoples

As in the European settlement of the United States, the interests and the way of life of indigenous populations have been threatened in the Russian settlement of Siberia and the Far East. Whether it be the native peoples of America or the small nations of the Russian far north, the advance of industrial society has posed for the indigenous population the same difficult alternatives. These alternatives range from forced assimilation into the majority society, to uneasy accommodation at the margins of society, to conscious preservation of traditional culture. What makes these alternatives so painful for the indigenous minorities, however, is that the majority society has colonized their territory and now claims it as its own.

To frame the situation in this way, however, is already to challenge those earlier Soviet apologists who maintained that the Siberian experience was very different from its American counterpart. According to this official Soviet view, Native Americans suffered near genocidal losses of population from European diseases, armed conflict with colonists, restrictions in location, and loss of herds. In contrast, Russian nineteenth- and twentieth-century settlement is said not to have resulted in native depopulation. Moreover, in those regions where natural resources such as oil or diamonds are extracted, the native population was able to secure gainful employment. Finally, unlike their American counterparts, Russian settlers have not, according to this view, hesitated to intermarry with the local indigenous population. In short, the argument is that the European settlement of America was associated with a pattern of violent domination and expropriation of land and resources, whereas the Russian settlement of Siberia and the Far East has been humane and understanding.

The discussion of modern Siberian and Far Eastern development and its impact upon the small nations of the north may now be addressed more openly, in a way hardly imaginable a decade ago before the advent of glasnost. In this debate, the basic demographic realities, which weigh heavily against the indigenous peoples, provide an appropriate starting point. Only in the small Republic of Tuva does the native population exceed that of the Russian settlers. In the Buriat republic, the Buriats constitute only about one-fourth of the total population. In the Sakha (Iakut) republic, the Sakha are about one-third the total population. Similarly, in the Altai republic, the Altai make up no more than one-third of the population. In other regions of the more sparsely populated north—for example, among the Evenk, Nenets, Khanti, Mansi, and Chukchi, the native peoples rarely constitute more than 10 percent of the population. Given the high concentration of Slavic population in the larger urban centers, as well, Siberia and the Far East have become a land where indigenous people live as minorities within a dominant Russian culture.

While the successive tsarist and Soviet governments have regarded their efforts as beneficial to the small nations of the north, the fact is that these regimes fundamentally sought to alter the basic nomadic patterns of the northern fishers, hunters, and reindeer herders. In the tsarist period, "ownership" of reindeer herds passed from the indigenous people to the more wealthy Russian adventurers and merchants. In the Stalinist and post–World War II periods, forced collectivization and consolidation of settlements effectively took the marketing of hunted game out of the hands of local people and placed it in the hands of Communist Party bureaucrats. The results have been devastating to those northern peoples who have lived for centuries by reindeer herding, fishing, and hunting. There have been dire predictions that unless management of the once-lucrative reindeer herding is

returned to the native tribes, reindeer herds will be overkilled and lost, and tribes' hunting and herd-management skills will not be passed along to the next generation. Estimates have been made that no more than 180,000 Paleo-Asiatic indigenous peoples still inhabit northern Siberia (less than the Native American population of Arizona alone).

Alongside its threat to traditional nomadic hunting, herding, and fishing patterns, the state has also been intrusive with respect to family life and religious patterns. Committed to literacy, the Soviet state in the 1920s established central bases in the Siberian north for the introduction of formal schooling. These cultural bases (sometimes called "red tents") became the locations for boarding schools that drew young native children away from their families, trained them in Russian language and culture, and established the authority of Soviet institutions. Because of these boarding schools, according to critics, young native students were not trained in basic family customs, including survival skills necessary for traditional life in the north, and their study of native languages was largely abandoned.

Soviet authorities also sought, without complete success, to eliminate the shamans from Siberian village life. This intrusion into local beliefs and practices was not coupled with any provision for alternative health care or social services. The consequent disruptions have, in the view of some, led to the widespread abuse of alcohol now afflicting many Siberian northern peoples. Prior to Russian settlement in Siberia, alcohol had never been available to the small nations of the north. (On these and other observations regarding the breakdown of local indigenous culture, see Kathleen Mihalisko, "Discontent in Taiga and Tundra," *Radio Liberty Research*, 7 July 1988.) It has been estimated that, since World War II, the life expectancy for indigenous northern peoples of Siberia has dropped by more than 10 years (45 for men, 55 for women).

Mounting fears over the fate of the Paleo-Asiatic peoples of Siberia and the Russian Far East led a Soviet State Commission for Arctic Affairs (formed in 1988) to broach the idea of establishing "zones of restricted economic activity," clearly a term for something similar to the Indian reservation in the United States. A frequently quoted Evenk writer, Alitet Nemtushkin, who has aired publicly his ecological concerns over both oil and gas exploration and the plans for yet further hydroelectric power stations, has added his strong support to the proposal for Siberian and Far Eastern "reservations" (quoted in Kathleen Mihalisko, "North American–Style Native Reservations in the Soviet North?" *Report on the USSR*, 21 July 1989). From the point of view of some of these northern peoples who seek to recover their nomadic traditions, the establishment of reservations can even be viewed as a positive force for arresting the physical, cultural, and ecological threats to the small northern nations of Siberia.

Although these smaller nations are peculiarly vulnerable to modern industrialization, a related set of concerns in the more southerly Republic of Tuva led to public demonstrations and violence directed against the Russian population. The Tuvinians, a Turkic-speaking Buddhist people numbering more than 200,000, constitute approximately two-thirds of the population of the Republic of Tuva (Russians make up approximately one-third of the population). The large post–World War II migration of European Slavs into Tuva was benefited by an industrialization policy that did little to assist the underemployed and more rural Tuvinians. Riots erupted in 1990, triggered by a dance-floor conflict between Tuvinian and Slavic youths. Violence between the two groups spread in May 1990 to Kyzyl, the capital of Tuva, where a young person was murdered for failing to answer a question in Tuvinian. Leaflets calling for Slavs to leave Tuva led to widespread Russian uneasiness and a substantial number of departures. Eventually, troops from the Soviet Ministry of Internal Affairs were called in to Tuva, a sign of how seriously this attack upon Russians and other Slavs was taken in Moscow. Subsequent declarations of Tuvinian sovereignty have only confirmed the potentially explosive interethnic friction, particularly in more southerly regions of Siberia.

Not unlike the Republic of Tuva, the Sakha Republic (formerly Iakutiia) has also been the scene of independence movements directed against Russian political and economic authority. The leadership of the Sakha Republic has used such movements effectively to challenge the Russian Federation's monopoly on marketing the republic's diamond reserves. In 1992 an agreement was reached whereby a jointly held Russian-Sakha company would control all diamond production and sales. According to this agreement, the Sakha Republic would keep 20 percent of the diamonds it produces, as well as 45 percent of all hard currency earnings derived from foreign diamond sales. Some unreconciled Sakha nationals nevertheless decry the diamond mining and its impact upon traditional Sakha pastoral ways of life. Others, including the republic's old-style political leadership, see the new Russian-Sakha profit-sharing arrangements as a significant improvement over earlier relations with Russia, especially the prospect of sharing in the estimated $1.4 billion annual diamond sales exported through the DeBeers South African diamond monopoly. For now, the Sakha diamond agreement, unlike the problems in Tuva, sug-

gests that the Russian Federation can continue to win local support by sharing the mineral rights it formerly controlled. It remains to be seen whether such concessions will guarantee lasting Russian ties with a Siberian/Far Eastern native population rediscovering its own ethnic and religious traditions.

From the indigenous Arctic peoples to the sovereign republics of Sakha and Tuva, the tension between Russian industrialization and natural resource exploitation, on the one hand, and non-Russian, rural, nomadic cultures, on the other, has become one of the greatest forces for conflict in contemporary Siberia.

Ecological Compromises in Modern Siberia

A second major dilemma faces those who seek to exploit the rich natural resources of Siberia and the Far East—namely, the long-term ecological well-being of Siberia and the Russian Far East can readily be damaged by bad planning and short-term thinking. The signs of such damage are already strewn across the land, with yet further dangers to the fragile Siberian environment clearly in the offing.

As a resource-rich frontier region, Siberia and the Far East now provide a disproportionate share of the Russian Federation's overall natural wealth. More than 60 percent of Russian mining production takes place in Siberia; more than 50 percent of its fuel production; nearly 40 percent of its production of nonferrous metals; and more than one-third of its wood and paper-product production. Yet, less than 25 percent of the Russian Federation's population lives in Siberia and the Far East. Such exploitation of Siberian and Far Eastern natural resources, including the current drive for foreign investment to access and market Siberian oil, natural gas, and timber, has become an absolutely essential part of the overall Russian economy. Yet, this exploitation has come with a great price, so much so that the ecological future of Siberia and the Russian Far East now hangs in the balance.

No area exemplifies the issue of ecological compromise in Siberia as strongly as the use and misuse of water resources. The northward-flowing rivers of Western and Eastern Siberia provide an abundant source of water for the region. In their effort to harness these water resources, however, Soviet engineers have put large parts of northern Siberia at risk. The large dams and hydroelectric power projects now dotting the Siberian landscape have limited the normal northward flow of river waters, which in some instances has affected the salinity of river deltas, in turn affecting the herding of reindeer and the grazing habits of other Arctic game animals.

More complicated has been the secondary impact of the hydroelectric stations. Launched early in the Soviet era, these plants provided electrical power beyond the needs of the sparsely populated Siberian tundra and taiga. In a classic case of "cart before the horse," the surplus electricity then became the rationale for transferring heavy industry to Siberia. Movement of industry into this cold, ecologically fragile region involved further immigration into regions with limited infrastructure. The urban communities that were built for industrial development led to fundamental environmental and health problems related to the Siberian climate. Weather extremes in winter, combined with normal industrial pollutants, have created serious temperature inversions and caustic air pollution. Even basic provisions for waste disposal have not always met elementary health standards. At stake in the debate over the construction of additional dams and hydroelectric power stations is the question of how much priority to give to the industrial and urban development of Siberia. This issue began to be discussed at higher policymaking levels only during the leadership of Soviet First Party Secretary Mikhail Gorbachev (1985–1991).

In the debate about Siberian water, the region's fledgling environmental movement found its first tenuous victory in the so-called Siberian Rivers Diversion Project. Drawn up by an army of Soviet hydroelectric engineers, this project sought to divert part of the flow of the Ob and Irtysh rivers southward into Kazakhstan to augment the Syr Darya and Amu Darya rivers and irrigate the Central Asian cotton fields. The appeal of this engineering plan was that it would also provide additional water to replenish the disappearing Aral Sea. Environmental critics of the plan, however, began to note the potentially dangerous impact of the project upon the Ob-Irtysh river valley. Not only would fishing, timber rafting, and navigation be affected, but the reduced flows would potentially alter the permafrost conditions of northern Arctic regions. In the end, perhaps the most damaging evidence came from those who projected that the reduced flows into the Arctic Ocean would increase the ocean's salinity, melting parts of the polar ice cap. In short, an impressive engineering plan, one of many such grandiose ideas proposed for Siberia, ended up having implications of truly global proportions. The Siberian Rivers Diversion Project appears to have been shelved during the Gorbachev years, but the plan occasionally has resurfaced, promoted by various land reclamation and water resource engineers who continue to hold posts in governmental ministries of the Russian Federation.

Related to the use and misuse of water resources is the ongoing pollution of Lake Baikal, the world's deepest lake and, by volume, the world's largest body of fresh water. Lake Baikal, because of its unique ecosystem—it contains numerous species that exist nowhere else in the world—has become a focal point of international attention from marine biologists, ecologists, and concerned environmental activists. While there is no single source of pollutants flowing into Lake Baikal, the most serious and easily identifiable culprits are the forest and wood-products industries located along streams and rivers flowing into the lake. Of these industries, the notorious Baikal Pulp and Paper Combine is the worst. Forced to make plans for conversion into a furniture manufacturing plant by 1993, the Combine continues to exist. Concern for workers disaffected by closure or conversion has held up the process, as have the conflicting signals of governmental ministries. Despite the hundreds of specialists who have focused in one way or another upon the pollution of Lake Baikal, there still seems to be no comprehensive assessment of the sources of the lake's pollution, nor any clear sense of the damage already inflicted (see Zeev Wolfson, "Anarchy Mirrored in Lake Baikal," *Report on the USSR*, 26 May 1989).

Related to the Baikal issue, forestry remains one of the most environmentally sensitive issues confronting Siberia. Possessing the largest coniferous forest in the world, an invaluable resource offsetting global warming, Siberia now must respond to contending interests covetous of those resources. On the one hand, the forest reserves hold great potential for revenue. International lumbering companies are already well represented in Russia and along with local cooperatives are seeking to utilize the forests for commercial gain. The Russian Federation and the local Siberian economies desperately need this revenue. At the same time, in the present chaotic state of the Russian economy, there is virtually no way of establishing what the real value of these forest reserves is. And while international corporations may seek to exploit this chaos to secure undervalued forest products, the fear also persists that wide-scale deforestation could compromise global environmental interests.

An indication of how unprepared Siberia and the Russian Far East are for the debate between environmental and economic interests can be seen in the region's forest fire policies. Outfitted with the largest aerial fire-fighting force in the world, Russian forest rangers confront a bewildering conflict over policy— or absence of policy—that reflects the fundamental dilemma over how best to evaluate the Siberian and Far Eastern forest reserves. In principle, the Russian aerial firefighters are committed to putting out all fires, but in practice, the control of fire over such a vast region is impossible.

Although the problem of establishing market value is not as great in the area of mining and oil drilling, associated environmental and occupational problems are just as troubling. Western and Eastern Siberia account for more than 70 percent of all oil drilled, more than 85 percent of all natural gas extracted, and more than 60 percent of all coal mined in the Russian Federation. Yet, environmental safeguards are woefully lacking. In Western Siberia alone it is estimated that "one million tons of oil are spilled annually onto the territory of Tyumen [Tiumen] and Tomsk oblasts" (Kathleen Mihalisko, "North American–Style Reservations in the Soviet North?" *Report on the USSR*, 21 July 1989). The strip mining of coal in the Siberian Kuzbass has left large swaths of territory denuded and unfit for habitation. The chemical industry in the Altai republic has contributed to levels of air pollution that have led to elevated rates of birth defects.

For workers in these industries, the effort to extract natural resources at minimal cost has yielded a shocking set of working conditions that violate elementary safety standards. Responding to these conditions and to the absence of consumer goods and basic infrastructure in the western Siberian mining towns of the Kuzbass region, local coal miners in July 1989 struck the Sheviakov mine. They presented a list of 42 demands that included safety improvements, longer vacations, more and better consumer goods (e.g., 80 grams of soap each month per worker), and better infrastructure (one mining community complained about having running water only 2 hours a day). Even political appeals were made for the independence of their mine and for local leadership on environmental issues. Not only did the strike extend to adjacent mining towns of the Kuzbass, affecting some 150,000 workers and enormous productive capacities, but also to the Ukrainian Donets coal mining region. Although the Soviet authorities ultimately sought to resolve the strike by providing higher salaries and seeking to guarantee access to consumer goods, the long-term problems remain in Siberian society. One of the ironies of the former Soviet Union, with its ideological commitment to the advancement of the proletariat, was its exploitative mining practices undertaken at the expense of workers.

The environmental crises and the grievances of local workers affect not only the indigenous native population of Siberia and the Far East, but also Siberian-born Russians and other Slavs who now consider Siberia their homeland. The talented Russian writer Valentin Rasputin has become a champion of Lake Baikal and has written widely on Siberian environmental concerns. Out of a common concern for the environment, there is the potential for alliance between indigenous peoples of Siberia and the far more numerous Slavic settlers. The long-term problem of coordinating economic development with respect for the fragile environment remains as much a dilemma for the Russian Federation as for Siberia's original native peoples.

Relations with Neighboring Regions

Siberia and the Russian Far East border Kazakhstan, Mongolia, North Korea, and China to the south; Japan on the Pacific; and Alaska in the far northeast. These borders, while not without occasional incident, have been relatively quiet. Nevertheless, the southeastern border with China, along the Amur River, has long been a sore point in Russian-Chinese relations, the Chinese believing that the "unequal" treaties ending World War II violated their interests. In the case of the Russian-Mongolian border, modern Trans-Baikal Buriat traditions are rooted in a Mongolic language and Buddhist religious practice, thus making for natural ties between the Buriat republic and Mongolia. Travel is now possible between the two.

The most troublesome current diplomatic relationship confronting Siberia and the Russian Far East is that with Japan. Although both Soviet leader Mikhail Gorbachev and Russian Federation President Boris Yeltsin traveled to Japan in the 1990s, the normalization of Russian-Japanese relations has foundered on the basic issue of the Kuril Islands, which lie south of the Kamchatka Peninsula and north of the main Japanese islands. The recent history of the Russian-Japanese dispute over these islands dates to World War II. At the Yalta Conference, the Allies promised the Soviet Union possession of the Kuril Islands in return for entering the Pacific war against Japan. Japan has never accepted the loss of the Kuril chain, particularly the four southernmost islands that are referred to in Japan as the "Northern Territories."

Despite the long-standing reluctance of the Soviet Union to reconsider any of the post–World War II peace terms, the assumption to power of Mikhail Gorbachev in the 1980s brought a fresh desire to relax tensions in Asia. For a time, it appeared as though the Soviet authorities might arrange a negotiated settlement regarding some of the southernmost islands in return for Japanese diplomatic support and foreign investment in the development of Siberian natural resources. The subsequent cancellation by Boris Yeltsin of his second visit to Japan and the Russian nationalist reaction against any concessions on the Kuril Islands seem, for the time being, to have closed the opportunity for renegotiation of the conflict. For Japan, which has taken a consistently hard-line position insisting on full sovereignty over all four of the southern Kurils, satisfactory resolution of the contending claims remains a prerequisite for full normalization of relations with the Russian Federation.

For the far northeastern peninsula of Chukotka, the most dramatic development in neighborly relations has been the opening of direct airline service between the regional center of Provideniia and Alaska. Initially started to allow relatives on either side of the Bering Strait to visit one another—something that had been impossible since the 1930s—flights can now be chartered between Chukotka and Nome, among other Alaskan cities. Regularly scheduled airline passenger service between major ports of call in Alaska and the Russian Far East is now possible.

Easier travel between the Russian Far East and Alaska, as well as the Pacific Northwest, points to the potential for expanded American and Japanese trade with this resource-rich region. The removal of barriers to travel is also a mark of the striking relaxation of East-West tensions in the region. Although still heavily fortified by military installations, the Russian Far East is nevertheless open to international trade and commerce in an atmosphere unrecognizable a mere decade ago when Soviet forces shot down a Korean passenger airliner that had strayed into Soviet air space.

PART TWO

BELARUS, MOLDOVA, AND UKRAINE

INTRODUCTION

The Russian Federation, which includes territory in both Europe and Asia, is the largest and most heavily populated successor state to the Soviet Union. In Europe, three other newly independent states of the former USSR—Belarus, Moldova, and Ukraine—are situated to the west of the Russian Federation (as are the three Baltic republics not covered in this volume). Belarus and Ukraine take their names from the two Eastern Slavic peoples who inhabit these republics— Belarusians and Ukrainians. Moldova, which borders the Balkan state of Romania, takes its name from the Moldovan (or Moldavian) people whose Romance language is virtually indistinguishable from that of modern Romanian.

The lands of present-day Belarus, Moldova, and Ukraine were first incorporated into the Russian Empire over the course of a 200-year period from the early seventeenth to the nineteenth century. Parts of Ukraine were brought into the Muscovite Empire even earlier, in the sixteenth century, but the Black Sea coastal areas and those lands west of the Dnieper River were annexed from the Crimean Khanate and the Polish-Lithuanian Commonwealth in the eighteenth century. Full incorporation of Ukraine into the Russian Empire awaited institutional changes of the later eighteenth and early nineteenth centuries. Belarus was annexed by the Russian Empire during the partitioning of Poland in the last third of the eighteenth century. Moldova, known as Bessarabia at that time, was then part of the Ottoman Empire. The annexation of Bessarabia first brought the lands of Moldova into the Russian Empire in 1812. Following World War I, parts of western Ukraine and Belarus again became a part of Polish territory, and Moldova rejoined Romania.

The present borders of Belarus, Moldova, and Ukraine were established by the Soviet Union at the end of World War II, with the exception of the Crimean Peninsula, which in 1954 was transferred from the Russian Soviet Socialist Republic to the Ukrainian Soviet Socialist Republic. Although the Belarusian, Ukrainian, and Moldovan nations have placed their own cultural stamp upon their newly independent states, there continues to be a large Russian minority in each of these three republics. Additionally, the region has an important Jewish heritage. The lands west of the Dnieper River constituted the traditional center of Jewish settlement during the centuries of the Polish-Lithuanian Commonwealth. Following Russian incorporation of the area, Jewish settlement was restricted to these lands, which came to be called the Pale of Settlement.

Heavily industrialized during the Soviet era, these republics have subsequently experienced repeated environmental and health crises. Along with other parts of Eastern Europe and the Baltic region, they suffered the worst of the impact of the 1986 nuclear reactor explosion in Chernobyl, which is situated near the Ukrainian-Belarusian border.

Three of the more troubling border disputes following the breakup of the Soviet Union have erupted in this region. Within Ukraine, there has been conflict over who owns and has the right to govern the Crimean Peninsula. In a related dispute, control of the former USSR's Black Sea naval fleet, which is porting at the Crimean city of Sevastopol, has been the subject of negotiations between the Russian Federation and Ukraine. And in Moldova, a Russian minority sought in the early 1990s to claim sovereignty over the slice of land north and east of the Dniester River, calling the region the Trans-Dniester Republic. This border dispute, yet to be fully resolved, has brought ethnic violence to a region long torn between rival Russian and Romanian claimants.

Bibliography

Batalden, Stephen K., ed. *Seeking God: The Recovery of Religious Identity in Russia, Ukraine, and Georgia.* DeKalb: Northern Illinois University Press, 1993.

Bociurkiw, Bohdan. *Ukrainian Churches under Soviet Rule: Two Case Studies.* Cambridge, MA: Harvard Ukrainian Research Institute, 1984.

Bruchis, Michael. *Nations, Nationalities, People: A Study of the Nationalities Policy of the Communist Party in Soviet Moldavia.* Boulder, CO: East European Monographs, distributed by Columbia University Press, 1984.

Conquest, Robert. *The Harvest of Sorrow: Soviet Collectivization and the Terror-Famine.* New York: Oxford University Press, 1986.

————. *Man-Made Famine in Ukraine.* Edmonton, Alberta: University of Toronto Press, 1986.

Dima, Nicholas. *From Moldavia to Moldova: The Soviet-Romanian Territorial Dispute.* Boulder, CO: East European Monographs, distributed by Columbia University Press, 1991.

Dolot, Mirom. *Execution by Hunger: The Hidden Holocaust.* New York: W.W. Norton, 1985.

Dyrud, Keith P. *The Quest for the Rusyn Soul: The Politics of Religion and Culture in Eastern Europe and in America, 1890–World War I.* Philadelphia: Balch Institute Press, 1992.

Encyclopedia of Ukraine. 5 vols. Toronto: University of Toronto Press, 1984–1993.

Gross, Jan Tomasz. *Revolution from Abroad: The Soviet Conquest of Poland's Western Ukraine and Western Belorussia.* Princeton, NJ: Princeton University Press, 1988.

Horak, Stephan M., ed. *Guide to the Study of the Soviet Nationalities: Non-Russian Peoples of the USSR.* Littleton, CO: Libraries Unlimited, Inc., 1982.

Hosking, Geoffrey, ed. *Church, Nation and State in Russia and Ukraine.* Basingstoke, England: Macmillan, 1991.

Hrushevsky, Michael. *A History of Ukraine.* New Haven, CT: Yale University Press, 1941.

Jewsbury, George F. *The Russian Annexation of Bessarabia, 1774–1828: A Study of Imperial Expansion.* Boulder, CO: East European Monographs, distributed by Columbia University Press, 1976.

Judge, Edward H. *Easter in Kishinev: Anatomy of a Pogrom.* New York: New York University Press, 1992.

Kipel, Vitaut, and Zora Kipel, eds. *Byelorussian Statehood: Reader and Bibliography.* New York: Byelorussian Institute of Arts and Sciences, 1988.

Kohut, Zenon E. *Russian Centralism and Ukrainian Autonomy: Imperial Absorption of the Hetmanate, 1760s–1830s.* Cambridge, MA: Harvard Ukrainian Research Institute, 1988.

Kravchenko, Bohdan. *Ukraine.* World Bibliographical Series. Santa Barbara: ABC-Clio, 1996.

Levin, Nora. *The Jews in the Soviet Union Since 1917: Paradox of Survival.* 2 vols. New York: New York University Press, 1988.

Marples, David R. *Chernobyl and Nuclear Power in the USSR.* New York: St. Martin's Press, 1986.

————. *Ukraine under Perestroika: Ecology, Economics and the Workers' Revolt.* London: Macmillan, in association with the Radio Free Europe/Radio Liberty Research Institute, 1991.

Motyl, Alexander J. *Dilemmas of Independence: Ukraine after Totalitarianism.* New York: Council on Foreign Relations Press, 1993.

RFE/RL Research Report, 1992–94. This publication of Radio Free Europe/Radio Liberty was formerly titled *Radio Liberty Research Bulletin* (through 1988) and *Report on the USSR* (1989–1991). Weekly. See also *Transition.*

Rudnytsky, Ivan L. *Essays in Modern Ukrainian History.* Edmonton: Canadian Institute of Ukrainian Studies, 1987.

————, ed. *Rethinking Ukrainian History.* Edmonton: Canadian Institute of Ukrainian Studies, 1981.

Solchanyk, Roman, ed. *Ukraine: From Chernobyl to Sovereignty. A Collection of Interviews.* London: Macmillan, in association with the RFE/RL Research Institute, 1992.

————. *Ukraine under Perestroika: Politics, Religion and the National Question.* London: Macmillan, in association with the RFE/RL Research Institute, 1991.

Transition: Events and Issues in the Former Soviet Union and East-Central and Southeastern Europe. 1995–. Prague: Open Media Research Institute. A biweekly journal that continues coverage of contemporary issues previously published in *RFE/RL Research Reports* (see above).

Ukraine: A Concise Encyclopedia. 2 vols. Prepared by the Shevchenko Scientific Society. Toronto: Toronto University Press, 1963–71.

Vakar, Nicholas P. *Belorussia: The Making of a Nation: A Case Study.* Cambridge, MA: Harvard University Press, 1956.

Wexler, Paul N. *Purism and Language: A Study in Modern Ukrainian and Belorussian Nationalism, 1840–1967.* Bloomington, IN: Indiana University Press, 1974.

Wilkinson, William. *An Account of the Principalities of Wallachia and Moldavia.* New York: Arno Press, 1971.

Wixman, Ronald. *The Peoples of the USSR: An Ethnographic Handbook.* Armonk, NY: M.E. Sharpe, 1984.

Zaprudnik, Jan. *Belarus: At a Crossroads in History.* Westview Series on the Post-Soviet Republics. Boulder, CO: Westview, 1993.

Belarus, Moldova, and Ukraine

BELARUS

Statistical Profile

Population: 10,297,000

Ethnic population

Belarusian	77.9%
Russian	13.2%
Polish	4.1%
Ukrainian	2.9%
Jewish	1.1%
Other	0.8%

Major urban centers and populations

Minsk	1,673,000
Homyel (Gomel)	507,000
Mahilyow (Mogilev)	368,000
Vitsyebsk (Vitebsk)	359,000
Hrodna (Grodno)	301,000
Brest	294,000
Babruysk (Bobruisk)	227,000
Baranavichy (Baranovichi)	173,000
Barysaw (Borisov)	155,000
Pinsk	130,000
Orsha	126,000
Mazyr (Mozyr)	106,000

Historic religious traditions

Christianity	98.1%
Judaism	1.1%

Languages: Belarusian, Russian

Population by age

Age	Total	Males	Females
0–14	22%	11.2%	10.8%
15–64	65%	31.5%	33.5%
65 and over	13%	4.2%	8.8%

Male/Female ratio: 46.9% male/53.1% female

Rural/Urban population: 31.4% rural/68.6% urban

Annual population growth rate: -0.2%

Population density: 128.5 persons per sq mi

Official name
Respublika Belarus (Republic of Belarus)

Capital: Minsk

Date of sovereignty/independence declaration
25 August 1991

Voting age: 18

Literacy (age 15 and over who can read and write)

total population	97%
male	99%
female	96%

Level of education for persons over 15

completed higher education	10.8%
completed secondary education	49.4%
incomplete secondary education	16.8%

Number of higher education institutions: 33

Higher education enrollment: 176,500 students

Selected institutions of higher education (and enrollment)

Minsk

Polytechnic Academy	22,500
State University	12,000
State University of Economics	10,000
State Linguistic University	3,000
Academy of Music	885

Brest

Polytechnic Institute	1,900

Homyel

F. Skaryna State University	7,000

Hrodna
State University 6,200

Mahilyow region
Agricultural Academy 11,000

Polatsk
Polytechnic Institute 3,750

Vitsyebsk
Technological Institute of Light Industry 3,500

Socioeconomic Indicators

Annual birth rate: 10.7 births/1,000 population

Fertility rate: 1.87 children/woman

Infant mortality: 13.2 deaths/1,000 live births

Average life expectancy
68.9 years (males 63.5, females 74.3)

Annual death rate: 12.6 deaths/1,000 population

Average family size: 3.2

Annual consumption of electrical energy
3,010 kWh/person

Hospital beds per 10,000 persons: 132.3

Physical Features

Area: 80,134 sq mi

Land use
cultivated 29%
pasture 9%

Highest elevation: 1,122 ft (Mt. Dzerzhin)

Rainfall: 24 in./yr

Temperature

Winter	Summer
southwest, average 24°F	southwest, average 66°F
northeast, average 18°F	northeast, average 63°F
lowest –42°F	highest 99°F

Economic Production

Estimated per capita GNP: $2,160 (1994)

Agricultural output
potatoes, dairy products, swine, grain, vegetables

Natural resources
forests, peat deposits, small quantities of oil and natural gas

Industrial output
agricultural machines, motor vehicles, televisions and radios, chemical fibers, fertilizer, textiles, refrigerators

Currency
Belarusian ruble (introduced May 1992)
1 ruble = 100 kopeks

Communications

Length of rail lines: 3,481 mi

Length of highways: 31,300 mi

Pipelines
crude oil ....919 mi
natural gas .... 1,238 mi

Telephones: 180 per 1,000 persons

Sources "Belorusskaia sovetskaia sotsialisticheskaia respublika," *Bol'shaia sovetskaia entsiklopediia* (Moscow, 1977); *Narodnoe khoziaistvo SSSR v 1990g.* (Moscow, 1991); *Naselenie SSSR* (Moscow, 1989); Matthew J. Sagers, "News Notes: Iron and Steel," *Soviet Geography* 30 (May 1989): 397–434; Lee Schwartz, "USSR Nationality Redistribution by Republic, 1979–1989: From Published Results of the 1989 All-Union Census," *Soviet Geography* 32 (April 1991): 209–48; *World of Learning*, 46th ed. (London, 1996); "Russia . . ." (National Geographic Society Map, 1993); *Europa World Yearbook, 1996* (London, 1996); *Demografischeskii ezhegodnik, 1995* (Moscow, 1995); "CIA World Factbook, 1995" (www.odci.gov/cia/publications/95fact/bo.html).

Belarus

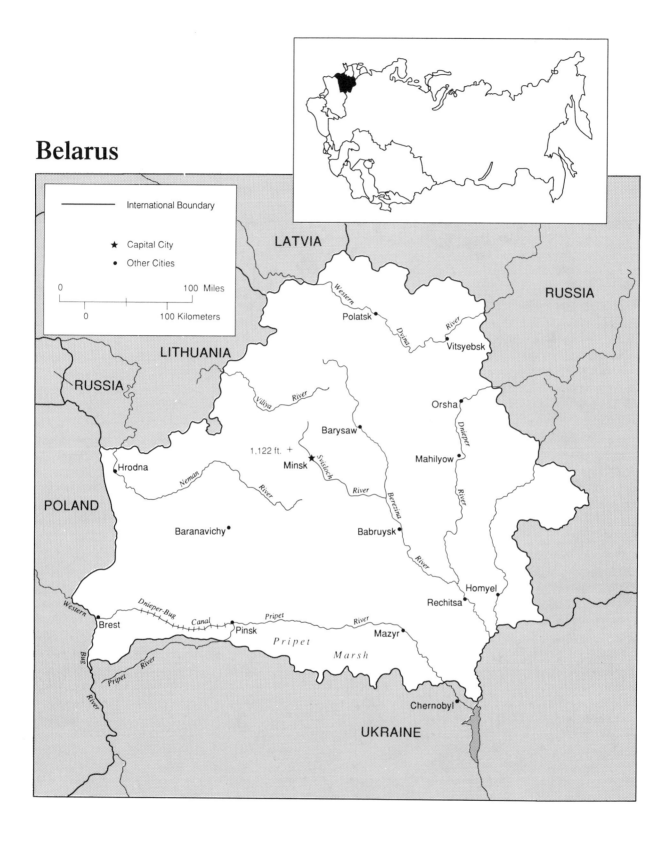

International Boundary

★ Capital City
● Other Cities

0   100 Miles

0   100 Kilometers

LATVIA

RUSSIA

LITHUANIA

RUSSIA

Polatsk

Western   Dvina   River

Vitsyebsk

Vilya   River

Orsha

Barysaw

Mahilyow

1,122 ft. +

Minsk

Svisloch

Dnieper   River

Hrodna

Neman

River

River

Berezina

POLAND

Baranavichy ●

Babruysk ●

River

Homyel ●

Rechitsa ●

Western

Dnieper-Bug

Canal

Pripet

River

Brest

Pinsk

Pripet

Mazyr ●

Bug

Pripet   River

Marsh

River

Chernobyl ●

UKRAINE

Belarus: History and Description

Physical Description

Borders Belarus, frequently referred to in English as "White Russia" (a translation of the Russian, Belorusiia), occupies a forested and lake-filled region in the northern part of Eastern Europe. Adjacent to the Baltic republics of Lithuania and Latvia along its northwest boundary, Belarus is bordered on the east by Russia, on the south by Ukraine, and on the west by Poland. Belarus is a small country (80,154 square miles), comparable in size to the state of Kansas. Its capital is Minsk.

Landscape The lands of Belarus make up part of the great East European Plain. Belarus is basically a lowland area divided by a ridge of hills running from the southwest to the northeast. In the northwestern part of the country, where rivers flow toward the Baltic Sea, a region of numerous lakes and a remnant of the primeval forest exist. In the southeastern part of Belarus, where rivers flow toward the Black Sea, the vast Pripet Marsh and its many crisscrossing waterways spread across the landscape.

Rivers The rivers of Belarus have, from earliest times, served as vital transportation links in a region generally unsuitable for travel by road. The exception to such river travel is along the upland ridge of hills: an ancient highway that constitutes the main Warsaw-Minsk-Moscow trade route. This highway has also served invading powers and was, for example, one of the strategic routes the Germans used to approach Moscow in 1941.

Major rivers in the southeastern part of Belarus are the Dnieper, flowing south before entering Ukraine on the way to the Black Sea; and the Pripet, flowing east through the southern part of Belarus to join the Dnieper just below Chernobyl. In the northwestern part of Belarus, the Western Dvina River flows north to the Gulf of Riga, the Neman (Nyoman) flows northwestward to the area of Kaliningrad, and the Western Bug flows west to join the Vistula above Warsaw. The latter three rivers tend to be slow, and they overflow often into adjacent marshy areas.

The Pripet River and the lowland region through which it flows, the Pripet Marsh, represent the type of landform remaining after glacial ice deposits had receded. A land of bogs, marshes, and swamps, the area has waterlogged soil but much good pine forest. When sufficiently drained, however, the soil yields a rich earth suitable for cultivation. Drainage projects, consequently, have often been attempted.

Climate The cool and damp climate of Belarus marks a shift between the coastal weather patterns of the Baltic republics to the north and the continental extremities of Russian lands to the east. Temperatures tend to stay in the mid-60s during the moderate summer season, when much of the annual average of 24 inches of rain falls. Winters are short with many thaws.

Agriculture Low temperatures and frequent cloudiness, combined with the generally poor soil, have made agricultural development a low priority in Belarus. Nevertheless, the raising of beef, dairy cattle, swine, and poultry for domestic and foreign consumption, as well as the growing of flax, grains, potatoes, and orchard crops, constitute a significant portion of the Belarusian economy. The forests of Belarus, a cross between the predominantly pine taiga of Russia and the deciduous woodlands of Europe, provide substantial timber resources. Lumbering and wood products, especially paper, plywood, furniture, and prefabricated housing, furnish much of the country's revenue.

Natural Resources and Industry Until the twentieth century, Belarus was thought to have few valuable natural resources. In recent years, however, oil has been discovered in the southeastern part of the country at the town of Rechitsa. In nearby Mazyr, an oil refinery has been built to complement the refinery already existing in the north at Polatsk, sited near a major oil pipeline between Latvian ports and Russia's Volga-Ural oil fields. Despite these limited new energy resources, Belarus remains oil dependent, having done little to make use of its newly discovered oil.

The major mined resource in Belarus is peat; found throughout the country, it has been used for centuries as the primary local energy source. Potash and reserves of various mineral salts have also been exploited. In addition, such building materials as quartz, limestone, clay, sand, and gravel are abundant.

The industrialization of the Belarusian economy under the Soviet system was well supported financially and theoretically provides a base for future development. Factories producing tractors, motorcycles, and trucks; metal-processing works that support auxiliary manufacturing; and plants turning out plastic and other synthetic products, especially fabrics, constitute much of the industrial activity in Belarus. Pianos, musical instruments, radios, and electronic equipment are also manufactured.

Cities The largest city in Belarus is its capital, Minsk (Mensk). Founded in the year 1067, it has suffered many invasions and endured control by foreign rulers. Almost totally destroyed in World War II, it has since been rebuilt and symbolizes for the Belarusians their survival as a people. Located in the very middle of Belarus, Minsk is both the cultural and commercial center of the country. Other Belarusian cities of historic importance are Polatsk, site of an eleventh-century cathedral; Brest (Brest-Litovsk), where the February 1918 peace treaty was signed, removing Russia from further participation in the First World War; Vitsyebsk (Vitebsk), native region of the artist Marc Chagall; and Hrodna, heart of Jewish life during the nineteenth and early twentieth centuries. During that time, Belarus was within the so-called Pale of Settlement, the territory west of the Dnieper River wherein the tsars sought to confine Jewish settlement. Jews constituted a majority or near majority of the population in most cities located within the Pale, and they were also settled in substantial numbers in surrounding rural areas.

Ethnic Background and Historical Development

The origin of the term Belarus or White Russia is unknown, and many theories have been put forward to explain its usage. For example, the attribute "white" could relate to white clothing commonly worn in the national dress of Belarus. It could refer, as in Turkic sources, to the pale skin coloration of western tribes. It could reflect local geographical terminology, in which the syllable "bel" is included in the names of rivers and towns. It could also refer to a god from early Slavic mythology. It could derive from a Tatar term for people free from taxation. Or "bel" could refer to the "sovereignty" of this early Slavic people. The term was first used in historical documents dating from the fourteenth century, but its meaning has since been altered and its precise etymology remains a mystery.

Belarusians are ethnic Slavs, and their language, written in Cyrillic, is closely related to Ukrainian and Russian. Belarusian belongs to the East Slavic branch of the Slavic language family. It is possible that Belarusians are descended from early Slavic tribes—in particular, the Krivichi—who migrated to the area between the Pripet and Dnieper rivers in approximately the sixth century A.D. The relationship between these migrant Belarusians and the early east Baltic tribes already inhabiting the region remains a matter of dispute.

Russian Conquest and Rule

By the ninth century, an East Slav principality, Polock (Polatsk), on the Western Dvina River within today's Belarus, was trading with the early Kievan Rus state. This principality, located on a major Baltic-Mediterranean trading route, eventually became one of the cities making up the medieval Kievan Rus state, and thus lay within the realm of Eastern Orthodox Christendom. By the fourteenth century, however, Belarusian lands had fallen under the domination of the neighboring Lithuanian Empire. Two hundred years later, after the subsequent establishment of the Polish-Lithuanian Commonwealth in 1569, a part of the Belarusian population converted to Roman Catholicism. Others maintained Eastern Orthodox practices, but were drawn into a form of ecclesiastical union with the Roman Catholic Church, forming what is known as the Uniate or Greek Catholic Church. The partitions of Poland by Russia at the end of the eighteenth century brought the area of Belarus entirely within the Russian Empire. Subsequent Russification was accompanied in the nineteenth century by coercive efforts to reconvert Belarusian Uniates to Eastern Orthodoxy.

The substantial Jewish presence in Belarusian territory (and throughout the lands of the former Polish-Lithuanian Commonwealth) dates, according to most accounts, from the invitation of the Polish King Casimir in the fourteenth century. Rarely possessing their own lands, Jewish settlers in the Commonwealth came to live on leased land or, more commonly, in the small towns and cities of the region. By the nineteenth century, the Jewish population constituted between one-third and two-thirds of most Belarusian cities, including Minsk, Hrodna, Vitsyebsk, and Pinsk.

Belarusian territory remained under imperial Russian administration until the end of the First World War. Although the nineteenth century had seen the development of a national consciousness amongst ethnic Belarusians, the Belarusian homeland was divided by the terms of the postwar Treaty of Riga. The western part of Belarus was joined to Pilsudski's interwar Polish Republic, while eastern Belarus was established by Moscow as the Belorussian Soviet Socialist Republic (Belorussian SSR). Such a division of Belarusian lands between two unfriendly powers did not, however, stem the desire of the Belarusians themselves to live together within their own unified state.

Soviet Rule

During the period between the two world wars, as Bolshevik power was being consolidated in Moscow, Soviet Belarusians endured both the trials of forced collectivization in the 1920s and Stalin's purges during the 1930s. By 1933, hundreds of thousands of small farms had been incorporated into collectives, in spite of active resistance by local peasant landholders. Those who objected were deported, and often died.

An intensive effort was made by Soviet authorities during the late 1920s and early 1930s to eliminate Belarusian nationalism. Anyone not oriented toward socialism was suspected of being a nationalist. Even those who merely affirmed the use of the Belarusian language, instead of Russian, fit the nationalist definition. In this manner, Moscow sought the destruction of Belarusian cultural identity. An early purge of Belarusian intellectuals in 1929–30 was followed by further periodic purges, including the Great Soviet Purges of 1937–38, in which thousands of innocent victims were killed in the Belorussian SSR and elsewhere in the Soviet Union. The recent discovery of mass graves in the Kurapaty Woods just outside Minsk has served to refocus national attention upon this period of Stalinist genocide.

On June 22, 1941, Germany broke the Nazi-Soviet Pact of 1939 and Hitler's forces attacked Russia. Heading east toward Moscow, the German army passed through Belarusian territory near Minsk, over the same terrain that Napoleon had traveled many years before. While Hitler's armies met with some support from Belarusian nationals, most of this backing could be explained by the persistence of strong anti-Stalinist feelings in the region and did not reflect widespread fascist ideological fervor. The subsequent German occupation and the battles that followed devastated Belarus. The countryside was ravaged, villages were flattened, and thousands of peasants burned alive. The many Jewish communities, urban and rural, that had been divided between Polish and Soviet territory after World War I were sacked, and millions of individuals were sent to concentration camps. Including its Jewish population, Belarus had lost more than 25 percent of its prewar inhabitants by the war's end. During the German retreat in 1944, the cities of Belarus were systematically destroyed on Hitler's direct orders. The Soviet Red Army eventually regained control of all of Belarus, and, following the postwar exchange of territory that shifted Poland's border westward, most of the lands historically considered Belarusian were brought together in 1945 as the new, larger, Belorussian Soviet Socialist Republic.

The most important task faced by Stalin in the immediate postwar period was to integrate within the Soviet system the western part of Belarus that had been part of Poland during the interwar years. First, however, citizens suspected of possible collaboration with the Nazis, including even former prisoners of war, were sent to the gulag, that vast network of Soviet prison and labor camps dotting the Russian and Siberian landscape (see page 36). The Communist Party proceeded to implement a cultural policy to make the country more firmly "Russian." Linguistic controls lay at the heart of this policy, and, in the attempt to bring the Belarusian language into greater conformity with Russian, Belarusian grammatical rules were changed. Belarusian words derived from Polish were eliminated, and the teaching of Russian was mandated in all schoolrooms, even when Belarusian remained as the primary language of instruction.

After Stalin's death in 1953 and the emergence of the more liberalizing leadership of Nikita Khrushchev, these Russification policies continued to be followed in the Belorussian SSR. Under the republic's Communist Party first secretary, Kirill Mazurov (1956–65), and his successor, Petr Masherov (1965–80), Belarus remained integrally tied to Moscow. Located at the western border of the Soviet Union and possessing nuclear weapons, the Belorussian SSR was considered by Soviet Communist Party leadership to be among the most strategically significant republics. In addition, Soviet concern about possible infiltration of Western ideas from the Polish Solidarity movement in the 1980s may also have played a part in the identification of the Belorussian SSR as one of the most important bastions of Soviet rule.

Belarus: Contemporary Issues

Belarusian Ecocide: The Aftereffects of Chernobyl

The explosion that rocked the Chernobyl nuclear generating plant in April 1986 occurred in what was then the Ukrainian Soviet Socialist Republic, less than 15 miles south of the Belarusian border. Carried aloft by southeasterly winds, the smoke cloud and debris from the Chernobyl explosion—including an estimated 50 tons of radioactive fallout—passed immediately to the north and west over much of Belarus, leaving large parts of the countryside contaminated. The cumulative radiation release from the fire that burned at the Chernobyl site for 5 days was 200 times that of the combined releases from the atomic bombs dropped at Hiroshima and Nagasaki in 1945.

Today, Belarus suffers more from the aftereffects of the Chernobyl disaster than any other region of the former Soviet Union, including even Ukraine. Some 2,000,000 people, including 800,000 children, live in contaminated areas. In measuring radiation levels, scientists typically use the unit of the kilobecquerel. As a baseline, one kilobecquerel per square meter (kBq/m^2) is the residual radiation level found on the earth's surface from above-ground nuclear weapons testing. In southern Belarus today, an area of about 1,000 square kilometers (386 square miles) has a surface contamination of more than 1,480 kBq/m^2. In that most-heavily polluted region, more than 10,000 people were still living as of 1990 in some 70 villages. In another larger area of 3,000 square kilometers (over 1,000 square miles), only slightly less contaminated (555 to 1,480 kBq/m^2), there remained in 1990 approximately 100,000 people in over 300 villages. According to the estimates of the International Atomic Energy Agency, still another 1,200,000 people are living today on lands where the contamination level is between 184 and 555 kBq/m^2 —an unsafe level, but one that has not been declared uninhabitable. Depending upon what contamination level is judged acceptable, anywhere between one-tenth and one-third of the newly independent Republic of Belarus continues today to be uninhabitable, based on international public health standards.

The magnitude of the Chernobyl disaster is too great for Belarus to address alone. Indeed, one of the primary concerns in Belarus, when it first separated itself from the old Soviet Union, was that it would not be able to call upon international sources of support to assist in the cleaning up of the health and environmental aftereffects. When, in May 1991, the International Atomic Energy Agency issued a report downplaying the existence of any serious international health problems, the Ukrainian and Belarusian officials quickly challenged the findings, noting that their local and regional health problems had not been taken into consideration. For Belarus, in particular, there remains an urgent need to maintain an international focus upon the aftereffects of Chernobyl in order to secure needed humanitarian aid.

In the meantime, the Chernobyl crisis has revealed the unusually complicated, closed political atmosphere within the former Belorussian Soviet Socialist Republic (Belorussian SSR) and its newly independent successor state, the Republic of Belarus. Responding to popular pressure, the newly elected Belorussian SSR

Supreme Soviet (the republic's parliament) formed in the spring of 1990 a Chernobyl investigatory commission charged with examining the actions of local government officials immediately after the 1986 explosion. The commission heard testimony revealing that local Belorussian SSR leaders, including Communist Party First Secretary Sliunkov, as well as the state security apparatus, knew of the dangers to the local population as early as the 29th of April, 1986, three days after the incident. Yet, in formal meetings held at the time, the decision was taken not to ask for international help and not to cancel the country's annual May Day celebrations, for fear of alarming the public. When the head of the investigatory commission released a preliminary report in June 1991, pointing the finger at high officials and agencies in the republic's government, the elected Belorussian SSR Supreme Soviet astonished everyone by abolishing its own investigatory commission.

In short, the country's Communist Party–dominated Supreme Soviet sought to control and suppress information about the Chernobyl events well into 1991. Much of that same conservative Belorussian Communist Party (BCP) leadership later supported the abortive Moscow coup in August 1991 and further discredited themselves in the process.

In the decade following the Chernobyl explosion, more than 5,000 deaths have been attributed directly to the catastrophe, including the heavy loss of life from those charged with putting out the fire at the reactor site. Many thousands more have died from diseases indirectly related to the Chernobyl disaster. Yet the full measure of the impact of the Chernobyl disaster is not found in the grim death toll, which continues to rise, but in the fear that has entered the lives of hundreds of thousands of people, mainly citizens of Belarus. The area most severely affected is southeastern Belarus, in the farmlands bounded by the urban centers of Homyel (a city of 500,000 people) and Mazyr. More than 2,000,000 people once lived in that region, and today, those who remain are plagued by the psychological aftereffects of Chernobyl as much as by the physical ailments produced by the radiation exposure (see Michael Specter, "10 Years Later, Through Fear, Chernobyl Still Kills in Belarus," *New York Times,* 31 March 1996, 1, 4; and David R. Marples, "Ten Years Later, the Tragedy Continues," *Transition* 2, no. 8, 19 April 1996, 46–51).

Political Volatility

In Belarus, citizen regard for established governmental authority has been eroded by the government's inadequate and misleading information following the

Chernobyl explosion, by cronyism and corruption, and, since 1994, by some of the most despotic and repressive leadership found in any of the former Soviet republics.

For Belarus, as for several other former Soviet republics, 1991 was a pivotal year for political change. The year's upheavals began inauspiciously in March with the referendum held throughout the Soviet Union on whether to preserve the Soviet Union itself. Of those voting in the Belorussian SSR, 83 percent supported preservation of the USSR, a margin of support exceeding the Union-wide average of 76 percent.

The majority sentiment in Belarus for preservation of the Soviet Union should not be construed, however, as widespread support for local Communist Party leadership. Belarusian workers launched a series of strikes in April 1991 that shattered the relative calm of Belarus political life. On April 4th, more than 100,000 workers demonstrated in Lenin Square in Minsk calling for wage increases, worker benefits, and, most significantly, the resignation of the political leadership of the Belorussian SSR. Neither the Communist Party first secretary, Anatolii Malafeyeu, nor the chairman of the republic's Supreme Soviet, Mikalai Dzemyantsei, supported the calls for an emergency meeting of the parliament. By the 23rd of April, the increasingly powerful independent workers' movement staged a highly successful one-day general strike, closing most large factories in Minsk and other cities. By May, the government was forced to concede across-the-board wage increases for Belarusian workers, even though the escalating demands of the workers for the nationalization of Communist Party property were rejected by a parliament that remained dominated by the old BCP leadership.

In this atmosphere of uneasy truce between workers and government, the events of the abortive Moscow coup in August 1991 reopened the process of political change in Belarus. The Belorussian Communist Party First Secretary Malafeyeu and most other local Party leaders openly supported the coup, a move that severely discredited the BCP. Moreover, even though most of the conservative bureaucratic heads of government ministries and the Supreme Soviet had remained "safely" noncommittal during the coup, Supreme Soviet Chairman Dzemyantsei was forced to resign after pointedly refusing to take sides when interviewed publicly during the coup itself.

Shushkevich Heads New Government

Threatened with their own demise, the BCP and the republic's Supreme Soviet quickly sought to adjust to the new realities following the collapse of the coup in late August. They issued a formal statement calling for support of Belarusian independence from the Soviet Union, and the Supreme Soviet then declared the country's independence on the 25th of August, 1991. In September, the republic's name was changed to the Republic of Belarus. October saw the newly-independent republic's Supreme Soviet elect a moderate political newcomer and ally of Russian President Boris Yeltsin, Stanislau Shushkevich, as chairman. As leader of the Belarus Supreme Soviet, Shushkevich remained the de facto head of state in Belarus, ruling in tandem with Prime Minister Vyacheslau Kebich as the new republic groped toward new forms of political life in the months following the turbulent events of 1991.

Stanislau Shushkevich was an unusual figure to be leading the new Belarus republic in its first years of independence. Born in 1934, he was the son of a recognized Belarusian poet who had spent time in the Soviet gulag. The young Shushkevich was trained in nuclear physics at the state university in Minsk. After earning the degree of doctor of science, he was later appointed to the faculty of the university in Minsk and subsequently rose to the position of corresponding member of the Belorussian Academy of Sciences. Having achieved recognition in academic circles, Shushkevich came very late to a career in politics. Although a member of the Communist Party, he did not hold political appointment until elected to the Belorussian SSR Supreme Soviet in the March 1990 open elections. During that campaign, he was supported by the Belarusian Popular Front and came to be identified as one of those seeking to expose official negligence in the aftermath of the Chernobyl disaster. Viewed as a moderate or centrist, Shushkevich was elected interim chairman of Belarus's Supreme Soviet on August 25, 1991, following the resignation of Dzemyantsei. He assumed the regular chairmanship by vote of the Supreme Soviet in October 1991. As with numerous other Communist Party leaders in republics of the former Soviet Union, Shushkevich formally abandoned his Party membership following the August 1991 abortive coup.

Under the moderate leadership of Shushkevich and Kebich, and with the Supreme Soviet still in the hands of former Communist Party leaders, Belarus followed a slow and uncertain path toward political reform. Steering a calculated centrist course between the more conservative Supreme Soviet and the reformist Belarusian Popular Front (chaired by Zyanon Paznyak), Shushkevich sought to avert a series of political crises. Rejecting the agenda of the Popular Front, which envisioned a more independent course for Belarus, Shushkevich led the new Republic of Belarus into full membership and collaboration in the post-Soviet Commonwealth of Independent States (CIS). The CIS, established in December 1991, is a loose organization of all the newly independent republics of the former Soviet Union (except the Baltic states). Launched by Boris Yeltsin of Russia, Leonid Kravchuk of Ukraine, and Stanislau Shushkevich of Belarus, the CIS has coordinated interstate affairs in the newly independent member states, particularly in military, defense, and environmental matters.

If Shushkevich's lead in the formation of the CIS constituted a bow toward supporters of the former Union, his early support for the nationalization of BCP property garnered him the momentary support of the Popular Front. In December 1991, Shushkevich secured Supreme Soviet majorities for both the renunciation of the 1922 treaty that formally tied Belarus to the Soviet Union and the nationalization of Communist Party property.

Following the breakup of the Soviet Union, Shushkevich seemed less inclined to pursue a reformist agenda. His conservative political posture reflected the continuing dependency of Belarus upon Russian energy resources, as well as the unabated strength of former Communist Party deputies in the Belarusian Supreme Soviet or parliament. The slow pace of political reform also served the interests of those who sought to keep control of key government security and policy-making offices in the hands of the nomenklatura. The nomenklatura—Communist Party–appointed bureaucratic managers—continued to exercise great influence over military and security matters. as well as over the press and economic policy.

Shushkevich Deposed

By late 1993, public disfavor with the new Belarusian government had reached a high point, and the Federation of Independent Trade Unions organized mass demonstrations to vent its frustrations over the collapse of the economy. In such a politically charged atmosphere, the Supreme Soviet seized upon the issue of political corruption to give vent to public hostility toward the government. The leader of the anticorruption commission within the Belarusian Supreme Soviet was a young and popular, if at times abrasive, collective farm manager, Alyaksandr Lukashenka. Founder of the Communists for Democracy faction of the Supreme Soviet, he had developed a public following in the months after independence by staking out a populist, anticorruption position. By early 1994, Lukashenka's anticorruption commission in the Supreme Soviet was leveling charges directly against Shushkevich—charges that were never fully confirmed—and the Supreme Soviet, exploiting the opportunity, deposed

Shushkevich as chair in February 1994. Within weeks of Shushkevich's fall, the Belarus Supreme Soviet had established a new constitution with an elected presidency, an arrangement that balanced power between the Supreme Soviet and the new presidency. Presidential elections were set for June 1994.

The Rise of Alyaksandr Lukashenka

The six candidates for the presidency included the deposed Shushkevich; Prime Minister Kebich (who had maintained control of ministerial appointments throughout the Shushkevich period); Zyanon Paznyak, the nationalist leader of the Belarusian Popular Front; Alyaksandr Lukashenka, who had achieved public recognition for his anticorruption campaign; and representatives of the new Communist and agrarian parties. To the surprise of most insiders, the flamboyant Alyaksandr Lukashenka received 45 percent of the vote in the first round, while Prime Minister Kebich received only slightly more than 17 percent. In the second round of balloting, Lukashenka was elected president of Belarus in a landslide victory, in which he received more than 81 percent of the votes cast.

In retrospect, Lukashenka's election reflected the discontent of Belarusian society with politics as usual. In voting for Lukashenka, the electorate sent a message of rejection to a government of professional officeholders and cronies who had proved ineffectual in addressing the failing Belarusian economy. Although it was relatively clear what citizens were voting *against,* it was much less clear what they were voting *for.* In the months since the 1994 election, the ramifications of the Lukashenka victory have become painfully clear. Lacking a reformist or national vision for Belarus, the brash young collective farm manager has sought to return Belarus to a Stalinist past in which the media is censored, the economy is state-controlled, governance is decreed by the executive, and the abuse of human rights and arrest of political opponents is normal. Sustaining this regime is a reinforced police and security apparatus modeled upon the one established by Lukashenka's historical hero, Felix Dzerzhinsky, the Belarusian head of Stalin's Cheka, a forerunner of the notorious Soviet KGB.

As a consequence of Belarus's political reversal, Western financial institutions such as the International Monetary Fund have refused to provide credits. Unable to solve the problem of the depressed Belarusian economy, the Lukashenka government has turned desperately to the Russian Federation for monetary and economic union. Until recently, the Russian government has been almost as careful as the West to keep the erratic Lukashenka regime at bay; in Moscow's case, to prevent Belarus from becoming a drain upon the Russian economy. At the height of the 1996 Russian presidential election campaign, however, Lukashenka managed to secure from President Boris Yeltsin a vague promise for monetary and financial integration of the Russian and Belarusian economies. That April 1996 agreement has only served further to alienate Lukashenka's regime from the Belarusian national intelligentsia. Outspoken opponents of the effort to reunite Belarus with Russia have even been forced, as in the case of Popular Front leader Zyanon Paznyak, to flee the country. Paznyak was granted political refugee status in the United States in August 1996.

Unable to pursue a steady course, and wedded to unrealistic visions of Stalinist stability, President Alyaksandr Lukashenka has dangerously isolated Belarus. Yet, as the republic falls into ever deeper political and economic crisis, Lukashenka remains relatively popular in Belarus itself, commanding considerable support from the country's rural and elderly population. It is among those people that Lukashenka's message of unification with Russia seems to make most sense. In 1995, more than 80 percent of the population supported a referendum put forward by the Lukashenka government calling for economic integration with Russia. Seeking public support in a November 1996 extra-constitutional referendum to extend his term of office beyond the year 2000, Lukashenka has been emboldened in his exercise of executive power. In the process, he has garnered the support of a rump parliament that has acceded to Lukashenka's autocratic ways. For the present, the development of an independent civil society in Belarus has suffered a serious reversal.

Military and Security

Belarus was forced to establish its own defense ministry following the collapse of the Soviet Union in late 1991. The majority of the officers, however, were Russians from the old Soviet regime's Belorussian Military District. Indeed, only approximately 20 percent of the officer corps within Belarus at the end of 1991 was Belarusian. As a result, there was initial resistance at highest military command levels to any break with the union-wide CIS military command structure. Today, Belarus's military policies continue to be closely harmonized with those of the Russian Federation.

These policies include the vital strategic question of nuclear weapons installations on Belarusian territory. The creation of an independent Belarus brought into existence a new nuclear power, for Belarus was one of the four former Soviet republics (along with Russia, Ukraine, and Kazakhstan) that possessed nuclear weapons. In 1991, Belarus fell heir to 82 single-warhead mobile SS-25 strategic nuclear missiles. Although its neighbor, Ukraine, was slow to address the issue of the decommissioning of nuclear weapons sites, Belarus immediately signed on to the Strategic Arms Reduction Talks (START-1) and the Nuclear Nonproliferation Treaty. In November 1992, prior to the deposing of Shushkevich, the Belarusian parliament adopted a military strategy that called for the removal of its nuclear weapons within two and a half years. On the strength of that commitment, Belarus was invited to join the NATO Partnership for Peace Program. Its nuclear weapons sites were placed under Russian/CIS command, and the decommissioning of the sites was advanced by the infusion of disarmament funds from the United States. U.S. President Clinton announced the commitment of $100 million during his visit to Minsk in January 1994.

However, as in other policymaking, the Lukashenka government has been unpredictable on the matter of nuclear decommissioning. In June 1995, approximately one year after taking office, the president halted the decommissioning and transfer of nuclear weapons out of Belarus into Russia. At the time, only 18 of the original 82 nuclear missiles remained on Belarus soil, and all of those sites were under Russian command. It appeared that President Lukashenka's purpose was to wrest further funds from the West for the decommissioning process, which Ukraine had been able to do with considerably greater success than Belarus. Lukashenka's official position, however, was that since Russia and Belarus would be reunited, there was no need to transfer weaponry into territory that would be under common sovereign authority. From June 1995, the decommissioning was continued at a slower pace, and with promise of further infusions of German and U.S. financial support for conventional and nuclear arms dismantling. Lukashenka's announcement in the fall of 1996 that all remaining nuclear weapons would be remanded to the Russian Federation constituted a major concession in what had been his hard-line policy. In November 1996, all remaining nuclear warheads and missiles in Belarus were finally handed over to Russia.

More indicative of the control maintained by the old Party nomenklatura is the continued role of the state security force, the KGB. Unlike the situation in other former Soviet republics, the KGB in Belarus has not even changed its name, much less its personnel, its policies, or its closed archives. Appointed head of the KGB in October 1990, while the republic was still part of the Soviet Union, General Eduard Shirkousky led the agency until his ouster by parliamentary vote in 1993. Despite changes in overall leadership, the Belarusian KGB has maintained its Communist deputy division heads and has continued to advance an agenda tied to the conservative Communist leadership of the Belarusian Supreme Soviet. The Belarusian KGB has also sought to strengthen preexisting ties with state security personnel in adjacent republics. Symbolic of this unreformed Belarusian security agency is the fate of a statue honoring Felix Dzerzhinsky, founder of the Soviet precursor to the KGB. Moscow's Dzerzhinsky statue was torn down in 1991, and the name of the square over which it presided was changed. In Minsk, however, the prominent figure of Felix Dzerzhinsky still stands opposite KGB headquarters, and portraits of Dzerzhinsky, a native of Belarus, continue to grace the offices of local KGB affiliates. (See Alexander Lukashuk, "Belarus's KGB: In Search of an Identity," *RFE/RL Research Report*, 27 November 1992, 18. Lukashuk was a writer and a reformist member of the Belarus Supreme Soviet.)

Despite proposals for political control over the Belarusian KGB, no such legislation has been adopted, and there is unlikely to be any reform of the Belarus KGB during a Lukashenka government. In the meantime, the KGB personnel who have retained their positions from the Soviet era argue that, in the face of economic corruption and rising crime, there is renewed need for the old security apparatus—regardless of its close ties to the former Communist government.

In September 1995, Belarus forces shot down an unarmed American hot-air balloon that had strayed over Belarusian air space. The two American pilots were killed. At the time, and in subsequent reconstructions, it was clear that the blame for this incident could be placed squarely on the reduction of Belarusian armed forces and the resulting confusion among competing jurisdictions for control of the country's air defense system. Military and arms reductions in Belarus pose continuing problems for morale and for international cooperation. Still, the reduction in forces and the dismantling of Belarus's nuclear arsenal ought not to be confused with the commitment that continues under the Lukashenka government to a well-funded, Soviet-style internal security apparatus. The combined forces of the interior ministry, the KGB, and Lukashenka's personal guard now number more than 120,000, while the army has been downsized to less than 75,000.

Economic Reform?

The Lukashenka government has undermined the process of economic reform already slowed in Belarus by the continued strength of bureaucrats appointed by the Communist Party before independence. Despite Lukashenka's occasional appeal for international investment in Belarus, he shows little understanding of, much less a commitment to, the development of a market economy. The process of privatization has advanced less in Belarus than in virtually any other former Soviet republic. Holding on to visions of a once-stable command economy, Belarus leaders, even before the onset of the Lukashenka government, were reluctant to shift the ownership of property and production into private hands. A 1992 project for privatizing state-owned enterprises ended up being limited to 147 plants. In the case of land reform, the popular support for a return to private farm holdings has been partially undermined by well-connected managers of large collective and state-run farms—individuals like Lukashenka, some of whom serve as deputies in the Supreme Soviet or have access to conservative Supreme Soviet leadership.

A series of conflicting laws on private property and foreign investment have generally tended to discourage Western corporations from doing business in Belarus. Until 1993, when Belarus developed its own currency, the country remained within the monetary zone of the Russian ruble. Today, despite the April 1996 agreement vaguely linking the Russian and Belarusian economies, the Russian Federation is understandably reluctant to tie its own freer banking and financial communities to the quite unreformed Belarusian economy. Although the Lukashenka government may want to return to the Russian ruble zone, it is unlikely that that will be possible, except in the world of black marketeering.

The single most difficult long-term problem confronting the Belarusian economy is that of its energy dependency. Belarus relies on Russia for 90 percent of its energy needs. Unable to meet the costs of this dependency, especially since Russia raised its energy prices to match world levels, Belarus has had to use some of its foreign credits to cover oil and natural gas needs. As a result, Belarus has developed a staggering debt to Russia—by 1995, that debt exceeded $500 million. There are other newly independent states of the CIS that have also become debtors to the Russian Federation, but none on the scale of Belarus, or with so little prospect for repayment. This energy dependency has fed popular interest within Belarus for reunification with Russia, yet it is unlikely that the Russian Federation, however much it may seek to restore parts of its once-great empire, will ever offer to assume the escalating Belarusian debt as an act of international philanthropy.

Religion, Language, and National Identity

As in other regions of Eastern Europe, national identities in Belarus have traditionally been linked to religious identity. Belarus, however, like Ukraine, confronts the reality of religious (or "confessional") division. Situated at the crossroads of Roman Catholic and Eastern Orthodox Christianity, Belarus has historically been home also to Jews and other non-Christian peoples. Thus, the Belarusian state lacks the advantage of a single faith, such as in Poland, to reinforce national identity.

Conflicts between Roman Catholicism and Eastern Orthodoxy date to the late sixteenth and early seventeenth centuries. It was then, under the Polish-Lithuanian Commonwealth, that Belarusian parishes of the Eastern Orthodox rite were wedded to the Roman Catholic hierarchy in a series of unions that created the Greek Catholic or Uniate Church. This Uniate Church, which came to dominate Belarusian lands in the seventeenth and eighteenth centuries, recognized the Roman Catholic hierarchy, but retained use of the Eastern Orthodox liturgy (worship services) in the Church Slavonic language. The Uniate parishes also were permitted to retain married clergy. Following Russian acquisition of Belarusian lands during the partitions of Poland in the late eighteenth century, Russian clerics made sustained efforts in the nineteenth century to bring the Belarusian Uniate parishes back into the Eastern Orthodox Church. In the Stalinist period, the Uniate Church was formally outlawed in both the Belorussian SSR and the Ukrainian Soviet Socialist Republic.

While there has been a reawakening of the Uniate Church in contemporary Belarus, the dilemma confronting the national movement is that both of the major denominations vying for the loyalty of Belarusian nationals—Roman Catholicism and Eastern Orthodoxy—draw their leadership and their ecclesiastical language from outside Belarus. In the case of the Roman Catholic Church of Belarus, its more than 200 parishes today are served overwhelmingly by Polish clergy, who continue to use the Polish language in church services. To be sure, as many as one-quarter of the estimated 1.5 million Roman Catholics in Belarus (15 percent of total population) are ethnic Poles living in Belarus. Nevertheless, the continued effort to Polonize the Roman Catholic Church of Belarus has been a source of aggravation within the Belarusian national movement. In particular, Pope John Paul II's appointment of Monsignor Tadeusz Kondrusiewicz of Hrodna as Roman Catholic archbishop of Belarus in 1989 reinforced the fear of Polish influence. Although born of ethnic Belarusian parentage, Kondrusiewicz was educated as a Pole and used only Polish in his Hrodna parish. Even Kondrusiewicz's consecration was conducted in Polish.

Responding to this concern over external domination of national religious life, the Belarusian Popular Front included specific proposals in its program known as Renewal (Adradzhen'ne) concerning the conduct of Christian denominations in Belarus. While the Popular Front sought to eliminate the registration of churches and other state interference in religious affairs, at the same time it recommended that all denominations in Belarus have their own territorial administration within Belarus. The Renewal program also proposed the translation of liturgical service books and Holy Scripture into Belarusian for use in all Belarusian Christian denominations—although these injunctions have not been applied to Islamic, Jewish, or other small religious minorities whose religious freedom has been explicitly recognized (Elizabeth Ambrose, "Language and Church in Belorussia," *Report on the USSR*, 9 February 1990, 18–24).

These proposals were directed not only at the Polonizing practices of the Roman Catholic Church in Belarus, but also toward the Eastern Orthodox Church, administered by the Belarus Exarchate of the Russian Orthodox Church. The designation of the diocese of Minsk and Belarus as an exarchate reflected the prestige of this post within the Russian Orthodox Church hierarchy. The Belarus Exarchate remains closely tied to the Russian Orthodox Church, a tie that is well illustrated in the person of the presiding Exarch of Minsk and Belarus, Metropolitan Filaret, an ethnic Russian and former head of the Moscow Patriarchate's Division of External Church Relations.

The Eastern Orthodox Church in Belarus faces two dilemmas in responding to the proposals from the Belarus National Front. First, Orthodox worship in all of the Slavic world has traditionally been conducted in Church Slavonic, an ecclesiastical language dating from the ninth-century Byzantine missions to the Slavs. Although there were efforts in the sixteenth century to translate Holy Scripture into a Belarusian dialect (the translations of Francis Skoryna, or Frantsishek Skaryna), the Orthodox faithful of Belarus have maintained the use of Church Slavonic in liturgical worship. The sudden introduction of a vernacular language into the church service will not necessarily appeal to the congregants.

A second and equally compelling reason for Orthodox reluctance to introduce modern translated Belarusian texts into the liturgy has to do with the national complexion of the Eastern Orthodox Church in Belarus. Just as the Roman Catholic Church includes thousands of Poles in its parishes, so, too, the Eastern Orthodox Church includes a great number of ethnic

Russians residing in Belarus. Not only do Russians make up more than 13 percent of the Belarusian population, but they are joined by a substantial number of Belarusian nationals who, over the course of the Soviet period, came to adopt Russian as their primary spoken language. (President Alyaksandr Lukashenka, for example, is alleged to speak only Russian in public because his Belarusian language skills are so poor.) The abrupt introduction of Belarusian into Eastern Orthodox Church services would little benefit those local parishes where Russian is the common spoken language of the faithful. In the meantime, both Roman Catholic and Eastern Orthodox Church leaders are sponsoring translation projects. One or more new editions of the Bible in modern Belarusian will shortly be in publication.

The wider question of the Belarusian language remains at the heart of the Belarus Popular Front's national agenda. Long before the onset of a more liberal Soviet regime in the 1980s under Mikhail Gorbachev, Belarusian intellectuals argued that there was insufficient Belarusian-language instruction in local schools and at higher education institutions. One of the early victories of the Belarusian intelligentsia was the passage by the Supreme Soviet in 1989 of a law on languages, which declared Belarusian to be the state language, while recognizing continued use of Russian. That legislation has now been superseded by a May 1995 referendum reinstating equal status for Russian alongside Belarusian. The 1995 referendum, which passed overwhelmingly, also revoked the new Belarusian flag and state emblem, replacing them with a flag and emblem that are virtually identical to pre-1992 symbols from the Soviet era.

The hurdle faced by those seeking to strengthen use of the Belarusian language in the republic is dramatized by circulation figures for the daily press. Even prior to the crackdown on the media under the Lukashenka government, more than a million copies of Russian-language dailies were distributed in Belarus, but only 80,000 copies of the Belarusian daily, *Zviazda* (Alexander Lukashuk, "Belarus after Glasnost," *RFE/RL Research Report*, 2 October 1992, 21). Circulation figures for weekly publications were even more one-sided. Some of the press initially sought to print bilingual editions, but the disproportionately high Russian-language readership demonstrates why the Belarusian Popular Front is so concerned about cultivation of the Belarusian language. There are simply many Belarusian nationals raised under Soviet Russian domination who continue to operate with Russian as the preferred language of communication.

As citizens of Belarus recover the legacy of their own diverse religious identity and struggle with the bilingualism of their Russian and Soviet imperial experience, they confront not only the devastation wrought by the Chernobyl disaster, but the burden of a political leadership remarkably isolated from the reformist spirit of its neighbors.

MOLDOVA

Statistical Profile

Demography

Population: 4,348,000

Ethnic population

Moldovan	64.5%
Ukrainian	13.8%
Russian	13.0%
Gagauz	3.5%
Bulgarian	2.0%
Jewish	1.5%
Other	1.7%

Major urban centers and populations

Chișinău (Kishinev)	667,100
Tiraspol	186,200
Bălți (Bel'tsy)	159,000
Bender (Bendery)	132,700

Historic religious traditions

Christianity	98.5%
Judaism	1.5%

Languages: Moldovan, Russian, Gagauz

Population by age

Age	Total	Males	Females
0–14	28.3%	14.5%	13.8%
15–64	64.3%	30.6%	33.7%
65 and over	7.4%	2.7%	4.7%

Male/Female ratio: 47.8% male/52.2% female

Rural/Urban population
53.2% rural/46.8% urban

Annual population growth rate: -0.1%

Population density: 334.2 persons per sq mi

Government

Official name
Republica Moldoveneasca (Republic of Moldova)

Capital: Chișinău

Date of sovereignty/independence declaration
27 August 1991

Voting age: 18

Internal region	Capital
Trans-Dniester	Tiraspol

Education

Literacy (age 15 and over who can read and write): 100%

Level of education for persons over 15

completed higher education	8.7%
completed secondary education	46.4%
incomplete secondary education	20.4%

Number of higher education institutions: 9

Higher education enrollment: 73,000 students

Selected institutions of higher education (and enrollment)

Chișinău

Technical University of Moldova	8,500
State Agricultural University of Moldova	7,500
Moldova State University	6,000

Socioeconomic Indicators

Annual birth rate: 14.3 births/1,000 population

Fertility rate: 2.2 children/woman

Infant mortality: 22.6 deaths/1,000 live births

Average life expectancy
67.5 years (males 64.3, females 71.0)

Annual death rate: 12.0 deaths/1,000 population

Average family size: 3.4

Annual consumption of electrical energy
2,491 kWh/person

Hospital beds per 10,000 persons: 121.3

Physical Features

Area: 13,012 sq mi

Land use
cultivated 50%
pasture 9%

Highest elevation: 1,339 ft (Mt. Balansi)

Rainfall: 20 in./yr

Temperature

Winter	Summer
average 25°F	average 72°F
lowest –33°F	highest 106°F

Economic Production

Estimated per capita GNP: $870 (1994)

Agricultural output
corn, sunflowers, grapes, sugar beets, livestock, tobacco

Natural resources: lignite, gypsum, phosphorites

Industrial output
processed food, wine, textiles, shoes, agricultural machinery, foundry equipment, household appliances

Currency
leu (introduced November 1993), 1 leu = 100 bani

Communications

Length of rail lines: 713 mi

Length of highways: 6,300 mi

Pipelines
natural gas .... 193 mi

Telephones: 134 per 1,000 persons

Sources "Moldavskaia sovetskaia sotsialisticheskaia respublika," *Bol'shaia sovetskaia entsiklopediia* (Moscow, 1977); *Narodnoe khoziaistvo SSSR v 1990g.* (Moscow, 1991); *Naselenie SSSR* (Moscow, 1989); Matthew J. Sagers, "News Notes: Iron and Steel," *Soviet Geography* 30 (May 1989): 397–434; Lee Schwartz, "USSR Nationality Redistribution by Republic, 1979–1989: From Published Results of the 1989 All-Union Census," *Soviet Geography* 32 (April 1991): 209–48; *World of Learning*, 46th ed. (London, 1996); "Russia . . ." (National Geographic Society Map, 1993); *Europa World Yearbook, 1996* (London, 1996); *Demograficheskii ezhegodnik, 1995* (Moscow, 1995); "CIA World Factbook, 1994" (http://www.ic.gov/94fact/country/161.html).

Moldova: History and Description

Physical Description

Moldova, a picturesque country of rolling hills and rich lowlands deeply cut by an extensive river system, lies in the southwestern corner of the former Soviet Union. Bordered on the north, east, and south by Ukraine, Moldova's western neighbor is Romania. The capital of Moldova is Chișinău (in Russian, Kishinev). Second smallest of the former Soviet republics, Moldova (13,012 square miles) is approximately half the size of West Virginia. With a population of well over four million, Moldova has the greatest population density of all the former republics.

Lying between the Prut (Pruth) River in the west and a stretch of territory along the left bank of the Dniester River in the east, Moldova is blessed with a climate conducive to agricultural success. Summers are mild and wet, and winters are not too harsh. Corn, wheat, sugar beets, and sunflowers are major crops, but Moldova is primarily known for the wines produced from its famous vineyards. In some years, it has yielded half of the former Soviet Union's grapes. Other fruits and vegetables are also intensively farmed, and food processing plants constitute an important part of the mainly agricultural economy, for Moldova has few natural resources.

The largest Moldovan city is Chișinău, situated on the Byk River among the Kodry Hills. It is the center of the main grape-growing region of Moldova. Bălți (Bel'tsy), a regional center in the north, is a transportation crossroads. To the south are Bender (Bendery) and Tiraspol, on the west bank and the east bank, respectively, of the Dniester. Both are important commercial towns. Tiraspol served as the capital during the years between the first and second world wars when Soviet authorities set up an autonomous republic of Moldavia east of the Dniester.

Ethnic Background and Historical Development

Moldovans, formerly called Bessarabians, are ethnic Romanians thought to be descended from Roman legions stationed in the ancient territory known as Dacia (similar in location to modern Romania). Over the course of many centuries, however, other peoples mixed with these Romanian peoples, among them Greeks, Slavs, and Turks. The Moldovans speak an eastern Romance language, basically a dialect of Romanian, although in writing they have most recently been using the Cyrillic alphabet rather than the Latin. The Moldovans are by tradition Eastern Orthodox Christians.

In the fourteenth century, two Balkan principalities (nation-states) were founded by the powerful Basarab family. These principalities, Wallachia and Moldavia, became the basis of the future Romania. In the fifteenth and sixteenth centuries, the Moldovan prince Stephen the Great (1457–1504) fought many battles against the Turks of the Ottoman Empire, and he has come to be regarded as the father of the Moldovan nation, despite its ultimate fall to the Ottomans.

By the eighteenth century, the Black Sea had virtually become an Ottoman lake. Russian military victories and conquests in southern Ukraine and Novorossiia (northern Black Sea coast), however, began to alter the power relations in the area. Russian troops, for the third time in a 40-year period, entered Moldovan territory during the Russian-Ottoman war of 1806–12. In the concluding Treaty of Bucharest, shortly before the Napoleonic invasion of Russia, Russia secured the annexation of Bessarabia (Moldova). Thus, Moldovan territory north and east of the Prut River came to be integrated into the Russian Empire in the nineteenth century. Russian Bessarabia, lying between the Prut and Dniester rivers, roughly equals present-day Moldova.

After the Crimean War (1853–56), Moldovan territory west of the Prut River, along with three southern Bessarabian districts, were united with Wallachia to form the foundation for what became in 1878 the independent state of Romania. In the aftermath of the Russo-Turkish War of 1877–78, the southern Bessarabian districts were returned to the Russian Empire. As a result of World War I, however, Bessarabia was reunited with the rest of Moldova into the greater Romanian state, a union that lasted only until 1940 and Soviet reannexation.

During the interwar period, in 1924, the Soviet Union established just east of the Dniester in western Ukraine a Moldavian autonomous republic, which was attached administratively to the Ukrainian Soviet Socialist Republic. Although this Moldavian republic represented but a fraction of the territory of greater Moldova, whose historic capital was Iași (Jassy, located west of the Prut), Romanians living east of the Dniester River were designated Moldavians by the Soviets in an attempt to influence the disposition of Romanian-held Bessarabian lands claimed by the Russians.

Moldova

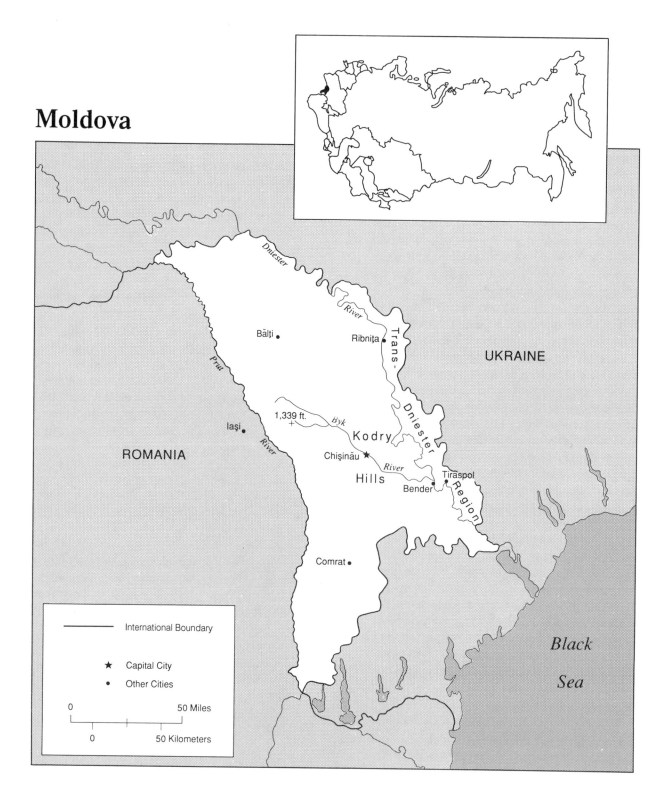

ROMANIA

UKRAINE

Dniester

River

Bălți

Ribnița

Trans-

Prut

River

1,339 ft.

Byk

Iași

Kodry

Chișinău

River

Hills

Dniester

Tiraspol

Bender

Region

Comrat

Black

Sea

International Boundary

★ Capital City

• Other Cities

0   50 Miles

0   50 Kilometers

In 1940, at the beginning of World War II, as Romania was moving into the German orbit, the Soviet Union demanded the return of Bessarabia, and the Romanian king acceded to the Russian ultimatum. In 1941, with German military assistance, Bessarabia was temporarily recaptured by Romania, only to be reconquered by Soviet troops in 1944. At the end of the war, the interwar Moldavian autonomous republic was abolished, and the new Moldavian Soviet Socialist Republic was established, including the lands of Bessarabia up to the Prut River. This republic lasted formally until the breakup of the Soviet Union in 1991, at which time Moldova declared itself independent.

The population of Moldova, although primarily Moldovan (64.5 percent), contains substantial minority groups, almost all of which live in urban centers. Ukrainians are the most numerous, due in part to the frequent shifting of the Moldovan-Ukrainian border. Many Russians also live in Moldova, a reflection of the long-term Russian imperial interest in the region. During the eighteenth century and up until the Russian Revolution of 1917, Russians, Ukrainians, and Jews were encouraged by the government to resettle in the Bessarabian lands of Moldova. In 1902, Jewish settlement in the Russian Bessarabian capital of Kishinev (Chișinău) was submitted to one of the worst of a series of pogroms, random racist acts of violence then frequently directed against Jewish people and their property.

Smaller percentages of Turkic peoples (Gagauz), Bulgarians, and others also inhabit Moldova. The origins of the Gagauz, who migrated to southern Bessarabia late in the eighteenth and early in the nineteenth centuries, are uncertain. They are thought to derive from either a Bulgarian or Turkish background.

The Gagauz speak a Turkish dialect but practice Eastern Orthodoxy as their religion. At the time of their immigration they received large land grants from the tsar, but under Soviet authority have known no cultural autonomy. In 1957, a Cyrillic alphabet was imposed on their language.

Soviet Leadership

Soviet policy in the post–World War II Moldavian Soviet Socialist Republic (Moldavian SSR) was devoted to integrating Moldova into the Soviet Union by promoting its culture as unique and separate from Romania. In keeping with this policy, relations with Romania were discouraged, and beginning in 1964, when Romania raised questions over the annexation of Bessarabia, contact was actually forbidden. Moldovan nationalists during the 1950s and 1960s struggled against the collectivization of agriculture (see *Collectivization* in the Glossary), as well as against the antireligious propaganda introduced by Soviet authorities. Following the brief tenure of Leonid Brezhnev as first secretary of the Moldavian Communist Party from 1950 to 1952, the leadership of the Moldavian SSR was given over to ethnic Moldovans, despite the continued Moscow orientation of local Communist Party decision making. In the late 1960s and 1970s, the first secretary of the Moldavian Communist Party, I. I. Bodiul, spoke publicly about the unacceptable nationalistic expressions that were of great concern to the Party. Bodiul's successor, Semen Grossu, continued the basic policy of subservience to Moscow in the leadership of the Moldavian Soviet Socialist Republic.

Moldova: Contemporary Issues

Moldovan Politics and the Language Question

The politics of the former Moldavian Soviet Socialist Republic (Moldavian SSR), now the newly independent Republic of Moldova, have been largely dominated by an attempt to reach political consensus within a multiethnic population. At the center of this effort has been the controversy over the Moldovan language and its status in the public life of the country.

Following the Soviet occupation of Bessarabia (Moldova) and its reabsorption as Soviet Moldavia after World War II, Soviet authorities declared that the Moldovan and Romanian languages were entirely separate. To bolster these claims, the Latin alphabet for Moldovan was replaced by Cyrillic, and Romanian literature was virtually banned from Soviet Moldavia. Although legally no official language was named, Russian became the effective language of the republic, and use of and instruction in Moldovan declined.

This Soviet language policy, which prompted both grievances from the Moldovans and anti-Soviet propaganda from Romanian nationalists, came under heavy fire during the mid-1980s as Moldovan writers and intellectuals pressed for greater use of Moldovan and for admission by the Soviet government that Moldovan and Romanian were essentially the same. The reemergence of the language issue in Soviet Moldavia was part of the greater openness in public discourse during the era of glasnost. The issue quickly became a major agenda item for newly formed groups, including the Moldovan Popular Front. At the same time, the language question stirred the fears of non-Moldovan nationals, particularly the Slavic (Russian and Ukrainian) inhabitants of the Trans-Dniester region and the Gagauz of southern Moldova. These non-Moldovan nationals feared that, if the Moldovan language were to be recognized as official and its linkage with modern Romanian confirmed, pressure for territorial reunification with Romania would intensify.

The Soviet Moldavian Communist Party and the Language Problem Soviet Moldavia's most powerful institution, the Moldavian Communist Party, found itself particularly ill-prepared to respond to the language issue. The Party in Soviet Moldavia had enjoyed special favor from the Soviet government during the Brezhnev era, a time that has since come to be known as the period of "stagnation" *(zastoi).* In fact, Leonid Brezhnev had served briefly as first secretary in the Moldavian Communist Party, from 1950 to 1952. Very much tied to the Brezhnev era, Semen Kuzmich Grossu, first secretary for the Moldavian Communist Party throughout the 1980s, came under mounting criticism during the reform-minded Gorbachev years because of his association with the legacy of corruption and inefficiency in the Moldavian SSR. Grossu's position was further weakened in the eyes of Moldovan intellectuals and writers because of the Communist Party's firm commitment to a Soviet language policy that subordinated Moldovan to Russian.

Seeking to reestablish support among ethnic Moldovans, the Communist Party of the Moldavian SSR announced in May 1987 two concessions on language policy. The first was a resolution calling for expanded use of Moldovan (then still called "Moldavian") in social life, literature, media broadcasts, and in the schools. A parallel resolution set forth policies for use of Russian, so as not to give the appearance that there had been any prior inadequacy in the use of Moldovan. In fact, there were wide areas of Moldovan life in which Russian continued to be used exclusively, including some higher education institutes.

While state and Party leaders sought to keep pace with rising public disaffection, by 1988, the language issue had become central to the platform of two significant informal political groups—the Alexe Mateevici Literary and Musical Group and the Demo-

cratic Movement in Support of Restructuring. The Mateevici Group, primarily concerned with cultural issues, was named for a Moldovan poet and Orthodox priest who agitated for Moldovan culture within the Russian Empire at the beginning of the twentieth century. The more directly political Democratic Movement laid out a comprehensive platform calling for democratic government, cultural autonomy for all ethnic groups, and privatization of industry. Both groups called for Moldovan to be the republic's official language, the return of a Latin script, and the recognition of Moldovan as identical to Romanian.

To quiet the agitation on the language issue, the Moldavian Supreme Soviet established, in 1988, the Commission on the Study of the History and Problems of the Development of the Moldavian Language. Although the commission was largely ineffective, it did recommend in December 1988, during the height of public demonstrations over the language question, that Moldovan be recognized as an official language of the republic. Semen Grossu remained opposed to such concessions but, nevertheless, authorized the publication in the Latin script of the works of popular dissident writer Ion Drutse. Grossu also tentatively approved publication of a new periodical, *Glasul,* also to be printed in the Latin script.

The slow pace of reform and the government's failure to make good on limited concessions regarding the language issue led to increasingly hostile confrontations between popular forces and the government. Failing to secure prompt publication of *Glasul,* the Writers' Union in Chișinău arranged to have it printed in Riga, Latvia. After the discovery that copies of the first issue were circulating in Chișinău, Grossu declared the publication illegal and ordered that searches be undertaken for the galley proofs of the second issue. Despite Grossu's declaration that the informal groups were illegal, these groups combined, in March 1989, to win three of the six seats in elections for the Soviet Union's Congress of People's Deputies. The defeat of three of the Communist Party candidates did little to halt Grossu's continued harassment of the informal groups.

New Language Law When the government formally proposed its new language laws in late March 1989 few people were satisfied. Although the proposals called for Moldovan to be the official language of the republic, Russian was identified as the official language of interethnic communication. For Moldovans, this was taken to mean the continued subordination of Moldovan to Russian, and 25,000 Moldovans demonstrated against the laws. Meanwhile, for the Gagauz and the Slavic peoples of Soviet Moldavia, the designation of Moldovan as the official language of the republic was also unacceptable, and these groups launched their own demands for separation and autonomy *from* the Moldavian SSR. In short, the failure to resolve the language issue forthrightly and effectively had created, by mid-1989, a dangerous situation that threatened to set the ethnic communities of the Moldavian SSR against one another.

The Moldovan Popular Front (MPF), acting as an umbrella group for the Democratic Movement, the Mateevici Group, the Moldovan Greens, and others, was established in May 1989. The MPF led the largest public demonstrations to date in June 1989. As many as 80,000 supporters rallied in Chişinău protesting the 1940 Soviet annexation of Bessarabia. The MPF further demanded that the former Bessarabian areas of northern Bukovina (north of the Moldavian SSR) and southern Bessarabia (between the Moldavian SSR and the Black Sea) be returned by Ukraine to Moldova.

By the end of August 1989, the Soviet Moldavian government offered to concede on the proposed language laws. The section making Russian the official language of interethnic communication was changed to make Russian coequal with Moldovan for such purposes. Moreover, the government conceded that the Cyrillic script would be replaced by the Latin script in printed Moldovan. In response, Russian workers in the Trans-Dniester region lashed out in strikes organized by a group calling itself Edinstvo (Unity). Up to half a million Moldovans, many of them peasants from outlying villages, crowded into Chişinău to join an MPF rally in support of the new provisions, which became law in September 1989. The law also provided cultural concessions to other ethnic groups, including the Ukrainians, Gagauz, Jews, and Bulgarians.

The Collapse of Soviet Authority

Behind the language question there festered the real political issue; namely, Soviet authority. World War I peace settlements had given Romania, not the Soviet Union, territorial control over Bessarabia, and it was not until 1940 that Soviet troops first moved into Moldavian Romania following the Nazi-Soviet Pact of 1939. Before the 1980s, the legality of this wartime Soviet occupation of Moldavia could not be openly questioned. By challenging the Soviet occupation of Moldavia, demonstrators in the streets of Chişinău were threatening the very foundation and legality of Soviet rule. The protests were, in turn, fanned by the presence of troops sent to Moldavia in 1989 by the Soviet Ministry of Internal Affairs. It was in the midst of this increasingly bitter outpouring of public disfavor with the government that Moscow authorities in

November removed Semen Grossu as Moldavian Communist Party first secretary.

In March 1990, the first open elections were held for the republic's Supreme Soviet. Supporters of the MPF gained control of this legislative body, securing 40 percent of the seats. Adherents of other informal groups took another 30 percent. When the Supreme Soviet convened, Grossu's replacement as chair, Petru Lucinschi, was ousted, and Mircea Snegur, a committed reformist, was named to the post.

New Moldovan Republic Breaks with Soviet Union

By June 1990, 18 months before the formal end of the Soviet Union, the Moldavian Supreme Soviet proclaimed the republic a sovereign state. Soviet occupation was declared illegal and, in subsequent legislation, the Soviet military draft was suspended. Enforcing the 1989 Moldovan language reform, Russian place names were converted to Moldovan (Kishinev became Chişinău, for example).

Mircea Snegur was chosen for the newly created position of president of the republic. Snegur staunchly opposed all efforts to revive the Soviet Union through a new union treaty, even rejecting the entreaties of Gorbachev himself, and called back Moldovan representatives to the Congress of People's Deputies in Moscow. The old Moldavian Communist Party then joined with the Edinstvo group in the Trans-Dniester region to oppose Moldovan sovereignty, but Soviet control was continuing to slip. In May 1991, the government formally changed the name of the country to the Republic of Moldova. Following the abortive coup d'état in Moscow in August 1991, the new Moldovan republic moved to outlaw the Moldavian Communist Party and to eliminate its special internal role in the former Moldavian SSR. After the crisis of August passed, the Moldavian Communist Party was banned and its assets were seized.

During the August coup, the Moldovan Supreme Soviet and a national assembly of informal political groups declared the Republic of Moldova independent. President Snegur sought formal diplomatic recognition for the new state and secured membership in the United Nations. He also opened negotiations for the removal of Soviet troops from Moldova and, simultaneously, began to establish a new Moldovan military force.

Since the declaration of independence, Moldovan officials have had to contend with a deteriorating economy, all the while facing challenges from both ends of the political spectrum—the Trans-Dniester Slav demand for reunion with Russia, and the drive of some of the former members of the Moldovan Popular Front for reunion with Romania.

The Trans-Dniester Issue

The Trans-Dniester region (also called Transnistria) is the narrow Moldovan corridor along the eastern side of the Dniester River, adjacent to the Ukrainian border. Before the Soviet occupation of Bessarabia in 1940, this tiny region and its capital Tiraspol formed the Moldavian Autonomous Soviet Socialist Republic within the larger Ukrainian Soviet Socialist Republic. The population of this region was subjected to the collectivizing and Russifying efforts of the 1920s and 1930s. The area was also inundated by a mass of Russian and Ukrainian workers. By the time this Trans-Dniester region was incorporated with Bessarabia as a Soviet union republic (the Moldavian SSR), it had become predominantly Eastern Slavic (Russian and Ukrainian). The region's 1990 population (approximately 600,000) was about two-thirds Slavic.

The Russians and Ukrainians in the Moldavian SSR began demanding autonomy as soon as the Moldavian government proposed Moldovan as the republic's official language. Although Russian would continue as the official language of interethnic communication, Trans-Dniester Slavs overwhelmingly opposed such an arrangement. The August 1989 designation of Moldovan as the republic's official language prompted strong reactions from the Trans-Dniester Slavs. Edinstvo called for strikes by Russian workers, and although the Moldovan Popular Front was able to keep factories in Chișinău open with volunteer antisabotage committees, strikes broke out in the Dniester cities of Tiraspol, Bender, and Ribnița.

When the Moldovan Popular Front gained control of the Supreme Soviet in 1990, tensions escalated in the Trans-Dniester, and Slavic deputies boycotted the Supreme Soviet. In September 1990, Slavs in the Trans-Dniester proclaimed their own state, the Dniester Soviet Socialist Republic (Dniester SSR), and elected their own Supreme Soviet. The new Dniester republic formed a militia that clashed with Moldovan police along the Dniester as well as in Chișinău. A violent showdown in Chișinău left six dead, hardening the positions of all sides in the dispute. The Moldovan government refused to negotiate with the Dniester republic.

In August 1991, the Dniester republic, along with the old Moldavian Communist Party and Edinstvo, supported the Moscow coup attempt, continuing to do so even after the coup had failed. Nevertheless, the collapse of the Communist Party, especially after the failure of the Moscow coup, put the Trans-Dniester Slavs in a very defensive position.

In March 1992, the Moldovan government declared emergency rule in the Trans-Dniester, sending in its own armed forces to respond to fighting that left 40 people dead. The violence continued into April, with Moldovan forces attacking separatist-held enclaves in Bender. In June 1992, despite assurances from Russian President Boris Yeltsin that Russian troops would withdraw from the Dniester region, the Russian army assisted Dniester separatists against Moldovan troops.

Responding to U.S. and European calls for a peaceful resolution of the conflict, Moldovan President Snegur met with Yeltsin, Romanian President Ion Iliescu, and President Leonid Kravchuk of Ukraine in an attempt to end the conflict. Although these talks ended with no satisfactory resolution of the impasse, the position of the Russian troops in the breakaway Dniester republic became increasingly unacceptable to the regional arbiters of the dispute.

Following two years of on-again, off-again talks over the impasse, the Russian and Moldovan presidents finally signed a formal agreement in October 1994 to provide for a three-year phased withdrawal of Russian troops from the Trans-Dniester region. The agreement undermined the position of the Russian Fourteenth Army in the Trans-Dniester, commanded by Lieutenant General Aleksandr Lebed. Lebed, who later would rise to prominence in the 1996 Russian presidential elections and in his negotiations with Chechen rebels in the Caucasus, first came to public attention in the wake of the negotiated settlement of the Trans-Dniester dispute. The 1994 settlement was not, however, without its detractors. The Russian majority in Tiraspol, who earlier had admired their flamboyant Russian commander, felt betrayed by news of the impending withdrawal of Russian troops. Indeed, in the years since the settlement, the negotiated withdrawal has led to widespread emigration of ethnic Russians from Moldova, particularly from the Trans-Dniester region.

The military showdown over the Trans-Dniester region appears to have ended with the Russian army in retreat. While this military resolution may pave the way for the ultimate integration of the Trans-Dniester region into the Republic of Moldova, such integration is neither assured, nor without potential consequences. The Moldovan economy stands to lose much of the productive human resources of Trans-Dniester cities such as Tiraspol in the face of the emigration of Slavic residents to neighboring Slavic republics to the north and east. Meanwhile, faced with elections, such as those for the office of president in November 1996, Moldovan leaders have been reluctant to sign onto any final compromise agreements.

The Gagauz and Bulgarians

Along with the Trans-Dniester Slavs, the Gagauz and the Bulgarians came to be alienated by the Moldovan language demands of the 1980s. The Turkish-speaking Gagauz and the Bulgarians both reside in the southernmost regions of Moldova. Under Soviet rule, the Gagauz and the Bulgarians occasionally protested the absence of instruction and of published literature in their own languages. According to the 1979 census, however, the overwhelming majority of both Gagauz and Bulgarians claim Russian as their first language. In concessions to the two groups, the Moldavian Soviet government in the mid-1980s granted monthly broadcasts, occasional news columns, and expanded instruction in their respective languages. In 1988, during demonstrations by Moldovans demanding language concessions, the Moldavian government launched two new journal publications, one in Gagauz *(Ana Sozu)* and one in Bulgarian *(Rodno Slovo)*.

Nevertheless, when the Moldavian government proposed to make Moldovan the official language of the Moldavian SSR, the Gagauz decided to seek their own autonomy. Largely Russianized, and with a very small percentage of Moldovan speakers, the Gagauz were afraid that if they did not learn Moldovan, they would face discrimination. Out of this concern came the creation of the Gagauz popular political group Khalky (The People), a cultural and debating society. After the language law was proposed in 1990, Khalky called for secession from Moldavia and the creation of a Gagauz Autonomous Soviet Socialist Republic (Gagauz ASSR). Another Gagauz informal political group, Arkalyk (Cooperation), proposed the creation of a Bulgar-Gagauz ASSR within the Moldavian Soviet Socialist Republic. In July 1990, the Khalky gathered in the town of Comrat (Komrat) and proclaimed the founding of the Gagauz ASSR. In Gagauz regions, the Gagauz flag—a white wolf's head in a gold circle on a blue field—was even flown at government buildings. When the Supreme Soviet responded by banning all Gagauz rallies, a 754-member Gagauz national congress convened in August 1990, voting unanimously to secede from the Moldavian SSSR.

The Moldovan Popular Front and its supporters in the Supreme Soviet sought to defuse the situation through concessions to the Gagauz. The Popular Front had always favored cultural autonomy for the Gagauz, and the Supreme Soviet made offers of such autonomy, also infusing financial aid into Gagauz regions and inviting Turkish performers and representatives of Turkish culture to Moldova. On the matter of secession, however, the Moldovan Supreme Soviet refused any territorial autonomy and condemned the Khalky group for generating such disruptive activity.

During the August 1991 Moscow coup, the Gagauz supported the junta and opposed Moldova's subsequent declaration of independence. When the Moldovan government banned the Communist Party and seized their assets, the Gagauz continued to support the Moldavian Communist Party. While the collapse of the Moldavian Communist Party posed problems for the Gagauz autonomy movement, it by no means stilled it. In December 1994, in a final effort to placate Gagauz nationals, the Moldovan parliament enacted legislation that provided for "territorial autonomous structures" in these southern regions of Moldova densely populated by Gagauz. In those regions, Gagauz and Russian would be recognized alongside official Moldovan or Romanian. Individual communities could hold referenda to determine whether they wished to be included in such an autonomous territorial structure. Gagauz have also secured under this legislation the right to self-determination should Moldova ever change its political status. As a result of this legislation, the Snegur government was largely effective in reaching understandings with Gagauz regional leaders.

Moldovan Politics and the Romanian Question

The Snegur government's ability to negotiate settlements with the Trans-Dniester and Gagauz regions was owed in good measure to internal political developments within the Republic of Moldova. Foremost among these developments were the elections of 1994 that brought into power a parliamentary majority for the Democratic Agrarian Party (PDAM). The PDAM, led by former Communist Party elite and longtime officeholders, ran on a platform that promised compromise solutions to the Trans-Dniester and Gagauz issues. Winning 43.2 percent of the ballots, the PDAM garnered, under the system of weighted voting, a working majority in the Moldovan parliament. A follow-up referendum in March 1994 on reunification with Romania yielded a solid 95 percent vote *against* unification and for the maintenance of an independent Republic of Moldova. The turnout for the referendum (75 percent of registered voters) and the overwhelming vote against union with Romania also had the result of marginalizing a remnant of the Moldovan Popular Front, the Christian Democratic Popular Front Alliance (AFPCD). The AFPCD, in advocating union with Romania, has become the major opposition and revisionist force in Moldovan politics. Finally, in liberalizing the 1989 language law to postpone required Moldovan language exams for teachers and civil servants, the parliament further sought in 1994 to placate the Slavic population of the republic.

If 1994 was the year of reconciliation in Moldovan politics, the months that followed were characterized by the splintering of old coalitions. In 1995, the ruling Democratic Agrarian Party (PDAM) broke into two new parties. On the left, the charismatic parliamentary chairman, Petru Lucinschi, bolted the PDAM to launch his own social democratic Party of Social Progress in Moldova (PPSM). More devastating to the PDAM coalition was the defection of President Snegur, who in the wake of student demonstrations in the spring of 1995 abandoned the PDAM and founded the Party of Revival and Coalition of Moldova (PRCM). Snegur's split with the PDAM may have been prompted by his support for the modification of the new Moldovan constitution, changing the name of the official language of the state to Romanian, instead of Moldovan. While Snegur was not rejecting the ideological commitment to a unique and independent Moldovan state, his concession on the language issue reflected the fact that the Moldovan and Romanian languages are, for all practical purposes, one and the same.

The presidential elections of late 1996 pitted the various splinter parties of the old PDAM against one another and tested the ability of Mircea Snegur to maintain his hold over post-independence politics in Moldova. In the end, the runoff elections of early December 1996 marked the defeat of Snegur and the electoral victory of his PDAM rival, Petru Lucinschi. Lucinschi had been the last Communist Party leader of Soviet Moldavia prior to independence. His reemergence in Moldovan politics parallels the success of former Communist Party leaders elsewhere in Eurasia, and reflects widespread Moldovan electoral dissatisfaction with economic conditions. Lucinschi, who was 56 at the time of his election, polled 53 percent of the vote to Snegur's 47 percent. Given Snegur's earlier acknowledgement of the identity of Moldovan and Romanian languages, his loss to Lucinschi no doubt marks a further weakening of Moldovan Popular Front forces. Whether the new Lucinschi government will be any more successful than its predecessor in satisfying the demands of Slavic population in the breakaway Trans-Dniester region remains to be seen.

Moldova's Agricultural Economy

The Moldavian Soviet Socialist Republic was one of the poorer European republics of the former Soviet Union. In attempting to strengthen its largely state-operated economy, the new Moldovan government has confronted both the advantages and disadvantages of a largely agricultural economic base. Theoretically, a country dependent largely on agriculture should not face the extreme levels of unemployment feared in the more industrialized areas of the former Soviet Union. In addition, Romanian officials have indicated an interest in processing Moldovan agricultural products. However, economic problems are faced by both countries, problems that are compounded by the lack of foreign investment and the political sensitivity of Moldovan-Romanian relations.

As elsewhere in the former Soviet Union, 1991 and 1992 were years when Moldovan industrial production dropped as consumer prices rose dramatically with the sudden absence of government subsidies. The result was a bitter "stagflation." As an agricultural producer with a more industrialized neighbor on its northeastern border, Moldova has also faced other, unexpected incursions. In January 1992, Ukrainians—with rubles that had been devalued in Ukraine—flooded across the border buying everything in sight. Ukraine, like Moldova, operated with mixed currencies. Such external pressures sped the drive for an independent and less inflation-prone Moldovan currency. The result was the introduction in November 1993 of the Moldovan leu, a currency that has now secured stable exchange rates with the U.S. dollar and German mark. Aided by the International Monetary Fund and the World Bank, Moldova has begun the privatization of state-owned enterprises. It has also overcome the worst of the inflationary pressures of 1991–92. At the end of 1994, the rate of inflation had dropped to a low of 5 percent. Ironically, it was Moldovan agriculture, plagued by poor marketing and processing, that held back yet further growth of the Moldovan economy.

Ecocide in Moldova

Moldova's environment has suffered much from the policies of the Soviet regime. Under Communist Party first secretaries Bodiul and Grossu, the republic's agriculture was "modernized," with nearly catastrophic results for the ecosystem. Excessively heavy pesticide applications polluted the soil to such a degree that over half a million acres had to be taken out of rotation. More than 90 percent of the beneficial insect population was destroyed, and virtually no birds were left in Moldova. The full impact upon topsoil has yet to be assessed. The republic's water supply was also affected by this chemical experimentation, and water shortages were made worse by pesticide pollution. Drinking water remains in short supply in many rural areas, and the river system shows signs of considerable pesticide contamination.

International Relations

The long-expected special fraternal ties between Romania and Moldova have yet to mature. Although Snegur during his February 1991 visit to Romania spoke often of a cultural confederation, economic cooperation has been slow to develop. The economies of both countries are still state-controlled, and Moldovan trade with Romania is small. Construction of desperately needed housing in Moldova, a project launched with Romanian aid, has run aground on Romanian insistence that only Romanian labor be used. Further complicating the relationship has been the demand of the Romanian democratic opposition party for reunification with Moldova, a demand that President Iliescu and his foreign minister had dismissed prior to Iliescu's own electoral defeat in the Romanian presidential elections of November 1996. Iliescu's visit to Moldova in May 1992 was kept very low keyed in a deliberate effort by the Moldovan government to quell any suspicions that the Moldovans desired reunification.

One area of Moldovan-Romanian relations that has grown, owing to the Dniester conflict, is that of military sales and training. The Romanian government has supplied Moldova with military equipment—mostly obsolete armored personnel carriers—and is training the newly created Moldovan military. Romania is also training Moldovan diplomats and attempting to offset renewed Moldovan ties with the Russian Federation and the Commonwealth of Independent States (CIS).

Since the 1994 negotiated Russian-Moldovan agreement over the Trans-Dniester region and the beginning of the phased withdrawal of Russian forces from Moldova, Moldovan relations with the Russian Federation have decidedly improved. Moldova's decision in April 1994 to enter the CIS economic alliance has been widely interpreted as signaling Moldova's renewed ties with the East. The decisive rejection of reunification with Romania in the spring 1994 referendum adds to the picture of an independent Moldovan state seeking the widest possible set of security alliances. In addition to the strengthened relationship with Russia and the CIS, these alliances include Moldovan membership in the U.S./NATO-initiated Partnership for Peace, as well as technical and scientific agreements with Germany and its immediate Central European neighbors.

Recovering the Past

During the process of their determined drive for language reform, the Moldovan people have rediscovered their own national heritage. The place of the Romanian or Moldovan language in Moldova's past became part of a widespread disaffection from Soviet rule. Literature by Romanian writers, outlawed in Soviet Moldavia, now circulates openly as cultural ties with Romania have become the only aspect of Romanian-Moldovan relations to flourish.

At the same time, a distinctly Moldovan national identity has also been fostered. The Moldovan demands for northern Bukovina (north of Soviet Moldavia) and southern Bessarabia (between Soviet Moldavia and the Black Sea) have aimed at recreating such an integrated Moldovan national identity. This Moldovan, as opposed to Romanian, identity has not been repudiated by the new Moldovan government, even with the more recent recognition of the unity of the Moldovan and Romanian languages. Demonstrations in 1989 included the tricolor flag of the brief 1917–1918 Democratic Moldavian Republic, and protesters frequently began their rallies around the statue of Stephen the Great (1457–1504), recognized as the father of the Moldovan nation. In 1991, the anniversary of Stephen's death became a state holiday, and the Moldovan Orthodox Church canonized him later that year.

The surge of nationalism has also brought with it popular religiosity. Before the Soviet occupation, Bessarabia was famous for its large number of churches and monasteries. Under Soviet rule, however, most of these buildings were converted to warehouses, theaters, and museums, or otherwise fell into disuse and disrepair. There were 1,120 active churches in Bessarabia before 1940, but only 300 in 1980. In 1988, volunteers began restoring many of the ruined churches. Despite occasional opposition from the Moldavian Communist Party, the restoration effort by the end of that year had brought 62 church structures back into service. In the 1990s, that restoration effort has greatly expanded. Historic preservation remains one of the most daunting tasks confronting the Moldovan nation.

Even in matters involving the Eastern Orthodox Church, Moldova continues to be pulled between Russian and Romanian spheres of influence. In December 1992, Patriarch Teoctist of the Romanian Orthodox Church reactivated the interwar Metropolitanate of Bessarabia, seeking thereby to bring the Orthodox Church in Moldavia under direct Romanian ecclesiastical authority. The Russian Orthodox Church has responded angrily, defending the authority of the Moldavian exarch, whose position is tied to that of the Moscow Patriarchate. The result is an Orthodox Church in Moldova split between rival jurisdictions.

As Moldova seeks to avoid the extremes of Romanian unification on the one side and Trans-Dniester and Gagauz secessionist moves on the other, the test of its internal success will be the ability to energize its multi-ethnic population while offering economic and political security to its many minorities. The record of the nineteenth and early twentieth centuries, scarred by the memories of the pogroms against the Jews in Kishinev, is not a particularly bright one to build upon, but President Snegur and his PDAM successor, Petru Lucinschi, have sought to position themselves in a more conciliatory light. The weakness of the Moldovan economy and its fragile multi-ethnic coalition remain the most severe tests to the newly independent Moldovan state.

UKRAINE

Statistical Profile

Demography

Population: 51,728,000

Ethnic population

Ukrainian	73%
Russian	22%
Jewish	1%
Other	4%

Major urban centers and populations

Kiev	2,643,000
Kharkiv	1,662,000
Dnipropetrovs'k (Ekaterinoslav)	1,190,000
Donets'k	1,121,000
Odessa	1,096,000
Zaporizhzhya	898,000
L'viv	807,000
Kryvyy Rih	729,000
Mariupol (Zhdanov)	523,000
Mykolayiv	515,000
Luhans'k (Voroshilovgrad)	505,000
Makiyivka	426,000
Vinnytsya	384,000
Sevastopol	371,000
Kherson	368,000
Simferopol	357,000
Horlivka	336,000
Poltava	324,000
Chernihiv	311,000
Zhytomyr	299,000

Historic religious traditions

Christianity	97.2%
Judaism	1.0%

Languages: Ukrainian, Russian

Population by age

Age	Total	Males	Females
0–14	20.5%	10.4%	10.1%
15–64	65.4%	33.9%	31.5%
65 and over	14.1%	9.6%	4.5%

Male/Female ratio: 46.1% male/53.9% female

Rural/Urban population
32.1% rural/67.9% urban

Annual population growth rate: -0.7%

Population density: 221.9 persons per sq mi

Government

Official name: Ukraina (Ukraine)

Capital: Kiev

Date of sovereignty/independence declaration
24 August 1991

Voting age: 18

Internal republic	Capital
Crimea	Simferopol

Education

Literacy (age 15 and over who can read and write)

total population	98%
male	100%
female	97%

Level of education for persons over 15

completed higher education	10.4%
completed secondary education	50.6%
incomplete secondary education	18.4%

Number of higher education institutions: 149

Higher education enrollment: 829,300 students

Selected institutions of higher education (and enrollment)

Kiev

Polytechnic Institute	27,700
T. G. Shevchenko State University	20,000
D. S. Korotchenko Institute of National Economy	10,000
Technological Institute of Light Industry	8,500

Technological Institute of Food Industry 8,000
Civil Engineering Institute 7,900
Road and Road Transport Institute 6,100
Mohyla Academy 500

Dnipropetrovs'k
State University 11,000
Metallurgical Institute 7,000
Dzerzhinskii Institute of Chemical
    Technology 6,300

Donets'k
State University 12,000

Kharkiv
State University 12,000
Institute of Radio Electronics 8,000
State Agricultural University 5,600
State Academy of Railway Transport 5,500
Institute of Engineering and Economics 5,000

Kryvyy Rih
Mining Institute 4,500

L'viv
Polytechnic Institute 23,000
Ivan Franko State University 13,000
Agricultural Institute 6,500

Mariupol
Metallurgical Institute 5,600

Odessa
Mechnikov State University 10,500
Institute of National Economy 7,200
State Music Conservatory 700

Poltava
Civil Engineering Institute 4,200

Sevastopol
Instrumentation Institute 12,000

Simferopol
Frunze State University 6,600

Zaporizhzhya
Chubar Engineering Institute 8,000
Industrial Institute 5,000
State University 4,500

Zhytomyr
Agricultural Institute 3,800

Socioeconomic Indicators

Annual birth rate: 10.0 births/1,000 population

Fertility rate: 1.8 children/woman

Infant mortality: 17.2 deaths/1,000 live births

Average life expectancy
66.3 years (males 64.0, females 69.0)

Annual death rate: 14.7 deaths/1,000 population

Average family size: 3.2

Annual consumption of electrical energy
3,200 kWh/person

Hospital beds per 10,000 persons: 135.5

Physical Features

Area: 233,089 sq mi

Land use
cultivated 55%
pasture 8%

Highest elevation: 6,762 ft (Mt. Goverl)

Rainfall
northwest, 26 in./yr
Crimea, 43 in./yr
Carpathian Mountains, 55 in./yr

Temperature

Winter	**Summer**
northwest, average 19°F	northwest, average 65°F
south, average 37°F	south, average 74°F

Economic Production

Estimated per capita GNP: $1,570 (1994)

Agricultural output
grain, vegetables, sugar beets, sunflowers, livestock, dairy products, poultry

Natural resources
iron ore, coal, manganese, natural gas, oil, salt, sulfur, graphite, titanium, magnesium, kaolin, nickel, mercury, timber

Industrial output
metallurgy, machinery, minerals, sugar refining, railroad cars, electrical power, transport equipment, chemicals

Currency
karbovanets (name for coupon introduced November 1992); the karbovanets is being replaced by the hryvna

Communications	Pipelines

Length of rail lines: 14,050 mi

Length of highways: 107,000 mi

Pipelines
  crude oil .... 1,256 mi
  natural gas .... 4,875 mi

Telephones: 151.4 per 1,000 persons

Sources "Ukrainskaia sovetskaia sotsialisticheskaia respublika," *Bol'shaia sovetskaia entsiklopediia* (Moscow, 1977); *Narodnoe khoziaistvo SSSR v 1990g.* (Moscow, 1991); *Naselenie SSSR* (Moscow, 1989); Matthew J. Sagers, "News Notes: Iron and Steel," *Soviet Geography* 30 (May 1989): 397–434; Lee Schwartz, "USSR Nationality Redistribution by Republic, 1979–1989: From Published Results of the 1989 All-Union Census," *Soviet Geography* 32 (April 1991): 209–48; *World of Learning*, 46th ed. (London, 1996); "Russia . . ." (National Geographic Society Map, 1993); *Europa World Yearbook, 1996* (London, 1996); *Demograficheskii ezhegodnik, 1995* (Moscow, 1995); "CIA World Factbook, 1995" (www.odci.gov/cia/publications/95fact/up.html).

Ukraine: History and Description

Physical Description

Borders Ukraine, a country whose very name means "borderland," occupies the great plains region between Europe and Asia. This Eurasian frontier, part of the East European steppe, is situated north of the Black Sea and south and west of the vast Russian Federation. After the breakup of the USSR and Ukraine's subsequent declaration of independence, this former Soviet republic became the largest country in Europe (233,000 square miles) except for Russia—nearly as large as the state of Texas. Along its many miles of frontier, Ukraine shares borders with six states in addition to the Russian Federation. To the northwest lies newly independent Belarus, while on the west, the boundary line touches four nations previously part of the Soviet bloc—Poland, Slovakia, Hungary, and Romania. The newly independent Republic of Moldova lies to the southwest. The southern border of Ukraine follows the coastline of the Black Sea and the smaller Sea of Azov. The Black and Azov seas feature significant international ports by virtue of their direct water access to the Mediterranean.

Landscape The Ukrainian landscape is typically one of rolling plains of rich black soil. With the exception of the mountains in extreme western Ukraine and the mountains along the southern edge of the Crimean Peninsula, these Ukrainian plains follow a pattern of wooded plateaus and lowlands in the north changing to flat steppe areas in the south. Broadleaf trees and various grasses grow in this steppe part of Ukraine. In the northern third of the country, however, where the lowland area constitutes a continuation of the Pripet Marsh in neighboring Belarus, the soil is poor. Al-though pine forests predominate in this region, marsh grasses flourish in the less-well-drained bog portions. The Carpathian Mountains extend into Ukraine from Slovakia. They reach their highest point in Ukraine at Mount Goverl (6,762 feet) in the vicinity of the head-waters of the Prut River.

Rivers The three main river systems of Ukraine are the Dnieper, the Southern Bug, and the upper Dniester, supplemented by important effluents and tributaries such as the Donets and the Desna. The Dnieper (Dnipro in Ukrainian), one of Europe's longest rivers (1,420 miles), has been used as a commercial waterway for centuries. It divides the country into what has historically been called right-bank (western) and left-bank (eastern) Ukraine.

Eastern Ukraine's Natural Resources and Industry In the heavily industrialized eastern half of Ukraine, the Donets Basin (Donbass) constitutes one of the world's richest areas of natural mineral wealth. First developed commercially in the late nineteenth century during the course of the industrialization of the Russian Empire, the heavily populated urban centers of the Donets Basin and the Dnieper Valley still contain reserves of coal, iron ore, natural gas, oil, manganese, mercury, uranium, graphite, phosphorite, kaolin, limestone, titanium, and zirconium. Steel production is of paramount importance in Donbass, and iron ore provides a vital export item to Europe and Asia. A modern petrochemical industry has grown up in the Donbass, turning out such products as nitrogen fertilizers, superphosphates, and sulfuric acid. Numerous machine manufacturing plants are also located in this part of Ukraine. To provide enough water to meet all

Ukraine

LITHUANIA

BELARUS

POLAND

RUSSIA

Pripet Marsh

Western

Bug

Chernihiv

Desna

River

Chernobyl

River

Galicia

L'viv

Zhytomyr

Kiev

Pereiaslav

Kharkiv

Carpathian

Dnieper

Poltava

Donets

River

SLOVAKIA

Dniester

Vinnytsya

Dnipropetrovs'k

Horlivka

Uzhhorod

Southern

River

Donets'k

Makiyivka

HUNGARY

+ 6,762 feet

Bug

Kryvyy Rih

Donets Basin

Mountains

Zaporizhzhya

River

Prut

MOLDOVA

Mariupol

River

Mykolayiv

ROMANIA

River

Odessa

Kherson

Sea

of

RUSSIA

Azov

Crimea

Black

Sea

Simferopol

Sevastopol

Yalta

International Boundary

Internal Republic Boundary

★ Capital City

• Other Cities

0   200 Miles

0   200 Kilometers

the human, agricultural, and industrial needs of Donbass, the Dnieper has been dammed in many places, and major hydroelectric plants have been constructed.

Western Ukraine's Natural Resources and Industry
Even though the western part of Ukraine is not as richly endowed with mineral and other natural resources as eastern Ukraine, small deposits of coal, oil, gas, sulfur, as well as potassium and magnesium salts, are found west of the Dnieper. In the 1970s, Ukraine turned to the use of nuclear power with the building of the Chernobyl nuclear power generating plant north of Kiev on the outer edges of the Pripet Marsh. Furthermore, the discovery in the south of oil and gas fields in the Crimea and the Sea of Azov may yield additional sources of these precious commodities. Yet another energy resource is to be found in the extensive peat bogs of the Pripet Marsh. The chemical industry of western Ukraine manufactures nitrogen fertilizers, plastics, synthetic fibers, and rubber products. Automotive manufacturing and food processing plants also strengthen the region's economy. Ukraine's international ports on the Black Sea and the Sea of Azov allow for vital military and trading ventures, and the local fishing industry provides food exports.

Agriculture The prosperous agricultural heartland of western Ukraine, blessed with rich black earth, a relatively mild climate, and sufficient rainfall, has traditionally grown a surplus of farm products. Formerly referred to as the breadbasket of the Soviet Union, Ukrainian lands excel in yields of sugar beets, grains, potatoes, flax, tobacco, sunflowers, legumes, and other vegetables and fruits, including grapes. The more densely populated rural areas of western Ukraine also support livestock breeding, especially swine and cattle, and dairying. Eastern Ukraine, in spite of heavy industrialization and lower rainfall, also intensively cultivates its own remaining rich farmland. Near the Sea of Azov, in the sunny Crimea, and around Odessa—locales where rainfall is insufficient—irrigation has helped improve yields, and the irrigated vineyards in these regions are crucial to Ukraine's wine industry. The success of irrigation has likewise led to the introduction of rice and cotton along the northern Black Sea coast.

Cities Ukraine has 50 urban areas with more than 100,000 inhabitants. The largest of these areas is the historic city of Kiev (Kyiv in Ukrainian), located on the high right bank of the Dnieper near its confluence with the Desna. Kiev, a picturesque city of wide boulevards lined with beautiful chestnut trees, offers magnificent views of both the Dnieper and the country-side beyond. The center of East Slavic civilization between the ninth and the thirteenth centuries, Kiev was the cultural and political capital of the grand princely state known as Kievan Rus. After adopting Christianity from Byzantium at the end of the tenth century (Grand Prince Vladimir, or Volodymyr, was baptized in A.D. 988), Kievan Rus drew upon the religious and cultural inheritance of Byzantium. The multidomed Cathedral of St. Sophia (A.D. 1037), the Monastery of the Caves (Kievo-Pecherskaia Lavra, A.D. 1051) on the hillside above the river, and the statue of St. Vladimir looking down on the Dnieper all call to mind the early conversion of Kievan Rus to Byzantine, Eastern-rite Christianity. Kiev is also the long-established seat of the Ukrainian Academy of Sciences and of the "red" Kievan State University (so called for its brightly painted red exterior), founded in 1834. Modern Kiev, having expanded to the east or left bank of the Dnieper to accommodate a population of more than 2.5 million residents, has become a center for manufacturing of computers and electronics, clothing production, and food processing industries. It is today the capital of the independent Republic of Ukraine.

Other important large cities in western and southern Ukraine include L'viv, a medieval university town founded in 1241 and previously part of both the Austro-Hungarian Empire and the Polish-Lithuanian Commonwealth; Odessa, an international port on the Black Sea as well as a resort and spa; Mykolayiv (Nikolaev), a shipbuilding center on the estuary of the Southern Bug; and Kherson at the mouth of the Dnieper. In the Crimean Peninsula, which was transferred administratively from the Russian to the Ukrainian Soviet Republic in 1954, the city of Sevastopol is a strategic naval port. The Crimean resort city of Yalta was the site of World War II meetings between Churchill, Roosevelt, and Stalin in February 1945, at which time controversial territorial divisions for postwar Europe were secretly worked out by the Allied powers.

The heavily industrialized Donbass region of eastern Ukraine, however, is where most of the country's largest urban centers are to be found. These include such cities as Dnipropetrovs'k and Donets'k with populations of more than one million, and Zaporizhzhya and Kryvyy Rih with populations approaching one million. Ukraine's second largest city, numbering more than 1.6 million, is Kharkiv, just north of the Donbass. Founded by Ukrainian Cossacks in 1650, Kharkiv became in the nineteenth century an important transport and railroad junction. Later, between 1922 and 1934, it served as the capital of Soviet Ukraine. Modern Kharkiv is a center of the machine construction industry, producing agricultural and transport vehicles. Poltava, site of Peter the Great's defeat of Sweden in

1709, is located less than 100 miles southwest of Kharkiv. The modern city of Poltava, near the battle site, is a regional agricultural processing center.

Ethnic Background

Ukrainians belong to the group of Slavic peoples known as the East Slavs. This group also includes the Russians, Belarusians, and Rusyns (Carpatho-Russians). Before 1917, within the Muscovite and Russian empires, Ukrainians were referred to as the Little Russians (Malorossian'e), a term that is now obsolete. This term dates from early Byzantine references to the territorial location of this people. Although Ukrainians are traditionally Eastern Orthodox by religion, there exists in western Ukraine a substantial population of Uniates or Greek Catholics—those who continue to follow Orthodox liturgical practices but are administratively within the ecclesiastical structure of the Roman Catholic Church (see page 59).

The Ukrainian language, which uses the Cyrillic alphabet, belongs to the eastern branch of Slavic languages, within the larger Indo-European family. The modern Ukrainian literary language that developed in the nineteenth century was based on the dialect used in the area of Kiev but was significantly affected by earlier Polish and German borrowings. Modern Ukrainian has also been influenced by the dialects spoken in the lands of Galicia and Transcarpathian Ukraine. In these western territories, the local Rusyn population—a population that most Ukrainians consider to be a part of the greater Ukrainian nation—found itself under more moderate Austro-Hungarian rule and was allowed to publish works in its own native language. Modern Ukrainian thus came to be influenced by Rusyn or Carpatho-Russian writers, who contributed significantly to the development of a modern Ukrainian literary tradition.

The majority of ethnic Ukrainians live in Ukraine, although substantial numbers can also be found in European Russia, Siberia, and Kazakhstan. Ukraine itself has been and continues to be the home of numerous other ethnic groups. Russification policies during both the tsarist and Soviet periods encouraged massive infiltrations of ethnic Russians to live and work in Ukrainian lands, especially in the more industrialized Donbass. Additionally, western or right-bank Ukraine constituted a major part of the Pale of Settlement, the zone to which Jewish settlement was restricted in Eastern Europe. The territory constituting the Pale of Settlement, divided in the 1920s between Poland and the Soviet Union, was home to many of the six million Jews who perished in the Holocaust during World War II. Ukrainian Jews suffered enor-

mous losses on both sides of the Polish-Soviet border. Other neighboring peoples have also long been a part of the Ukrainian demographic picture, especially Belarusians, Moldovans, Bulgarians, and Poles.

Historical Development

Although Ukrainians date their own political history from the unification of East Slavs under the Kievan Rus grand princedom in the ninth century, the early modern history of Ukraine dates from the sixteenth and seventeenth centuries when geographical references to "Ukraine" commonly came to denote the region roughly equivalent to present-day Ukraine. In the seventeenth century, the leadership of the Dnieper or Zaporizhzhian Cossacks fought the Polish-Lithuanian Commonwealth to secure greater autonomy for Ukraine. Despite the legendary efforts of the famous Cossack leader, or *hetman,* of the Zaporizhzhian Cossacks—Bohdan Khmelnytsky—the Cossacks failed to secure Ukrainian independence. Indeed, Khmelnytsky's efforts to enjoin Muscovite armies in the fight against Poland (the Union of Pereiaslav, 1654) led instead to the eventual subordination of Ukraine to Muscovite Russia. In spite of the leadership of Khmelnytsky during the ill-fated "national liberation wars," the Union of Pereiaslav has been associated with the period of "the Ruin" in latter-day Ukrainian historical writing. With the exception of Ukrainian lands in Galicia and Transcarpathia, the Russian Empire gradually extended its centralized control over Ukraine during the eighteenth and early nineteenth centuries. (On this process, see Zenon E. Kohut, *Russian Centralism and Ukrainian Autonomy: Imperial Absorption of the Hetmanate, 1760s–1830s,* Cambridge: Harvard Ukrainian Research Institute, 1988.)

Russian Revolutions and Ukrainian Independence

The Russian revolutions of 1905 and 1917 unleashed the modern drive for Ukrainian national independence. In March 1917, Ukrainian national leaders formed a Ukrainian Central Council, or the Central Rada as it was called, briefly led by the Ukrainian historian Michael Hrushevsky. Initially the Central Rada called for Ukrainian autonomy within a Russian federal republic, and the Rada was duly recognized as the autonomous Ukrainian government by the Russian Provisional Government in July 1917. In November 1917, however, following the October Bolshevik Revolution, the Central Rada adopted a proclamation of independence and formed the Ukrainian National Republic.

Facing Bolshevik opposition and without the Ukrainian military forces still mobilized by World War I, the Rada eventually fell to Bolshevik insurgency in Kiev in late January 1918. The defeated Ukrainian republican government moved its headquarters temporarily to Zhytomyr. Soon, however, the besieged Ukrainian government, with German assistance, successfully recaptured Kiev in the spring of 1918. Having defeated the Bolshevik forces, the Ukrainians then remained under the influence of the German military until the armistice of November 1918 signaled the end of World War I.

In the wake of the evacuation of German troops, the Central Rada, with the support of Ukrainian military forces, was quickly able to reassert its power, reuniting eastern and western Ukraine in January 1919. Led by General Simon Petliura, the independent Ukrainian government held out against Soviet forces during the ensuing Russian Civil War, even striking a temporary accord with the Poles during the Polish-Soviet war of 1919–20. By 1921, however, the Soviet government had established itself throughout most of Ukraine, bringing an end to the brief period (1917–20) of Ukrainian independence.

Soviet Rule

While nationalist sentiment continued to make itself felt in the 1920s within the new Ukrainian Soviet Socialist Republic, Stalin's collectivization and industrialization campaigns launched in 1928 fell bitterly upon Ukrainian soil. Collectivization of agriculture meant the forcible resettlement of peasant communal residents into large new collective farms (kolkhozy), a process that caused widespread dislocation. Even though these Stalinist policies were implemented throughout the Soviet Union, agricultural Ukraine seemed targeted for particularly harsh and cruel enforcement of the new regulations. During the ensuing famine of the 1930s, as many as six million peasants were condemned to starvation (see Robert Conquest, *The Harvest of Sorrow: Soviet Collectivization and the Terror-Famine,* New York: Oxford University Press, 1986).

World War II brought yet further devastation to Ukraine as German armies invaded the Soviet Union during Operation Barbarossa, launched in June 1941. Kiev, Odessa, and other Ukrainian cities were all heavily damaged before being captured by the German war machine. Millions of ethnic Ukrainians, alongside countless Poles, Jews, and Belarusians on Ukrainian soil, lost their lives in the fighting. One of the most sensitive issues in Ukrainian historiography involves the extent of Ukrainian collaboration with Nazi forces in World War II. The issue arises particularly in connection with the Ukrainian Insurrectionary Army (UPA) and its main leader, Stepan Bandera. The UPA was the military arm of the Organization of Ukrainian Nationalists (OUN), an authoritarian, rightwing organization founded in interwar Poland. Bandera and the OUN/UPA saw their primary goals as Ukrainian independence and the overthrow of Soviet rule in Ukraine, and they were prepared to use terrorism to accomplish their ends. In the aftermath of the Nazi-Soviet Pact of 1939, Bandera's organization openly fought the Soviet army. While Bandera's struggle against the Soviet forces has earned him recognition among Ukrainian nationalists, some in the OUN/UPA collaborated with the Nazis. At the same time, however, Bandera's followers fought against both German and Soviet forces.

Following World War II, efforts were redoubled to integrate the Ukrainian Soviet Socialist Republic into the Soviet Union. These efforts included such measures as outlawing the Uniate Church and encouraging the use of the Russian language in public education and the mass media. The effective integration of the Ukrainian Communist Party into the Communist Party of the Soviet Union (CPSU) was reflected in the occasional rise of key Ukrainian Party leaders to the highest positions of Soviet power. Both Nikita Khrushchev and Leonid Brezhnev held leadership posts in Ukraine before assuming the office of CPSU general secretary in Moscow. Brezhnev, whose Ukrainian accent was often lost amidst a more general slurring of his speech in later years, hailed from the industrial river city of Dnipropetrovs'k (Ekaterinoslav). Out of this ideologically correct Ukrainian Communist Party, the first president of newly independent Ukraine, Leonid Kravchuk, also rose to power. First a regional Party head, then an official in the Central Committee of the Ukrainian Communist Party, and finally in 1979 placed in the Party's ideology and propaganda department (a department he came to head in 1988), Kravchuk became chair of the Ukrainian Supreme Soviet in 1990. Although his earlier impeccable Communist Party credentials discredited him in the eyes of some Ukrainian nationalists, Leonid Kravchuk's personal metamorphosis into the political leader of the newly independent republic mirrored the wider transformations occurring in contemporary Ukraine.

Ukraine: Contemporary Issues

The Politics of Independence

On the 24th of August, 1991, the Ukrainian Supreme Soviet formally proclaimed the independence of the republic of Ukraine. Although the timing of the promulgation obviously related to the abortive coup attempt earlier that same week in Moscow, the declaration of Ukrainian independence also reflected the ascendancy in Ukrainian politics of a new voice for political reform and national sovereignty. The leading edge of this reformist voice was, from its gestation in 1988 and its official founding in 1989, the political movement known as Rukh.

Rukh, meaning "movement" in Ukrainian, was established during the Gorbachev years of perestroika. Its full title was initially the Ukrainian Popular Movement for Perestroika. Following the pattern of national front movements in the Baltic region, Rukh sought democratization, economic reform, and Ukrainian sovereignty. In its earliest documents, however, Rukh called for the rule of law (the legal protection of individual citizens) inside a restructured Soviet federation. In this sense, Rukh carefully positioned itself within the larger spectrum of Ukrainian politics. With respect to the nomenklatura (the established bureaucratic apparatus) and the Ukrainian Communist Party, Rukh was a voice of political dissent. With respect to the goals of Gorbachev's perestroika, however, Rukh could claim to be loyally supportive. Its 1989 platform endorsed market-oriented economic reforms, the broad application of human rights and the rule of law, and the religious toleration of all faiths on Ukrainian soil (it specifically recognized the formerly outlawed Greek Catholics, and it noted the historic role in Ukraine of the Jewish population). Rukh's central message, however, was its call for the national sovereignty of Ukraine, which was seen unmistakably as a threat to the Soviet order.

The success of this national front movement became readily apparent in the March 1989 parliamentary elections, elections that occurred simultaneously in all republics of the Soviet Union. In the vote for the Ukrainian Supreme Soviet, Rukh won approximately 100 seats. With its allies in other fringe parties, Rukh came to control about one-third of the seats in the roughly 400-member Supreme Soviet. The elections revealed that Rukh's position had become so popular that, had the elections not entailed a cumbersome party registration procedure effectively keeping Rukh candidates off many slates, their parliamentary minority might well have been an outright majority.

Sensing the mood of the public, the majority Communist Party within the Supreme Soviet shifted its position, endorsing the notion of Ukrainian sovereignty. In July 1990, the Supreme Soviet voted overwhelmingly to proclaim Ukrainian state sovereignty—but *not* independence from the USSR. Leonid Kravchuk, a leading Communist Party supporter of the 1990 sovereignty declaration, was elected chair of the Supreme Soviet that same summer. Politically adept, Kravchuk sought to ride the Rukh-inspired wave of Ukrainian nationalism while maintaining his commitment to the leading role of the Communist Party in Soviet Ukrainian life.

The Moscow Coup and Aftermath

As elsewhere in the former Soviet republics, the failed Moscow coup d'état of August 1991 turned out to be a watershed event in Ukrainian politics. Within days of the abortive coup, the Ukrainian Supreme Soviet declared Ukraine independent. Local Communist Party leaders changed their tone. Kravchuk, who had indicated his support for the coup in the early stages of the August events, quickly reversed his position and issued a strong statement against the conspiracy. Shortly thereafter, he resigned from the Communist Party and then banned the Party in Ukraine (just as Boris Yeltsin later did in Russia). By October 1991, the Communist Party had renamed itself the Socialist Party. Kravchuk—using the former Communist Party's bureaucratic structure, but effectively positioning himself behind the national message of a strong Ukrainian state—went on to win in the December 1991 open election for the newly created office of president of Ukraine.

The August 1991 events and the declaration of Ukrainian independence exerted a profound impact upon the Rukh organization. On one side of the Rukh coalition, Vyacheslav Chornovil, a former political prisoner and opponent to Kravchuk in the December 1991 presidential election, led a "constructive opposition" that claimed Kravchuk was not carrying through the process of political reform to its natural end. Calling the process "an unfinished revolution," the Chornovil faction of Rukh decried Kravchuk's reliance upon the nomenklatura (composed of old Communist Party appointments) at all levels of the bureaucracy. Chornovil also called for a speeding up of market-oriented economic reform. By the fourth Rukh congress in December 1992, Chornovil was clearly in control of the organization and was elected head of Rukh by a vote of 423 to 8. Under Chornovil's leadership, Rukh seemed to be on the path toward becoming a powerful political opposition party, the largest such independent political group in Ukraine (see Roman Solchanyk, "Ukraine: A Year of Transition," *RFE/RL Research Report* 2, no. 1, 1 January 1993, 58–63).

Another important faction within the original Rukh movement, however, supported the Kravchuk government in the months following August 1991. The first head of Rukh, Ivan Drach, typified those Ukrainian nationalists within the Rukh movement who believed the central goal of the movement should be to defend and consolidate the independence of the Ukrainian state, even at the expense of far-reaching political and economic reforms. For Drach and his supporters, including several Rukh deputies in the Supreme Soviet, the goal of state consolidation came to be identified increasingly with support for Leonid Kravchuk. For his part, Kravchuk openly sought to co-opt Rukh support in 1992 by creating an independent State Council that included notable Rukh members. As Kravchuk sought to defend the republic of Ukraine against Russian claims to the Black Sea fleet and Crimean territory (see page 84), Rukh support for Kravchuk seemed justifiable in order to advance Ukrainian state independence. Drach's elimination from the co-chairmanship of Rukh at the December 1992 congress nevertheless demonstrated that Rukh remained, at its core, a dissenting Ukrainian national opposition committed to more rapid democratization and economic reform.

Offsetting the Ukrainian national agenda of Rukh have been the less reform-minded forces of the former Ukrainian Communist Party, now renamed the Socialist Party. Drawing its greatest support from the easterly, more Russian, regions of Ukraine, the Socialist Party has been able to capitalize on the pent-up frustrations of urban and agricultural workers over the general deterioration of the Ukrainian economy. As with other newly independent states of the former Soviet Union, the stability of political life in Ukraine and the relative strength of opposing political agendas have rested in good measure on the shifting fate of the state economy. By the end of 1993, these shifting currents were responsible for a major turnover in Ukrainian political life.

Leonid Kuchma Becomes President

Most observers credit the coal miners' strike of June 1993 with launching the change in Ukrainian leadership. Rather than accede to the miners' demand for a public referendum of confidence in the president and legislature, President Leonid Kravchuk and the Ukrainian parliament agreed to hold early presidential and parliamentary elections. The initial round of parliamentary elections began in late 1993. Of the 338 deputies elected, the Socialist Party and related communist and agrarian followers collected the biggest bloc: 118 seats. Nonparty, regional candidates accounted for the largest number of deputies: 171. The liberal and national parties, including Rukh, were left with a representation much smaller than they had in the previous parliament.

In the ensuing presidential elections, held in June and July 1994, Leonid Kuchma, the pro-Russian prime minister whose resignation from his post in September 1993 helped to force early parliamentary elections, defeated incumbent President Leonid Kravchuk, garnering more than 52 percent of the vote. Kravchuk, a former Communist Party leader who had refashioned himself as a Ukrainian nationalist, drew his heaviest support from the western regions of Ukraine where nationalist sentiment is strongest. Kuchma, on the other hand, was unpopular in western Ukraine because of his perceived willingness to compromise with Russia over controversial issues such as the status of the Black Sea naval fleet. However, the pro-Russian stance that rendered Kuchma less popular in western Ukraine strengthened his candidacy in the more populous eastern Ukraine, where the ethnic Russian representation is greatest. Kuchma's newly created Interregional Reformist Bloc, based largely in eastern Ukraine, advocated the maintenance of economic ties with Russia and the restoration of Russian as an officially recognized language in Ukraine.

Despite the fears of Ukrainian nationalists that a Kuchma presidency would undermine Ukrainian sovereignty, the new Kuchma era has brought a measure of unexpected stability to Ukrainian politics. Cultivating financial and banking ties with the West, the Kuchma government has sought to overcome Ukraine's economic production declines and energy dependency by securing major credits from the International Monetary Fund, as well as aid from Western governments for the dismantling of Ukraine's nuclear weapons arsenal. In advocating a strong presidency, the Kuchma government has confronted internal opposition from both socialists and liberal nationalists in the parliament. On several occasions, the president has threatened to bypass parliament and use public referenda to preserve executive powers. Yet, in June 1996, Kuchma successfully overcame parliamentary opposition by compromising on the terms of a landmark new Ukrainian constitution. That constitution includes the following provisions: (1) a unicameral legislature elected every four years (Kuchma had originally sought a bicameral body); (2) an autonomous status for the Crimea, including its own constitution; (3) a right to ownership of private property; (4) a prohibition against foreign military bases on Ukrainian soil, but with provision for temporary Russian use of Crimean naval installations for its Black Sea fleet; and (5) the retention of new Ukrainian national symbols and of Ukrainian as the sole official language of the state (see Ustina Markus, "Rivals Compromise on Constitution," *Transition* 2, no. 15, 26 July 1996, 36–37).

The Economics of Independence

The most serious problem facing Ukraine is its deteriorating economy and related energy dependency. All sectors of the Ukrainian economy have suffered significant declines in production. Industrial and consumer goods manufacturing was down by more than 20 percent in 1992 from comparable periods in 1991. Food production was down by over one-third in 1992. These declines have resulted in price increases, even at a time when real wages adjusted for inflation have been dropping. Given the changes underway in the ownership of some enterprises, the statistical measurements of productivity may be unreliable. Nevertheless, there was undisputed deterioration of the Ukrainian economy in 1992–93. Subsequent improvement in international trade after 1994 only reflects how profoundly weakened the Ukrainian economy has become since the early 1990s and the drop-off in production.

Energy Dependency

Other former Soviet republics have suffered comparable levels of decline in production as new market-oriented sectors of the economy seek to offset sharp drops in the output of state-subsidized heavy industry. In the case of Ukraine, however, the economic problems are compounded by the republic's energy dependency. Even though Donbass oil reserves have not run out, Ukraine lacks sufficient oil production to meet its basic energy needs. Ukraine must turn to the purchase of Russian, Turkmen, and Kazakh oil—now being offered at world market prices, and needing to be paid for with internationally floatable hard currency. In the 1960s and 1970s, Ukrainian energy dependency was addressed by the construction of nuclear power generating stations, notably the complex at Chernobyl. Today, the human disaster surrounding the Chernobyl explosion is coupled with the reality of energy shortfalls, a problem that the architects of Ukrainian political independence must face (for analysis of the

Chernobyl nuclear disaster of 1986, see pages 53–54). Those who would seek short-term answers for Ukarinian energy problems must also contend with the reality that, in the period from 1986 to 1994, as many as 125,000 people may have died in Ukraine alone from diseases related to the Chernobyl disaster (*Europa World Yearbook*, London: 1996).

The country's energy dependency has led to short-term solutions that do not fundamentally solve the long-term Ukrainian energy problem. First among these solutions has been the rapid reactivation of the remaining Chernobyl nuclear power station, and the recommitment of Ukraine to nuclear energy. Although international agencies have deplored the renewed operation of the remaining generating stations at Chernobyl, two-thirds of the energy needs of the city of Kiev continue to be met by Chernobyl, which is situated less than 70 miles from the Ukrainian capital. Even though the population of the immediate region of Chernobyl has been evacuated, workers at the reactivated portion of the Chernobyl power station are paid high wages and transported daily onto the site in protective clothing to permit the ongoing operation of remaining Chernobyl units. Given Ukraine's overall energy dependency, it is uncertain how Ukraine's commitment to nuclear power, including the continued use of Chernobyl, will be affected by international opinion. Still, in late 1996 Ukraine closed one of the two reactors at Chernobyl still operating and restated its commitment to close the entire Chernobyl site by the year 2000.

A second short-term solution is the use of Western credits to pay off mounting energy debts to Russia and Turkmenistan. The Ukrainian energy debt to the Russian natural gas conglomerate Gazprom has reached nearly $1 billion. The debt to Turkmenistan is not far behind. Faced with threats of cutoffs, the Ukrainian government, like its counterpart in Belarus, has used International Monetary Fund credits to avert a crisis. Ukraine has also secured promises from Western powers for the provision of safety improvements in its nuclear power industry.

Ukraine has made far less progress, however, in implementing long-term energy conservation. At a time when Ukrainian economic production still lags well behind pre-independence levels, the country's leaders are not willing to allow energy conservation goals to block efforts to increase industrial production.

Market Reforms

In fashioning economic policy for the 1990s, Ukrainian political leadership has been particularly indecisive, emphasizing short-term political responses instead of longer-term structural solutions. In the debate over the pace of market reforms and privatization, the Kravchuk government essentially sought to steer a middle ground between rapid privatization and state economic control. Faced with the liberalization of prices by the Russian Federation in January 1992, Kravchuk appointed as minister of economics a liberal advocate of rapid privatization, Volodymyr Lanovyi. By July 1992, however, Kravchuk had sacked Lanovyi, who openly criticized the government for its antimarket response to rising Russian prices. Dismayed over the performance of the Ukrainian economy, the parliament in October 1992 adopted a resolution of no confidence in the government, forcing Kravchuk to undertake a major cabinet reshuffling.

In this reshuffling, the future president of Ukraine, Leonid Kuchma, was chosen as prime minister. Director of the largest state-run missile production plant in the world (at Dnipropetrovs'k), Kuchma let it be known that he intended to support market reforms only on a gradual basis, beginning slowly with the privatization of smaller firms and consumer-oriented businesses, while continuing state support for large industrial enterprises. As president, Kuchma subsequently came to realize that economic restructuring was critical for Ukraine's international credit-worthiness, as well as for the prevention of runaway inflation. Still, the danger to the government from economic restructuring is that market-oriented policies can create destabilizing unemployment. Given its energy dependency and need for international credits, the Kuchma government has been far more receptive to privatization and economic restructuring than was anticipated by its electoral opponents. Ukraine still faces, however, the grim realities of high unemployment; ongoing inflationary pressures caused by inefficient, subsidized state-run enterprises; and long-term energy dependency.

The Diplomacy of Independence

The problems of the Ukrainian economy are intimately tied to international diplomacy. From questions of currency reform to the relationship of Ukraine with the Commonwealth of Independent States (CIS), from the possibilities of privatization measures to the status of financial ventures with the West—all of Ukraine's international affairs have been affected by the needs of the economy. On the matter of currency reform, for example, Russian insistence upon payment for its oil and gas with internationally negotiable hard currency helped to speed Ukrainian independence from the Russian "ruble zone." After experimenting with an interim coupon introduced in November 1992, the karbovanets, Ukraine began planning for the introduction of its new currency, the hryvna.

Status of the Crimea Especially pressing for the Republic of Ukraine is the normalization of its relations with the Russian Federation. The relationship is complicated by Ukraine's mounting energy debt to Russia and by occasional Russian nationalist sentiment that continues to reject the notion of a Ukraine fully independent from Russia. Beyond the issue of the Ukrainian debt, the two international hot spots in this Russian-Ukrainian relationship have been the status of the Crimean Peninsula and the disposition of the Black Sea naval fleet.

The question of Crimea's status dates to the immediate post-Stalinist era when, in 1954, Moscow formally transferred the Crimean Peninsula to the jurisdiction of the Ukrainian Soviet Socialist Republic. In May 1992, however, the Russian Supreme Soviet adopted a resolution declaring that the 1954 transfer lacked the force of law. Current Russian claims to the Crimea derive mainly from the fact that the majority population on the peninsula is Russian or Russian-speaking. Additionally, in December 1992, the Russian Congress of People's Deputies specifically challenged Ukrainian claims to the Crimean port city of Sevastopol, the home of the Black Sea naval fleet.

For Ukraine, the issue of Crimea's status is perceived as a strictly internal matter between Ukraine and the peninsula's residents, the 1954 transfer having made the Crimean Peninsula a part of the Ukrainian republic. Nevertheless, concerned Ukrainian policymakers have been moving swiftly to appropriate funds (7 billion rubles by 1992) to assist Crimea's "deported nations," a reference to the Crimean Tatars, Greeks, and other residents of the peninsula exiled to Central Asia by Stalin during World War II. These returning deportees are perceived as potential allies in defense of Ukraine's claim to the Crimea. With the Crimea's election in 1994 of its own first president, Iurii Meshkov, the tensions between the Ukrainian government and Crimean autonomists grew to alarming proportions. In 1995, the Ukrainian parliament, seeking to marginalize the separatist Crimean President Meshkov, annulled the Crimean constitution approved by voters in 1992—a constitution providing for Crimea the right of secession from Ukraine. The compromise provisions of the new 1996 Ukrainian constitution provide for Crimean autonomy within a sovereign Ukraine. While such compromise will not end the conflict over the status of the Crimea, divisions within the Crimea itself have paved the way for broader agreement on the issue (see Abraham

Brumberg, "Whose Crimea?" *New York Review of Books*, 22 October 1992, 63–64).

The Black Sea Naval Fleet The port facility at Sevastopol, on the Crimean Peninsula, links the Crimean autonomy issue with the Russian-Ukrainian dispute over the Black Sea naval fleet—potentially, a more serious conflict. Each backed by their national parliaments, Ukrainian President Kravchuk and Russian President Yeltsin initially took a hard line on the sovereign claims of their countries to the ownership of the Black Sea fleet. Both Ukraine and the Russian Federation have coastal lands on the Black Sea and the Sea of Azov, but port facilities at Sevastopol have traditionally served as headquarters of the fleet. Facing a showdown over the ownership of the fleet, the two presidents met on the Crimean Peninsula at Yalta in August 1992 to seek resolution of their differences. The interim resolution reached there placed the fleet under a joint Ukrainian-Russian command for three years, after which time it would be divided into two fleets, one Russian and one Ukrainian.

In ensuing Russian-Ukrainian discussions, an impasse continually arose during efforts to designate the future basing of these respective Black Sea fleets. The disposition of the ships, however, was finally resolved in April 1994, when Kravchuk and Yeltsin agreed to a 50-50 split of the vessels in question. Of the 833 vessels, Ukraine would ultimately retain only 164, the remainder (beyond the 50 percent split) would be purchased by Russia. The sale price of the vessels took the form of Russian forgiveness of part of the Ukrainian energy debt. At the same time, agreement on the porting of the fleets continued to elude the negotiators, partly because the only deepwater Crimean harbor that could accommodate the fleet's larger ships and submarines is Sevastopol. In June 1995, the new Kuchma government reached a tentative agreement with Russia over porting. Under the terms of the agreement, the Russian Black Sea fleet will be allowed to port at Sevastopol, but must pay for port privileges.

Nuclear Policy Cordial Ukrainian diplomatic ties with the West have been crucial in securing financial investment and economic development funds. Yet, in 1992–93, concerns over Ukrainian nuclear policy threatened to undermine Western support for the Ukrainian republic. While Ukraine had transferred its tactical nuclear weapons out of Ukrainian territory, it had retained "administrative authority" over its strategic nuclear weapons, an authority that preserved Ukraine's status as one of the leading nuclear powers in the world. Operational management of Ukraine's nuclear arsenal was placed under CIS armed forces, but Ukraine continued to demand the right to "administer" its weapons. Furthermore, Ukraine sought full representation at nuclear arms negotiations, a representation which it felt had been unfairly given over to the Russian Federation. Finally, Ukraine, unlike Belarus and Kazakhstan, stalled its ratification of the START agreements and did not immediately sign the Nuclear Non-Proliferation Treaty.

These Ukrainian signals served to elicit from the West expressions of concern over Ukraine's independence on the nuclear issue and raised the possibility that such independence might jeopardize normal trade and economic relations. With Leonid Kuchma's accession to the presidency, however, Ukrainian policy on nuclear weapons shifted significantly. Impressed that International Monetary Fund credits would be tied to Ukraine's signature on the Nuclear Non-Proliferation Treaty and to full participation in nuclear weapons dismantling, Kuchma persuaded the Ukrainian parliament (the Ukrainian Supreme Soviet) that Ukrainian interests would best be satisfied by joining a Central European nuclear weapons-free zone. In December 1994, the Ukrainian parliament finally agreed to the nonproliferation treaty, receiving in turn security guarantees from the United States, Russia, and Great Britain, as well as more than $1 billion in energy credits and compensation for dismantling costs. On June 1st, 1996, President Leonid Kuchma proclaimed that all strategic nuclear warheads had been effectively withdrawn from Ukrainian territory.

Religion and the National Question in Ukraine

Perhaps nowhere in the European lands of the former Soviet Union has religious identity been so closely tied to the national question as in Ukraine. Dating from the conversion of St. Vladimir (Volodymyr) in the tenth century, Ukraine has been a center of Eastern-rite Christianity in Europe. Yet, these Eastern-rite Christians are deeply split into regional and ecclesiastical divisions—divisions that mirror complex regional and historical distinctions within Ukrainian society.

Setting aside the presence of smaller Protestant groups in Ukraine, the Eastern Christian community in Ukraine is today divided into at least four major ecclesiastical or church subdivisions—a single Eastern-rite Ukrainian Catholic Church and three contentiously divided Eastern Orthodox churches. As recently as the 1988 celebrations of the millennium of the conversion of St. Vladimir and the eastern Slavs to Christianity, these subdivisions continued to be held together artificially by the dominating presence of the Moscow-based Russian Orthodox Church. Then headed by Metropolitan Filaret of Kiev, the Russian Orthodox Church controlled virtually all official Eastern-rite religious life in Ukraine. When Ukrainian independence was declared in 1991, the artificial unity of the Eastern-rite divisions was broken. In its stead, four distinct groups emerged—the Ukrainian Catholic Church (UCC), formerly known as the Uniate or Greek Catholic Church; the Ukrainian Autocephalous Orthodox Church; the Ukrainian Orthodox Church of the Moscow Patriarchate (the Russian Orthodox Church); and more recently, the Ukrainian Orthodox Church of the Kiev Patriarchate.

Ukrainian Catholic Church Dating from the sixteenth century and the Union of Brest (1596), the Uniate or Greek Catholic Church, now the Ukrainian Catholic Church, was dominant among Eastern-rite Christians of Galicia and Transcarpathia until those areas were annexed by the Soviet Union at the end of World War II. Many of the Eastern-rite Greek Catholics emigrated from this region to the United States during the late nineteenth and early twentieth centuries (establishing the Rusyn communities of western Pennsylvania, for example). Those remaining in Galicia and Transcarpathia suffered the formal dissolving of their Uniate or Greek Catholic Church by the Soviet government in 1946. Despite subsequent decades of persecution, an underground Greek Catholic or Uniate Church maintained its loyalty to the union with the Roman Catholic Church (see page 59 for discussion of the Uniate Church), and both clergy and laity were ready to resume their activities aboveground when religious toleration was extended to non–Russian Orthodox believers in the late 1980s. Thus, nearly half of the parishes of the Russian Orthodox Church in Galicia were threatened with takeover by forces loyal to the Ukrainian Catholic Church in the westernmost provinces of Ukraine. By 1991, when Cardinal Myroslav Liubachivs'kyi returned to L'viv from exile in Rome, the Ukrainian Catholic Church could already claim as many as 2,000 parishes in western Ukraine.

Ukrainian Autocephalous Orthodox Church Even more dramatic was the rebirth of the Ukrainian Autocephalous Orthodox Church (UAOC). Twice in the twentieth century, Ukrainian Orthodox Church leaders had founded an autocephalous (independent) Eastern Orthodox Church on Ukrainian territory. First, during the brief period of Ukrainian independence from 1917 to 1921, the Ukrainian Church movement led to the self-consecration of the Ukrainian Autocephalous Orthodox Church in 1921. Quickly liquidated by the Soviet authorities, the UAOC survived among Ukrainian émigré communities abroad. Again, during the German occupation in 1942, the UAOC was revived on Ukrainian soil. As in the 1920s, the revived UAOC of 1942 was abolished by Soviet authorities when they regained power after the war. However, Ukrainian émigrés of both the 1921 and the 1942 consecrations perpetuated this Ukrainian Autocephalous Orthodox Church in the West.

As noted in Frank Sysyn's recent essay on Ukrainian church politics, the failure of the Russian Orthodox Church to learn from these attempts at Ukrainian Orthodox independence meant that a renewed drive for independence would again yield conflict and schism in Orthodox ranks (Frank Sysyn, "The Third Rebirth of the Ukrainian Autocephalous Orthodox Church and the Religious Situation in Ukraine, 1989–1991," in *Seeking God: The Recovery of Religious Identity in Russia, Ukraine, and Georgia*, DeKalb: Northern Illinois University Press, 1993). Typical of such lack of understanding was the visit of Moscow Patriarch Aleksii II to Kiev in November 1990, ostensibly for the purpose of recognizing the "autonomy" of the Kievan Exarchate (diocese) of the Russian Orthodox Church. What the Moscow patriarch encountered, among other things, were Ukrainian protesters who objected to the patriarch's use of the St. Sophia Cathedral in Kiev. The cathedral had been, until its forcible closure in 1930, the center of the UAOC. In the end, 1990 was decisive for the autocephalists, who won over significant numbers of clergy and parishes for a revived UAOC. It was in that year that Patriarch Mystyslav, then head of the UAOC, returned to Ukraine from his post abroad. Despite his advanced age, the patriarch provided a visible symbol of continuity in Ukrainian Orthodox independence, as well as a signal of the church's important ties with Ukrainians living outside the country. Today, the UAOC has more than 1,000 parishes functioning in Ukraine, most of them in the far western provinces. Since 1993, its patriarch has been Dymytrii Yarema of L'viv.

Ukrainian Orthodox Church of the Moscow Patriarchate Formerly a diocese within the Russian Orthodox Church, the Moscow Patriarchate's newly renamed Ukrainian Orthodox Church of the Moscow Patriarchate (UOCMP) still maintains the largest number of active parishes in Ukraine, claiming more than 6,600. This church remains under the jurisdiction of the Moscow Patriarchate, even though its current Kievan metropolitan, Volodymyr (Sabodan), supports the middle-ground position of an independent Ukrainian church ecclesiastically tied to Moscow.

Ukrainian Orthodox Church of the Kiev Patriarchate

Drawn from elements of the UOCMP and from the UAOC, the Ukrainian Orthodox Church of the Kiev Patriarchate was founded in 1992. Its origins date to a leadership crisis within the UOCMP. In 1991, the individual then head of the UOCMP, Kievan Metropolitan Filaret (Denysenko), inexplicably began calling for the establishment of a new, independent Ukrainian Orthodox Church. Although he claimed to be concerned about the potential loss of support for the UOCMP in Ukraine following independence, Filaret's break with the Moscow Patriarchate may well have reflected his personal alienation from Russian Orthodox Church leaders, who were embarrassed by widely circulated stories regarding Filaret's past personal indiscretions. In May 1992, UOCMP Moscow Patriarch Aleksii II, with the support of a Russian Orthodox Church synod, denounced Filaret's call for an independent Ukrainian Orthodox Church and replaced him with a new prelate, Kievan Metropolitan Volodymyr (Sabodan). Reeling from this decision, the ousted Metropolitan Filaret sought to increase support for an independent Eastern Orthodox Church in Ukraine. Not only did he accept backing from an ultranationalist paramilitary group, the Ukrainian National Self-Defense Organization, he also managed for a time to secure the support of the leadership of the UAOC. The merger of the ousted Metropolitan Filaret and his supporters within the UAOC in June 1992 constituted the formal establishment of the Ukrainian Orthodox Church of the Kiev Patriarchate (UOCKP). Patriarch Mystyslav of the UAOC agreed to serve as patriarch of the new church, with Filaret serving as a deputy. The newly merged church committed itself to the use of the Ukrainian language in liturgical worship and actively cultivated the support of Ukrainian national leaders, notably President Kravchuk. At its high point in 1993, the new UOCKP may have commanded the loyalty of as many as 2,000 parishes.

Religious Politics Turn Violent

The subsequent history of the UOCKP is one of the more bizarre and tragic chapters in modern Eastern Orthodox Church history. Before his death at the age of 95 in 1993, Patriarch Mystyslav broke with Filaret, claiming that Filaret had discredited himself by his personal and political associations. Mystyslav further charged that Filaret had duped him into the merger. Several of the bishops from Mystyslav's former UAOC abandoned the UOCKP after Patriarch Mystyslav's death in order to revive the UAOC. The result was a three-way split in the Eastern Orthodox Church in Ukraine. Meanwhile, the newly formed UOCKP maintained much of its nationalist following and elected Volodymyr (Romaniuk) as its new Kievan patriarch in June 1993. Conflicts between the UOCKP's new patriarch, Volodymyr, and the nationalist supporters of former Metropolitan Filaret continued to dominate the UOCKP.

In July 1995, the unexpected death of UOCKP Patriarch Volodymyr became the occasion for an ugly demonstration that dramatized the extent to which religious politics were dividing the new Ukrainian state. Nationalist followers of ousted Metropolitan Filaret (Denysenko) sought to use the funeral of Patriarch Volodymyr to confront state authorities with the demand for burial of the patriarch in St. Sophia Cathedral in Kiev, the ancient Kievan landmark claimed by each of the republic's three competing Eastern Orthodox jurisdictions. The government of Leonid Kuchma, more inclined to seek religious neutrality than the preceding Kravchuk government had been, refused to let Filaret and the UOCKP bury Volodymyr in St. Sophia. Nevertheless, Filaret and his followers decided to turn the funeral into an open challenge to the authorities. They marched to St. Sophia as a part of the funeral procession and proceeded to bury Volodymyr in a makeshift grave just outside the cathedral. Riot police arrived, tear gas was fired, and unarmed mourners were caught in the crossfire, along with numerous priests. In all, more than 70 mourners and police were treated for injuries. "Black Tuesday," as the event came to be called, revealed the deep schism in the religious culture of contemporary Ukraine. In the aftermath of the funeral, Filaret was elected patriarch of the UOCKP. While the UOCKP continues to receive support from some nationalist elements, the defection of a number of priests, bishops, and parishes from its ranks reflects the ongoing controversies surrounding the person of Filaret Denysenko.

Two larger realities can be seen in the tripartite split of the Eastern Orthodox Church in Ukraine. On the one hand, the rebirth of the Ukrainian Autocephalous Orthodox Church has demonstrated the pivotal importance that the Ukrainian émigré community, especially the Ukrainians of Canada and the United States, have played in Ukrainian cultural life. There is little question that the UAOC in North America contributed mightily, both in terms of leadership and finances, to the revival of the UAOC on Ukrainian territory. The linkages of Ukrainian émigrés with their homeland carry important lessons not lost upon a Ukrainian political leadership anxious to cultivate commercial ties and financial support in the West.

A second reality beneath the current Eastern Orthodox schism in Ukraine is the manner in which religious divisions highlight ongoing Ukrainian-Russian tensions. Having been forced in 1992 by powers in the

Moscow patriarchate of the Russian Orthodox Church to resign from his post as metropolitan of Kiev, and deprived of all priestly functions amidst allegations of immoral sexual behavior, Metropolitan Filaret returned to Kiev in April of that year to announce that he would not depart, after all, because his resignation had been made under duress. Such signs of independence had no doubt contributed to Filaret's undoing in Moscow; nevertheless, his appeal for an independent Ukrainian Church temporarily endeared the beleaguered prelate to the government of Leonid Kravchuk and to ultra-nationalist followers. Indeed, ousted Metropolitan Filaret had managed to capitalize upon Ukrainian national sensitivities in such a fashion as to secure the support of the Ukrainian government. In the ensuing showdown between Ukrainian governmental supporters of Filaret and backers of the Moscow patriarchate, almost all bishops and most clergy within the UOCMP sided with what they perceived to be the canonical authority of the Moscow Patriarchate in disciplining Metropolitan Filaret. But Filaret had demonstrated the way in which it was possible to play upon perceptions of Russian imperial rule in the new era of Ukrainian national sovereignty. The final chapter in this bitter conflict within Eastern Christendom has yet to be written.

Fundamental national and cultural issues, such as the language of liturgical worship, continue to be hammered out in a Ukraine rent by profound confessional, regional, and ethnic divisions. Underlying all of these divisions are the contending interests of Ukrainian independence and the continued presence of Russian influence in Ukraine. Although the Kuchma government has managed to improve the state of Ukrainian-Russian relations significantly—from energy debt accords, to negotiations over the Black Sea fleet, to nuclear arms dismantling—the tensions evidenced within the Ukrainian religious culture demonstrate how critical the Russian question continues to be for the future of modern Ukraine.

PART THREE

TRANSCAUCASIA

INTRODUCTION

Situated south of the greater Caucasus Mountains between the Caspian and Black seas is the region known as Transcaucasia, or Transcaucasus, home of the three newly independent states of Georgia, Armenia, and Azerbaijan. Bordering Transcaucasia on the south and west are Iran and Turkey. Along the northern slopes of the Caucasus Mountains lies a group of former "autonomous republics" of the Soviet Union. These eight territories, now considered simply "republics" within the Russian Federation, are Adygeia, Karachai-Cherkessiia, Kabardino-Balkariia, North Ossetiia, Dagestan, Kalmykiia, Ingushetiia, and Checheniia (Chechnya). Until 1992, the last two of these formed the single autonomous republic of Checheno-Ingushetiia.

Torn by ethnic and political conflict, Transcaucasia has become in the 1990s the Yugoslavia of former Soviet lands. As in Yugoslavia, ethnic conflict has been driven in part by religious differences. The Georgian and Armenian churches constitute two of the oldest branches of the Christian faith. The Azerbaijanis are a people of mixed Turkic, Iranian, and Caucasian roots, who practice, in the main, a conservative, Shi'ite, form of Islam. As in Yugoslavia, the absence of clear ethnic and religious borders within Transcaucasia has contributed to the impasse. Pockets of minority ethnic population dot the entire Caucasus region. The newly independent Transcaucasian state of Georgia alone contains three autonomous republics within its borders.

The conflicts that exist both within and between the Transcaucasian republics have been readily manipulated to the advantage of rival nationalist leaders. Within Georgia, the minority Abkhazian and Ossetian people have sought greater measures of autonomy and independence—movements that have encountered the stiff resistance of Georgian national leaders. In this Georgian instance, the conflicts pit mountain highlanders against Georgians who seek a homogenous state. The most widely recognized dispute in Transcaucasia is that between the newly independent states of Armenia and Azerbaijan. At stake in this conflict is the status of two important territories—Nagorno-Karabakh and Naxçivan (Nakhichevan). Nagorno-Karabakh, with its capital in Xankändi (Stepanakert), is a predominantly Armenian, Christian enclave fully surrounded by and, during the Soviet period, legally incorporated into the Azerbaijan republic. Naxçivan, adjacent to Turkey, is an autonomous region of Azerbaijan separated from the rest of the Azerbaijani state by Armenian territory.

Since the late 1980s, the rival ethnic and religious claims over Nagorno-Karabakh and Naxçivan have generated numerous military offensives and counteroffensives between Armenian and Azerbaijani forces, resulting in hundreds of casualties on both sides. As in former Yugoslavia, the collapse of independent third-party mediation in the form of a central political authority—in this case, the Soviet Union—has complicated the resolution of these long-standing territorial, ethnic, and religious divisions.

Despite these conflicts, the natural beauty of Transcaucasia—with its mountainous terrain and extensive seashores—makes it one of the most picturesque regions of Eurasia. Access to the Caspian Sea oil fields and valuable mineral resources makes the region important also for economic development. As the ancient lands separating the Slavic Christian world of the north from the Islamic Middle East, Transcaucasia marks an important cultural divide in the modern world.

Russian annexation of Transcaucasia dates from the early nineteenth century. Despite the strength of national independence movements and civil war in the region following the Bolshevik Revolution of 1917, Transcaucasia was integrated into the Soviet Union in the 1920s. Unlike the Baltic region, into which there was heavy Russian migration after World War II, Soviet rule did not radically alter the ethnic composition of Transcaucasia. Today, the legacy of Soviet economic and political rule continues to be felt, however, and Russian influence in the region has rebounded since the collapse of the Soviet Union. Nevertheless, the economic and political life of the three newly independent states of Transcaucasia is now being defined from Erevan, Baku, and Tbilisi, not from Moscow.

Bibliography

Allen, W. E. D. *A History of the Georgian People: From the Beginning down to the Russian Conquest in the Nineteenth Century.* New York: Barnes and Noble, 1971 (originally published in 1932).

Altstadt, Audrey L. *The Azerbaijani Turks: Power and Identity under Russian Rule.* Stanford, CA: Stanford University Press, 1992.

Atamian, Sarkis. *The Armenian Community: The Historical Development of a Social and Ideological Conflict.* New York: Philosophical Library, 1955.

Curtis, Glenn E., ed. *Armenia, Azerbaijan, and Georgia: Country Studies.* Washington, DC: Library of Congress, 1995.

Edwards, Mike. "The Fractured Caucasus." *National Geographic,* February 1996: 126–31.

Goldenberg, Suzanne. *Pride of Small Nations: The Caucasus and Post-Soviet Disorder.* Atlantic Highlands: Zed Books, 1994.

Hewsen, Robert H. *Russian-Armenian Relations, 1700–1828.* Cambridge, MA: Society for Armenian Studies, 1984.

Horak, Stephan M., ed. *Guide to the Study of the Soviet Nationalities: Non-Russian Peoples of the USSR.* Littleton, CO: Libraries Unlimited, Inc., 1982.

Hunter, Shireen. *The Transcaucasus in Transition.* Washington, DC: Center for Strategic and International Studies, 1994.

Lang, David Marshall. *A Modern History of Soviet Georgia.* Westport, CT: Greenwood Press, 1975 (originally published in 1962).

———. *Armenia: Cradle of Civilization.* London: George Allen and Unwin, 1978.

———. *The Armenians.* London: George Allen and Unwin, 1981.

Matossian, Mary. *The Impact of Soviet Politics in Armenia.* Leiden: E.J. Brill, 1962.

Nissman, David B. *The Soviet Union and Iranian Azerbaijan: The Use of Nationalism for Political Penetration.* Boulder, CO: Westview Press, 1987.

RFE/RL Research Report, 1992–. This publication of *Radio Free Europe/Radio Liberty* was formerly titled *Radio Liberty Research Bulletin* (through 1988) and *Report on the USSR* (1989–91). Weekly. See also *Transition.*

Schwartz, Donald V., and Razmik Panossian, eds. *Nationalism and History: The Politics of Nation Building in Post-Soviet Armenia, Azerbaijan, and Georgia.* Toronto: University of Toronto Center for Russian and East European Studies, 1994.

Suny, Ronald Grigor. *Looking toward Ararat: Armenia in Modern History.* Bloomington: Indiana University Press, 1993.

———. *The Making of the Georgian Nation.* Bloomington: Indiana University Press, in association with Stanford University Press, 1988.

———, ed. *Transcaucasia, Nationalism and Social Change: Essays in the History of Armenia, Azerbaijan, and Georgia.* Revised edition. Ann Arbor: University of Michigan, 1996.

Swietochowski, Tadeusz. *Russian Azerbaijan, 1905–1920: The Shaping of National Identity in a Muslim Community.* Cambridge, England: Cambridge University Press, 1985.

———. *Soviet Azerbaijan Today: The Problems of Group Identity.* Washington, DC: Kennan Institute for Advanced Russian Studies, 1986.

Transition: Events and Issues in the Former Soviet Union and East-Central and Southeastern Europe, 1995–. Prague: Open Media Research Institute. This biweekly journal continues the coverage of *RFE/RL Research Reports.*

Walker, Christopher J. *Armenia: The Survival of a Nation.* New York: St. Martin's Press, 1980.

Wixman, Ronald. *The Peoples of the USSR: An Ethnographic Handbook.* Armonk, NY: M.E. Sharpe, Inc., 1984.

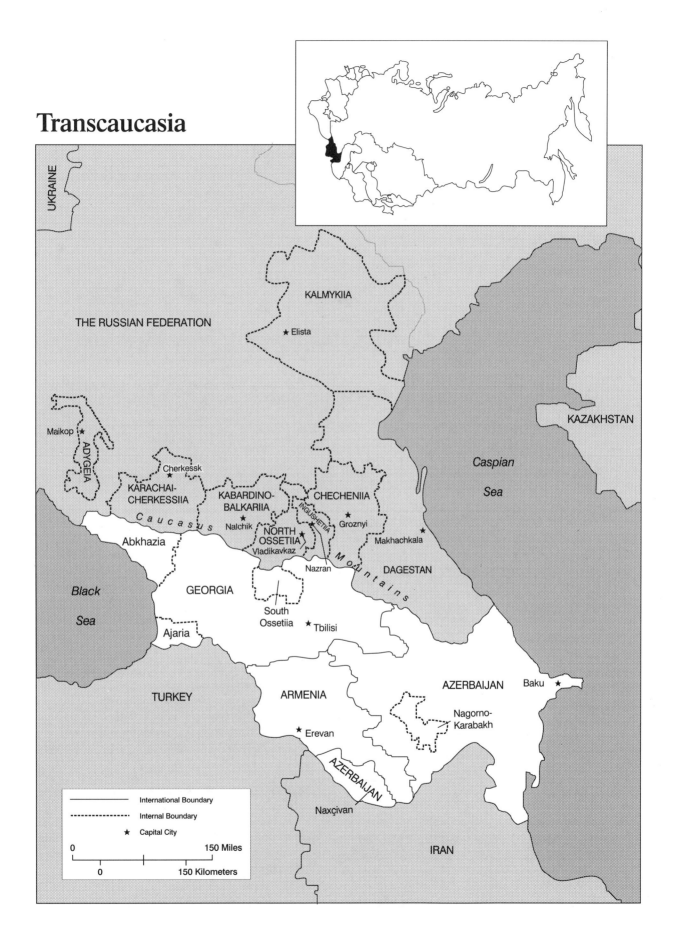

Transcaucasia

UKRAINE

THE RUSSIAN FEDERATION

KALMYKIIA

★ Elista

KAZAKHSTAN

Maikop ★

ADYGEIA

Caspian

Sea

Cherkessk ★

KARACHAI-
CHERKESSIIA

KABARDINO-
BALKARIIA

CHECHENIIA

C a u c a s u s

Nalchik ★

INGUSHETIIA

Groznyi ★

Makhachkala ★

Abkhazia

NORTH
OSSETIIA ★

Vladikavkaz

Nazran

M o u n t a i n s

DAGESTAN

Black

GEORGIA

South
Ossetiia

Sea

★ Tbilisi

Ajaria

AZERBAIJAN

Baku ★

TURKEY

ARMENIA

Nagorno-
Karabakh

★ Erevan

AZERBAIJAN

Naxçivan

IRAN

———————	International Boundary
- - - - - - - -	Internal Boundary
★	Capital City

0   150 Miles

0   150 Kilometers

ARMENIA

Statistical Profile

Demography

Population: 3,754,000

Ethnic population

Armenian	93.3%
Azerbaijani	2.6%*
Kurdish	1.7%
Russian	1.5%
Other	0.9%

Major urban centers and populations

Erevan	1,254,000
Gyumri (Leninakan)	207,000
Kirovakan	170,000

Historic religious traditions

Christianity	94.9%
Islam	4.3%*

Languages: Armenian, Russian

Population by age

Age	Total	Males	Females
0–14	31.4%	16.1%	15.3%
15–64	61.3%	30.3%	31.0%
65 and over	7.7%	3.1%	4.4%

Male/Female ratio: 49.5% male/50.7% female

Rural/Urban population
31.8% rural/68.2% urban

Annual population growth rate: 0.3%

Population density: 326.3 persons per sq mi

*These figures do not reflect the recent exodus of most Azerbaijanis from Armenia.

Government

Official name
Hayastani Hanrapetut'yun (Republic of Armenia)

Capital: Erevan

Date of sovereignty/independence declaration
21 September 1991

Voting age: 18

Special area	**Capital**
Nagorno-Karabakh	Xankändi

Education

Literacy (age 15 and over who can read and write)

total population	99%
male	99%
female	98%

Level of education for persons over 15

completed higher education	13.8%
completed secondary education	57.7%
incomplete secondary education	18.6%

Number of higher education institutions: 14

Higher education enrollment: 68,400 students

Selected institutions of higher education (and enrollment)

Erevan

State Engineering University of Armenia	11,000
State University	10,000
Academy of National Economy	5,600
Armenian Agricultural Institute	4,000
State Pedagogical Institute of Russian and Foreign Languages	2,800

Socioeconomic Indicators

Annual birth rate: 14.2 births/1,000 population

Fertility rate: 3.1 children/woman

Infant mortality: 16.2 deaths/1,000 live births

Average life expectancy
70.6 years (males 67.9, females 73.4)

Annual death rate: 6.8 deaths/1,000 population

Average family size: 4.7

Annual consumption of electrical energy
1,620 kWh/person

Hospital beds per 10,000 persons: 89.8

Physical Features

Area: 11,506 sq mi

Land use
cultivated 17%
pasture 20%

Highest elevation: 13,419 ft (Mt. Aragats)

Rainfall
12 in./yr, up to 28 in./yr in the mountains

Temperature

Winter	Summer
average 23°F	average 72°F
lowest −51°F	highest 108°F

Economic Production

Estimated per capita GNP: $670 (1994)

Agricultural output
vegetables, grapes, sheep, cattle

Natural resources
gold, copper, molybdenum, zinc, alumina

Industrial output
wine, brandy, machinery, tires, textiles, chemicals, trucks, watches, microelectronics

Currency
dram (introduced November 1993)
1 dram = 100 luma

Communications

Length of rail lines: 525 mi

Length of highways: 4,780 mi

Pipelines
natural gas .... 563 mi

Telephones: 177 per 1,000 persons

Sources "Armianskaia sovetskaia sotsialisticheskaia respublika," *Bol'shaia sovetskaia entsiklopediia* (Moscow, 1977); *Narodnoe khoziaistvo SSSR v 1990g.* (Moscow, 1991); *Naselenie SSSR* (Moscow, 1989); Matthew J. Sagers, "News Notes: Iron and Steel," *Soviet Geography* 30 (May 1989): 397–434; Lee Schwartz, "USSR Nationality Redistribution by Republic, 1979–1989: From Published Results of the 1989 All-Union Census," *Soviet Geography* 32 (April 1991): 209–48; *World of Learning*, 46th ed. (London, 1996); *Europa World Yearbook, 1996* (London, 1996); "Russia . . ." (National Geographic Society Map, 1993); *Demograficheskii ezhegodnik, 1995* (Moscow, 1995); "CIA World Factbook, 1995" (www.odci.gov/cia/publications/95fact/am.html).

Armenia

GEORGIA

GEORGIA

AZERBAIJAN

Spitak

Gyumri   Kirovakan

Dilijan

+
13,419 ft.

Sevan

Sevana Lich

Ejmiatsin

★ Erevan

TURKEY

Ararat

Mt. Ararat ▲

Nagorno - Karabakh

Zangezur Region

Aras River

Naxçivan

AZERBAIJAN

International Boundary

Internal Republic Boundary

★ Capital City

● Other Cities

0   50 Miles

0   50 Kilometers

Armenia: History and Description

Physical Description

Borders Heir to an ancient culture that flourished in eastern Asia Minor, modern Armenia is situated high on the Armenian Plateau in the lesser Caucasus Mountains of southern Transcaucasia. A tiny, landlocked country, Armenia is bordered on the north by Georgia and to the east by Azerbaijan, both also former republics of the Soviet Union. Nearby, but within the borders of Azerbaijan, lies the mountainous Armenian enclave of Nagorno-Karabakh (literally "mountainous Karabakh"). Long a part of historic Armenia, Karabakh was not included within the Soviet-designed borders of modern Armenia. To the south is the Islamic state of Iran and the isolated piece of Azerbaijani territory called Naxçivan (Nakhichevan). Finally, Armenia shares a lengthy southwestern border with Turkey. The smallest of all the former Soviet republics, Armenia (11,506 square miles) is approximately the size of the state of Maryland. Its capital is Erevan.

Mountains The high Armenian Plateau is a volcanic region with many snow-capped peaks, the highest of which is Mt. Ararat, in Turkey. The similarly named Mt. Aragats, an extinct volcano northwest of Erevan, is the tallest summit within Armenia itself; it soars to 13,419 feet. The eight ranges of the Lesser Caucasus exhibit considerable seismic activity, and major earthquakes have periodically devastated areas of Armenian population, the latest being in 1988.

Lake Sevan Armenia's water system is dominated by Lake Sevan (Sevana Lich), the largest lake in Transcaucasia and one of the largest high-elevation lakes in the world. Located 6,234 feet above sea level, its main outlet is the Razdan River. The Razdan drops 3,300 feet in 65 miles as it rushes south to join Armenia's longest river, the Aras (also known as the Araks, or Araxes). The Aras, augmented by mountain tributaries, follows Armenia's border with Turkey, Naxçivan, and Iran before it joins the Kura River in Azerbaijan and empties into the Caspian Sea.

Natural Resources, Agriculture, and Manufacturing The Armenian climate is continental, cold, and dry. Average winter temperatures fall to 20°F or lower. Summer readings average 72°F. Rainfall is a scant 12 inches per year, except in the mountains, where there may be up to 28 inches.

Agriculture constitutes only 12 percent of the Armenian economy. The population tends to be clustered in the Erevan basin through which the Razdan flows and along the valley of the Aras. These areas, assisted by irrigation projects, provide the best settings for the growing of vegetables and fruit, especially grapes for wine. Grains and some other crops are grown at higher altitudes. Pastureland for sheep, goats, and cattle is found at yet higher elevations.

Armenia is not rich in natural resources and must import all of its petroleum, gas, and coal. Electricity, on the other hand, is produced in greater abundance because of the considerable hydroelectric power available from steep mountain streams such as the Razdan. Armenia has long mined copper and more recently molybdenum. It manufactures aluminum and synthetic rubber. In the 1970s, a gold mine was opened east of Lake Sevan.

Cities Erevan is a center of machine manufacturing and light industry. Before the establishment of Soviet Armenia after World War I, Erevan was a small provincial outpost of the Russian Empire, yet in the post–World War II period, it had one of the highest growth rates for large Soviet cities. Gyumri (Leninakan), Armenia's second-largest city, was previously called Alexandropol. It has suffered massive earthquakes; those of 1926 and 1988 killed thousands. Gyumri is a center of the textile industry and a transportation crossroads.

Armenian Diaspora

Although Armenians constitute an overwhelming majority of the population of Armenia, many Armenians live abroad. There have traditionally been such large groups of Armenians living outside historic Armenian lands throughout the 2,000 years of the nation's history that the term *diaspora* has come to refer to these people. The largest populations of expatriate Armenians are found in Georgia and Russia, as well as in neighboring states of the Middle East. Armenian communities also exist in Europe, and a substantial Armenian-American population is settled in the United States.

Ethnic and Historical Background

The origins of the Armenian people lie in the region surrounding Mt. Ararat, where Indo-Europeans migrated at the end of the third millennium B.C. Modern Armenia is but a small part of the area historically inhabited by Armenians, and the modern republic does not include Mt. Ararat. The mountain is visible, however, from much of Armenia and still adorns the state seal. It is symbolic both of Armenian origins and of the roots of conflict between Armenia and its neighbors.

The most extensive kingdom in Armenian history was achieved by Tigran the Great (95–55 B.C.), who ultimately came to control lands that stretched from the Caspian to the Mediterranean, and from the Caucasus to Palestine, lands that included parts of modern Georgia and Azerbaijan. Such an extension of power brought the Armenians into conflict with the Roman Empire. After eventually being brought under Roman control, Armenia became at times a buffer state used by other empires to protect themselves against nomadic peoples north of the Caucasus Mountains.

Armenians speak a language that exists as an independent branch of the Indo-European language family. They use the word Hai to refer to themselves. The unique Armenian script was created at the beginning of the fifth century A.D. Having a written language served the early Armenians well in maintaining their identity and culture during the centuries in which they were a subject people. The contemporary Armenian literary language is based on the so-called Ararat dialect.

The Armenian Church Armenia adopted Christianity in the year 301, when St. Gregory the Illuminator converted the ruler Tiridates III. Armenia thus preceded Byzantium as the first nation to receive Christianity as a state religion. Since the seventh century, the Armenian Church has been headed by the supreme catholicos (bishop) who resides at the monastery of Ejmiatsin (Echmiadzin) west of Erevan. The Armenian Church has remained one of the few manifestations of greater Armenian sovereignty, performing a national as well as a religious role.

Domination of Armenia by Other Empires Late in the fourth century, much of Armenia was partitioned between Byzantine and Persian rulers. Persian forces continued to fight for the remaining Armenian lands until succumbing to the Arab invasions in the seventh century. For the next 300 years, Armenians lived under Arab control, although many fled to Byzantine-controlled western Armenia to avoid the religion of Islam brought by the Arab conquerors. During this period, Armenians made important contributions in the administration of both the Byzantine state (several Byzantine emperors were Armenian) and the Arab empire. *David of Sassoun,* the Armenian national epic of the ninth century, presents colorful accounts of Armenian heroes during this period of Arab domination.

As Armenian lands continued to be controlled by competing regional powers, a new military presence entered the scene. The Seljuk Turks came out of Persia and fought against the Byzantine Empire for control of Asia Minor. In 1236, however, Mongol hordes conquered the entire region. The Armenians fell under the control of the Ottoman Empire in the late sixteenth century. In 1555, the Ottomans divided eastern Armenia with Persia, and in 1620, the Persians annexed Karabakh and the surrounding territory from the Ottomans.

Even though Armenia came to be dominated by other empires, Armenians who had migrated abroad kept alive the notion of an independent Armenian homeland, which they sought to reestablish in the lands of eastern Asia Minor. In the eighteenth century, these expatriate Armenians first formulated ideas of a sovereign Armenia, or an Armeno-Georgian union. Proposals were sent to the Russian Empire, location of the largest Armenian community outside the Ottoman Empire, where there was thought to be sympathy for the Armenian cause.

Russian Conquest

In 1827, by the end of the Russo-Persian wars, the Russian Empire had wrested control of Transcaucasia from the Persians. All Persian territory north of the Aras River came under Russian control. This included most of modern Azerbaijan, the predominantly Armenian Khanate of Karabakh, and the area that ultimately became the modern Republic of Armenia. The rest of historic Armenia remained within the Ottoman Empire.

In the first half of the nineteenth century, Russian tsars Alexander I and Nicholas I encouraged Armenians to move from Ottoman to Russian-held Armenian territory. There followed a migration of Armenians into what became modern Armenia, often into territory with insufficient dwellings and arable land to support the new immigrants. This migration, nevertheless, created a predominantly Armenian region, as Muslims in the area left for Azerbaijan or Persia (now, Iran) to avoid the large numbers of incoming Christians. Erevan, which in 1830 was 50 percent Muslim, underwent a dramatic demographic shift as Armenians arrived from historic Armenian lands outside the new Russian borders. It is estimated that as much as one-half of the 1850 Armenian population of Transcaucasia had immigrated there only since 1830.

The dream of Armenian sovereignty under the tsars never materialized. The settlement of Russian immigrants in Transcaucasia was also encouraged, and Russification policies prevailed at the expense of the

Armenian population. Anti-Russian sentiment grew as Armenians felt increasingly frustrated over unfulfilled Russian promises to protect Armenians still living in the Ottoman Empire.

Armenian Resistance to Turkish and Russian Rule

During the last quarter of the nineteenth century, Armenians in the Ottoman Empire (now, Turkey) formed political parties to press for change. The Hunchak party (established 1886) called for an independent socialist Armenia, while the Dashnak (Dashnaktsutiun) party (established 1890) sought autonomy within a reformed Ottoman Empire. Both groups turned to terrorism. Ottoman suspicions that Armenians were attempting to dismember the Ottoman Empire culminated in a series of massacres from 1894 to 1896, in which an estimated 200,000 Armenians were killed. Russia and the European powers protested—but did little to stop the carnage.

Armenian nationalist groups, angered by Russian inaction and by intensified Russification policies in Armenia, became increasingly anti-Russian. In 1903, when the Russian government advanced a measure to confiscate Armenian Church lands, the Dashnak party mobilized residents in every Armenian village, attacking and killing Russian authorities and Armenians who cooperated with them. The Russians responded by generating anti-Armenian sentiment among the Azerbaijanis, a policy that would be repeated under Soviet commissars. Armed resistance continued until the attacks on the Armenian Church ended in 1905.

At the turn of the century, Armenians participated in socialist groups in Alexandropol and Erevan, as well as in Georgia and Azerbaijan, and helped to organize workers in Baku under the guidance of the Georgian Josef Dzhugashvili (Stalin). In spite of the presence of Armenian workers in the industrial centers of Transcaucasia, however, most of Russian Armenia remained agricultural. The problems generated by the immigrations of the 1830s remained, such as the lack of sufficient good land to support the population. Almost half of the agricultural inhabitants owned no land.

The Armenian Holocaust World War I brought the single greatest tragedy in the history of the Armenian people. This tragedy—known as the Armenian holocaust—is still commemorated annually by all Armenians, in church services and elsewhere, on April 24. The Ottoman government of the Young Turks, amid calls for a holy war and a pan-Turkic empire, began deporting Armenians, who were considered pro-Russian, from Ottoman territory. In forced marches across Turkey in 1915, one million or more Armenians perished from starvation, exhaustion, or raids by Kurdish and Turkish troops. While some Turkish gov-ernors refused to carry out deportation orders, the policy of genocide continued.

At the end of World War I, after the collapse of the tsarist government in Russia and the rise to power of the Bolsheviks, an independent Republic of Armenia was declared in Russian Armenia in May 1918. Although the Ottoman Empire retired from the war and from Russian Transcaucasia in October, Armenia was still at risk from Turkish troops in neighboring Azerbaijan, who avoided disarmament by acquiring Azerbaijani citizenship.

Soviet Conquest

Receiving no help from the West and threatened on all sides, the Armenian Republic turned to the Bolsheviks for assistance by the fall of 1920. The new Soviet government took control of Armenia under an agreement signed on the 2nd of December, 1920, that included grants to Armenia of Nakhichevan and Karabakh. What followed was the incorporation of Armenia into the Soviet Union. In violation of agreements made by the Soviet government, Dashnaks and other nationalists were arrested. Local resistance resulted and continued into 1921 when the Dashnaks recaptured Erevan on the 28th of February, taking revenge for the executions of Dashnak prisoners. After the end of resistance in neighboring Georgia, however, the Red Army retook Erevan in April and the rest of Armenia by late summer.

Armenia was incorporated into the Soviet Union as part of the Transcaucasian Soviet Federated Socialist Republic (TSFSR) in 1922. Despite the earlier promise by the Communists to grant Armenia control of Karabakh and Nakhichevan, the two regions were placed under Azerbaijani governance. The latter, however, was separated from Azerbaijan by the narrow strip of Zangezur, under Armenian control. These border arrangements, intended by the Soviet authorities to continue tsarist policies of playing the Armenians against the Azerbaijanis, have been the subject of ongoing dispute in the aftermath of Soviet power in Transcaucasia. Under the 1936 Stalin constitution, the TSFSR was eliminated, and Armenia became the Armenian Soviet Socialist Republic.

Soviet Leadership

The first priorities of the Soviet regime were to neutralize nationalist forces in Armenia. The Dashnaks were banned in November 1923. The city of Alexandropol was renamed Leninakan in 1924. Persecution of the Armenian Church began in the 1920s by closing places of worship and religious presses. The

Ejmiatsin monastery was expropriated in 1928, and gifts of the Armenian diaspora to the catholicos and the church were confiscated.

Purges of suspect Armenians began in 1929, continuing virtually to the beginning of World War II. The first purge, aimed at old Bolsheviks and nationalists, was largely carried out by the first secretary of the Armenian Communist Party (ArCP), Aghasi Khanchian. As Khanchian himself resisted Russian attempts to curtail Armenian culture, he became less and less reliable to the Communists. In 1936 he died, alleged by the authorities to have committed suicide.

Following Khanchian's death, the purges intensified, devouring most of the newer members of the Party as well as Armenian nationalists. Khanchian's successor as first secretary was Grigor Arutiunov, from a Georgian-speaking family. Arutiunov had risen through the ranks of the Georgian Communist Party and was an associate of Stalin's chief of secret police, Lavrentii Beria.

Although the Russification of Armenia achieved the elimination of age-old rural practices such as bride sales, child marriage, and vendettas, it also led to the destruction of Armenian literature and culture. The purges of 1936 destroyed the works of contemporary Armenian writers. Literature by nineteenth-century authors, such as Hakob Melik Hakobian (Raffi), was banned.

Another goal of the Communist Party was to reform Armenia's economy enough to absorb the masses of refugees it sheltered. In the 1920s, the republic, already short of provisions, was forced to submit to the requisition of food by the Communists. Western aid was critically important as Armenians sought to avoid starvation.

Following the subjugation of Transcaucasia, Communist authorities began a policy of rapid industrialization in Armenia to help employ the excess labor population. By the 1930s, Armenian copper mines were operating at a profit, and Armenia was second only to Kazakhstan in copper production. The Soviet government also built plants for producing sulfuric acid and other chemicals.

A destructive aspect of Soviet economic policies was the forced collectivization of agriculture in the 1930s (see *Collectivization* in the Glossary). Both Armenian and Azerbaijani peasants in Armenia put up armed resistance to these measures, slaughtering cattle to prevent their seizure and attacking Communist officials, both Russian and Armenian, who attempted to collectivize their holdings. The resistance was largely unorganized, although some groups received arms and aid from exiled Dashnaks across the border in Iran. Collectivization slowed in 1930 as a result of the resistance, with collectivized households dropping from 63 percent in February to 9 percent in the fall. Since Armenian Red Army troops were considered unreliable, Russian soldiers were used to put down local revolts, some of which continued into 1934. By 1936, however, the resistance was largely broken, and 80 percent of the peasants in Armenia were collectivized.

Soviet policies changed with the advent of World War II. Moscow reversed itself and attempted to use Armenia as a showcase for the diaspora. The Armenian Church was called upon to rally Armenians to the Soviet war cause, and expressions of nationalism were tolerated. Later, during the tensions of the postwar era, the Soviet government temporarily encouraged some signs of Armenian nationalism in an effort at anti-Western propaganda. For a time, Moscow encouraged Armenians from around the world to move to Soviet Armenia, but the policy was stopped in 1948 after 100,000 Armenians had immigrated. Discriminatory Soviet policies led many of these newcomers to warn relatives not to join them, and some escaped to Iran.

After the death of Stalin in 1953, pressure on Armenian nationalism and culture lessened. Arutiunov was arrested in 1953 for his association with Beria. His successor as first secretary, Suren Tovmasian, encouraged the rehabilitation of some of the nationalist victims of the purges. Previously banned literature was republished. From that time, Armenia was given greater leeway than other Soviet republics in ideological matters. Arutiunov's other successors, Iakov Zarobian (1958–66), Anton Kochinian (1966–74), and Karen Demirchian (1974–88), suffered little criticism, despite the inability of Armenian officials to discourage religion, nationalism, and increasing corruption. Armenian autonomy was due in part to the high efficiency of local industry, which met and exceeded almost all production quotas. Soviet officials were also reluctant to crack down on a republic that they touted as an Armenian homeland, made possible only under benevolent Russian tutelage. It was not until Gorbachev assumed control of the central government and initiated perestroika and glasnost that Demirchian came under fire, both from the government and from Armenian citizens.

Armenia: Contemporary Issues

Nagorno-Karabakh and Armenian Politics

The overriding issue in Armenian politics since 1987 has been the Nagorno-Karabakh conflict—a conflict posed by the existence of an autonomous Armenian enclave that, for most of the twentieth century, has been surrounded by and included in the predominantly Turkic Azerbaijan Soviet Socialist Republic. (For a comprehensive discussion of the Nagorno-Karabakh conflict, see pages 112–14.) The issue of Nagorno-Karabakh has often pressed Armenia into conflict not only with Azerbaijan, but also with Turkey, Iran, and even Moscow. As support for the Armenians in Karabakh increasingly became a litmus test of Armenian national identity, the plight of Nagorno-Karabakh led eventually to open military support for the enclave. Ultimately, the defense of Karabakh became intertwined with nationalist aspirations for Armenian independence from the Soviet Union. Today, a decade after the renewal of the conflict, there is still no political settlement over the contested ethnic and territorial issues posed by Nagorno-Karabakh. Meanwhile, the future of Nagorno-Karabakh stands squarely in the way of the normalization of Armenian relations with its Turkic neighbors, Azerbaijan and Turkey.

In 1987, Armenians appealing for the independence of the Nagorno-Karabakh oblast from Azerbaijan formed the Karabakh Committee. The Karabakh Committee organized demonstrations in Erevan and other parts of Armenia, increasingly criticizing Soviet policies on the dispute. In May 1988, the removal from office of Armenia's Communist Party First Secretary Karen Demirchian signaled Moscow's intention to maintain central control over contested territorial issues such as Karabakh. The selection of Demirchian's successor, Suren Gurgenovich Arutiunian, an official who had spent most of his political life in Moscow, was widely interpreted as an indication that Soviet President Mikhail Gorbachev himself wished to oversee the resolution of the conflict in Nagorno-Karabakh.

Despite the success of Armenian efforts to gain military control over Nagorno-Karabakh—or perhaps, ironically, because of the success—the escalation of fighting in the region would later claim Party First Secretary Arutiunian, for the Karabakh issue quickly became a liability for the Armenian Communist Party. Armenian nationalists were increasingly wary of a Soviet policy that insisted on the maintenance of Azerbaijani authority over Nagorno-Karabakh, while Armenian Communist Party leaders were faced with the prospect of defying Soviet authorities if they went along with the rising tenor of Armenian nationalism on the Karabakh issue. Although Armenian Communist Party loyalists at first deferred to Moscow for resolution of the territorial dispute, the Armenian Supreme Soviet, dominated by Communist Party members, declared Nagorno-Karabakh a part of Armenia in December 1989. Fresh outbreaks of violence in Nagorno-Karabakh in March 1990, and a general refusal of Armenians to accept military service in the Soviet army (as few as 7.5 percent of eligible Armenian men were fulfilling their obligatory military service) led to the dismissal of Arutiunian in April 1990. Arutiunian had openly supported the independence of Nagorno-Karabakh from Azerbaijan prior to his ouster. It was assumed that his successor, Vladimir Migranovich Movsisian, would be an official more pliant to Moscow's demands.

Nevertheless, Moscow's hold over Armenia continued to deteriorate. In May 1990, clashes between Armenians and Soviet troops in Erevan crystallized anti-Soviet sentiment throughout the republic. Presidential elections were held in August 1990, with Movsisian losing to Levon Ter-Petrosian, a philologist who chaired the Armenian Pan-National Movement and was a founding member of the Karabakh Committee. In November, the Armenian Communist Party declared itself independent from the Communist Party of the Soviet Union, and Movsisian was replaced as first secretary by Stepan Pogosian. The Union for National Self-Determination, an Armenian popular front movement, called for immediate secession from the Soviet Union.

Soviet-Armenian tensions increased in 1991. In January, Gorbachev deployed Soviet airborne troops to Armenia to enforce the draft. The Armenian government refused to take part in the March 1991 all-Union referendum on maintaining the Soviet Union, instead choosing to hold a September 1991 referendum on Armenian secession. Following the abortive Moscow coup in August 1991, Ter-Petrosian endorsed the decision to secede. On 21 September, 94.4 percent of the electorate turned out to vote, with 99.3 percent supporting secession. The formal declaration of secession was issued on 23 September 1991. In October, Ter-Petrosian was reelected to the Armenian presidency, garnering over 80 percent of the vote.

As president, Ter-Petrosian has sought to distance himself from unofficial Armenian military groups operating in Nagorno-Karabakh and in adjoining Azerbaijani territory. His goal has been to defuse the Nagorno-Karabakh issue while ostensibly seeking a long-term political settlement of the dispute. Toward that end, he has sought to normalize relations with both Turkey and Iran. In the case of Turkey, his efforts at international mediation have brought considerable domestic criticism, especially in the wake of Turkish blockades of vital Western energy resources.

In the years since Ter-Petrosian's first election as president in 1990 (he has most recently been reelected for a third time in the September 1996 elections), his commitment to democratization has been subject to debate. Ter-Petrosian's administration was initially marked by considerable openness, as in his encouragement of Armenian nationalist groups of the diaspora to return to Erevan. This initial openness toward potential rivals brought with it political opposition to the Ter-Petrosian government. Most notably, the legalization of the Dashnaktsutiun or Dashnak party (the Armenian Revolutionary Federation) in 1992 gave opportunity to nationalist opponents of Ter-Petrosian's policies. The Dashnaks, appealing to a more chauvinist audience with visions of a greater Armenia, have charged the government with failure to recognize the "Nagorno-Karabakh Republic." Aided by minor opposition parties, the Dashnaks have not only challenged Ter-Petrosian's more cautious policies on Nagorno-Karabakh, but have also sought to block the creation of a new constitution that would, in their view, centralize too much power in the office of the presidency. Curiously, the Russian right-wing political figure, Vladimir Zhirinovsky, spoke out in 1995 in support of the Dashnak nationalist efforts.

Conflict between the Ter-Petrosian government and various opposition parties came to a head in the months prior to the parliamentary elections of July 1995. Charging that the Dashnaks were linked to the KGB and to acts of state terrorism, Ter-Petrosian banned the Dashnak party from participation in the elections. His crackdown, just six months before the elections, was interpreted by many as an indication of Ter-Petrosian's increasingly repressive policies toward political opposition. Ter-Petrosian and his ruling coalition, the Armenian National Movement (Hanrapedutiun), defended the ban by seeking to link the Dashnaks with an underground terrorist organization, Dro, whose members have allegedly been responsible for acts of political assassination, such as the murder of the former mayor of Erevan in late 1994.

The elections of July 1995 yielded a solid parliamentary majority for the government's Hanrapedutiun coalition. They secured well over 100 seats in the 190-member National Assembly. The elections were marred, however, by charges that repressive policies were limiting the range of candidates. Approximately 55 percent of the electorate participated in the voting, which was conducted in the presence of international observers. Also on the July 1995 ballot was a referendum on the new Armenian constitution, which was supported by slightly more than two-thirds of those who voted.

Despite the charges that Ter-Petrosian has been engaged in repressive domestic politics, the 1995 elections indicate that the ruling coalition of the Armenian National Movement has captured, for the present, a working majority of Armenians who have come to support the government despite its caution on the volatile Nagorno-Karabakh issue. At the base of this political support are those civil servants, military and police officers, and local representatives who have come to benefit from their own positions in the Ter-Petrosian government.

Armenian Economic Recovery Ter-Petrosian's support also reflects the relative turnaround of Armenian economic life. The desperate state of the Armenian economy in the early 1990s, plagued by the blockade of vital energy resources from Azerbaijan and Turkey, led to the exodus of thousands of Armenians who sought to avoid the economic collapse by joining Armenian émigré communities in the West. Nevertheless, after introducing its new currency, the dram, in November 1993, Armenia by late 1994 began to come out of the downward cycle of inflation and falling production. Inflation rates have fallen to under 10 percent per year, consumer prices and the currency exchange rate have stabilized, rapid privatization has been launched (the World Bank noted in October 1994 that over 40 percent of Armenia's gross domestic product was generated from privatized sources), and national income and industrial production have increased. For 1994, Armenia exhibited the highest per capita gross domestic product (GDP) of any of the newly independent states of the former Soviet Union.

The 1988 Earthquake

Still complicating Armenia's position is the damage wreaked by the earthquake that ravaged its northern provinces on the 7th of December, 1988. The strongest earthquake registered in the region for over 80 years (measuring 6.7 on the Richter scale), it destroyed 75 percent of Gyumri (Leninakan), 50 percent of Kirovakan, the entire town of Spitak, and 55 villages. Soviet officials admitted later that they lacked the equipment for a timely response to the quake. Early estimates placed the death toll at 50,000–70,000, although in January 1990 the figure was lowered to 30,000–40,000 (up from an official count in 1989 of 25,000). Relief efforts by the Soviet and Armenian governments were slow and badly organized. One week after the quake, the official Moscow news agency Pravda reported that many earthquake survivors had died from exposure. Patriarch-Catholicos Vasken I of the Armenian Church called for a requiem mass similar to the annual mass to commemorate the 1915 Armenian holocaust.

The cost of rebuilding the three cities was estimated in January 1989 at eight billion rubles. In the days that followed the quake, 67 countries sent assistance of some sort. By Christmas, international aid had reached $97 million. Pope John Paul II sent a personal message of sympathy to Soviet President Gorbachev, who cut short his attendance at international meetings to return to the Soviet Union. On Christmas Day 1988, a son and grandson of U.S. President George Bush visited the region, distributing gifts to Armenian children.

The earthquake exacerbated existing Armenian-Azerbaijani and Armenian-Soviet tensions. Some Armenians reportedly refused aid from Azerbaijan, and four men bringing relief supplies from Azerbaijan were allegedly turned back by groups of Armenian citizens. Armenian officials were criticized by Moscow for their handling of the crisis, but many Armenians expressed fears that evacuees were being sent to Siberia. Meanwhile, efforts to rebuild the destroyed towns and villages were delayed by Azerbaijani rail blockades in 1989, and the Nagorno-Karabakh conflict generally distracted energy and attention from reconstruction.

Energy

The Nagorno-Karabakh conflict and resultant blockade of Armenia by Azerbaijan has resulted in a critical shortage of energy. Although before the 1960s Armenia produced its own hydroelectric power, such energy accounted for only about 5 percent of Armenian consumption. The Medzamor nuclear power plant, closed after the 1988 earthquake, had been producing an estimated 36 percent of Armenia's energy needs. Prior to the opening of the Medzamor plant—and again after its closure—Armenia, with no coal, oil, or natural gas of its own, was forced to import virtually all of its fuel for energy production. The largest share of such fuels (82 percent) traditionally came from Azerbaijan. Imports of oil and coal from Russia and other republics also reached Armenia through Azerbaijan.

Compounding this picture of energy dependency, Armenia's energy infrastructure remains badly out-

dated and unable to withstand severe seismic activity. The Sevan-Razdan hydroelectric plant, for example, is 42 years old. Although plans to shift to solar production appear promising, with some regions receiving 300 days of sunshine per year, energy shortages led to a near-desperate situation in the early 1990s (see John Tedstrom, "Armenia: An Energy Profile," in *Report on the USSR* 3, no. 8, 22 February 1991, 18–20). By the end of 1992, apartment dwellers in Erevan could hope for little more than one or two hours of electricity a day.

Responding to the energy crisis and the continuing Azerbaijani oil blockade, Armenian authorities have turned to the Russian Federation, which pledged over 110 billion rubles in 1994 for technical assistance in reactivating the Medzamor nuclear power plant. Despite the opposition of neighboring states and expressions of concern from the West, the International Atomic Energy Agency (IAEA) approved the plant's newly installed safety measures, and one Medzamor reactor was restarted in June 1995. Armenian President Ter-Petrosian attended the ceremony marking the occasion, and the successor to Vasken I, the Armenian Church's Patriarch-Catholicos Karekin I, offered an official blessing (see Ara Tatevosyan, "Living Dangerously with Nuclear Power in Armenia," *Transition* 2, no. 9, 3 May 1996, 23–25, 63).

The Medzamor plant is still very much a matter of domestic and international concern. Although it can supply over one-third of all Armenia's energy needs, it is located in an area of frequent seismic activity, about 25 kilometers west of Erevan near the Turkish-Armenian border. In 1995, the IAEA provided sophisticated devices for monitoring seismic activity in the area of Medzamor, although the plant was not built to withstand earthquakes. The Medzamor plant is a thermal neutron reactor, different from the carbon-uranium reactor at Chernobyl. Concerned Armenian ecologists have alleged that an incident involving radioactive release occurred at the Medzamor plant in May 1988, but public documentation of such a claim has not been made. The plant was closed, however, shortly after the December 1988 earthquake, reflecting widespread uncertainty over its safety. The plant's reopening in 1995 met with protest from Turkey and Azerbaijan, yet ironically it was the Azerbaijani oil blockade in 1989 and the Turkish blockade in 1993 that created the urgent need for the plant's reactivation.

Environmental Issues

The rapid industrialization of Armenia since the 1930s has left its mark on the environment, most notably in the air pollution generated by chemical plants and the drainage of Lake Sevan that resulted from ambitious hydroelectric power projects. Protests over air and water pollution and the potential dangers of nuclear power began in the late 1980s. The issues raised at that time remain matters of great national concern.

In March 1986, 350 Armenian intellectuals addressed environmental pollution in an open letter to Soviet President Gorbachev. The letter noted that in the Ararat valley, stomach cancer, cardiac and respiratory diseases, and birth defects had increased fourfold from 1965 to 1985. From 1970 to 1985, instances of mental retardation had increased by 500 percent, mental illnesses 600 percent, and leukemia and abnormal and premature births had increased 400 percent. The Armenian press further noted that 60 percent of the air pollution in Erevan was caused by automobiles, while the other 40 percent came from chemical plants (quoted in Elizabeth Fuller, "Is Armenia on the Brink of an Ecological Disaster?" *Radio Liberty Research Bulletin* 30, no. 34, 20 August 1986). In 1985, the Soviet Council of Ministers passed a resolution to combat air pollution in Erevan, but by 1987 none of the council's recommendations had been implemented.

Part of Armenia's environmental problem arose from the fact that fines for pollution were assessed at a much lower rate than were fines for not meeting industrial production targets, thus discouraging changes in plant processes. In March 1987, Demirchian announced plans to reduce pollution at the major chemical plants in Kirovakan and Erevan. In October, the Party's first secretary from Kirovakan announced that air pollution there was "tens of times higher than permissible" (quoted in Elizabeth Fuller, "USSR Ministry of Health Cites Data on Infant Mortality and Infectious Diseases in Two Transcaucasian Republics," *Radio Liberty Research Bulletin* 31, no. 43, 28 October 1987). Later that month, thousands of Armenians in Erevan protested environmental pollution.

Lake Sevan has suffered from both irrigation projects and hydroelectric plants. By the 1950s, the water level of the lake was down by 50 feet, and the original 547 square miles of surface area had decreased substantially, with drastic repercussions for the local ecosystem. Construction of tunnels to reroute rivers into the lake began in 1963, but the work was not completed until 1980. In 1985 the tunnels collapsed, and water flow into the lake stopped completely. The collapse was not reported for a year, during which time the lake's water level continued to fall. Although the tunnels were subsequently repaired in 1987, the newly independent Armenian government has insufficient resources for such projects. Furthermore, the tunnels do not work as well as required, and Lake Sevan has never been fully replenished. Given the energy situation, it is unlikely that hydroelectric projects will be

shut down, and Lake Sevan will likely be further depleted (see Elizabeth Fuller, "Glasnost in Armenia: The Lake Sevan Cover-Up," *Radio Liberty Research Bulletin* 30, no. 45, 5 November 1986).

As a result of the political and economic problems facing the republic, environmental issues are likely to remain of lesser concern in the near term. Energy needs will necessitate the continued operation of the Medzamor plant and hydroelectric plants, while economic needs stemming from the blockades will make the Armenian government reluctant to reduce the productivity of their chemical production plants.

The Diaspora

The Armenian diaspora represents one of the largest and oldest emigrations out of Eurasia. Dating from the medieval period when Armenian communities were first established in west European centers, the spread of Armenian émigrés has been a constant source of enrichment for Armenian culture. Informal estimates of the size of this Armenian diaspora in the 1970s included 1,400,000 in non-Armenian republics of the Soviet Union; 500,000 in the United States and Canada; 250,000 in Lebanon; 180,000 in Iran; 150,000 in France; 130,000 in Syria; and 125,000 in Turkey. These figures from the 1970s do not reflect the subsequent exodus of Armenians from the Middle East, and they do not reflect the population of Soviet Armenia which was then approximately 2,600,000. Armenian emigrants residing abroad have tended to maintain a strong Armenian identity. This tendency has corresponded to a lively consciousness within the diaspora of an historic Armenia, as well as the potent memory of the Armenian holocaust during World War I (see Ronald Grigor Suny, *Looking toward Ararat: Armenia in Modern History*, Indiana University Press, 1993, 213–230, 270–71).

For Armenians, the diaspora has served as the wellspring from which their community, both in the homeland and abroad, has drawn inspiration and incentive to survive as a people. By the eighteenth century, Armenian enclaves—composed primarily of an urbanized middle class and intelligentsia—were established in Italy, Persia, and India, as well as Russia. The first Armenian book was published in Venice in 1512. The first Armenian journal, *Azdarar,* was published in Madras from 1794 to 1796.

Armenians in the diaspora have, during the twentieth century, found themselves divided into opposing political camps based primarily on their attitude toward Soviet Armenia. The Ramkavar (Democratic Liberal) faction and the Hunchak faction (Social Democrats) have been open to cooperation with the Soviet Socialist Republic of Armenia, viewing the

Soviet (or Russian) state as offering important protection to their Armenian homeland against its traditional enemy, Turkey. The Dashnaks, on the other hand, have traditionally been anti-Soviet and irredentist, insisting upon the extension of Armenian borders by adding Turkic lands considered to be historically Armenian. Extremist Dashnak sympathizers have occasionally engaged in acts of terrorism, both against Turkish officials in Turkey and abroad, and occasionally against fellow Armenians who oppose their views.

Since the 1960s, events in Soviet Armenia have led to the beginnings of reconciliation between the diverse elements of the Armenian diaspora, and even between these groups and Armenians in the homeland. The goal of international recognition of the genocide during the Armenian holocaust of 1915 has come to be seen by most Armenians as so important that differences on other matters might be put aside. Armenian cultural and educational organizations have created a day of remembrance on April 24th, a day that is recognized officially in Armenia and also commemorated in many other countries.

The Armenian Church

A key feature of Armenian nationalism is its identification with the Armenian Church, one of the earliest churches of Eastern Christendom. Factions within the Armenian diaspora have invariably played out their political battles within the framework of the Armenian Church, leaving the Church split between the See of the Armenian Apostolic Church at Ejmiatsin (Echmiadzin) in Armenia and a Catholicosate located in Lebanon.

Operating under the constraints of the Soviet government, political conflicts arose within the Armenian Apostolic Church as Dashnaks at home and abroad struggled for control of the Church against Soviet-recognized Ramkavar church leaders. The latter have viewed Dashnaks as part of an illegal church, and in most cases have been able to elect sympathetic Ramkavar officials to church boards. The See of the Armenian Church at Ejmiatsin, too, has defrocked or refused to recognize pro-Dashnak clergy.

Central in this struggle between Dashnak and Ramkavar factions was the stable postwar leadership of Vasken I, patriarch-catholicos of the Armenian Apostolic Church. For nearly 40 years he headed the See at Ejmiatsin until his death in 1994 at the age of 85. He has been succeeded in the office of patriarch-catholicos by Karekin I. The Armenian Church, still evolving in its response to the dissolution of the Soviet Union, occupies a critical position that can potentially serve to mediate domestic political divisions and en-courage support for Armenia from within the diaspora.

The diaspora remains a potent force in providing Armenian support. The strength of its connection to Armenia was particularly visible in its response to the 1988 earthquake. Prosperous Armenians in the United States and Europe have long taken an interest in the republic, encouraged by Soviet policies to see Soviet Armenia as their homeland. Just as the diaspora played a role in Russian-Armenian cultural relations in the eighteenth and nineteenth centuries, so also the diaspora is likely to continue to play an important role in the survival of independent Armenia.

International Relations

Armenia's geopolitical position is almost as delicate now as it was following World War I and the Armenian genocide of 1915. Facing both a hostile Azerbaijan and an energy blockade, Armenia must rely on help from other countries. Although Ter-Petrosian has sought to normalize relations with Turkey and Iran, he faces the traditionally strong anti-Turkish sentiment within the ranks of his domestic Armenian opposition.

While there has been financial assistance for Armenia from the International Monetary Fund and humanitarian aid from the United States—support that was reaffirmed during Ter-Petrosian's official state visit to Washington in August 1994—Armenia's most important international ties have been with the Russian Federation. Russia has sought to create a special sphere of interest in Transcaucasia, echoing the situation that prevailed when Armenia was part of the Russian Empire and the Soviet Union. Russian technical and financial support for the reactivation of the Medzamor nuclear power plant is only one part of a strong Armenian-Russian bilateral relationship that is now widely perceived to be the closest between any of the newly independent states and the Russian Federation. Russia also continues to see itself as a broker in matters such as the issue of Nagorno-Karabakh. The unwillingness of the United Nations or other international or Western agencies to mediate effectively the ethnic and territorial disputes within Transcaucasia has reinforced this image of Russia as an important continuing presence in Transcaucasian politics. After the August 1991 coup attempt in Moscow, Armenian President Ter-Petrosian called for a union similar to that of the European Community, led by a democratic Russia. Now a member of that informal union, the Commonwealth of Independent States, Armenia has given every indication that it will continue to rely upon the support of Russia in the contested world of Transcaucasian politics.

AZERBAIJAN

Statistical Profile

Demography

Population: 7,487,000

Ethnic population

Azerbaijani	90.0%
Dagestani	3.2%
Russian	2.5%
Armenian	2.3%
Other	2.0%

Major urban centers and populations

Baku	1,149,000
Gäncä (Kirovobad)	281,000
Sumqayit	235,000
Naxçivan (Nakhichevan)	<100,000
Xankändi (Stepanakert)	<100,000
Shusha	<100,000

Historic religious traditions

Islam	93.4%
Christianity	4.8%

Languages: Azerbaijani, Russian, Armenian

Population by age

Age	Total	Males	Females
0–14	32.8%	16.9%	15.9%
15–64	60.9%	29.6%	31.3%
65 and over	6.3%	2.4%	3.9%

Male/Female ratio: 48.9% male/51.1% female

Rural/Urban population: 47.1% rural/52.9% urban

Annual population growth rate: 0.8%

Population density: 224.0 persons per sq mi

Government

Official name
Azerbaycan Respublikasi (Republic of Azerbaijan)

Capital: Baku

Date of sovereignty/independence declaration
30 August 1991

Voting age: 18

Special areas / **Capitals**

Special areas	Capitals
Naxçivan	Naxçivan
Nagorno-Karabakh	Xankändi

Education

Literacy (age 15 and over who can read and write)

total population	97%
male	99%
female	96%

Level of education for persons over 15

completed higher education	10.5%
completed secondary education	58.1%
incomplete secondary education	19.2%

Number of higher education institutions: 17

Higher education enrollment: 105,100 students

Selected institutions of higher education (and enrollment)

Baku

State Petroleum Academy	14,600
Baku State University	12,390
Technical University	9,680
Gadzhibekov Academy of Music	800

Socioeconomic Indicators

Annual birth rate: 21.4 births/1,000 population

Fertility rate: 2.64 children/woman

Infant mortality: 25.2 deaths/1,000 live births

Average life expectancy
70.6 years (males 66.6, females 74.2)

Annual death rate: 7.4 deaths/1,000 population

Average family size: 4.8

Annual consumption of electrical energy
2,270 kWh/person

Hospital beds per 10,000 persons: 102.2

Physical Features

Area: 33,436 sq mi

Land use
cultivated 18%
pasture 24%

Highest elevation: 14,652 ft (Bazardbiuzi peak)

Rainfall
10 in./yr, up to 69 in./yr on the Caspian coast

Temperature

Winter	Summer
average 29°F	average 79°F
14°F in the mountains	41°F in the mountains
lowest –22°F	highest 109°F

Economic Production

Estimated per capita GNP: $500 (1994)

Agricultural output
cotton, grain, rice, grapes, vegetables, tea, tobacco, livestock

Natural resources
petroleum, natural gas, iron ore, nonferrous metals, alumina

Industrial output
petroleum products, oil field equipment, petro-chemicals, textiles

Currency
manat (introduced August 1992)
1 manat = 100 gopik

Communications

Length of rail lines: 1,306 mi

Length of highways: 19,875 mi

Pipelines
crude oil .... 706 mi
natural gas .... 775 mi

Telephones: 90 per 1,000 persons

Sources "Azerbaidzhanskaia sovetskaia sotsialisticheskaia respublika," *Bol'shaia sovetskaia entsiklopediia* (Moscow, 1977); *Narodnoe khoziaistvo SSSR v 1990g.* (Moscow, 1991); *Naselenie SSSR* (Moscow, 1989); Matthew J. Sagers, "News Notes: Iron and Steel," *Soviet Geography* 30 (May 1989): 397–434; Lee Schwartz, "USSR Nationality Redistribution by Republic, 1979–1989: From Published Results of the 1989 All-Union Census," *Soviet Geography* 32 (April 1991): 209–48; *World of Learning*, 46th ed. (London, 1996); "Russia . . ." (National Geographic Society Map, 1993); *Europa World Yearbook, 1996* (London, 1996); *Demograficheskii ezhegodnik, 1995* (Moscow, 1995); "CIA World Factbook, 1995" (www.odci.gov/cia/publications/95fact/aj.html).

Azerbaijan

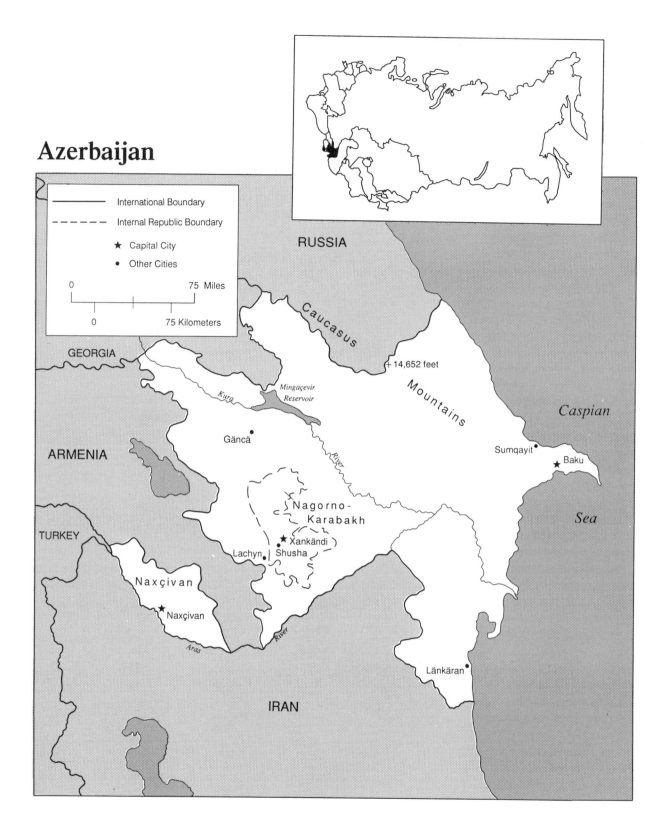

RUSSIA

International Boundary
Internal Republic Boundary
★ Capital City
● Other Cities

0   75 Miles

0   75 Kilometers

GEORGIA

Caucasus

Kura

Mingaçevir
Reservoir

+ 14,652 feet

Mountains

Caspian

ARMENIA

Gäncä

River

Sumqayit ●

★ Baku

Sea

TURKEY

Nagorno-
Karabakh

★ Xankändi
Lachyn ● | ● Shusha

Naxçivan

★ Naxçivan

Aras

River

IRAN

Länkäran ●

Azerbaijan: History and Description

Physical Description

Azerbaijan, largest of the republics of former Soviet Transcaucasia, is located along the western shore of the Caspian Sea. On the north, Azerbaijan is bordered by the Russian Federation, while Georgia and Armenia lie on its northwestern and western borders, respectively. To the south, Azerbaijan shares a border with Iran. The small territorial region of Naxçivan (or Nakhichevan)—approximately 3,420 square miles—is geographically separated from the rest of Azerbaijan by a 25- to 30-mile-wide strip of Armenian territory. Naxçivan borders Turkey and Iran. The isolated Armenian enclave of Nagorno-Karabakh (2,730 square miles), under Azerbaijani control, is the object of a violent conflict with Armenia that escalated to armed warfare in 1987.

The main waterways in Azerbaijan are the Aras (also known as the Araks, or Araxes) and the Kura rivers, both of which begin in the mountains of northeastern Turkey. From there, the Kura flows north into Georgia before entering the extreme northwestern part of Azerbaijan. It then flows through Azerbaijan in a southeasterly direction all the way to the Caspian Sea. The Aras, from its Turkish headwater, flows southeast, eventually running parallel to the Azerbaijani-Iranian border on the Iranian side. It then turns north into Azerbaijan and joins the Kura, which empties into the Caspian Sea.

Elevations in Azerbaijan rise from near sea level on the Caspian coast and in the river basins of the Kura and Aras to almost 15,000 feet in the northern mountains and close to 12,000 feet in the west. Between the central lowlands and the surrounding mountains lie several different climatic regions, from the mild, semi-arid weather near the coast to the much colder and wetter weather found in higher elevations.

This variation of climate allows for the cultivation of several different crops; in particular, grapes and cotton. Some areas are suitable for growing wheat, tea, figs, pomegranates, saffron, and mulberry trees (for the silk-production industry), as well as for raising sheep and cattle. Natural resources include copper, salt, and iron ore, although the single most important Azerbaijani resource is oil. Baku, the Azerbaijani capital and the fifth-largest city in the former Soviet Union, is located in the richest of the oil-bearing regions, on the Apsheron Peninsula.

Ethnic and Historical Background

Although the terms Azeri and Azerbaijani are sometimes used interchangeably, Azeri more correctly applies to an ancient Iranian language of the fourth century B.C. The most accurate term for an inhabitant of modern Azerbaijan is Azerbaijani. Modern Azerbaijanis are a Turkic people whose language is known, simply, as Azerbaijani. It is similar to the language spoken in Turkmenistan and is easily understood by speakers of modern Turkish. Azerbaijanis are primarily Shi'ite Muslims, unlike the other Turkic peoples of the former Soviet Union, who are predominantly Sunni Muslims. Azerbaijani Shi'ism is basically a reflection of the historical ties between Azerbaijan and Iran, a center of Shi'ite Muslim life.

The origins of the name Azerbaijan are a matter of question. The term is generally thought to come from the fourth-century figure, Atropat, who ruled the area of what is now northwestern Iran. Indeed, the name Azerbaijan is used for the northernmost province of Iran. The term Azerbaijan may also derive from *azer,* the Persian word for fire, relating to the oil-fed flames that burned on the altars of the Zoroastrians, followers of an ancient Persian religion.

The area of present-day Azerbaijan was conquered by Persians in the sixth century B.C. Thus, the earliest inhabitants of the region were probably subjected to a heavy Persian/Iranian influence in both language and culture. During the third and fourth centuries B.C., Baku, Gäncä, Naxçivan, and other cities that still exist in modern Azerbaijan were founded as trading centers for silk and lamp oil.

With the rise of Islam in the seventh century A.D., Arab Muslims brought a new religion to the area, and Islam thereafter prevailed. By the eleventh century, under the Seljuk Turks, the Persianized peoples of Azerbaijan were becoming Turkicized. Then the Oghuz Turks, whose descendants inhabit Turkmenistan, migrated from the east and came to influence the linguistic development of the Azerbaijanis. With the Mongolian invasions of the thirteenth century, the region fell under the domain of Genghis Khan. Later came rival Turkmen clans who completed the Turkicization of Azerbaijan.

Yet another stage in the development of the Azerbaijanis came in the sixteenth century, when the Persian ruler Ismail Safavi conquered Azerbaijani lands. Ismail established Shi'ism as the official religion, thus antagonizing the Ottoman Turks, who were Sunni. In subsequent wars, although Azerbaijan was held by the Ottomans from 1578 to 1603, it remained a province of Safavid Persia until 1747, when Persian rule was replaced with that of Turkic Muslim khanates based in Baku, Naxçivan, Erevan, and elsewhere.

Russian involvement in Transcaucasia began in the early eighteenth century with efforts to secure raw materials such as copper, silk, and cotton. Russia also wished to acquire a militarily strategic position on the Caspian Sea. Peter I's Persian expedition led to the conquest of the Caspian coast in the 1710s and 1720s. Although the territory soon had to be relinquished, Russian interest in the Caucasus influenced the policies of Azerbaijani khans and Georgian princes. In 1783, Catherine II brought Georgia under Russian protection by treaty, and in 1783, the Russians seized the Crimea and western Transcaucasia. At the beginning of the nineteenth century, with the Russo-Persian wars of 1804–13 and 1826–28, the Russian Empire detached northern Azerbaijan from Persia (the land now called Iran).

Russian Conquest

Official Russian rule in Transcaucasia began in 1801, when Alexander I established Georgia as an administrative unit within the Russian Empire. This unit also included adjacent Azerbaijani territory. The 1812 Treaty of Gulistan and the 1828 Treaty of Turkmanchai ended the two Russo-Persian wars and brought Azerbaijani khanates north of the Aras River under Russian control.

Armed resistance to Russian rule was led by several Sunni khanates of Dagestan that had been fighting a holy war against the Russians since the eighteenth century. Shi'ite Azerbaijanis often fought with the Russians against the Dagestanis, not only because of Islamic sectarian differences, but also because many Azerbaijani khans saw Russian overlordship as preferable to that of the shahs of Persia.

Russia governed Azerbaijan as part of a Transcaucasian administration. For most of the early nineteenth century, this was done through existing khanates and local structures. As the century wore on, however, policies leaned more toward assimilation. Provinces were combined, eliminating a number of governmental personnel; most of the positions remaining went to Russians. During the 1860s and 1870s, Russian courts and law codes replaced the Islamic system of laws (sharia). For local Muslims, simply imprisoning a thief or murderer seemed inappropriate, and the subsequent vigilante justice added to tensions between Azerbaijanis and Russians. During the 1880s, with the influx of Russian settlers, Russification intensified.

Ethnic tensions between Azerbaijanis and Armenians have their roots in this period, as well. Following the Treaty of Turkmanchai, Tsar Nicholas I established in the Erevan and Naxçivan khanates a refuge for Armenian immigrants from Turkey and Persia. These Christian Armenians were seen by the Azerbaijanis, however, as the beneficiaries of preferential treatment. When local parliamentary bodies (dumas) were established in Azerbaijani areas in 1892, non-Christians were limited to a one-third representation. As a result, Azerbaijanis became a legal minority in their own native territories. Non-Christians were also disadvantaged in property ownership and taxation.

Under Russian rule the Azerbaijani economy, especially the oil industry, experienced rapid expansion. In 1872 the system of granting oil concessions was replaced by giving long-term leases to the highest bidder. This led to increased efficiency, including the swift introduction of power drilling in place of hand-dug wells. By 1901, peak oil production at Baku topped that of the entire United States. As the oil industry brought in foreign companies, Baku turned into a classic boom town, with an influx of Russians and Armenians.

These newcomers edged Azerbaijanis out of the highest-paying positions in the oil industry. Azerbaijanis still controlled Caspian shipping and silk production, but the majority of the native population involved in the oil industry worked in low-paid labor positions. The industrial development of Baku left the rural areas of Azerbaijan relatively untouched.

Russian Revolutions and Azerbaijan Independence

In Azerbaijan, the 1905 and 1917 revolutions were dominated by Armenians and Russians who were the laborers most involved in the mass demonstrations and strikes launched by social democratic groups in Baku. Azerbaijani parties, such as Himmat (Endeavor) and Musavat (Equality) were much less interested in class conflict than in combating Russian imperialism. They were also less hostile to religion, although Azerbaijani intellectuals tended to be critical of Muslim provincialism. These intellectuals watched with great interest the 1908 Young Turk revolution in the Ottoman Empire and the 1909 revolution in Persia as possible evidence of incipient pan-Turkic unity.

Following the October Revolution of 1917, Musavat, the most popular party among the Azerbaijanis, initially supported the Bolsheviks because of Lenin's speeches on self-determination. The Russian- and Armenian-dominated Baku Communist

Party apparatus, however, edged Azerbaijani socialists out and demonstrated an unwillingness to allow the nationalities to govern themselves. Distrust led to armed conflict in March 1918, when Armenian nationalists and Bolsheviks turned against the Azerbaijanis. When the latter surrendered, the Armenians engaged in a killing and looting spree, remembered today by the Azerbaijanis as the March Days, during which more than 3,000 people were killed.

Outside Baku, the Azerbaijanis and Georgians cooperated to create the short-lived Transcaucasian Federation, a sovereign state that in April 1918 negotiated peace with the Ottoman Turks. When Georgia withdrew from the Transcaucasian Federation, the Azerbaijanis remaining in the government declared themselves to be the Azerbaijani National Council, and on the 28th of May, 1918, they declared the formation of the Azerbaijani Democratic Republic.

Although the Azerbaijanis repelled attacks by the Baku Soviet (Council) and captured Baku in September 1918 (taking revenge on the Armenians for the March Days), the Azerbaijani Democratic Republic failed to get the recognition it sought from other nations. With the Armenians revolting in Karabakh, the Azerbaijani Communist Party pressuring the republican government, and the Red Army marching into Azerbaijan, the republican parliament signed the government over to the Bolsheviks on the 27th of April, 1920. Armed opposition throughout Azerbaijan followed, and resistance to Soviet rule continued to smolder until 1924.

Azerbaijan was incorporated into the Soviet Union along with Armenia and Georgia as part of the Transcaucasian Soviet Federated Socialist Republic (TSFSR) in 1922. The boundaries drawn between Azerbaijan and Armenia demonstrated the willingness of Soviet leaders to carry on the tsars' ethnic policies. After an earlier promise to grant control of Karabakh to the Armenians, it was instead placed under the control of Azerbaijan. Predominantly Azerbaijani Naxçivan was also given to Azerbaijan, but the Zangezur province between Naxçivan and the rest of the republic was given to Armenia. It was not until 1936, under the Stalin constitution, that the TSFSR was eliminated and Azerbaijan became a full union republic, officially the Azerbaijan Soviet Socialist Republic.

Soviet Leadership

As armed resistance continued in Azerbaijan, rule from Moscow in the 1920s began with the elimination of nationalists and resistance leaders. Mosques were closed, and a more aggressive Russification policy inaugurated. Azerbaijani resources, notably oil, were expropriated to serve other regions; in particular, Russia and Armenia. In the Azerbaijani Communist Party, only Nariman Narimanov, a doctor, spoke against these policies, and he was removed from local government and sent to Moscow. In 1925 he died of unknown causes.

The repression, which grew into the broader purges under Stalin, was carried out by Mir Jafar Bagirov, commissar for internal affairs from 1921 to 1933 and first secretary of the Azerbaijani Communist Party from 1933 to 1953. Under his leadership, the native party was virtually destroyed, as one after another of the old guard was denounced and executed or deported. It is estimated that between 1921 and 1940, 120,000 Azerbaijanis died from Soviet acts of repression, and it was not until the 1970s that the Baku government again had an ethnic Azerbaijani majority.

When Stalin died in 1953, Bagirov was removed from office and arrested. Three years later he was executed. His replacement as first secretary was Imam Dashdemiroglu Mustafaev, a plant geneticist. During Mustafaev's tenure, steps were taken to restore some autonomy to Azerbaijan, such as maintaining the republic's oil ministry separate from central control and amending the republican constitution to make Azerbaijani the official language. Moscow, however, considered Mustafaev too nationalistic, and in 1959 he was removed from office.

Mustafaev's successor, Veli Akhundov, was also an outsider to the Party structure. Although he lasted until 1969, he was blamed for Azerbaijan's poor economic performance and accused of fostering widespread corruption. His replacement was Gaidar Aliev, an Azerbaijani product of the Party system, who had worked his way up the ranks in the Naxçivan KGB. He was chosen to improve the republic's economy and wipe out corruption. He was praised for having achieved these objectives when he assumed higher office in Moscow at the beginning of 1983, but it was later discovered that Aliev had merely replaced Akhundov's patronage system with one of his own. All three of Aliev's successors have been members of that same system, chosen primarily from the Naxçivan Communist Party apparatus and the KGB. Azerbaijan's Party leadership continued to reflect the influence of hard-liners such as Aliev until 1991, when he was relegated to Party leadership in Naxçivan.

Azerbaijan: Contemporary Issues

Ethnic Disputes: Nagorno-Karabakh and Naxçivan

Azerbaijan's long-standing conflict with Armenia over Nagorno-Karabakh (mountainous Karabakh) has been the most critical problem facing the newly independent state. During the course of the twentieth century, Karabakh has been incorporated into several different republican and state units, but its population majority has remained Armenian. Dating from border arrangements imposed by the Caucasian Bureau of the Russian Communist Party, control of this Armenian region was awarded to Azerbaijan, which, along with Armenia and Georgia, became constituent parts of a larger Transcaucasian Soviet Federated Socialist Republic (1922–1936). Throughout the Soviet period, the Karabakh issue came to mirror the wider reality of Transcaucasia, in which pockets of tribal and ethnic minorities found themselves in conflict with more powerful imperial or majority rule. The Karabakh issue has also reflected the way in which ethnic tensions in the region have been exacerbated by Russian and Soviet manipulation.

The ethnic development of Nagorno-Karabakh is as much a political as a historical matter. As far back as the sixteenth century, Armenian-Muslim tensions surfaced in Karabakh when the holdings of Armenian farmers there were encroached upon by Muslim herders, who brought their flocks to the highlands of mountainous Karabakh during the summer. Russian tsarist policies of the nineteenth century shifted the demographic balance heavily in favor of the Armenian population. Armenian emigrants from the Ottoman Empire and Persia were encouraged to settle in Karabakh, and the Azerbaijani population there declined. By the time of the Russian Revolution in 1917, the region had become predominantly (75 percent) Armenian.

Under the short-lived Azerbaijani Democratic Republic (1918–20), the Armenians in Karabakh revolted in a futile attempt at national self-determination. After the Red Army took control of Azerbaijani territory in April 1920, the Bolshevik government in Baku agreed to place both Karabakh and Naxçivan under Armenian control. The Bolsheviks subsequently changed their position, giving over to Azerbaijan territorial control of the Naxçivan oblast in 1921, and of the Nagorno-Karabakh oblast in 1923. As a part of Azerbaijani territory (first in the Transcaucasian Soviet Republic and subsequently in the Soviet Republic of Azerbaijan), the capital of the newly established

Nagorno-Karabakh Autonomous Oblast was located in the predominantly Armenian town of Stepanakert, rather than in the Azerbaijani town of Shusha. Naxçivan, while also under Azerbaijani control, came to be physically separated from the main body of Azerbaijani territory by the Armenian region of Zangezur.

Armenian Appeals to Moscow From the 1960s, Armenia began appealing to Moscow to turn Nagorno-Karabakh over to Armenian control, arguing that Azerbaijanis discriminated against the Armenian population there, that cultural and educational facilities were lacking, and that the oblast was economically neglected by the government of Azerbaijan. Azerbaijanis, however, believed that Nagorno-Karabakh consistently received a larger share of the republican budget and more Soviet funding than its population warranted.

In October 1987, 1,000 Armenians demonstrated in Erevan for the return of Nagorno-Karabakh to Armenian control. The demonstration, organized by the Karabakh Committee (a group formed in Armenia to assist the Armenians of Nagorno-Karabakh), was sparked in part by an incident days earlier when a bus containing Armenians was surrounded by a group of Azerbaijanis and pelted with stones.

Escalating Violence On the 20th of February, 1988, the Nagorno-Karabakh oblast council declared Nagorno-Karabakh officially separate from Azerbaijan and asked Moscow to take formal action in support of the declaration. In the ensuing protest demonstrations, two Azerbaijani young people were killed. The announcement of their deaths led Azerbaijanis in the Caspian seaport town of Sumqayit to attack Armenian residents there. Thirty-two people perished in the fighting. The immediate and urgent appeal of the Karabakh Committee to modify republican borders was rejected by Moscow. Gorbachev, not wanting to encourage nationalistic aspirations, called instead for accelerated development of Nagorno-Karabakh by the Azerbaijani government.

Strikes and demonstrations continued throughout 1988. The trial of Azerbaijanis involved in the Sumqayit violence polarized the situation, and in May both the Azerbaijani and the Armenian Communist Party first secretaries were replaced. In November, hundreds of thousands of Azerbaijanis demonstrated in Baku's Lenin Square, protesting plans to build an Armenian rest home on the site of an eighteenth-century battle with Iran. Most disturbing to Soviet officials were the demonstrators who carried portraits of Ayatollah Khomeini and the green flags of Shi'ite Islam. By December 1988, the number of dead had reached 80, and the count of refugees (mainly Armenian and Russian) topped a quarter of a million. With mediation attempts rejected by both sides, Gorbachev in January 1989 placed Nagorno-Karabakh under the direct control of Moscow.

Azerbaijani refugees streamed out of Armenia as new campaigns of violence were directed against Armenian residents of Baku. Moved by the widening demonstrations in Azerbaijan in 1989, the Azerbaijani government instituted a rail blockade of Armenia that not only impeded Armenian industrial activity, but also restricted energy and related supplies destined for Armenian areas devastated in the 1988 earthquake. Through November 1989, Nagorno-Karabakh stayed under Moscow's direct control.

January 1990 witnessed the outbreak of such violence against the remaining Armenians and Russians in Baku that Gorbachev sent Soviet troops to intervene. Order was eventually restored, but only at the expense of many lives. In Erevan, meanwhile, anti-Soviet sentiment came to a head when, in May 1990, Armenians clashed with Soviet forces in Theater Square, leaving 24 dead. That August, Levon Ter-Petrosian, a high official in the Karabakh Committee, was elected president of Armenia.

The "transition to all-out war," as described by Ara Tatevosyan, the Erevan correspondent for *Moscow News* ("Nagorno-Karabakh's New Army of 'Iron Will and Discipline,'" *Transition* 2, no. 16, 9 August 1996, 20), occurred during Operation Ring, between April and June of 1991. During that time, despite Armenian resistance, the combined forces of the Soviet army and units of the Azerbaijani interior ministry deported 5,000 Armenians from Karabakh, emptying as many as 19 villages. A similar deportation operation launched in August 1991 in northern Nagorno-Karabakh prompted the besieged Armenians to begin coordinating their own defense efforts to avoid what seemed like the inevitable ethnic cleansing of Karabakh. The result was the creation of between 40 and 50 small Armenian self-defense units eventually cooperating under a single leader.

In October 1991, as a follow-up to their Supreme Soviet's declaration of independence, the Azerbaijani parliament voted to eliminate the autonomous status of the Nagorno-Karabakh oblast. The Armenians of Karabakh, facing the complete blockade of the territory by Azerbaijan, declared their independence in December 1991, and requested admission to the Commonwealth of Independent States. Azerbaijan contin-

ued its attempt to take control of the oblast, launching an intense bombardment of the Karabakh capital, Stepanakert.

As Nagorno-Karabakh became increasingly isolated, armed units from Armenia joined the struggle. In May 1992, combined Armenian forces managed to take control of Shusha and soon thereafter established a corridor of land between Nagorno-Karabakh and Armenia, in the process capturing the westerly Azerbaijani town of Lachyn. In June, disorganized and poorly trained Azerbaijani military forces counterattacked in Nagorno-Karabakh, sustaining heavy casualties but managing, with the deployment of heavy artillery, to recapture several villages. With financial aid from the Armenian diaspora, the Karabakh Armenians gradually began to acquire more technically advanced military equipment. Radar systems and anti-aircraft machinery enabled the Karabakh Armenians to down Azerbaijani bombers during air attacks on the enclave. Strengthened by the consolidation of Armenian Karabakh forces, the Armenians in Nagorno-Karabakh proclaimed in September 1992 the independence of the "Republic of Nagorno-Karabakh," and named a supreme military commander to fuse local defense units into the new republic's well-structured and effective armed forces.

The spring of 1993 witnessed important advances by the Karabakh Armenians, in which they managed not only to gain complete control of Nagorno-Karabakh, but also to conquer additional Azerbaijani territory immediately to the north and to the east of their republic, as well as a portion of land along the Azerbaijani-Iranian border to the south. The Karabakh Armenians thus came to control more than 20 percent of the territory of Azerbaijan, but their victory had created over 100,000 additional refugees. The lengthy fighting resulted in the displacement of virtually all Azerbaijanis from Armenia, and of Armenians from Azerbaijan, more generally jeopardizing minority population in both republics. The massive relocation of population since 1988 has produced one million refugees on the Azerbaijani side alone.

After 10 months of intense pressure, a Russian-mediated cease-fire was worked out in May 1994 and has survived since then, despite periodic flare-ups. For now, despite the absence of international recognition, Nagorno-Karabakh is nominally independent, although geographically and militarily linked to Armenia. Western-sponsored peace talks seeking a long-term political settlement to the conflict have become deadlocked. The diplomatic process seems to offer few prospects to the opposing sides, thus making war an ever-present danger. The Karabakh Armenians will not give up occupied Azerbaijani territory crucial to Karabakh security, while the Azerbaijanis refuse to participate in peace negotiations without an agreement on the restoration of their territory and the return and resettlement of their refugees.

The new constitution of Azerbaijan, approved by referendum on the 12th of November, 1995, reaffirms the territorial integrity of Azerbaijan, implying thereby the continued claim of Azerbaijan to Nagorno-Karabakh, although Karabakh is not mentioned by name in the constitution. The constitution does, however, seek to clarify the status of Naxçivan, no longer referring to it as an "autonomous republic" within Azerbaijan, but rather as a fully integrated "state" within the Azerbaijani republic.

Politics and Informal Groups

The conflict over Nagorno-Karabakh has occurred during a period of prolonged internal political turmoil in Azerbaijan. Communist Party leaders of Azerbaijan were among the last to support internal political reform or recognize local resistance to Communist rule. Under the regime of Party First Secretary Kiamran Bagirov, who succeeded Gaidar Aliev in 1982, problems of economic and political corruption resurfaced in Azerbaijan. Kiamran Bagirov was still first secretary when the Nagorno-Karabakh conflict flared in 1987, and his removal from office in May 1988 was linked in part to how he handled that crisis. Abdul-Rakhman Vezirov, an Aliev protégé, succeeded Bagirov, but was in turn removed in 1990.

During Vezirov's tenure, an Azerbaijani Popular Front (APF) formed in resistance to Soviet rule. In 1988, Azerbaijani intellectuals, previously more concerned with keeping their culture alive than with political action, joined the hundreds of thousands of demonstrators in Baku's Lenin Square protesting the Nagorno-Karabakh conflict. As grievances broadened to include the stifling of native Azerbaijani cultures, the concealment of environmental problems, and the concern for Azerbaijani self-determination, the APF instituted a series of demonstrations and strikes. Also from 1988, the Birlik (Unity) Society, made up primarily of immigrants from the Azerbaijani-populated region of northern Iran, united with the APF. Birlik, along with several groups within the APF, such as the Social Democratic Party, the Azerbaijani Liberal Democratic Party, and the National Democratic Party (New Musavat), all called for a referendum on secession from the Soviet Union. With the outbreak of violence in January 1990, Gorbachev sent Soviet troops into Baku. When the media blackout ended, it was learned that 131 Azerbaijanis had been killed and 744 wounded. A report on the Soviet intervention called it a "carefully planned and cynically executed punitive action" (quoted in "Azerbaijan Commission on January 1990 Military Intervention," *Radio Free Europe/ Radio Liberty Research Report* 1, no. 5, 31 January 1992, 69).

Nearly one-third of Azerbaijani Communists destroyed their membership cards as Vezirov's successor, Ayaz Niyaz Mutalibov, was chosen. Refusing to yield on the Nagorno-Karabakh issue, Mutalibov concentrated on developing ties with other Soviet republics and encouraging foreign investment in Azerbaijan. After Mutalibov's failure to condemn the Moscow August 1991 coup attempt, however, the Azerbaijani Popular Front called for his resignation and demanded Azerbaijani independence. The parliament, still dominated by ex-Communists, unanimously voted to "restore" Azerbaijan's independent status of 1918–20. In the ensuing September presidential elections, Mutalibov went on to win more than 80 percent of the vote (a figure disputed by the APF). The candidate of the Azerbaijani Social Democratic Party had withdrawn from the race, complaining of unfair campaigning. The referendum on Azerbaijani independence meanwhile resulted in a 99 percent approval, with 54 percent of those eligible voting.

Pressure from the APF and Mutalibov's failure to maintain control of Nagorno-Karabakh led to his forced resignation by parliament in March 1992. Elections were set for June. In May, however, Mutalibov reclaimed the presidency, canceled the elections, and imposed a curfew and censorship. Although a democratic bloc boycotted the vote, the parliament reinstated Mutalibov. In response, the APF, in a bloodless coup conducted with the cooperation of the army, occupied the parliament building, took control of airport and broadcasting facilities, and directed the government under a temporary national council.

In statewide elections in June 1992, Abulfaz Elchibey was chosen as the new president of Azerbaijan. A 54-year-old historian and chairman of the APF, he gained 59 percent of the vote in a contest monitored by foreign observers. This was to be the high point of popular support for the Azerbaijani Popular Front. Although most Azerbaijanis accepted the election outcome, one of the challengers, Nizami Suleymanov, candidate of the Democratic Union of the Intelligentsia of Azerbaijan, charged fraud.

Political Volatility from Elchibey to Aliev

President Abulfaz Elchibey, despite his electoral majority and the support of the Azerbaijani Popular Front, failed to provide effective leadership in the two areas most vital to the young Azerbaijani nation. First of all, the Elchibey government continued to sustain reversals in Nagorno-Karabakh. The victorious Armenians, having carved out a corridor linking Armenia-proper to Karabakh, badly embarrassed Elchibey and his commanders. After dismissing the Azerbaijani military leader, Surat Husseinov, whom he charged with responsibility for Azerbaijani losses, Elchibey faced the personal revenge of Husseinov. In June 1993, Husseinov led his rebel followers from the city of Gäncä in a direct assault upon the Elchibey government, forcing the elected president of Azerbaijan to flee to Naxçivan.

On a second and equally important matter, President Elchibey failed to turn around the misfortunes of the Azerbaijani economy, despite the presence of substantial untapped oil reserves. One of the ironies of Elchibey's fall in June 1993 was that prior to the domestic uprising, negotiations with a five-party Western consortium for joint development of the Baku oil fields were on the verge of completion. The five Western negotiating parties—British Petroleum, Amoco, Pennzoil, Unocal, and McDermott International—were prepared to invest sizable new development funds into the rich Caspian Sea oil fields.

The Reemergence of Gaidar Aliev

With Elchibey's withdrawal to Naxçivan—without a formal resignation from the presidency—Gaidar Aliev, one-time head of the Azerbaijani KGB and Brezhnevite Communist Party leader, became chair of the parliament and was elected president in September 1993. Aliev's reemergence as a power broker in Azerbaijan has paralleled developments elsewhere in the newly independent states of Eurasia where, following the euphoria of independence and subsequent disillusionment, former Communist leaders reassumed or retained their hold upon power. Gaidar Aliev's return was a particularly striking example of the familiar pattern—a one-time Communist Party leader embracing the modern nationalist cause resurfaces with a new ideological identity, but with powerful ties to the old Party bureaucracy or nomenklatura. (That pattern, in varying degrees, can be used to describe Eduard Shevardnadze of Georgia, Islam Karimov of Uzbekistan, and Nursultan Nazarbaev of Kazakhstan.) From his post as KGB chief in Azerbaijan, Aliev had been tapped by Brezhnev to be Communist Party first secretary of the republic in 1969. In 1983, he was named to the central Soviet Politburo, the effective governing body of the Communist Party of the former Soviet Union. He served during Gorbachev's leadership as deputy prime minister of the Soviet Union before being ousted in October 1987. Following a period of oblivion in Moscow, Aliev resurfaced in the spring of 1990 and, after resigning his Party membership, led protests in Moscow against Soviet military intervention in Baku—protests that marked the emergence of a new, more nationalistic Aliev. From the summer of 1990, the reincarnated nationalist Aliev took residence in Naxçivan until his return to Baku in mid-1993.

The Aliev government has been no more able than the Elchibey government to restore national honor in its relationship with Armenia, and the stability of Azerbaijan has been threatened by a series of coup attempts. Closely related to the political instability that prevails in Azerbaijan is the Aliev government's official stifling of many popular movements and its institution of restrictions on the press and other forms of free expression. Aliev's first decree upon his return to power was to appoint a chief censor. Censorship is present at every stage of publication, and is managed by an agency subordinated directly to Aliev. Despite his reported commitment to democratization (Lowell Bezanis, "Azerbaijan: Clear Trends behind Kaleidoscopic Change," *Transition* 1, no 18, 6 October 1995, 70), dictatorial measures from Aliev's office have now been codified in 1995 constitutional provisions that ensure the perpetuation of a strong presidency.

Ecological Issues

Azerbaijan's agricultural and oil industries pose grave ecological dangers for the new state. Azerbaijan has a long-standing pollution problem arising from nineteenth-century oil drilling in Baku and resultant contamination of the Caspian Sea. Most of the air pollution in cities along the Caspian coast is caused by the petroleum and chemical industry. In 1987, the Soviet minister of health noted that the air throughout the republic contained five times the maximum permissible concentration of pollutants (cited in Elizabeth Fuller and Mirza Michaeli, "Azerbaijan Belatedly Discovers Environmental Pollution," *Radio Liberty Research Bulletin* 32, no. 1, 6 January 1988). Another potential threat to Azerbaijan's air quality comes from its energy blockade on Armenia, as a result of which the Armenians have restarted the dangerous nuclear power plant at Medzamor (see page 103).

The Caspian Sea has suffered badly from the dumping of raw sewage and petroleum waste. Dumping was supposed to cease by 1985, but in that year alone, an estimated 104,000 tons of oil and sediment was released into the sea. Worsening the situation, dam projects from the 1930s limit the flow of fresh water from the Aras and Kura rivers.

The use of fertilizers and pesticides in Azerbaijan has left dangerously high concentrations of chemicals in the soil and the air of agricultural regions. In 1987, the Soviet minister of health noted a high infant mortality rate—30.5 per 1,000 live births (higher than the official figure of 23 per 1,000 released in the census)—and high rates of infectious diseases. Both the infant mortality rate and the rates of infectious diseases were increasing at alarming rates. These high rates were linked to chemicals used in cotton growing. Also in 1987, 10 percent of the melon crop was found to have dangerously high concentrations of nitrates. A 1989 article by the head of the Health Science Research Institute of Epidemiology, Hygiene, and Occupational Diseases showed that the concentration of pesticides in Azerbaijan was 20 times the average in the Soviet Union (cited in Yasin Aslan and Elizabeth Fuller, "Azerbaijani Press Discusses Link between Ecological Problems and Health Defects," *Radio Liberty Report on the USSR* 1, no. 31, 4 August 1989: 20–21). These problems have been compounded by an unwillingness to deal with them openly. Many studies on the effects of pesticides and chemical pollution have been suppressed by governmental authorities.

Economic Issues

Azerbaijan faces the most severe economic difficulties of the three former Soviet Transcaucasian republics, but because of its rich natural resources, it should have the best chance to solve its problems. Azerbaijan is burdened with high unemployment and a long tradition of economic corruption, both of which have affected production. During 1991, gross industrial output decreased by 8 percent, while consumer prices rose 816.7 percent (cited in Douglas Stanglin, "A Victory Gone Sour: Yeltsin and His Compatriots Are Struggling, a Year after the Failed Coup," *U.S. News & World Report*, 24 August 1992, 43–45, 48). The republic's agriculture, although more diversified than the cotton monocultures of Central Asia, was troubled by Gorbachev's anti-alcoholism campaign. Azerbaijan, a major wine producer, found reduced markets for its grapes and viticulture.

Complicating all economic activity in Azerbaijan, however, is the massive refugee problem. With 15 percent of its population rendered homeless by the Nagorno-Karabakh war, the resources of Azerbaijan are strained to the limit. Production of all goods has plummeted and Azerbaijan has become dependent on international aid to assist the refugees.

In its favor, Azerbaijan has sufficient potential oil revenues to improve living standards, if funds are not diverted into misguided ventures. In September 1994, Azerbaijan signed the "deal of the century" with an international consortium that is further developing the republic's off-shore oil fields on the Caspian shelf (see Elizabeth Fuller, "Transcaucasus: Between Anarchy and Despotism, *Transition*, 15 February 1995, 63). According to terms of the agreement, Azerbaijan will receive $7.4 billion from 8 Western oil companies in return for a 70 percent share of 3 Caspian oil fields that have an estimated reserve of 4 billion barrels. Subsequent debate has centered on how best to export this oil. While the consortium and Turkey favor a pipeline that crosses through Armenia, Iran, and Turkey to the Aegean coast, Russia (due to receive a percentage of Azerbaijan's 30 percent take on all oil extracted) wants the oil routed through an existing pipeline by way of Chechnya (Checheniia) to Novorossisk on the Sea of Azov.

Islam in Azerbaijan

Azerbaijan's Muslim population experienced a resurgence of Islamic sentiment in the mid-1980s when mosques, closed since the 1930s, were reopened. The green banners and portraits of Iran's Ayatollah Khomeini at the 1989 Baku demonstrations, however, were condemned by intellectuals in the APF, who sought a secular democracy. Mutalibov, on the other hand, appealed to Islamic sentiment by reading verses from the Koran during his presidential campaign.

Until the twentieth century, most Azerbaijanis identified themselves as Muslims rather than Azerbaijanis or Turks. The idea of a nation was generally subordinated to the idea of a spiritual community of Islam. Turkish intellectuals in the Ottoman Empire placed the idea of a Turkish nation above that of religious identification. Members of the intelligentsia in Azerbaijan took up the discussion, arguing over whether they were Muslims, Turks, or even Azerbaijani Turks. Such debates, however, were confined to the intellectuals, and the majority of Azerbaijanis identified themselves simply as Muslims. Arguably, this remains the case today. While a national identity is present, its status is closely interwoven with religious identity.

The Shi'ite-Sunni split means little in Azerbaijani religious or social life. Although the Shi'ite Azerbaijanis fought with the Russians against the Sunni Dagestanis in the eighteenth and nineteenth centuries, Azerbaijanis today have no clear idea of the differences between Sunni and Shi'ite doctrine. Sectarian variations in general were deemphasized by the Muslims themselves in the face of cultural conflict with Christian rulers. Although separate Sunni and Shi'ite hierarchies exist, the differences between the two for the average Muslim are not clearly apprehended.

Russian and Soviet rulers sought to recognize and influence the official leadership of the Muslim spiritual jurisdiction in Azerbaijan as a means of exercising control over the population. Unlike Eastern Orthodoxy or Roman Catholicism, however, Islam has little need for an established clergy. Spiritual leaders are primarily scholars and judges. The principal obligations of Islam are carried out at the individual level— the five daily prayers, the month of fasting, charity to the poor, and the strictures against alcohol and some foods. During the tsarist period, Azerbaijanis had learned not to trust religious officials, and this mistrust continued during the Soviet era. Azerbaijani Muslims therefore stayed away from the mosques but still carried out the individual rituals in private or in small groups. Further, Shi'ite Muslims may deny their faith if under duress, and Azerbaijanis have done so to avoid scrutiny from Communist authorities.

Russian and Soviet co-optation of the official organs of Islam meant that only reliable Muslims could receive education at official seminaries. The most talented fled to Iran or even Turkey to complete their studies, leaving behind unofficial religious teachers who lacked higher levels of education. By the end of the nineteenth century, there were probably no religious scholars left in Azerbaijan (see Audrey L. Altstadt, *The Azerbaijani Turks: Power and Identity under Russian Rule*, Hoover Institution Press, 1992, 57–62). Trusted religious leaders in contemporary Azerbaijan tend to be more reactionary, tied to local and communal interests. This situation exposes them to criticism by Azerbaijani intellectuals who would prefer that a more secular version of Islam determine the course of Islamic revival among the masses. Although Iran has been assisting Azerbaijanis in religious study, the Azerbaijani religious scholarly community is still recovering from Russian and Soviet rule.

Thus, the picture that emerges is far from clear. While many Azerbaijani Turks strive to establish a secular democracy, and the Azerbaijani state has been the first Muslim state to allow women to vote, there remains the possibility of growing popular support for a republic grounded upon Islamic principles. In the Nagorno-Karabakh conflict, battle cries have occasionally taken on a decidedly religious tone, as in the June 1992 Radio Baku call for a "Holy War at the state level against the Armenian infidels" (quoted in Elizabeth Fuller, "Azerbaijan after the Presidential Elections," *Radio Free Europe/Radio Liberty Research Report* 1, no. 26, 26 June 1992, 1–7).

International Relations

Azerbaijan has historically traveled a course between Turkey and Iran in its foreign relations. Both of these countries have tried to establish ties with the Turkic and Muslim republics of the former Soviet Union. Turkey has been held up as the model of secular democracy by Central Asian and Azerbaijani intellectuals. For their part, Turkish political leaders have emphasized the links of Turkey to the Turkic peoples of the former Soviet Union. Although the prospect of a resurgent pan-Turanian (pan-Turkic) movement is unlikely to affect Azerbaijan as much as its Central Asian counterparts, Turkey has begun transmitting cultural programming to these republics.

Elchibey's promise to remove Azerbaijan from the Commonwealth of Independent States signaled a rejection of Russian influence. During Elchibey's tenure, relations with both Turkey and Iran were explored. Turkish merchants expressed interest in Baku as a trading center to link them to the Central Asian republics, and Turkish officials toured Azerbaijan frequently in 1992 and 1993. The darker side of this relationship is Turkey's potential role in the Nagorno-Karabakh conflict, a role reflected in APF contacts with Turkish fascist groups, such as that led by Arpaslan Turkesh, whose gray wolf insignia is worn by Azerbaijani military units. Turkey, however, has not found the financial means to support Azerbaijani military efforts in Nagorno-Karabakh, and instead has limited its support to educational and cultural ties with the new republic.

In aspiring to serve as spiritual head for the world's Muslims, Iran has also sought to assist Azerbaijan. In late 1991, Iran tried to broker a cease-fire in the Nagorno-Karabakh conflict. There were also initial Iranian efforts to provide state-supported stipends for Azerbaijani students in Iran. Elchibey rejected Iran's fundamentalism, however, and Azerbaijanis have been wary of possible Iranian support also for Armenia. For its part, Iran has been concerned about potential Azerbaijani sentiment for uniting with the Azerbaijani population in northern Iran. Such was the aim of Azerbaijan's Birlik (Unity) Society in 1989. Northern Iran has much of the oil and resources of Iran, and its Turkic population (between 8 and 13 million) has agitated for greater cultural and linguistic autonomy since the 1980s. In 1920, shortly after Azerbaijan's fall to the Bolsheviks, Azerbaijanis in Iran (Persia) revolted against Tehran, declaring northwestern Iran to be

Azadistan (Land of Freedom). In the post–World War II period, the Azerbaijani-populated region of Iran was a base for the pro-Soviet communist Tudeh Party. The principal city of northern Iran, Tabriz, would today be the center within Iran for any such clandestine moves toward Azerbaijani reunification. Meanwhile, in Azerbaijan itself, the Azerbaijani Popular Front has never rejected reunification as a long-term goal.

The perceived tilt of Russia toward Armenia has provided a constant theme in recent Russo-Azerbaijani relations. It explains, for example, the fact that under Elchibey the Azerbaijani parliament in October 1992 voted unanimously against ratifying Azerbaijani membership in the CIS. Upon Aliev's return to power, however, Azerbaijan did join the CIS, albeit with Aliev's strong proclamations that Azerbaijan was the only CIS member with no Russian troops on its soil. A current round of jousting over the development of Caspian oil reserves pits the Azerbaijanis against the Russians as the Yeltsin government tries to promote its strategic and economic interests in the region (see Elizabeth Fuller, "The Tussle for Influence in Central Asia and the Transcaucasus," *Transition* 2, no. 12, 14 June 1996, 11–15).

United States relations with Azerbaijan are presently muted by the 1992 legislation preventing aid to Azerbaijan as long as it continues its blockade of Armenia. Tense relations between the United States and Azerbaijan consequently have served to strengthen Russian influence in Azerbaijan.

Redefining the Past

Despite the purges of the Stalinist period and the retrenchment of the Brezhnev era, Azerbaijanis were among those least likely to criticize the central regime or voice nationalist sentiments. Histories of nineteenth- and twentieth-century Azerbaijan were heavily endowed with Marxist-Leninist ideology. Ancient history was safer, being distant from more contemporary issues, while at the same time indirectly counteracting Soviet assertions that Russia had been the older, benevolent brother to Azerbaijan.

Historical novels were the other escape valve for nationalist sentiment—so much so, in fact, that at the 1986 Congress of the Azerbaijani Union of Writers, authors who limited their writings to historical novels were criticized. Writers were urged to deal with more contemporary issues and to display glasnost more openly. Younger writers were criticized for being too eager to get their works published in Russian.

Under Gorbachev, but particularly since Azerbaijan's independence, the past has been reexamined. As early as 1987, a young critic urged historians

to study those individuals whom Soviet histories have ignored, and in 1988, Mahmoud Ismailov, a corresponding member of the Azerbaijani Academy of Sciences, urged historians to undertake an objective evaluation of the Azerbaijani Democratic Republic (Annette Bohr and Yasin Aslan, "Independent Azerbaijan, 1918–1920: Call to Reevaluate History of Former Nation-State," *Radio Liberty Research Bulletin* 32, no. 35, 31 August 1988).

Language and Orthography

One problem that faces all the Turkic republics of the former Soviet Union is deciding which alphabet to use. Conversion of Azerbaijani Turkish from an Arabic to a Latin script, as was ultimately done in Turkey, was contemplated by nineteenth-century intellectuals. From 1922 to 1928, a Latinized alphabet was developed in cooperation with intellectuals from the Central Asian republics, and it was implemented in 1929. In 1940, however, Stalin mandated a change from the Latin to the Cyrillic alphabet. Most contemporary Azerbaijanis have become literate through schooling in an Azerbaijani language that employs the Cyrillic alphabet. Today, very few academic personnel can read either the Latin or the Arabic script, even though there have been some efforts to reintroduce the Latin script.

More threatening to Azerbaijani intellectuals has been the declining status of Azerbaijani Turkish alongside Russian. Prominent Azerbaijani poet Bakhtiyar Vahabzade noted in 1989 that Azerbaijani Turkish, the official language of the republic since the 1950s, had not been used to conduct state business since World War II (Yasin Aslan and Elizabeth Fuller, "Azerbaijani Intellectuals Express Concern over Native Language," *Radio Liberty Research Bulletin* 1, no. 9, 3 March 1989, 22–23). During the 1920s, Azerbaijani Turkish words for ideological concepts were replaced by their Russian counterparts. Higher education most often took place in Russian. Before 1958, students were required to pass examinations in both Russian and their native language, but since then they have been allowed to choose between the two, placing Azerbaijani Turkish in jeopardy. Youths in Baku tend to speak either a mixture of Azerbaijani Turkish and Russian, or pure Russian, and educated Azerbaijani professionals often have difficulty expressing themselves in their native language. At the turn of the last century, linguistic autonomy was an issue for Azerbaijani intellectuals; today, 100 years later, it is again one of the issues defining the Azerbaijani search for its national identity.

As in Tajikistan, the newly independent state of Azerbaijan appears to be following its own violent rebellion of 1993 with the implementation of firm authoritarian measures, albeit to the accompaniment of renewed nationalist rhetoric. Alongside this tide of authoritarian reaction, however, the long-term economic future for Azerbaijan is somewhat brighter because of the presence of significant oil reserves.

Internationally, the test for Azerbaijan will be seen in its ability to develop these reserves effectively while normalizing relations with Armenia, as well as with its southern neighbors, Turkey and Iran.

GEORGIA

Statistical Profile

Demography

Population: 4,600,000

Ethnic population

Georgian	70.1%
Armenian	8.1%
Russian	6.3%
Azerbaijani	5.7%
Ossetian	3.0%
Greek	1.9%
Abkhazian	1.8%
Ukrainian	1.0%
Kurdish	0.6%
Jewish	0.2%
Other	1.4%

Major urban centers and populations

Tbilisi	1,268,000
Kutaisi	236,000
Rustavi	160,000
Batumi	137,000
Sokhumi	122,000
Tskhinvali	30,000

Historic religious traditions

Christianity	83%
Islam	11%

Languages

Georgian, Russian, Armenian, Azerbaijani, Turkish

Population by age

Age	Total	Males	Females
0–14	24.2%	12.3%	11.7%
15–64	64.5%	31.4%	33.1%
65 and over	11.5%	4.3%	7.2%

Male/Female ratio: 48.0% male/52.0% female

Rural/Urban population
43.8% rural/56.2% urban

Annual population growth rate: -0.4%

Population density: 170.9 persons per sq mi

Government

Official name
Sakartvelos Respublika (Republic of Georgia)

Capital: Tbilisi

Date of sovereignty/independence declaration
9 April 1991

Voting age: 18

Internal regions / **Capitals**

Internal regions	Capitals
Abkhazia	Sokhumi
Ajaria	Batumi
South Ossetiia	Tskhinvali

Education

Literacy (age 15 and over who can read and write)

total population	99%
males	100%
females	98%

Level of education for persons over 15

completed higher education	15.1%
completed secondary education	57.4%
incomplete secondary education	15.2%

Number of higher education institutions: 19

Higher education enrollment: 103,900 students

Selected institutions of higher education (and enrollment)

Tbilisi

Technical University	28,000
Ivan Dzhavakhiladze University	16,000
Tbilisi State Medical Institute	3,500
Saradzhishvili State Conservatory	700

Kutaisi

Muskhelishvili Technical University	6,400

Socioeconomic Indicators

Annual birth rate: 10.7 births/1,000 population

Fertility rate: 2.2 children/woman

Infant mortality: 18.3 deaths/1,000 live births

Average life expectancy
72.1 years (males 68.1, females 75.7)

Annual death rate: 8.6 deaths/1,000 population

Average family size: 4.1

Annual consumption of electrical energy
1,526 kWh/person

Hospital beds per 10,000 persons: 108

Physical Features

Area: 26,911 sq mi

Land use
cultivated 11%
pasture 27%

Highest elevation: 16,558 ft (Mt. Kazbek)

Rainfall
22 in./yr in the plains and foothills
up to 79 in./yr in the mountains

Temperature

Winter	Summer
average 40°F, 29°F	average 73°F
in the mountains	
lowest –40°F	highest 101°F

Economic Production

Estimated per capita GNP: $560 (1993)

Agricultural output
tea, grapes, citrus, vegetables, livestock, tobacco

Natural resources
forest lands, hydropower, manganese, iron ores, copper

Industrial output
steel, machine tools, electrical machinery, textiles, shoes, chemicals, wood products, wine

Currency
lari (introduced October 1995), 1 lari = 100 tetri

Communications

Length of rail lines: 981 mi

Length of highways: 18,438 mi

Pipelines
crude oil ....231 mi
natural gas ....275 mi

Telephones: 117 per 1,000 persons

Sources "Gruzinskaia sovetskaia sotsialisticheskaia respublika," *Bol'shaia sovetskaia entsiklopediia* (Moscow, 1977); *Narodnoe khoziaistvo SSSR v 1990g.* (Moscow, 1991); *Naselenie SSSR* (Moscow, 1989); Matthew J. Sagers, "News Notes: Iron and Steel," *Soviet Geography* 30 (May 1989): 397–434; Lee Schwartz, "USSR Nationality Redistribution by Republic, 1979–1989: From Published Results of the 1989 All-Union Census," *Soviet Geography* 32 (April 1991): 209–48; *World of Learning*, 46th ed. (London, 1996); "Russia . . ." (National Geographic Society Map, 1993); *Europa World Yearbook, 1996* (London, 1996); *Demograficheskii ezhegodnik, 1995* (Moscow, 1995); "CIA World Factbook, 1995" (www.odci.gov/cia/publications/95fact/gg.html).

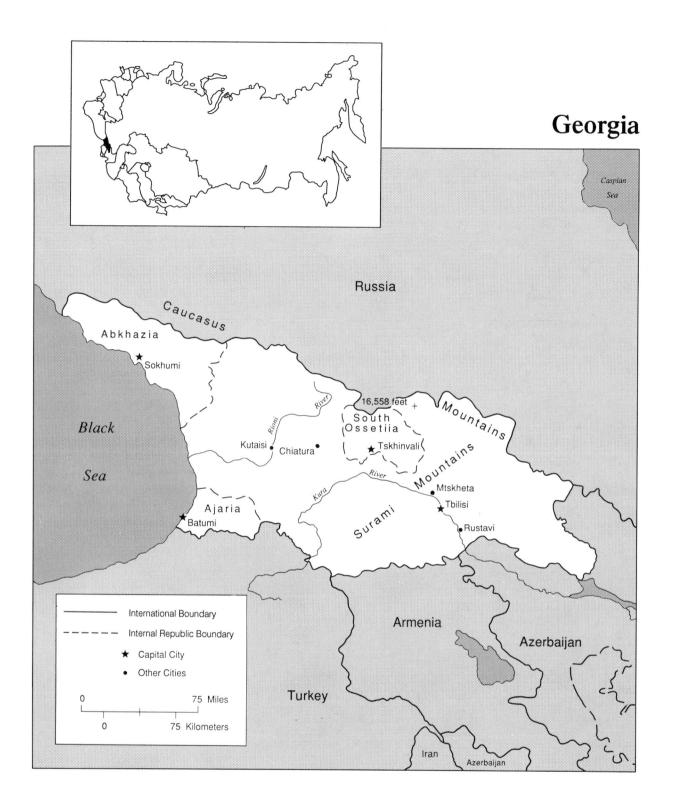

Georgia

Caspian Sea

Russia

Caucasus

Abkhazia

★ Sokhumi

16,558 feet +

South Ossetiia

Mountains

Rioni River

Black

Kutaisi • Chiatura •

★ Tskhinvali

Mountains

Sea

Kura River

Mtskheta •

Ajaria

★ Batumi

Surami Mountains

Tbilisi ★

• Rustavi

Armenia

Azerbaijan

Turkey

Iran   Azerbaijan

International Boundary

- - - Internal Republic Boundary

★ Capital City

• Other Cities

0   75 Miles

0   75 Kilometers

Georgia: History and Description

Physical Description

Borders An ancient country with a long and complex history, Georgia is situated amongst the magnificent mountains of Transcaucasia. Essentially part of an isthmus between the Black and Caspian seas, Georgia is bounded on the north by the greater Caucasus Mountains and on the south by the lesser Caucasus. Georgia's mountainous plateaus and river valleys contrast with lowland areas lying to either side of the Surami mountain range, which bisects the country along a northeast-southwest axis. Much volcanic activity takes place in this region of Transcaucasia.

To the north and northeast of Georgia lies the Russian Federation, the frontier at many points distinguished by the snow-clad peaks of the greater Caucasus range, including Mt. Kazbek (16,558 ft.), one of the highest points in Europe. To the east and southeast of Georgia are the arid plains of Azerbaijan, separating Georgia from the Caspian Sea. Georgia is today linked to the Caspian by oil and gas pipelines connecting Georgian cities to the Azerbaijan port of Baku. To the south lie Armenia and Turkey. The shoreline of the Black Sea makes up Georgia's western boundary.

Transcaucasian Climate Slightly smaller than South Carolina, Transcaucasian Georgia (26,911 square miles) consists of two quite separate geographic areas. The western part of the country is characterized by a humid, subtropical climate and landscape that is very different from the dry, continental conditions prevailing in the eastern part. The swampy lowlands of western Georgia, drained by many rivers and streams, present a hot, damp climate conducive to the intensive cultivation of agricultural products such as citrus fruits, tea, and tobacco, which cannot be grown elsewhere in Transcaucasia or in Russia. Georgia has long been noted for wines and cognacs produced from grapes grown in this region. By contrast, the Kura lowland in eastern Georgia offers a primarily arid plain with occasional low mountains used for livestock grazing. Agricultural production in the east is devoted to grains, vegetables, and fruits, especially grapes.

Rivers The streams and rivers of Georgia, as they cascade from mountainous heights, provide abundant hydroelectric power for local use. Georgia's main river, the Kura, enters the country from Turkey, slices through the Surami mountains at Tbilisi, and then continues southeasterly through the Kura River valley, across the border into Azerbaijan, and farther east until it empties into the Caspian Sea. The Rioni River in western Georgia flows into the Black Sea, watering the formerly marshy region of Kolkhida (known as Colchis in Greek mythology, the place where Jason searched for the golden fleece). This area was drained and reclaimed for agricultural purposes during the Soviet period.

Natural Resources Georgia's natural resources include rich reserves of manganese, much of which is exported to other parts of the world. Petroleum, low-grade coal, and barite are also found in Georgia. A large petroleum-refining industry has been developed at the Black Sea port of Batumi. Copper and silver have been mined in Georgia for centuries.

Cities Large cities in Georgia include its modern capital, Tbilisi (formerly Tiflis). A beautiful city spread out along the gorge formed by the Kura River, Tbilisi has long been the center of Georgian cultural life. Taking its name from the warm sulfur springs on which it sits, Tbilisi is known to tourists for the funicular railway and cable cars that carry passengers to the summit of Mt. Mtatsminda for a spectacular view of the city. Rustavi, a town designated for development in the 1940s to accommodate the growing iron and steel industry in eastern Georgia, has grown into an important metallurgical center. Kutaisi, the industrial center of western Georgia, lies on the Rioni River. Chiatura, a center of manganese mining operating since 1879, is also in western Georgia. Sokhumi, a resort on the Black Sea, and Batumi, an industrial seaport, also support the economic life of Georgia.

Internal Regions Well over 90 percent of the world's Georgians live in the Republic of Georgia. Very few have emigrated beyond the borders of their homeland, although some Georgian émigré enclaves exist in western Europe. Because of the existence of numerous minority groups within Georgia, however, the percentage of Georgians as part of the country's total population stands at just 70 percent.

Under the Soviet system, Georgia administered three separate autonomous regions within its national borders. These regions are inhabited by peoples of ethnic or religious backgrounds different from those of the Georgians. The collapse of the Soviet Union has complicated the status of these regions. The largest and most populous of them is the Republic of Abkhazia in northwestern Georgia, along the Black Sea. There are approximately 540,000 people living in Abkhazia today. Its capital, Sokhumi (Sukhumi), was one of the premier resort sites in the former Soviet Union, having a climate similar to that of southern Florida. The people of Abkhazia speak a Caucasian language belonging to the northern branch of that language family. Many of the Muslim Abkhazians emigrated to Turkey in the nineteenth century, with the result that those remaining within Abkhazia today compose a minority (less than 20 percent) of the total population. Although Eastern Orthodoxy is practiced by some Abkhazians, others adhere to traditional Islamic practice.

South Ossetiia, another internal region within Georgia, is located in the extreme north of the country on the southern slopes of the Caucasus, west of the pass where the Georgian Military Highway crosses the Caucasus Mountains. Its capital, Tskhinvali, was formerly named Stalinir, after Josef Stalin, a Georgian. South Ossetiia is inhabited by an Iranian-language-speaking people called Ossetians. On the other side of the Caucasus Mountains live the Ossetians of North Ossetiia, which is a formerly autonomous region (oblast) of the USSR, now an internal republic within the Russian Federation. Although the majority of the South Ossetians come out of the Eastern Orthodox, Christian tradition, both Christian and Islamic religious traditions are represented in the Ossetian communities north and south of the Georgian-Russian border.

The smallest internal region within Georgia is the Ajari republic on the Black Sea in southwestern Georgia. Its capital is Batumi, known for its warm tropical climate, as well as for its importance as Georgia's major seaport. Ajaris are those largely rural Georgians who converted centuries ago to Islam while under Ottoman rule. Although their language exhibits many Turkic elements, they continue to speak Georgian. Ajaria was added to the Soviet Union as a part of the Turkish-Soviet peace negotiations following World War I and the Russian Civil War.

In addition to the ethnic groups whose territories were given autonomous standing in the former Soviet republic of Georgia, many other minorities also live in present-day Georgia. Some represent the people of neighboring countries, such as the Armenians, Azerbaijanis, and Russians. Many are members of distinct groups who speak dialects of Georgian and live in isolated mountain valleys. The Mingrelians, the Svans (Svanetians), and the Laz are among these smaller groups slowly being assimilated by the Georgians. The Meskhetians, a Georgian-speaking Muslim people, were relocated to Central Asia during World War II, and few remain today in Georgia.

Ethnic Background and Historical Development

Georgians are thought to derive from early indigenous inhabitants of the Caucasus region. Historical and archeological records reveal evidence of agricultural activity in eastern Georgia as early as the fifth century B.C. The Roman, Persian, Byzantine, Arabic, Mongol, and Turkish empires all influenced Georgian politics well before the advent of Russian domination in the eighteenth century. Although Christianity was adopted by Georgian kings in the fourth century, inspired by the activities of St. Nino, religious life followed a distinctly Georgian pattern as the country struggled to maintain its independence between competing powers.

Georgians as an ethnic group are part of the so-called Kartvelian people, and they call their land Sakartvelo. Their language belongs to the southern branch of the Caucasian language family. The alphabet, written in a beautiful script dating to the fourth century or before, has undergone several modifications or reforms. Georgians identify themselves as Kartveli, Russians use the name Gruziny, and Turks employ the term Gurcu. In the classical period, Georgia was known as Iberia to the Greeks and Romans. English usage of the term Georgia comes from the Turkish Gurcu.

Formation of the Georgian Nation

For over two millennia during the formation of the Georgian nation, ethnically related groups inhabiting the mountains of the Caucasus region and speaking distinct Kartvelian dialects gradually came together under a series of different rulers. Because of the strategic location of Georgian lands as a crossroads between East and West, an important commercial trade route emerged there, and many empires vied for influence or control over Georgia. From the Romans in classical times to the Russians in the modern period, the Georgian nation often found itself responding to the conflicting claims of great empires.

Mtskheta, ancient capital of the Kartli or eastern Georgians, existed as early as the third century B.C., but by the reign of Vakhtang in the late fifth century A.D., a new capital had been established at Tbilisi. As Persian domination gave way to Arab invasion and then to Byzantine influence, the lands of eastern and western Georgia were finally brought together under one Georgian ruler in the eleventh century. The accession to power of King Bagrat III in 1008 marked a culmination in the process of Georgian national unification. Subsequent Turkish campaigns later in the eleventh century were quelled by David the Builder (1089–

1125), leading to the memorable reign of Queen Tamar (1184–1212), under whom Georgia reached the apogee of its early national and cultural achievement. During Tamar's reign, Georgia's national poet Rustaveli wrote his great epic tribute to the Georgian nation, *The Knight in the Tiger's Skin*. Peace did not last, however, for during the thirteenth and fourteenth centuries, Mongol hordes nearly destroyed Georgia. Turkish forces of the Ottoman Empire became the next warring power to dominate Georgian lands until finally, in 1783, a Russian protectorate was sought to help preserve the Georgian nation.

Russian Rule

Contrary to the expectations of the Georgian aristocracy and other national leaders, the autonomous protectorate was not long honored by the tsar. In 1801, Georgia was effectively annexed into the Russian Empire during the reign of Alexander I. The Georgian Orthodox Church, independent for centuries, was made subordinate to the Holy Synod of the Russian Orthodox Church. The economy of the country stabilized, however, under the rule of its northern neighbor, and Russian and European ideas came to influence the educated class of Georgians. Intellectual life flourished, serious literary publications appeared, and by the end of the nineteenth century, political concerns mirrored to a great extent important issues being debated in Moscow and St. Petersburg. Georgian political radicals participated within wider Russian revolutionary circles, in which Georgian Marxists were largely Menshevik, as opposed to Bolshevik, in their sympathies.

Georgia under the Soviet System

In May 1918, following the Bolshevik Revolution in Moscow the previous October, Georgia declared its independence. This independence, although later recognized by other countries and looked upon favorably by the League of Nations, did not last. In February 1921, less than nine months after Moscow had signed a treaty accepting the sovereignty of the Georgian Democratic Republic, the Red Army, led by a Georgian named Sergo Ordzhonikidze, secretly crossed into Georgia from Azerbaijan and quashed the young state. Later, in 1922, under the personal direction of Stalin (also a Georgian, whose real name was Josef Dzhugashvili), Georgia was established as one of three nations (the others being Armenia and Azerbaijan) making up the Transcaucasian Soviet Federated Socialist Republic (TSFSR). Violent resistance to Soviet power continued until 1924 when a last uprising was crushed by Bolshevik authorities. As many as 4,000 rebels were executed and countless others imprisoned. The TSFSR prevailed until 1936. At that time it was divided, and Georgia was declared a full union republic of the Soviet Union.

During the long period of Stalin's dictatorship, Georgia might have been expected to enjoy a special status within the Union of Soviet Socialist Republics. The more Stalin came to identify himself as a Russian nationalist, however, the less he seemed willing to show any favoritism to Georgia. Instead, the incredible horrors of the purges of the 1930s, carried out among Georgian political leaders and the intelligentsia, took as high a toll in Georgia as elsewhere. During this time, Georgia came under the personal authority of Stalin's close associate, a fellow Georgian of Mingrelian origin, Lavrentii Beria, who served as first secretary of the Communist Party of Georgia throughout the 1930s. Through Beria's firm grip, Georgia came to be just as tightly controlled by Moscow as were the other Soviet republics.

Although the battles of World War II were all fought north of the Caucasus, Georgia's military loss of life was comparable to that experienced by other Soviet nationalities because of the large number of Georgian soldiers who perished in battle. During the war, a substantial population of minority groups was transferred out of the Caucasus because Stalin feared that these minority groups (mainly Turkic) would support the invading Axis powers. Following the war, Stalin's personal control of the Soviet Union became even stronger. Lavrentii Beria, having been elevated to a position in Moscow to head the Soviet secret police, collaborated with Stalin, intensifying Moscow's authority not only over Georgia, but over all of Soviet society.

After Stalin's death in 1953, Beria was executed by rivals in the Stalinist succession struggle. Meanwhile in Transcaucasia, Vasilii Mzhavanadze became first secretary of the Georgian Communist Party. Ensuing de-Stalinization (a liberalizing process originating with the new Soviet premier, Nikita Khrushchev) resulted in pro-Stalin demonstrations in Tbilisi in March 1956. A large, but peaceful, demonstration threatened to take over the local radio station until police regained control. In the clash between police and demonstrators, several were killed. There continue to be those in Georgia who view Stalin as a positive national figure.

In 1972, Eduard Shevardnadze was appointed the new first secretary of the Georgian Communist Party, a post he held for 13 years, until named by Gorbachev to head the Soviet Ministry of Foreign Affairs in 1985.

As the new Communist Party leader in Georgia and former leader in the security police, Shevardnadze was called upon to deal with the remaining legacy of Stalinism—namely, widespread corruption, poor economic (especially agricultural) growth, and a revival of Georgian nationalism. The strength of the latter may be attested to by the reaction in 1978 to an attempt to remove Georgian as the sole official language of the republic. Moscow wanted to add a second official language, Russian. The attempt failed as thousands of students protested in Tbilisi. This time, however, the demonstrations remained peaceful.

Georgia: Contemporary Issues

Abuladze and Sakharov

Two landmark statements of the 1980s help to clarify the complex world of contemporary Georgian society. The first of these was a Georgian statement, the most dramatic cinematographic work produced in the Soviet Union in the 1980s—the award-winning film, *Repentance (Monanieba),* directed by Tengiz Abuladze. Released first in Tbilisi, and later in Moscow and the West in 1986, *Repentance* depicted a dictatorial figure, Varlam Aravidze, who, with his villainous followers dressed as medieval knights, visited a reign of interrogation, death, and forcible exile upon innocent victims. Patterned after Lavrentii Beria, but understandably associated in the public imagination with Stalin himself, Varlam and "Varlamism" readily came to be identified with the realities of twentieth-century Georgian and Soviet history.

In one particularly gripping moment of the film, Varlam's grandson Tornike learns of the complicity of his father (Abel) in the crimes of the grandfather Varlam. Unable to forgive his father, Tornike shoots himself with a rifle given him by the late Varlam. Profoundly affected by the suicide of his son, Abel digs up the corpse of Varlam and heaves it from a mountain top. For Georgians, even more than for other Soviet citizens (who had to view the film with Russian subtitles), the haunting question of the grandson Tornike to his father Abel became a matter of riveting, existential importance: "Did you know about all this?"

For Georgians young and old who crowded into movie theaters, the agony of *Repentance* rested in the memories and unanswered questions over Stalinism that the film unearthed. In the years since 1986, the violent political upheavals wrenching Georgian society have been, in many ways, the legacy of this Stalinist, Soviet inheritance. Driven by passionate and heroic ambition to erase this legacy, some political leaders have paid scant attention to human rights and democratic processes as they sought to eliminate by force the remnants of the old Soviet order. In appealing too readily to violence and to limitations upon free expression, some of these resurgent Georgian nationalists may have demonstrated, unwittingly, their own roots in the Soviet system.

While Abuladze's film called forth a searching Georgian reassessment of the Soviet past, another statement from the 1980s—this time from a Russian Nobel laureate—posed a more subtle problem for Georgian national consciousness. In the summer of 1989, the late Andrei Sakharov, a celebrated Russian nuclear physicist and human rights advocate, granted an interview to the popular Russian journal *Ogonek,* in the course of which he described the union republics of the Soviet Union, specifically including Georgia, as "miniature empires" (*Ogonek*, no. 31, 1989; cited in Elizabeth Fuller, "South Ossetiia: Analysis of a Permanent Crisis," *Report on the USSR*, 15 February 1991). While Georgians were quick to challenge the venerable human rights activist, the reference to Georgia as a "miniature empire" could not be easily dismissed. The Soviet state had, after all, consciously awarded to certain "winners"—the union republics—the right to control minorities within their own borders in an internal political game intended to divide and conquer. For Georgia, Sakharov's comments made unmistakable reference to the status of those South Ossetians, Abkhazians, Ajaris, Azerbaijanis, and others, who found themselves "autonomous," but still subordinate to the dominant Georgian nation.

These two dramatic public statements—a pathbreaking Georgian film and an uncensored comment from an unimpeachable Soviet dissident—point to the fundamental and unavoidable conflict confronting the Georgian nation. For as it seeks to establish its own territorial sovereignty and independence—its own "post-Varlamian," post-Soviet identity—the Georgian nation also confronts the reality that some of the same territory claimed by Georgians as their own has also been home to non-Georgian nationalities who today seek a measure of independence and self-determination not unlike that sought by Georgians themselves.

Tragically, since 1989, the tensions posed by responding to these two statements have led to violence and political crisis. While there are long-term economic problems that still must be solved, the immediate future for Georgia will be determined by how well it is able to reconcile its own national ambitions with the hopes and aspirations of minorities who see in Georgian nationalism a new form of imperialism. In the Georgian case, no less than in the case of the other Transcaucasian states of Armenia and Azerbaijan—and no less than in the war-torn regions of former Yugoslavia—there is the violent conflict between national agendas and minority rights.

Prelude to a National Crisis

Georgian national politics entered into a period of profound crisis following the events of the 9th of April, 1989, a day that has come to be known as Bloody Sunday. On that fateful day, the use of chemical weapons upon thousands of Georgian participants in peaceful Tbilisi demonstrations resulted in the initial loss of 19 innocent lives. But the prelude to this national crisis antedated the April events by months. In the time preceding the Tbilisi demonstrations, Abkhazian nationals had approached the Moscow Party Central Committee authorities, seeking their support to offset what the Abkhazians considered to be Georgian efforts to assimilate Abkhazians into greater Georgian society. Specifically, the Abkhazians sought status as a full union republic within the USSR. Meanwhile, the Ossetians of the South Ossetiia Autonomous Oblast sought secession from Georgia and merger with their North Ossetian co-nationals in the Russian republic.

While Georgian Communist Party officials were slow to respond to these developments, Georgian public opinion, galvanized by a more open daily press, reacted strongly. First of all, the Abkhazian allegations against Georgian policies were judged to be false. Georgians viewed themselves as simply trying to preserve the interests of those Georgians who composed over 45 percent of the population of the autonomous Abkhazian republic (ethnic Abkhazians constituted approximately 17 percent). Second, Georgian public opinion was aroused by the blatant effort of the Abkhazians, as well as similar attempts by the Ossetians, to circumvent the Georgian republic in their appeals. Why were the Abkhazians and the Ossetians taking their grievances to Moscow, rather than to Tbilisi?

In the events that followed, Georgians reacted to the pent-up frustrations of Soviet rule by challenging the authority of their own Georgian Communist Party leadership. The inclination to do so was all the greater in the face of the graphic symbols of Soviet abuses presented to them in Abuladze's *Repentance*. Sensing that national honor was at stake, and that Soviet rule simply perpetuated the ability of non-Georgian nationals to manipulate the Moscow center against Georgian interests, thousands of demonstrators, most of them young people, took to the streets in organized protests focused upon the Georgian Council of Ministers' building in April 1989.

For Georgian Communist leaders, the dilemma was that they could appeal only to Moscow to reinforce their position. At work was the classic trade-off operating in the Kremlin's relations with outlying union republics: Moscow would provide military support to back up the union republic's recognized government, but at the same time, Moscow retained the right to undermine the credibility of that same local Communist Party leadership by appearing to support the independent initiatives of autonomous republics and oblasts operating within that union republic. This fundamental principle of Soviet rule was being challenged in Georgia during a scheduled week of peaceful, national protests that began in Tbilisi in early April 1989.

Bloody Sunday, April 1989

Having been forewarned of the planned demonstrations that were scheduled to run until the 14th of April, Georgian Communist Party First Secretary Dzhumber Patiashvili (successor to Shevardnadze) turned to the Communist Party Central Committee in Moscow with an appeal for additional forces to maintain public order. The Soviet Politburo met in Gorbachev's absence (he was in England at the time) to consider the request. From the investigations that followed the massacre, Patiashvili appears to have received news from Moscow by early on the 8th of April that reinforcements would be provided to terminate the mass demonstrations. Soviet Defense Minister Dmitrii Iazov apparently designated Colonel General Igor Rodionov to take charge of the effort, and Rodionov met with Patiashvili in Tbilisi on the 8th of April.

Early on the morning of April 9th, while peaceful demonstrations continued in the square in front of the Council of Ministers' building, combined troops of the Soviet Ministry of Internal Affairs and the Soviet army launched tanks, tear gas, and, most controversially, chemical weapons upon the demonstrators, effectively dispersing the crowd, but not before thousands were harmed by the chemicals and 19 were killed. In the martial law that followed, more questions than answers were forthcoming. Who made the final decision to attack the demonstrators? What advance knowledge did

Gorbachev have of this military action taken directly against citizens of the Soviet Union? Why was there no effort to disperse the crowd nonviolently?

The immediate impact of the April 1989 massacre was to galvanize support for those informal Georgian political and cultural groups that had been marginalized during the years of Georgian Communist Party rule. By August 1989, the Georgian Supreme Soviet, despite the dominant role of the Communist Party, had voted to declare Georgia's sovereignty. Although Eduard Shevardnadze's image in the West was that of a reformist foreign minister close to Mikhail Gorbachev, his very association with Moscow politics tended to relegate him in 1989 to outsider status in Georgian politics. Clearly, the institutions and political leaders having the most to gain were those perceived to be the least encumbered by the old Soviet-style leadership.

Georgian Orthodox Church

One such institution surfacing during the April 1989 events was the Georgian Orthodox Church. Having reclaimed its independence from the Russian Orthodox Church, the Georgian Orthodox Church in the Soviet period still found itself in an ambivalent position. On the one hand, it rightly laid claim to a role in preserving the identity of the Georgian nation over centuries when that identity was in jeopardy from foreign imperial powers. On the other hand, the Church was weakened by official state atheism and governmental oversight that had curtailed freedom of religious expression during the worst of the Stalinist and Khrushchev years. With the renewal of Georgian national identity, however, the Georgian Orthodox Church, its clergy, and its monasteries, became a focal point for the national movement. Its leader, the articulate catholicos, Patriarch Ilia II, came to be revered for his devotion to nonviolence as the right way to achieve Georgian independence.

On the evening of April 8th, Patriarch-Catholicos Ilia II came before the assembled crowds, praised them for their honorable intentions, and asked that they disperse so as to avoid the possibility of bloodshed. When the crowds refused to leave, the patriarch-catholicos steadfastly remained with the demonstrators. Thus, with candles in hand, and with the leader of the Georgian Orthodox Church before them, the demonstrators peacefully confronted the Soviet tanks. While the symbolic authority of the Georgian Church triumphed on that occasion, the subsequent divisions of the national movement, and its resort to violence, have posed difficult problems for the Church. It is unlikely that

any lasting national reconciliation will occur, however, without the involvement of this oldest of Georgian national institutions.

The Rise and Fall of Zviad Gamsakhurdia, 1989–92

More unpredictable is the legacy of Zviad Gamsakhurdia, the charismatic Georgian intellectual who, with useful credentials as a Soviet dissident, emerged as a popular national hero and political leader in the months following April 1989. The son of Georgia's national poet, Zviad Gamsakhurdia never made a significant mark as an original writer, but he claimed attention as an outspoken opponent of Georgian Communist officialdom, earlier having served time in prison for his underground activities. The dissident Gamsakhurdia used the months following the April demonstrations to galvanize the support of a coalition of informal political groups. This coalition, called Round Table/Free Georgia, pressed for prompt parliamentary elections to the Georgian Supreme Soviet and demanded the restoration of the constitution that had governed the Georgian Democratic Republic (1918–21) prior to Soviet takeover.

In the elections of October 1990, Gamsakhurdia's Round Table/Free Georgia coalition won a solid victory in the Georgian Supreme Soviet, securing 54 percent of the vote. Two weeks later, in mid-November 1990, Gamsakhurdia was elected without opposition to head the new parliament. Initially his post was that of chairman of the Georgian Supreme Soviet, the de facto Georgian head of state. (Later, the office of president was created, and presidential elections were held in May 1991.)

Claiming as his goals the liberation of Georgia and the restoration of its state sovereignty—goals entirely in line with the anti-Soviet theme of the day—Gamsakhurdia appointed a coterie of loyal anti-Communists to the new government, many of them without prior professional governmental experience. Viewing himself as a moral savior of the Georgian nation, Gamsakhurdia proclaimed, "The Almighty has imposed a great mission on Georgia. The day is not far off when Georgia will become an example of moral greatness for the whole world" (cited in Elizabeth Fuller, "Gamsakhurdia's First 100 Days," *Report on the USSR*, 8 March, 1991, 10). Gamsakhurdia, in conspicuously identifying himself with the Georgian Orthodox Church—despite earlier conflicts with Patriarch-Catholicos Ilia II—was clearly appealing to Georgian chauvinism and anti-Communism.

This moral, chauvinist appeal was coupled with a ruthless and vindictive approach toward political opponents, an approach that quickly began to raise concern among Georgians, as well as among the national minorities within the Georgian state. These concerns were well substantiated, as evidenced by several policy reversals that marked his first months in office. For example, during the election campaign, Gamsakhurdia had committed himself to the preservation of autonomous regions for the Abkhazians and South Ossetians, but by the end of 1990, he had reversed his position, arguing rather that South Ossetiia should be abolished.

What most disheartened political moderates in Georgia, however, was Gamsakhurdia's attempt to restrict access to the media and the threats he made to his opponents. Also, the promising economic program of Round Table/Free Georgia was largely abandoned as the Georgian economy suffered from high rates of inflation and chronic shortages.

What ought to have concerned political democrats in Georgia even before the election was Gamsakhurdia's suggestion that only parties demonstrating electoral strength throughout Georgia should gain access to the ballot. Such measures would effectively disfranchise local minorities—Abkhazians, South Ossetians, Ajaris, the Azeris of Marneuli, and other groups. While Gamsakhurdia proceeded to blame Georgian Communists, former Soviet rulers, and opposing political parties for the failings of his new government, there were ample signs by the spring of 1991 that he himself was carelessly reopening old ethnic and regional wounds without securing the economic and political stability of the new Georgian government.

Responding to Gamsakhurdia's suggestion, the Georgian parliament formally declared Georgian independence in April 1991. An earlier referendum submitted to the republic's electorate had garnered almost 100 percent support for the restoration of Georgian independence. The critical term "restoration" referred to a situation based upon the terms of the 1918 independent Georgian state. Even this matter revealed ominous signs of conflict and coercion, for Gamsakhurdia had made it known that any district voting against the referendum would face the prospect of its voters losing citizenship, and thereby the right to land ownership. Moreover, Gamsakhurdia dismissed outright the fact that the far-reaching 1918 declaration of independence had guaranteed equal rights for all citizens of Georgia without regard to nationality, religion, or sex.

While there was modest erosion in support for Gamsakhurdia in the first Georgian presidential elections (May 1991), he still polled more than 85 percent of the Georgian vote. The election process, however, was colored by threats and intimidation directed at some of Gamsakhurdia's opponents—several having been kept off the ballot and one having been assaulted during the campaign. Gamsakhurdia's continuing popularity among the Georgian populace reflected the strength of the national desire for independence from Moscow. No other national figure could so charismatically draw upon the anti-Soviet feelings of the Georgian electorate. For Gamsakhurdia, the results only strengthened his anti-Communist resolve.

Given the electoral plurality of May 1991, no clearer sign of the instability and violence of Georgian politics was to be found than the violent ouster of Gamsakhurdia from power just six months later in January 1992. After barricading himself in the parliament building for over two weeks against the combined rebel forces of the Georgian National Guard and the Mkhedrioni (a paramilitary group of "Georgian Knights"), Gamsakhurdia fled in early 1992 beyond the Georgian border. Why did a charismatic national leader who six months earlier had received an 85 percent vote of confidence as the new president of Georgia end up being unceremoniously hounded out of office?

Beyond the challenges that Gamsakhurdia had posed to the sensibilities of a democratic Georgian intelligentsia, several concrete incidents contributed to his fall. First, he had irreparably broken with minority nationalities in Georgia. Contradicting his own election promises, he abolished the autonomous status of the South Ossetiia Autonomous Oblast. Indeed, Georgian troops ended up fighting the South Ossetians to establish Georgian authority in the Ossetian city of Tskhinvali. Furthermore, Gamsakhurdia arrested many political opponents and introduced far-reaching curbs on freedom of the press. At one point he even used his presidential powers to strip Georgian Communist Party deputies of their status in the Georgian parliament, the Supreme Soviet.

The most serious of Gamsakhurdia's problems began with the celebrated incident in early September 1991 when he used National Guard troops to fire on peaceful demonstrators. Calling to mind the innocent victims of Bloody Sunday, this single incident quickly eroded popular support for Gamsakhurdia. Large sections of the National Guard, a new Georgian army that Gamsakhurdia wished to put under his own Ministry of Internal Affairs, were disaffected. The split between loyalist (Gamsakhurdia followers) and rebel factions in the Georgian National Guard became the basis for a violent civil conflict played out on the streets of Tbilisi from December 1991 until Gamsakhurdia's flight in early January 1992.

The Reemergence of Eduard Shevardnadze in Georgian Politics

The violent departure of the dictatorial Gamsakhurdia left Georgian society split between those who favored and those who opposed this first post-Soviet Georgian president. By forcibly ousting him, the rebel National Guard, the Mkhedrioni, and their political allies—a coalition that formed its own Military Council for the purpose of establishing law and order—had clearly operated unconstitutionally. Thus, from the perspective of international law, the Georgian state entered 1992 facing charges of flagrant human rights abuses directed not only against its minority populations but against its own nationals as well. Furthermore, an extra-legal coup d'état had been used to secure political power by brute force.

Under these circumstances, the Military Council quickly sought new elections to add legitimacy to the political situation. In a step that would have been unthinkable a year earlier during the first months of the Gamsakhurdia government, Eduard Shevardnadze was invited back in 1992 to head a new interim State Council. The summer of 1992 was spent readying a complex election law in time for the scheduled October 1992 elections. A timely alliance of former Communist Party figures, members of the intelligentsia, and other center-left political interests formed itself into an effective political bloc, the Mshvidoba, under whose umbrella Eduard Shevardnadze ran for office. The Mshvidoba bloc, buoyed by the support of a populace that once more was looking to the Communists to restore economic stability to Georgia, carried the largest number of seats in the October elections. Shevardnadze was elected parliamentary chair, or acting head of state.

Georgia and the Abkhazian Question

No question has proved more troublesome for the Shevardnadze government than that of the autonomous republic of Abkhazia. While the deterioration of the Georgian economy has necessarily focused the energies of the Georgian state on its own domestic recovery, the long-term issue that poses the thorniest problem is that defined by Andrei Sakharov—namely, the dilemma of a "miniature empire." The complexity of the Abkhazian question defies easy generalization. In August 1992, Eduard Shevardnadze, chair of the then-ruling Military Council, sent loyal national guard units into Sokhumi, the Abkhazian capital. Using as a pretext the need to rescue Georgian officials abducted by Gamsakhurdia's followers, Shevardnadze's Geor-

gian National Guard sought to capture Gamsakhurdia himself. The invading National Guard went on a virtual rampage in Abkhazia, killing tourists on the beach and destroying several scientific research institutes and museums. More than 50 were killed. Protesting this invasion of their territory by Georgian troops, the forces of the Abkhaz Internal Affairs Ministry returned fire on the Georgian National Guard. The August 1992 fighting led to a rapid deterioration in Georgian-Abkhazian relations, and more than 250,000 refugees (mainly Georgian) fled Abkhazia for other parts of Georgia. Fighting continued until July 1993 when a United Nations–brokered truce set up talks for a long-term political settlement of Georgian-Abkhazian differences. Aided by initial Russian military support, the Abkhazians had secured in the truce the temporary autonomy of their own breakaway republic, but at the price of regional devastation and isolation.

Although ethnic Abkhazians constituted less than 20 percent of the pre-1992 population of the Abkhaz republic, they have demanded their own independence and sovereignty. Perhaps influenced by Gamsakhurdia's confrontational politics, the chairman of the Abkhaz Supreme Soviet, Vladislav Ardzinba, has pressed for Abkhazian separation from Georgia in any political settlement.

Seeking to counteract Abkhazian separatism, Shevardnadze has called for a negotiated settlement of the Abkhazian question that would recognize Abkhazia as a federal republic, but within the overall sovereignty of the Georgian state. Shevardnadze has also been insistent upon implementation of an April 1994 agreement coming out of the United Nations talks that called for repatriation of all refugees to Abkhazia.

Although the violent events of 1992–93 discredited Georgian political and military authorities, Georgia's position on the Abkhazian question has come to be appreciated by the international audience. Shevardnadze's assertion that Abkhazia must not violate the territorial integrity of Georgian borders has tended to be supported by politicians and diplomats wary of the consequences of nationalist and separatist movements such as those in former Yugoslavia. At the same time, Russia's own deepening involvement in the breakaway Republic of Chechnya (Checheniia) tended to make it far less sympathetic to Caucasian (including Abkhazian and South Ossetian) splinter movements—movements that have occasionally sided with Chechen rebels. Having already joined the Commonwealth of Independent States, Georgia successfully turned to the CIS in January 1996 for support of economic and trade sanctions against Abkhazian separatists. These CIS sanctions document the reversal of

Russia's position on the Abkhazian question, at the same time that they reflect the increasingly close understanding between Russia and Georgia in the Caucasus.

Finally, on the international level, the United Nations Security Council in July 1996 passed a resolution expressing concern about the deteriorating situation in Abkhazia and calling for all sides to settle their differences without resorting to violence or the violation of international borders. Shevardnadze has interpreted the United Nations resolution as supportive of his own position on Abkhazia and has threatened force if Abkhazia does not submit to refugee repatriation and a negotiated political settlement. While the years of political violence and the uncertainties over ethnic and minority rights in Abkhazia have undermined Georgian-Abkhazian understanding, the new constellation of forces—altered also by substantial Russian support for the strengthening of Georgia's internal police and military—undoubtedly places Georgia in an ascendant position on the Abkhazian question.

South Ossetiia and Ajaria

Not lost amidst the violence of the Abkhazian question are parallel questions involving the autonomous regions of South Ossetiia and Ajaria. The problems in South Ossetiia arose in 1989 when the Ossetians sought to secede from Georgia and unite with North Ossetiia (a republic within the Russian Federation). In late 1990, South Ossetiia's autonomous status within Georgia was abolished by the Gamsakhurdia government. Fighting broke out between Ossetians and Georgians, and hundreds of people were killed. In June 1992, Shevardnadze and Russian President Boris Yeltsin agreed to the use of joint peacekeeping forces in the Ossetian region. By 1996, Georgia and South Ossetiia had pledged to avoid the mutual use of force against one another, thus precluding for the near term the kind of violence associated with the Abkhazian question.

In the case of Ajaria, a region populated largely by Muslim Georgians or Ajarians, there has been no comparable conflict between central Georgian authorities and local citizens. Aslan Abashidze, the Ajarian leader, and his All Georgia Revival Union have become allies of the Shevardnadze government. Batumi, the capital of Ajaria, figures to remain prominent in efforts to stimulate the Georgian economy because of the efforts to reactivate the Baku-Batumi oil pipelines.

Contemporary Georgian Politics and Economic Life

Edouard Shevardnadze continues to dominate Georgian political life, as he has done since his return to Georgia in 1992. Overcoming threats to his life from former Mkhedrioni paramilitary forces and clamping down on the street violence in Tbilisi, he has put his own stamp upon this independent Georgian state. Since the summer of 1995, Georgia has been functioning under a new democratic constitution bearing Shevardnadze's imprint. In November 1995, garnering 74 percent of the vote, Shevardnadze was reelected to the Georgian presidency. In simultaneous parliamentary elections, Shevardnadze's ruling party, the Union of Citizens of Georgia (SMK), won 106 seats of the 235-member parliament, and his political allies from Ajaria and elsewhere have yielded a commanding majority for the government.

The Georgian economy has confronted the Shevardnadze government with a much more daunting set of problems. The influx of refugees, massive unemployment, underproductive industrial enterprises, and major energy shortfalls have combined to make the Georgian economy the weakest among those of the three newly independent states of Transcaucasia. There are, however, a few early signs of economic recovery. Inflation has been brought under some control. The potential for foreign investment in the Baku-Batumi oil pipelines and the ability of the Shevardnadze government to secure International Monetary Fund financial support offer grounds for hope of economic recovery, although unemployment remains high. The new Georgian currency introduced in October 1995, the lari, is now being maintained by market forces that include a growing privatized sector.

Despite Georgia's independence and international recognition, the past decade has brought political violence, conflicts with an internal minority population, and massive economic dislocations. With increasingly strong support from Russia, however, and with a strategic location on the Black Sea, Georgia's geopolitical position is markedly stronger today than it was when it first declared its independence in 1991. The beauty of its natural terrain, its deep historical and religious roots, and its energetic people offer promise for the future. That promise awaits the resolution of regional disputes that are still the most serious threat to Georgian stabililty.

PART FOUR

CENTRAL ASIA

INTRODUCTION

Strategically located between Russia, the Middle East, and China, the five republics of Central Asia—Kazakhstan, Kyrgyzstan, Tajikistan, Turkmenistan, and Uzbekistan—all declared their formal independence in the weeks following the abortive Moscow coup d'état in August 1991. The Central Asian region where these five newly independent republics are situated has several important characteristics.

First of all, the native populations are, by religious tradition, Islamic. Although great numbers of European Slavs, particularly Russians, migrated into the cities of Central Asia in the twentieth century, the tradition of Islam is one of the region's major distinguishing features. Most of the area's Islamic peoples have Turkic ethnic roots and speak a Turkic language. Thus, it is still possible for Kazakhs of Kazakhstan to be understood by Uzbeks of Uzbekistan or Kyrgyz of Kyrgyzstan. The very homogeneity of this once-nomadic local population raises important questions regarding the potential for a unified "Turkestan." When the region was conquered and annexed to the Russian Empire in the nineteenth century, it was referred to as Russian Turkestan. In the Soviet period, Turkestan was divided into separate union republics. Today, any effort to integrate the newly independent Central Asian states into a single Turkestan faces the barrier of ancient divisions, as well as 70 years of Soviet and post-Soviet historical development.

Despite the common Islamic heritage, a second point to be made about Central Asia is, indeed, its rich diversity. The Tajiks of Tajikistan (and of Uzbekistan, where they constitute an important minority) are not Turkic, but rather derive from a Persian background. Even within the Turkic nations of Central Asia there are significant regional and tribal differences. Moreover, despite the massive exodus of Russians from the area in the years since the breakup of the Soviet Union, the important role of the Slavic population in the urban, industrialized sectors of Central Asia is likely to continue into the twenty-first century.

The diversity of Central Asia is also to be seen in the topography and physical characteristics of the territory. From the mountainous regions along the southern and eastern borders, to the fertile Farghona (Fergana) Valley, to the deserts of Turkmenistan, Central Asia exhibits a wide range of climates and vegetation. From the rich oil deposits of Kazakhstan to the mines of Kyrgyzstan, there is a wealth of natural resources in the region, much of it untapped or difficult to access.

The wealth of natural resources, however, must be set alongside the grating poverty and economic deterioration of the region. Heavily committed to growing cotton during the Soviet period, the rural poverty of Central Asia is the worst of any region of the former Soviet Union. Dependent upon external imports for basic consumer goods, the area faces acute shortages of foodstuffs and household items. Compounding the poverty of Central Asia are the environmental problems left as a consequence of production-oriented Soviet central planning. The disastrous depletion of the Aral Sea, located in the center of the region, is symptomatic of the wider ecological dilemma faced by these newly independent countries. As the poor of rural Central Asia migrate into the more Slavic-dominated urban centers throughout the region, the potential for ethnic conflict looms. The underlying sources of civil strife and political turmoil, however, are to be found not only in ethnic conflict, but in the shortages of clean water, medical care, basic housing, and safe foodstuffs.

Amid serious disruptions and political conflicts such as those ongoing in Tajikistan, the process of democratization has either slowed or has been reversed in virtually all of Central Asia. Not only does the old Soviet bureaucracy remain in control of much of the governmental machinery in these newly independent states, but recent parliamentary elections and referenda have tended to exclude significant sectors of the political opposition from the process. Ever increasing power has been vested in executive authority. Although informal political groups, such as the environmental movement (the Nevada-Semipalatinsk group) in Kazakhstan, played important roles in the initial drive toward independence, such informal political activity has increasingly been thwarted as the prospects for a more open civil society in Central Asia have become clouded in the 1990s.

Despite the limits placed on political debate, the intelligentsia of Central Asia have seized upon the spirit of independence to reopen hidden chapters of their respective national and regional histories. In this pro-

cess, the Russian imperial role in the region has been put on the defensive as ethnic identity becomes an increasingly important part of public consciousness. The recovery of ethnic identity has invariably resulted in the rehabilitation of members of the Central Asian intelligentsia who suffered during the worst of the Stalinist era. The rewriting of local and national history has only begun, and although it can lead to ethnic conflict and turmoil, the redefinition of Turkic and other Central Asian identities is likely to be among the most enduring features of the current transition.

Bibliography

Akiner, Shirin. *Islamic Peoples of the Soviet Union.* London: KPI, 1986.

Allworth, Edward A. *The Modern Uzbeks from the Fourteenth Century to the Present: A Cultural History.* Stanford, CA: Hoover Institution Press, 1990.

———, ed. *The Nationality Question in Soviet Central Asia.* New York: Praeger Publishers, 1973.

———. *Soviet Nationality Problems.* New York: Columbia University Press, 1971.

———. *Uzbek Literary Politics.* The Hague, Netherlands: Mouton & Co., 1964.

Atkin, Muriel. *Subtlest Battle: Islam in Soviet Tajikistan.* Philadelphia: Foreign Policy Research Institute, 1989.

Bennigsen, Alexandre, and S. Enders Wimbush. *Muslims of the Soviet Empire: A Guide.* London: C. Hurst and Company, 1985.

Critchlow, James. *Nationalism in Uzbekistan: A Soviet Republic's Road to Sovereignty.* Boulder, CO: Westview Press, 1991.

Ellis, William S. "The Aral: A Soviet Sea Lies Dying." *National Geographic,* February 1990: 73–92.

Fierman, William, ed. *Soviet Central Asia: The Failed Transformation.* Boulder, CO: Westview Press, 1991.

Horak, Stephan M., ed. *Guide to the Study of the Soviet Nationalities: Non-Russian Peoples of the USSR.* Littleton, CO: Libraries Unlimited, Inc., 1982.

Index Islamicus, 1981–1985: A Bibliography of Books and Articles on the Muslim World. 2 vols. Compiled and edited by G. J. Roper. London: Mansell, 1991. (This index began in 1958, covering material published from 1906–1955.)

Mandelbaum, Michael, ed. *Central Asia and the World: Kazakhstan, Uzbekistan, Tajikistan, Kyrgyzstan, and Turkmenistan.* New York: Council on Foreign Relations Press, 1994.

Olcott, Martha Brill. *Central Asia's New States: Independence, Foreign Policy, and Regional Security.* Herndon, VA: U.S. Institute of Peace Press, 1996.

———. *The Kazakhs.* Stanford, CA: Hoover Institution Press, 1987.

Park, Alexander G. *Bolshevism in Turkestan, 1917–1927.* New York: Columbia University Press, 1957.

Rakowska-Harmstone, Teresa. *Russia and Nationalism in Central Asia: The Case of Tadzhikistan.* Baltimore, MD: The Johns Hopkins University Press, 1970.

RFE/RL Research Report, 1992–. This publication of Radio Free Europe/Radio Liberty was formerly titled *Radio Liberty Research Bulletin* (through 1988) and *Report on the USSR* (1989–91). Weekly. See also *Transition.*

Ro'i, Yacov. *The USSR and the Muslim World.* London: Allen and Unwin, 1984.

Rywkin, Michael. *Moscow's Muslim Challenge: Soviet Central Asia.* Rev. ed. Armonk, NY: M.E. Sharpe, 1990.

Shabad, Theodore. *Geography of the USSR: A Regional Survey.* New York: Columbia University Press, 1951.

Transition: Events and Issues in the Former Soviet Union and East-Central and Southeastern Europe, 1995– . Prague: Open Media Research Institute. This biweekly journal continues the coverage of *RFE/RL Research Reports.*

Wheeler, Geoffrey. *The Peoples of Soviet Central Asia: A Background Book.* London: The Bodley Head, 1966.

Wixman, Ronald. *The Peoples of the USSR: An Ethnographic Handbook.* Armonk, NY: M.E. Sharpe, 1984.

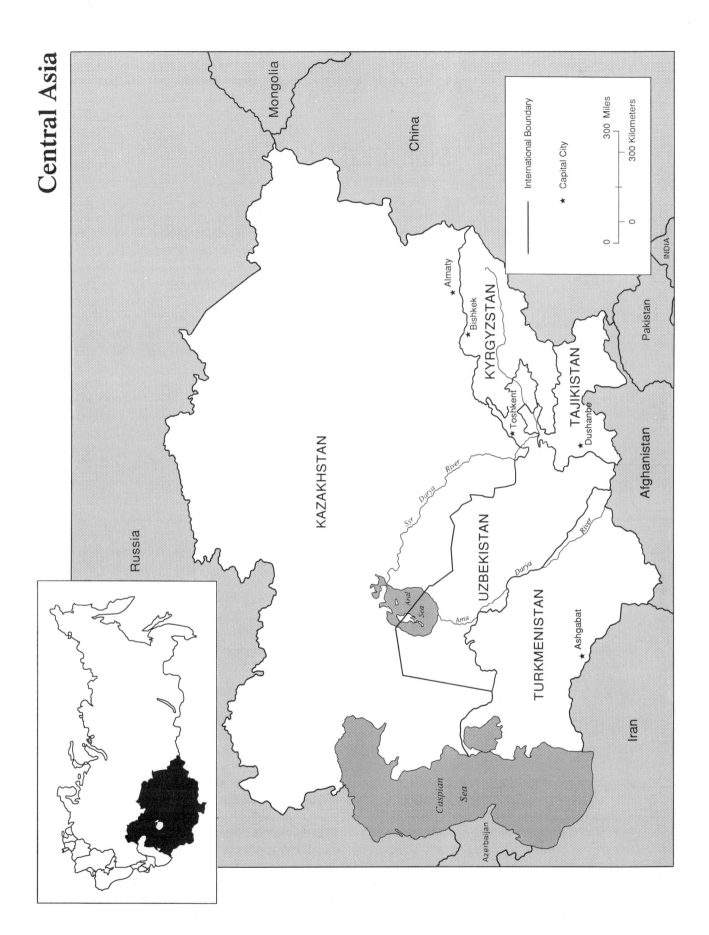

Central Asia

KAZAKHSTAN

Statistical Profile

Demography

Population: 16,679,000

Ethnic population

Kazakh	44.3%
Russian	35.8%
Ukrainian	5.1%
German	3.6%
Uzbek	2.2%
Tatar	2.0%
Uighur	1.1%
Belarusian	1.1%
Korean	0.6%
Azerbaijani	0.6%
Other	3.6%

Major urban centers and populations

Almaty (Alma-Ata)	1,147,000
Qaraghandy (Karaganda)	613,000
Shymkent (Chimkent)	401,000
Semey (Semipalatinsk)	339,000
Pavlodar	337,000
Öskemen (Ust-Kamenogorsk)	330,000
Zhambyl	311,000
Aqmola (Tselinograd)	281,000
Aqtöbe (Aktiubinsk)	260,000
Petropavl (Petropavlovsk)	245,000
Qostanay (Kustanai)	228,000
Temirtau	213,000
Oral (Uralsk)	207,000
Aqtau (Shevchenko)	165,000
Qyzylorda (Kzyl-Orda)	156,000

Historic religious traditions

Islam	50.5%
Christianity	48.0%

Languages: Kazakh, Russian

Population by age

Age	Total	Males	Females
0–14	30.2%	15.3%	14.9%
15–64	62.7%	30.9%	31.8%
65 and over	7.1%	2.3%	4.8%

Male/Female ratio: 48.5% male/51.5% female

Rural/Urban population
44.0% rural/56.0% urban

Annual population growth rate: -1.6%

Population density: 15.9 persons per sq mi

Government

Official name
Qazaqstan Respublikasy (Republic of Kazakhstan)

Capital: Almaty

Date of sovereignty/independence declaration
16 December 1991

Voting age: 18

Education

Literacy (age 15 and over who can read and write)

total population	98%
male	99%
female	96%

Level of education for persons over 15

completed higher education	9.9%
completed secondary education	54.1%
incomplete secondary education	19.8%

Number of higher education institutions: 55

Higher education enrollment: 287,400 students

Selected institutions of higher education (and enrollment)

Almaty

Al-Farabi State National University	14,000
Animal Husbandry and Veterinary Institute	5,670
Power Engineering Institute	4,720
State University of World Languages	2,350

Aqmola
    Agricultural Institute 10,000
Öskemen
    Institute of Construction and Road
      Building 6,700
Pavlodar
    Pavlodar State University 3,570
Qaraghandy
    State University 8,440
    State Medical School 5,080

Socioeconomic Indicators

Annual birth rate: 18.7 births/1,000 population

Fertility rate: 2.4 children/woman

Infant mortality: 27.4 deaths/1,000 live births

Average life expectancy
    68.3 years (male 63.6, female 73.1)

Annual death rate: 9.6 deaths/1,000 population

Average family size: 4.0

Annual consumption of electrical energy
    3,750 kWh/person

Hospital beds per 10,000 persons: 132

Physical Features

Area: 1,049,150 sq mi

Land use
    cultivated 13%
    pasture 58%

Highest elevation
    14,783 ft (Belukha peak in the Altai Range)

Rainfall
    12–18 in./yr; 10 in./yr on the steppe
    4–8 in./yr in the desert
    16–64 in./yr in the mountains

Temperature

Winter	**Summer**
north, average 0°F	north, average 66°F
south, average 27°F	south, average 84°F
lowest, –45°F	

Economic Production

Estimated per capita GNP: $1,110 (1994)

Agricultural output
    cotton, spring wheat, meat, wool, apples

Natural resources
    oil, coal, lead, iron, copper, manganese, chrome, nickel, cobalt, molybdenum, zinc, bauxite, gold, uranium, sulfur, titanium, silver

Industrial output
    petroleum products, mining, steel, nonferrous metals, agricultural machinery, electric motors, construction materials

Currency
    tenge (introduced November 1993)
    1 tenge = 100 tein

Communications

Length of rail lines: 8,800 mi

Length of highways: 51,300 mi

Pipelines
    crude oil .... 1,781 mi
    natural gas .... 2,175 mi

Telephones: 126.6 per 1,000 persons

Sources "Kazakhskaia sovetskaia sotsialisticheskaia respublika," *Bol'shaia sovetskaia entsiklopediia* 11 (Moscow, 1977) 145–73; *Narodnoe khoziaistvo SSSR v 1990g.* (Moscow, 1991); *Naselenie SSSR* (Moscow, 1989); Matthew J. Sagers, "News Notes: Iron and Steel," *Soviet Geography* 30 (May 1989): 397–434; Lee Schwartz, "USSR Nationality Redistribution by Republic, 1979–1989: From Published Results of the 1989 All-Union Census," *Soviet Geography* 32 (April 1991): 209–48; *World of Learning,* 46th ed. (London, 1996); "Russia . . ." (National Geographic Society Map, 1993); *Europa World Yearbook, 1996* (London, 1996); *Demograficheskii ezhegodnik,* 1995 (Moscow, 1995); "CIA World Factbook, 1995" (www.odci.gov/cia/publications/95fact/kz.html).

Kazakhstan

International Boundary

★ Capital City
● Other Cities

0   400 Miles

0   400 Kilometers

RUSSIA

Petropavl

Qostanay

Pavlodar

Oral

Altai Mtns.
14,783 ft.

Aqtöbe

Aqmola

Semey
Öskemen

Temirtau
Qaraghandy

Ural River

Gurev   Oil

Emba River

Fields

Baikonur
Cosmodrome

Balqash
Köl

Mangyshlak
Peninsula

Aral
Sea

Aqtau

Novyi Uzen

Caspian
Sea

Qyzylorda

Syr Darya River

Chu   River

Almaty

Zhambyl

UZBEKISTAN

Shymkent

KYRGYZSTAN

Tian Shan
Mtns.

CHINA

TURKMENISTAN

Samarqand

TAJIKISTAN

Kazakhstan: History and Description

Physical Description

Borders Kazakhstan is located at the crossroads of Europe and Asia. The second largest republic of the former Soviet Union, Kazakhstan extends from the Caspian Sea in the west to the Altai Mountains in the east and from western Siberia in the north to the Tian Shan Mountains in the south. A vast expanse made up primarily of grasslands known as the steppe (flat, desert-like terrain), Kazakhstan has only one truly mountainous region, a range that is located along its lengthy eastern border with China. Kazakhstan shares its southern boundary with the three Central Asian countries of Kyrgyzstan, Uzbekistan, and Turkmenistan. To the west lies the Caspian Sea and to the north the Russian Federation.

Water Resources The rivers of Kazakhstan are overshadowed in importance by the republic's large inland lakes. Largest of these is the Caspian Sea, the shoreline of which is shared with Turkmenistan, Azerbaijan, Russia, and Iran. Second in size is the shrinking Aral Sea, divided between Kazakhstan and Uzbekistan. Third largest is Balqash Köl (Lake Balkhash), a freshwater basin located entirely within the boundaries of Kazakhstan, north of its capital city, Almaty (Alma-Ata).

Topography Three distinct types of landforms are found within Kazakhstan. Soviet-designed borders gave the Kazakhs a share in the agriculturally valuable oases watered by the glacial rivers of the region's mountains. Apart from these irrigated lands in the southeastern part of the country along the Syr Darya and Chu rivers, Kazakhstan is made up almost entirely of a vast desert steppe that cannot sustain intensive farming and supports only a sparse population. A single region of black-earth farmland along the northern fringe of the Kazakh steppe does yield some wheat, cereal, and forage crops. This region was developed agriculturally in the 1950s as part of the famous Virgin Lands experiment begun by Soviet Communist Party leader Nikita Khrushchev.

Economic Resources Kazakhstan holds a wealth of natural resources comparable to its great size. The oil fields along the eastern shore of the Caspian Sea, particularly on the Mangyshlak Peninsula near Aqtau (Shevchenko), and the petroleum sources located in a region between the mouths of the Ural and Emba rivers are productive enough for the Kazakhs to export oil to other republics of the former USSR, and soon to other places in the world. In addition, coal deposits exist near the city of Qaraghandy (Karaganda) in an industrialized area of central Kazakhstan, with supplementary sources elsewhere, principally to the northeast in the Pavlodar region. Iron ore, copper, and lead deposits in the north and in other areas of Kazakhstan add to the intrinsic value of the country's mineral riches. In the arid central desert regions, Kazakhstan has been the home of the famous Soviet nuclear test site at Semipalatinsk (Semey) and the space Cosmodrome at Baikonur.

Agriculture Agriculturally, cotton is the major crop grown in the irrigated lands of southern Kazakhstan. In the north, grain, wheat, and fodder crops are grown for the many livestock traditionally raised by local herders. Fruits, vegetables, rice, and tobacco are cultivated in some of the less arid parts of the country, notably in the river valleys of the southeast. The city of Almaty takes its name from the apples grown in that region.

Ethnic and Historical Background

The origins of the Kazakhs date from the thirteenth-century incursions by the Mongol horde of Genghis Khan and his Tatar warriors into Central Asia. The intermingling of tribes of indigenous peoples, who had inhabited the area of present-day Kazakhstan from the prehistoric Bronze Age period, with Turkic peoples who had migrated to the area from other parts of Central Asia was then augmented by the assimilation of Mongol elements. By the end of the fifteenth century, when a union of Kazakh khans began to control the vast steppe territories making up contemporary Kazakhstan, a sense of ethnic identity had developed amongst the tribal groups formed from this assimilation.

The term Kazakh, as applied linguistically to a particular group of people, may come from the Turkish word *qaz* (to wander). For an ethnic definition, however, the meaning is rooted in the complex web of Central Asian tribal relationships. Historian Martha Brill Olcott, in her book, *The Kazakhs* (Stanford: Hoover Institution Press, 1987), describes these people as primarily "Turkic-speaking nomadic tribes of Uzbek-Turkic stock," who, despite a shared language and ethnic background, viewed themselves as Kazakhs, and thereby separate from Uzbeks.

By the beginning of the sixteenth century as many as one million Kazakhs inhabited a common Kazakh Khanate under Kasim Khan. This population was later joined by additional Kazakh tribes drawn from adjacent scattered hordes. The term Kazakh came to be identified with those who expanded into the territories north and east of the Uzbeks. The Uzbeks, for their part, had moved south into the historic area of Samarqand.

After the rule of Kasim Khan (A.D. 1511–1518), the Kazakhs divided into three nomadic hordes led by independent khans (tribal leaders). The Great Horde (also called the Elder Horde) roamed in the area of Semireche, the southern part of present-day Kazakhstan; the Middle Horde migrated within central and northern Kazakhstan; and the Small Horde ranged over the area of western Kazakhstan. During the seventeenth and eighteenth centuries, these hordes found it almost impossible to maintain themselves against invading armies from the east. As a result, some Kazakh leaders appear to have sought cooperation with the Russian state. Other Kazakhs did not seek Russian protection. They turned for assistance to Turkic leaders within Central Asia and strongly opposed Russia's expansion into the steppe regions. Such divided loyalties led to confrontation and warfare throughout the eighteenth and nineteenth centuries.

Russian Conquest

By the 1820s, tsarist influence had penetrated the life of the Kazakhs. Russian administrations were established in the territories occupied by the Middle Horde and the Small Horde. By mid-century, even some Kazakhs from the Great Horde had joined the Russians. In 1854, the Russian military command constructed a fortified settlement called Vernyi (later named Alma-Ata) to advance Russian imperial control of the Central Asian steppe. During the 1860s, more Kazakh lands came under the domination of Russia. An influx of Russian peasants into Kazakhstan followed. In the last two decades of the nineteenth century, hundreds of Russian and other Slavic peasant villages came to dot the Kazakh steppe. The indigenous population, which by the end of the century numbered close to 1.5 million "tents," or households, could not continue its traditional nomadic way of life under the land restrictions imposed by the new authorities and the Russian settlements. Uprisings that occurred were routinely repressed, as more and more European migrants continued to settle on Kazakh lands. After the turn of the century, as part of a more general tsarist agricultural policy, nearly a half million households were relocated from Russia to the Kazakh region. The Kazakhs continued to lose their most valuable pastureland to this influx. The Trans-Siberian Railroad, completed in 1904, made it possible to transport food products from the newly settled agricultural communities to the rest of the empire.

Until the nineteenth century, the Kazakhs appeared to be only nominally connected to the religious world of Islam within which the other Turkic peoples of Central Asia moved. Tsarist policy at first encouraged Islamization of the Kazakhs, believing that such a "civilizing" influence would make it easier to rule them, but later the tsar changed his mind and instead sent Christian missionaries. By then, however, the Kazakhs showed little interest.

The events of the First World War made heavy demands on the Kazakhs to support the tsarist military effort. Contributing to Kazakh resentment of the Russian presence, the requisitioning of farm products for the troops, including livestock, was accompanied by a demand for higher taxes. A 1916 mass mobilization order for Kazakhs to perform noncombatant work in the rearguard area brought Kazakh feelings into the open, resulting in widespread revolts aimed particularly at the local Russian inhabitants. Many were slain on both sides, and extensive material damage occurred. Thousands of Kazakhs fled with their livestock to China to escape conscription.

Soviet Rule

The tumultuous events of the Russian Revolution in 1917 inspired the Kazakh nationalist movement, Alash Orda, to proclaim for a brief period the independence of Kazakhstan. Bolshevik sympathizers opposed the Alash Orda and sought, instead, the integration of the region into the new Soviet state. Alongside Vladimir Lenin's special appeal to the Muslim workers of Russia and the east, the Kazakh leader of the Alash Orda, Ali Bukeikhanov, held out for a national government in Kazakhstan. Other Kazakhs critical of the aristocratic connections of Alash Orda joined the Communist Party, believing that its program would better assist in the formation of a modern, democratic Kazakh state. The ensuing civil war between revolutionary and anti-revolutionary factions brought a period of intense military struggle accompanied by great physical suffering. The inhabitants of Kazakhstan, both nomads and settled farmers, suffered appalling deprivations. Eventually, the Red Army prevailed and the Kazakh nationalists had to succumb to Soviet power. Not until August of 1920, however, was the whole of the Kazakh region finally linked to Russia and a capital established at Orenburg northwest of Aqtöbe.

The Kazakhs had been called Kyrgyz by European travelers and later settlers, and in 1920, the Soviet authorities duly established them as the Kyrgyz Autonomous Republic within the larger Russian republic. Those known today as Kyrgyz, in turn, found themselves called the Kara Kyrgyz. Not until 1925 did the Soviet government change the name assigned to the Kazakhs. Their country was then officially designated, still within the Russian republic, as the Kazakh Autonomous Republic. The capital was located at Kzyl-Orda but was moved to Alma-Ata in May 1929. The autonomous oblast of Karakalpak, whose people were closely related to the Kazakhs, was placed administratively within Kazakhstan until 1936 when it was joined to the Uzbek republic. It was also in 1936 that Kazakhstan was raised from autonomous status within the Russian republic and became a full union republic of the Soviet Union.

As the postrevolutionary period began and Soviet officials sought to include Kazakhstan in their new order, the economic needs of the republic required immediate attention. Land redistribution held priority in the social program proposed by the Bolsheviks. In a country where a pastoral nomadic way of life prevailed, however, the fixed assignment of land to those who annually migrated between summer and winter pastureland did not make sense. Nevertheless, the Soviets wanted Kazakh nomads to change their traditional ways and settle permanently in fixed areas. During the ensuing disruptions of the 1920s, Russian and Kazakh political figures vied for power amidst hunger and hardship, while failing to solve the severe economic problems pressing the new republic. Plagued by poor harvests, Kazakhs were unable to set aside seed meant for planting, using it instead to satisfy their immediate food needs. The resulting famine of the early 1920s left hundreds of thousands of Kazakhs dead.

A gradual recovery occurred between 1924 and 1929 as the state attempted to gain control of economic activities, taking authority out of the hands of local clans and tribes whose long-standing rivalries impeded the Soviet desire for change. Moscow promised to provide land for those Kazakhs who would give up their nomadic ways and assume a sedentary farming life. Very little good land, however, was offered, and Kazakhs resented the fact that Russian settlers had already received the best of the pasturelands. This legacy from the colonial period—the fact that the Russian settlers had been favored over the local peoples—needed to be overcome by the new Soviet authorities if economic recovery were to take place. Nevertheless, the Russians within the local Kazakh Communist Party structure persisted in trying to implement the land policy dictated from Moscow. The lack of such farming necessities as seed, plows, and tractors, not to mention decent land, doomed these efforts. Often those Kazakhs who tried to settle down and farm found their efforts unsuccessful and returned to the previous nomadic way of life.

Collectivization In 1929, collectivization of land was introduced throughout the Soviet Union. Under collectivization, farm land was first nationalized and then administered by the state. The peasants were resettled on *kolkhozy* (collective farms) and worked cooperatively, pooling their labor and supplies. After the land reform failures of the 1920s, Party officials were determined to make the new method work. In Kazakhstan, however, collectivization was strongly resisted, and defiant peasants were sent to prison camps or executed. The Communist Party sought to fix blame for yet another unsuccessful round of land reform. Local leaders, including Party First Secretary Goloshchekin (an ethnic Russian) and those who had shown sympathy for the Alash Orda, were accused of nationalist motivations at the expense of a concern for the country as a whole. Numerous activists were purged from their posts and replaced by newcomers.

Stalinist Purges and World War II Throughout the 1930s, political turmoil continued. The height of the Stalinist purges occurred in Kazakhstan in 1937 and 1938. Not only errant Party members, including the new first secretary, L. I. Mirzoian, but also Kazakh intellectuals were arrested, tried, and executed. The terror eventually yielded one of its Stalinist goals: by the end of 1938, 98 percent of Kazakhstan's rural population was living on collective farms.

World War II brought a halt to some of the harshest practices that Stalin had introduced into the Kazakh republic. Antireligious campaigns were softened to gain the support of certain sectors of the population, and many controversial policies were put on hold until the war was over. Alma-Ata and other Kazakh cities became the destination for thousands of Russian mothers and children seeking refuge from the military front. These cities also served as the new locale for factories and other enterprises from European Russia that were moved away from the threat of battle to keep up their wartime production. In addition, Russian engineers came searching for new caches of valuable natural resources to aid the war effort.

Post-Stalin Era A long period of economic recovery followed the end of the war, but even as late as the early 1950s, agricultural production was still not meeting the requirements of the recurring five-year plans. In 1953, after Stalin's death, Nikita Khrushchev proposed a new land-use program for northern Kazakhstan and southern Siberia. His proposal advocated cultivation of a huge area of 35 million hectares in an intensive wheat farming program. Khrushchev believed that this Virgin Lands program, which would bring much untilled land under cultivation, would solve shortages that might occur if Ukrainian harvests failed. As a result, still more Kazakh pastureland disappeared. The project yielded mixed results. After Khrushchev's ouster in 1964, the policy was phased out, with only scattered remnants of the Virgin Lands remaining.

From the early 1960s, Kazakh Communist Party leadership was assumed by Dinmukhamed Akhmedovich Kunaev, a native Kazakh whose administration during the Brezhnev years was noted for its corruption and favoritism. Yet, alongside the graft, it was during those Kunaev years that unprecedentedly large numbers of Kazakhs came to assume leadership posts in the republic.

Kazakhstan: Contemporary Issues

The Demographics of Multiculturalism: Kazakhs and Russians

The lands of Kazakhstan have been subjected to recurring demographic revolutions in the twentieth century. The Soviet efforts to impose fixed settlements and to eliminate the traditionally nomadic existence of the Kazakhs led to real losses in Kazakh population in the 1920s and 1930s. Some of that loss occurred during the violence of forced settlement. But hundreds of thousands of Kazakhs also fled to other regions, including the Xinjiang province of China. The result was that between the censuses of 1926 and 1939, during a period when natural population growth would have yielded a substantial increase, the Kazakh population dropped from approximately four million to just over three million.

This real loss of Kazakh population was in sharp contrast to the dramatic in-migration of Russians and other European Slavs during the 1920s and 1930s. The 1939 census revealed that, for the first time, Russians outnumbered Kazakhs in the Kazakh Soviet Republic. Russians constituted 40.2 percent of the population, while the Kazakh percentage had dropped to 38 percent.

The 1959 census shows that Russians were 42.7 percent of the population, while the Kazakh population percentage had dropped to just 30 percent. These population percentages reflected considerable ongoing immigration of Europeans into the republic. During World War II, large German communities from the Ukrainian and Volga regions were transferred into Kazakhstan, and further migration of Russians occurred during the Virgin Lands policies of the 1950s. Although this European population influx began to be reversed in the 1970s, the Kazakhstan capital of Alma-Ata, along with other large urban centers of Central Asia, became largely Russianized. As recently as the 1979 census, Kazakhs represented only 16.3 percent of the population of Alma-Ata.

In the context of this historic Russian demographic transformation of Kazakhstan, Kazakh demographers, most notably Makash B. Tatimov, began in the 1980s to rebel against the idea occasionally advocated in Moscow that there ought to be a "differentiated demographic policy" in the Soviet Union. Advocates of such a policy wanted to counter the accelerating Turkic birthrates and the much lower Slav birthrates by a state policy that would be pronatalist in the case of the Slavs and restrictive in the case of the Turkic population. But Tatimov, among others, welcomed the disproportionately high birth rates among the Kazakhs, seeing increased Kazakh population as a response to the earlier deterioration of Kazakh demographic power.

Since the 1970s, an equally dramatic demographic revolution has been occurring. As in other parts of Central Asia, Kazakhstan has witnessed an emigration of much of the European population from the country, and a corresponding rise in the percentage of the urbanized Turkic population. During the 1980s, and with increased momentum since 1989, German settlements have been depleted by out-migration to Germany. There has also been a considerable exodus of European Slavs, only partly moderated by the entry into Kazakhstan of Russians departing other Central Asian states. The result is that, for the first time since 1939, the 1989 census reflects a larger percentage of Kazakhs (39.7 percent) than of Russians (37.8 percent). Still, if other Slavs are added to the Russians in the census figures, European Slavs continue to outnumber Kazakhs in Kazakhstan. This relatively even mixture of Slavic and Turkic population in present-day Kazakhstan, although it is rapidly changing as birth rates and emigrations alter the equation, is unique to the newly independent states of Central Asia. Nowhere else in Central Asia is the percentage of Slavic population so high.

With the establishment of independence in 1991, the status of Russians in Kazakhstan has changed in subtle, but unmistakable ways. The Kazakh government has passed legislation declaring Kazakh the official language of the state. This legislation has not precluded ongoing use of Russian, however, especially for interethnic communication, because large numbers of urbanized Kazakhs (perhaps as many as 40 percent) are not fully fluent in their own language. Still, the gradual Islamization and Turkicization of Kazakh national life have transformed the position of Kazakhstan's Russian citizens who could, less than a decade ago, feel secure with a Russian-dominated Soviet empire ruling over the region.

One of the curious side issues related to Kazakh-Russian ethnic relations involves the recent decision to transfer the capital of Kazakhstan from Almaty in the south to Aqmola in the north. In September 1994, following action in the Kazakhstan parliament, President Nazarbaev decreed that the capital would be moved to Aqmola by the year 2000. Founded as a nineteenth-century Russian settlement, Aqmola (in Russian, Tselinograd or Akmolinsk) has always been a Russian city. Today, only about one-fourth of the approximately 300,000 residents are Kazakh, the vast majority being Russian. While there has been considerable speculation as to why the decision was taken to transfer the capital to Aqmola, most observers cite three factors in the change. First, the burgeoning city of Almaty, surrounded by mountains, has only limited capacity for growth. Second, President Nazarbaev appears concerned that Kazakh regions bordering Russia have been less well integrated into Kazakhstan, thereby raising the potential for secessionist moves by Russian majority population in those areas. Finally, Nazarbaev may be sensitive to rival clan and tribal loyalties that have brought southern Kazakhs into power in most government ministries. In this view, the movement of the capital to Aqmola would liberate the Kazakh government from exclusive domination by southern Kazakhs. It seems likely that, as in any interpretation of Kazakh politics, the concern for interethnic relations lies just beneath the surface.

While the Russians of Kazakhstan constitute the largest Russian percentage in any Central Asian country, they seem to be the least able of any Russians in the "near abroad" (Russian residents of the non-Russian states of the former Soviet Union) to acquire the local language. Less than one percent of all Russians

of Kazakhstan can speak or read Kazakh. Far from presenting a picture of multiculturalism and interethnic harmony, the population of Kazakhstan has become increasingly segregated into separate zones of Russian and Kazakh cultural life.

Faced with the new political realities, many Russians in Kazakhstan, as elsewhere in Central Asia, have decided to leave for Russia. From the collapse of the Soviet Union in late 1991 to 1996, more than three million Russians migrated to Russia from the near abroad (see Constantine Dmitriev, "Hostages of the [Former] Soviet Empire," *Transition* 2, no. 1, 12 January 1996, 18–21). The single greatest point of origin has been Kazakhstan. In 1996 alone, more than 200,000 Russians emigrated from Kazakhstan to the Russian Federation.

This exodus—likely to be the largest single population migration of the late twentieth century—could, over time, effect a general "ethnic cleansing" of Russians from Central Asia. In the case of Kazakhstan, however, Russian majorities in the north and east would seem to assure the continued existence and relative stability of an ethnic Russian population there. To combat Russian flight, the Kazakhstan government, like its counterparts throughout Central Asia, has encouraged the largely urbanized Russian population to stay. Frightened by restrictive language legislation and the ascendancy of Islamic and Turkic identifications, however, ethnic Slavs speaking only Russian are now agonizingly reassessing their commitment to their birthplace, the newly independent state of Kazakhstan.

The Politics of Multiculturalism: The December 1986 Riots

On the 16th of December, 1986, long-time first secretary of the Kazakh Communist Party, Dinmukhamed Kunaev, was replaced by an ethnic Russian more closely fitting the mold of Mikhail Gorbachev's policy of perestroika. The new Party secretary, Genadii Kolbin, appeared to be a reformer in the likeness of Gorbachev and Eduard Shevardnadze. Moscow hoped the new Kolbin regime would be able to eliminate the corruption, inside appointments, and graft that had come to be associated with the Kunaev government.

Even though the Kolbin appointment may have been only an interim measure, the selection of an ethnic Russian as first secretary constituted an aberration in post–World War II Central Asia. Typically, first secretaries had been chosen from indigenous nationals, with the second party post reserved for a European Slav. In Alma-Ata, the reaction to Kolbin's appointment was swift and overwhelming, rocking a calm

Central Asian capital accustomed to the quiescence of the local population.

Within a week of the December 1986 appointment, uncontrolled rioting broke out in Alma-Ata. Official reports proclaimed that only a few hundred students, designated "hoodlums," were responsible for the rioting. Unofficial sources, however, put the numbers as high as 10,000 and indicated that some rioters had even died in the fighting. During the two days of disturbances, the headquarters of the Communist Party were raided. So serious was the fighting that highly placed Moscow officials from the Central Committee of the Communist Party of the Soviet Union were dispatched to Alma-Ata. At the height of the confrontation, the demonstrators openly chanted, "Kazakhstan for the Kazakhs."

Although the December 1986 riots were quickly suppressed, they remained for some years the subject of secret investigations and hidden reports. The basic outlines of the confrontation quickly became clear. Central to any explanation of the demonstrations were the Kazakh ethnic sensitivities set off by the unexpected appointment of Genadii Kolbin, a Russian. Even though leading figures in Moscow had deplored the deterioration of the Kazakh economy and the corruption in governmental life during the quarter century of Kunaev's leadership, these leaders may not have appreciated the level of internal support that the Russified Kunaev generated as he appointed numerous Kazakhs to government positions. His replacement by a Russian was perceived as a threat not only to a younger generation of Kazakh nationals fed up with official politics, but also to many Kazakh Communist Party officials who had risen to power under the patronage of Kunaev. At the very least, the fear that riots against officialdom could easily turn into direct ethnic conflict motivated those who quickly suppressed the uprising.

The Language Question Since 1986

Indication of the potentially explosive ethnic dimension of the riots was seen in the number of efforts to assuage Kazakh ethnic sensitivities after the December events. Conferences were held on "international education" and on the teaching of Kazakh in the schools. As Ann Sheehy noted in her report on the "Conference on International Education in Alma-Ata" (*Radio Liberty Research Reports*, 30 April 1987), fewer than one percent of Russians living in Kazakhstan possessed good knowledge of Kazakh. Government-sponsored conferences addressing problems of multiculturalism focused upon inadequate Kazakh lan-

guage preparation by Russians. For Kazakhs, the problem was equally great. Even though Kazakh students were heavily represented in republican institutions of higher education, the language of instruction was invariably Russian. At primary education levels, out of the nearly 9,000 schools operating in the republic in 1987, fewer than 2,500 offered instruction in Kazakh. Kazakh was taught as a second language in another thousand schools. Of the approximately four million students in Kazakh schools, the number enrolled in institutions offering Kazakh (either as the language of instruction or as a second language) was estimated to be little more than one million. The ethnic character of the December 1986 uprising pointed to the inadequate training and support for study of the Kazakh language.

By mid-1987, although the Kazakh Communist Party was calling for the reassertion of Leninist principles of bilingualism, party leadership was falling behind the curve of public opinion. Pressure mounted to declare Kazakh the official language of the Kazakh Soviet Republic. Following the establishment of full Kazakhstan independence in 1991, the issue of language policy continued to be at the center of Kazakh political culture. Although the issue is still being debated, the new 1993 Kazakhstan constitution identifies Kazakh as the sole official language, while recognizing Russian as a language of communication between nationalities. (This latter provision was strongly criticized by Kazakh nationalists.) Russian continues to be used alongside Kazakh in most government communications.

Politics in Kazakhstan: The Limits of Democratization

As in other newly independent Central Asian states, the relative openness that accompanied the policies of perestroika and glasnost gave rise in Kazakhstan to informal public groups that served as agents of political and cultural change. Already by the end of 1988, some 300 informal groups had been formed. Although the participants were few at first, the number of freely organized informal groups grew steadily from that time forward.

Not all of these groups desired status as a political party; many attempted, instead, to highlight particular environmental, economic, or religious concerns. The Nevada-Semipalatinsk antinuclear movement, for example, became a prominent early environmental group. The goals of this movement included the cessation of nuclear testing, the responsible handling and disposal of radioactive materials, the conversion of military industry to environmentally responsible industry, and the closure of the Semipalatinsk nuclear test site. Founded in early 1989 and headed by the Kazakh writer, Olzhas Suleimenov, the Nevada-Semipalatinsk group began holding well-attended rallies as early as the fall of 1989.

Although the Nevada-Semipalatinsk movement has retained its following, some strictly political movements have been less successful in adjusting to Kazakhstan's shift from Soviet republic to independent state. Since the establishment of independence, even those political movements that initially found popular support have tended to be overshadowed, or sometimes closed, by the centralization of political authority in the executive office of the Kazakhstan president. The early loser in this politics of transition was the Kazakh Communist Party, which was initially outlawed after the August 1991 coup in Moscow. Other political parties, such as the Kazakh Free Party and the Social Democratic Party (the latter claiming to have followers from among all major ethnic groups of Kazakhstan), surfaced and initially gained strength. On the right, the nationalist Kazakh Alash Party, along with the Azat Movement and the Republican Party, capitalized upon the discrediting of the Communist Party, calling for a coalition government and a division of Communist Party assets. After independence, however, the ruling government in Kazakhstan became increasingly wary of informal political groups and oppositionist political parties. Since 1992, it has allowed only limited registration of formal opposition political parties (with submission of membership lists).

Kazakh politics today is a blend of the old and the new. Much of the old Party-appointed bureaucracy (the nomenklatura) remains, but political change has occurred at the upper levels of the Kazakhstan government. By mid-1989, two and a half years into his leadership of Kazakhstan, Party Secretary Genadii Kolbin had been transferred to a post in Moscow. The resulting vacancy at the head of the Kazakh Soviet Republic was filled by the Party election of Nursultan Nazarbaev as first secretary of the Kazakh Communist Party. Born in 1940, the relatively young Nazarbaev had worked his way through lower-level Communist Party posts, distinguishing himself both by his support of reform and by his outspoken opposition to government corruption. A firm supporter of perestroika, Nazarbaev had already risen to the chairmanship of the Kazakhstan Council of Ministers in 1984. His selection as Party leader brought reformist tendencies to the Kazakh Communist Party earlier than

they appeared in other parts of Central Asia. Nazarbaev's assumption of power in Kazakhstan also ended the brief period in which an ethnic Russian served as the foremost political leader of the republic.

After the abortive August 1991 coup attempt in Moscow, Kazakhstan followed the pattern of other former Soviet republics by declaring its own independence. Not lost upon local Kazakhs was the fact that the declaration of independence came on the 16th of December, 1991, exactly five years after the Alma-Ata riots. Since becoming president of the newly independent Kazakhstan, Nazarbaev has proven to be a resilient, independent political leader, despite his ascent to power through the Communist Party. In the fall of 1991, while he contributed to the dismantling of the old Kazakh Communist Party, he refused a post in the newly created socialist party. Nazarbaev argued that he must be president of "all the people." In that same vein, he has sought to rise above political squabbles. He took the lead in October 1991 in establishing a new superparty, the People's Congress of Kazakhstan. This independent People's Congress, headed by former parliamentary deputy and environmental activist Olzhas Suleimenov, now finds itself in opposition to the majority presidential parties identified with President Nazarbaev and his expansion of executive authority.

The consolidation of political power by Nazarbaev has been evident in a series of recent measures undertaken by the Kazakh president. After the March 1994 election and the fractious infighting of the Kazakh parliament that followed, Nazarbaev used a constitutional court ruling on election irregularities to invalidate the election. He then dismissed parliament and—ruling by executive decree in the absence of a legislative body—called for new elections and a national referendum to extend his term of office, originally slated to end in June 1996. The referendum, which passed with over 90 percent of the vote in his favor, extended Nazarbaev's term to the year 2000. In the aftermath of this referendum, Nazarbaev proposed a new constitution with an even greater centralization of power in the executive presidency.

The December 1995 parliamentary elections that followed yielded a predictable landslide for pro-presidential candidates. Opposition candidates complained of difficulties in filing for office. They faced exorbitant filing fees and, according to some, presidentially generated intimidation. In one widely reported incident, an ethnic Slav leader Nikolai Gunkin was arrested in October 1995 when he sought to register as a candidate.

Nazarbaev may not fit the Western model of a democratic leader concerned about the division of powers within government. He has created a weak parliament, with virtually all power assigned to the executive. Yet, Nazarbaev retains considerable popular appeal, drawing upon the support of civil servants, the military, and the police, as well as a broad spectrum of Slavic and Kazakh nationals, who see the president as the person most capable of directing the process of reform. Positioning himself above politics and subtly reminding his followers of the potential for disaster, as in the riots of 1986, Nazarbaev defends a multinational state, arguing that narrow ethnic chauvinism could lead to a situation in Kazakhstan worse than that in former Yugoslavia (see James Critchlow, "Kazakhstan: The Outlook for Ethnic Relations," *RFE/RL Research Report*, 31 January 1992).

The Recovery of Kazakh Identity

Among the cultural changes occurring in the past decade, perhaps the most revealing has been the drive for the recovery of Kazakh identity. The initial leader of this effort, as in the Nevada-Semipalatinsk movement, was the first secretary of the Kazakh Union of Writers, Olzhas Suleimenov. In early 1987, Suleimenov urged the rapid rehabilitation of two Kazakh literary figures who perished in the Soviet purges of the 1920s and 1930s, Maghjan Jumabaev and Shakerim Qudayberdiev (see Ann Sheehy, "Call for Rehabilitation of Two Kazakh Poets," *Radio Liberty Research*, 9 June 1987).

The drive to rehabilitate Maghjan (1896–1938) and Shakerim (who died in the 1930s) reflected a desire to reopen Kazakh religious and political issues that were systematically excluded from consideration during the Soviet period. The poet Maghjan's verses were patriotic in nature, appealing to the rich heritage of the Kazakhs, the Turks more generally, and the Kazakh homeland. For official Soviet ideology, Maghjan's literary output was unacceptable because of his leadership in the Alash Orda, the liberal nationalist movement that briefly came to power in Kazakh lands following the October Bolshevik Revolution of 1917. The Alash nationalist party proclaimed the autonomy of these lands in December 1917, and held out for Kazakh interests during the years of the wider Russian Civil War. By the time of the collapse of the Alash Orda, Maghjan's views had become ever more pan-Turkic, reflecting a not uncommon view (found also in the Basmachi movement) that the salvation of any one Turkic people rested in the unification of all Turkic peoples against the Bolshevik Revolution and against

Western innovations. For subsequent generations of Soviet writers, Maghjan was consigned to the number of those reactionary figures viewed as opponents of the liberating role of the Bolsheviks.

Shakerim Qudayberdiev, nephew of the founder of modern Kazakh literature (Abay Kunanbaev, 1845–1904), was a Kazakh intellectual of the early twentieth century who understood Russian thought and culture, but maintained a deeply religious, Islamic way of life. Alongside his *History of the Kazakh Clans,* he also published before World War I a religious treatise on *The Basic Tenets of Mohammedanism.* According to the traditional Soviet interpretation, Shakerim was viewed unfavorably as a reactionary religious mystic.

The effort to rehabilitate Maghjan Jumabaev and Shakerim Qudayberdiev (along with other writers discredited during the Soviet period) culminated in 1988 with their formal recognition. Republication of literary, political, and religious works from the early twentieth century is flourishing. The rehabilitation of these leading cultural and political figures from the early twentieth century has been central to the recovery of Kazakh identity. New publications of works by and about them have highlighted the hidden history of nationalist leaders from the era of the Alash Orda, an era that formally ended in 1920 with the abolition of the Alash party. The rehabilitations constitute, in the present context, a repudiation of Soviet (and, to some extent, Russian) influence upon Kazakh culture.

Equally important are the Islamic and pan-Turkic themes in the current reevaluation of the Kazakh past. The renewed popularity of Islamic writers of the early twentieth century, the recovery of Islamic religious identity, and the linkage of ethnic and religious themes in the popular consciousness are all parts of the larger reawakening of Kazakh ethnicity.

Economic and Environmental Problems

In the worst public violence since the December 1986 riots, thousands of Kazakhs demonstrated in the oil city of Novyi Uzen in June 1989. At least five people died in the conflict. A city of more than 50,000 inhabitants, Novyi Uzen was established in 1968 after discovery of oil in western Kazakhstan along the Caspian Sea. Set astride a desert steppe frontier, Novyi Uzen is one of the least inhabitable cities of the former Soviet Union. Recurring dust storms frequently make it necessary for drivers there to use headlights in the middle of the day. The development of the oil fields contributed to the overnight growth of this city that was established only for its industrial output and without regard to necessary urban infrastructure. Compounding the tensions within the city was the mixed ethnic population made up of both Kazakhs and workers from the Caucasus hired for jobs in the oil industry. The rush to cities such as Novyi Uzen also led to unemployment by the 1980s, for there were limits to the sudden oil boom.

When Kazakhs took to the streets in Novyi Uzen in June 1989, the fighting seemed to be directed at ethnic Lezghins from Dagestan, as well as against Chechen, Ingush, Ossetian, and other transplanted workers from the Caucasus region. As in the case of the Alma-Ata riots of 1986, however, the appearance of ethnic conflict covered deeper, underlying causes. The sudden growth of the oil economy had led to massive transfers of human population, without regard to satisfying basic needs such as housing, health care, education, transportation, and food. For central planners, the only goal was production, or industrial output. Similar problems have plagued the coal mining region of Qaraghandy (Karaganda).

Despite the disquieting events in Novyi Uzen, Kazakh government officials have continued to press for the development of the country's oil industry, Kazakh authorities recognize that development of the oil reserves offers a powerful inducement for foreign investment in the Kazakh economy. In turn, Russia has demonstrated its interest in maintaining a foothold in the Kazakh oil industry. At the center of the oil question are the Tengiz oil fields. These oil fields, located on the northeast coast of the Caspian Sea, contain a proven reserve of six billion barrels of crude oil. To develop such a potential, Kazakhstan must be able to market these petroleum resources. The Nazarbaev government has actively sought to reach international agreement on the construction of a major oil pipeline. Although there have been proposals for an extended pipeline reaching from Kazakhstan through China to the Pacific Ocean, the route decided on in 1996 for the pipeline will take it across the northern coast of the Caspian Sea to Russian port facilities to be built on the Black Sea.

Under a 1993 accord, the Chevron Corporation secured a $10 billion contract to develop the Tengiz oil fields, but progress on the development of these reserves has awaited the more protracted negotiations over construction of the oil pipeline. In April 1996, eight Western, Russian, and Kazakh oil companies agreed to form a consortium for construction of the pipeline, a project that is expected to cost $1.2 billion. Under terms of the agreement, Russia, Kazakhstan, and Oman will own approximately 50 percent of the consortium's interests. Notable for the size of its share in the venture was the Russian government's portion (24 percent), along with the participation of the larg-

est Russian oil company Lukoil (12.5 percent) and Russia's Rosneft (7.5 percent). Among the Western firms participating in the consortium will be Chevron (15 percent ownership), Mobil Oil (7.5 percent), British Gas (2 percent), and the Dallas-based Oryx Energy Company (1.75 percent); (see Michael R. Gordon, "New Pact for Kazakh-Russian Oil Pipeline," *New York Times*, 29 April 1996, A7).

While the presence of natural resources in Kazakhstan offers considerable promise and feeds the drive to secure Western investment, the reality is that the industrial and mining sectors of the Kazakh economy are fragile and prone to boom and bust cycles. The absence of infrastructure, especially the housing shortages that plague much of Central Asia, has added to labor unrest. High birth rates and rapid urbanization only aggravate the problems of poor infrastructure.

Equally troubling for Kazakhstan is its dependence upon external sources for consumer goods. Prior to declaring independence, Kazakhstan imported as much as 60 percent of its consumer products. Potentially capable of growing enough food, Kazakhstan continues to use scarce water resources for heavy irrigation and the cultivation of cotton. As a consequence, Kazakhstan shares with Uzbekistan the environmental nightmare of the depleted Aral Sea. While more diverse than the cotton monoculture of Uzbekistan, the Kazakh economy also exhibits the results of centrally planned Moscow decision making, in which unrealistic goals were often set for production and local self-sufficiency was sacrificed for agricultural mass production.

To its credit, Kazakhstan has moved aggressively in seeking Western capital investment. Despite exercising inordinate caution in implementation, the Kazakhstan government has also mapped out a privatization formula intended to divest the state of most of its assets and launch an effective market economy. Progress has been particularly noticeable in Almaty, where as much as 40 percent of the housing market has been sold or divested. Because of its delicate ethnic balance, however, the perils of economic failure are potentially very great for Kazakhstan. The social unrest that can accompany rises in unemployment, and the political disruptions that can attend the process of democratization, are daily concerns for the new government. Not unexpectedly, Nazarbaev has sought massive foreign credits to ease the transition to privatization.

Because of its ability to attract foreign investment, the prospects for the Kazakh economy are among the brightest in Central Asia. The new Kazakh currency, the tenge, was introduced in November 1993. Despite initial problems in handling money supply and overcoming runaway inflation—the inflation rate in 1994 was 1,250 percent before dropping to single digits in 1995—the tenge is now among the strongest currencies of Central Asia. Kazakh foreign trade, which initially was dominated by exports to Russia, is showing signs of substantial diversification. The prospects for economic development, however, must be matched against real shortages of basic foodstuffs, health supplies, and housing—shortages that continue to threaten the very fabric of society in Kazakhstan.

Finally, the environmental costs of production-oriented central planning remain present everywhere. The clean-up efforts needed to make the Semipalatinsk nuclear test site safe are far beyond the capacities of the Kazakh government. The Aral Sea disaster is every bit as serious for Kazakhstan as it is for Uzbekistan. Meanwhile, the costs of basic pollution control devices for cleaning smokestack industries and guaranteeing safe drinking water greatly exceed the government's ability to pay.

Strategic Importance of Kazakhstan

Western concerns for the stability of Kazakhstan are all the greater because of the country's considerable military and strategic capacity. Kazakhstan houses more than 100 enterprises from the military-industrial complex of the former Soviet Union. Among these are the nuclear weapons testing site of Semipalatinsk and the Baikonur Cosmodrome space center. Western concern has been most focused upon the strategic nuclear weapons sites located on Kazakh soil. At the time of its independence, Kazakhstan was, owing to its status within the former Soviet Union, one of the world's nuclear powers. Following extensive agreements with the United States and within the Commonwealth of Independent States, Kazakhstan has now demobilized its nuclear arsenal and brought these nuclear weapons sites under CIS military authority. Kazakhstan's willingness to accede to the terms of the Nuclear Non-Proliferation Treaty and its dismantling of its nuclear weapons sites have been accompanied by United States military aid for peacetime conversion of Kazakh military forces.

Maintaining a lengthy international border with the Xinjiang province of China, Kazakhstan has expanded the range of its economic ties to include China. Imports from China have dramatically increased since independence. More than one million Kazakhs reside in the Xinjiang-Uighur Autonomous Republic of China. The normalization of relations between Kazakhstan and China answers the concerns of both states over illegal border crossings.

Strategically situated between Russia and China, Kazakhstan is a country rich in natural resources and with a determined, if at times dictatorial, political leadership. Its unique, multi-ethnic population provides a resource for economic advancement, while also posing the potential for nationalistic reaction and political instability. Its mixed economy is the most robust of the Central Asian region, but its more urban, industrially advanced population could suffer the most serious reverses should the transition to a market economy be marked by high unemployment, massive Russian out-migration, unmet consumer needs (particularly in the area of housing), and chronic agricultural shortages.

KYRGYZSTAN

Statistical Profile

Demography

Population: 4,483,000

Ethnic population

Kyrgyz	52.4%
Russian	21.5%
Uzbek	12.9%
Ukrainian	2.5%
German	2.4%
Tatar	1.6%
Uighur	0.9%
Kazakh	0.9%
Tajik	0.8%
Other	4.1%

Major urban centers and populations

Bishkek (Frunze)	627,800
Osh	219,100
Przhevalsk	64,000
Naryn	26,000

Historic religious traditions

Islam	70.0%
Christianity	24.0%

Languages: Kyrgyz, Russian

Population by age

Age	Total	Males	Females
0–14	37%	18.7%	18.3%
15–64	57%	28.1%	28.9%
65 and over	6%	2.0%	4.0%

Male/Female ratio: 48.8% male/51.2% female

Rural/Urban population
64.9% rural/35.1% urban

Annual population growth rate: 0.5%

Population density: 58.5 persons per sq mi

Government

Official name
Kyrgyz Respublikasy (Republic of Kyrgyzstan)

Capital: Bishkek

Date of sovereignty/independence declaration
31 August 1991

Voting age: 18

Education

Literacy (age 15 and over who can read and write)

total population	97%
male	99%
female	96%

Level of education for persons over 15

completed higher education	9.4%
completed secondary education	56.4%
incomplete secondary education	18.4%

Number of higher education institutions: 9

Higher education enrollment: 63,900 students

Selected institutions of higher education (and enrollment)

Bishkek

State University	13,000
Agricultural Institute	4,500

Socioeconomic Indicators

Annual birth rate: 28.6 births/1,000 population

Fertility rate: 3.3 children/woman

Infant mortality: 29.1 deaths/1,000 live births

Average life expectancy
68.1 years (male 63.9, female 72.6)

Annual death rate: 7.2 deaths/1,000 population

Average family size: 4.7

Annual consumption of electrical energy
2,700 kWh/person

Hospital beds per 10,000 persons: 119.0

Physical Features

Area: 76,641 sq mi

Land use
cultivated 7%
pasture 42%

Highest elevation: 24,406 ft (Pobeda peak)

Rainfall: 30 in./yr

Temperature

Winter	Summer
lower elevations, average 23°F	lower elevations, average 75°F
higher elevations, average –18°F	higher elevations, average 41°F
lowest, –64.5°F	highest, 109.4°F

Economic Production

Estimated per capita GNP: $610 (1994)

Agricultural output
wool, tobacco, cotton, livestock, vegetables

Natural resources: coal, gold, uranium, mercury

Industrial output
machinery, textiles, metallurgy, food-processing products, cement, shoes, refrigerators, furniture

Currency
som (introduced May 1993), 1 som = 100 tyiyns

Communications

Length of rail lines: 211 mi

Length of highways: 13,900 mi

Pipelines
natural gas .... 120 mi

Telephones: 76 per 1,000 persons

Sources "Kirgizskaia sovetskaia sotsialisticheskaia respublika" *Bol'shaia sovetskaia entsiklopediia* (Moscow, 1977); *Narodnoe khoziaistvo SSSR v 1990g.* (Moscow, 1991); *Naselenie SSSR* (Moscow, 1989); Matthew J. Sagers, "News Notes. Iron and Steel," *Soviet Geography* 30 (May 1989): 397–434; Lee Schwartz, "USSR Nationality Redistribution by Republic, 1979–1989: From Published Results of the 1989 All-Union Census," *Soviet Geography* 32 (April 1991): 209–48; *World of Learning*, 46th ed. (London, 1996); "Russia . . ." (National Geographic Society Map, 1993); *Europa World Yearbook, 1996* (London, 1996); *Demograficheski ezhegodnik, 1995* (Moscow, 1995); "CIA World Factbook, 1995" (www.odci.gov/cia/publications/95fact/kg.html).

Kyrgyzstan

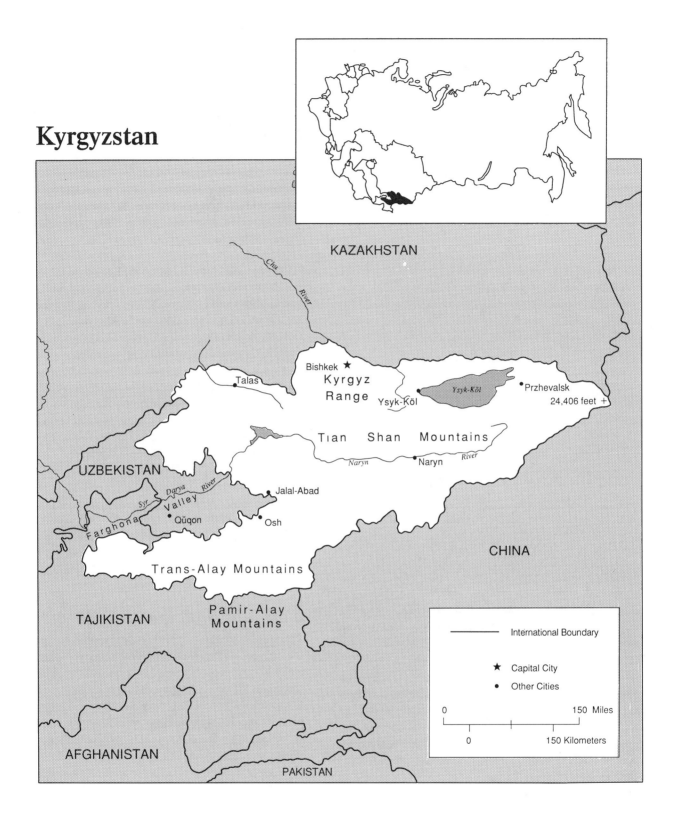

KAZAKHSTAN

Chu River

Bishkek ★

Talas

Kyrgyz Range

Ysyk-Köl

Ysyk-Köl

Przhevalsk

24,406 feet +

Tian Shan Mountains

Naryn

Naryn River

UZBEKISTAN

Jalal-Abad

Syr Darya River

Farghona Valley

Qŭqon

Osh

CHINA

Trans-Alay Mountains

Pamir-Alay Mountains

TAJIKISTAN

AFGHANISTAN

PAKISTAN

International Boundary

★ Capital City

● Other Cities

0   150 Miles

0   150 Kilometers

Kyrgyzstan: History and Description

Physical Description

Borders Kyrgyzstan (previously identified in English as Kirgizia or Kirghizstan) is located in the eastern part of Central Asia. A highly mountainous country, Kyrgyzstan shares its borders with three other newly independent, former Soviet republics—Tajikistan to the south, Uzbekistan to the west, and Kazakhstan to the northwest and north. On the eastern frontier, across a lengthy series of frozen peaks, lies China. Kyrgyzstan's oddly contorted western boundary, established during the Soviet period, allows this country of steep and forbidding heights to share a part of the fertile Farghona (Fergana) Valley. Other parts of this ancient irrigated valley belong to Tajikistan and Uzbekistan. The capital of Kyrgyzstan, Bishkek (formerly Frunze), was once the nineteenth-century Russian military fortress of Pishpek. In the Soviet period the capital was renamed Frunze after the Russian general Mikhail Frunze, who was born in the city and served in the region through the period of the 1917 Russian Revolution. In 1991, the name Bishkek was restored.

Kyrgyzstan is composed of several distinct natural regions. These include the irrigated Chu River valley in the north, where Bishkek is situated; the extremely mountainous area in the northeast around the large natural lake Ysyk-Köl; another mountainous area along the Naryn River in central Kyrgyzstan; the Kyrgyz portion of the Farghona Valley (from the ancient silk center of Osh in the south to Jalal-Abad in the north); and the more isolated Talas river valley in the northwest, separated from the rest of Kyrgyzstan by high mountains.

Mountains Two major mountain ranges, the Tian Shan and the Pamir-Alay systems, form the contours of Kyrgyzstan, unfolding along a generally east-west axis. In the north, the Kyrgyz Range, a spur of the Tian Shan Mountains, looms over Bishkek. To the east, on the other side of Ysyk-Köl, near the Chinese border, is the highest point in Kyrgyzstan, Pobeda (Victory) Peak, towering 24,406 feet. Southern and western Kyrgyzstan are occupied by the Trans-Alay Mountains. They constitute the northernmost part of the Pamir-Alay mountain system extending from Tajikistan.

Rivers The river systems of mountainous Kyrgyzstan provide enough hydroelectric power to make Kyrgyzstan an exporter of electricity. The longest and

most important river, the Naryn, originates in the Tian Shan mountains and flows in a southwesterly direction through Kyrgyzstan, eventually joining with other rivers to form the Syr Darya, a major river that brings water to the heavily irrigated Farghona Valley before continuing to the Aral Sea far to the west. Other notable rivers in Kyrgyzstan are the Chu and Talas in the north. In addition to these rivers, Kyrgyzstan has 3,000 lakes, including Ysyk-Köl.

Climate The climate of Kyrgyzstan depends very much on the altitude. From the ice and snow of its high peaks to the relatively moderate temperatures of its mountain valleys and lowland areas, great variation in temperature exists. Such variation has led to the widely practiced tradition known as transhumance, in which herders take their animals to cool summer pastures high in the mountains and then return them to warmer valleys in the winter.

Economic Resources The economy of Kyrgyzstan is largely based on energy sources: hydroelectric power, coal deposits, and some reserves of oil. Since World War II, it also has exploited a rich supply of mercury and antimony. The country's main agricultural crops are cotton, sugar beets, and grains. Livestock breeding is extremely important in mountainous areas. Sheep, pigs, cattle, and the traditional small Kyrgyz horse play a vital role in the economy.

Ethnic and Historical Background

The ethnic origin of the Kyrgyz people has become the subject of much debate. One theory suggests that early Kyrgyz peoples inhabited an area in Siberia near the upper Enisei River. A nomadic people, these Kyrgyz eventually made their way southwestward toward present-day Kyrgyzstan. By the sixteenth century, they were trading with other Turkic peoples of the region while continuing to raise and herd livestock. The Kyrgyz language is Turkic, belonging to the Nogai subdivision of Kypchak Turkic, a non–Indo-European tongue related to Kazakh. A literary Kyrgyz language was established during the Soviet period, based primarily on dialects spoken in the northern part of Kyrgyzstan. The territory now occupied by the Kyrgyz was long fought over by competing Turkic and Mongol warlords before the early nineteenth century, when the Kyrgyz were subjugated by the powerful ruling khanate at Kokand (Qŭqon, now in Uzbekistan). During the years of vassalage to the Kokand state, the Islamization already accomplished in the southern part of Kyrgyz lands in the previous century spread northward. Today, most ethnic Kyrgyz profess the moderate Sunni form of Islam, although some elements of the more fundamentalist, mystic Sufi form are found in the southern regions of Kyrgyzstan, particularly at Osh, a popular destination of Muslim pilgrimages.

Russian Conquest

Russian influence in Kyrgyzstan, the result of ongoing nineteenth-century tsarist campaigns in Central Asia, began in 1862 with the capture of the fortress at Pishpek (Bishkek) from the Kokand Khanate. Soviet historians have maintained that some Kyrgyz clan leaders had already sought Russian protection against Turkic enemies much earlier in the century. The surrender of Pishpek led eventually to the complete defeat of Kokand in 1876. At that point, the Kokand Khanate and all the lands it controlled became a protectorate of tsarist Russia. The colonization of Kyrgyz lands by Slavic peoples then began in earnest as tens of thousands of Russian and Ukrainian settlers emigrated from the European part of the Russian Empire to start farms, thereby carrying out the central government's Russification policies. An inevitable result of this great land rush was the loss of the best farmland to the influx of Slavic newcomers and an accompanying reduction in the pastureland available for Kyrgyz livestock.

In 1916, as tsarist armies struggled during World War I to conduct successful military operations against the Germans, the government in Petrograd issued an order for mobilization of the Muslim peoples of Russian Turkestan (the administrative term for Central Asia). The indigenous Central Asian peoples, already overtaxed by wartime demands for the provision of both military and civilian supplies, and long resentful of their treatment under tsarist colonialism, refused to cooperate. Revolts against the mobilization order soon erupted throughout the Muslim territories, most of which had not been fully integrated into the Russian Empire. Thousands of people were massacred on both sides as the widespread rebellion was put down mercilessly by the Russian authorities. In Kyrgyzstan alone more than 2,000 European settlers perished and an uncounted number of Kyrgyz fell. An estimated 300,000 Central Asians fled into the eastern mountains or across the border into China. As many as half of them were ethnic Kyrgyz.

Soviet Rule

Following World War I, the Kyrgyz slowly returned to their lands, where the Revolution and the Bolshevik assumption of power may have seemed far removed from local problems. The Bolsheviks, however, in spite of promises of national sovereignty for the Muslims of Central Asia, were determined to rule this remote part of the former tsarist empire. In 1918, after taking control of the greater part of Russian Turkestan and proclaiming it the Turkestan Soviet Republic, the Bolsheviks declared victory in Central Asia. The victory soon proved temporary as opponents of the new government rallied to defeat it. Nevertheless, the Red Army eventually prevailed, and Moscow launched a series of political and economic policies that ultimately led to repression, anarchy, hardship, and deprivation for the Kyrgyz and other peoples of Central Asia.

Early Years of Communist Rule The Kyrgyz found themselves confronted by a different and potentially more threatening way of life than any inflicted on them by previous conquerors. Lenin's new government promulgated a program of atheism, the emancipation of women, and communal land ownership, breaking longstanding tribal landholding patterns. These new policies, countering nearly all the religious and cultural traditions of the Kyrgyz peoples, prompted yet more revolts. The Basmachi movement, made up of armed Muslim rebels, cooperated with other enemies of the Bolsheviks and fought a long guerrilla war against Red Army soldiers throughout the 1920s.

During this time, amidst bitter Kyrgyz opposition to much of the Communist political program being imposed by outsiders from Moscow, the new Soviet authorities were continuing to reorganize the territories within the newly named Turkestan Soviet Republic. The Soviet government distinguished amongst the various ethnic groups of the region by identifying the Kyrgyz as the Kara Kyrgyz, while the Kazakhs to the north were identified as the Kyrgyz. Not until well into the Soviet period were the labels changed. Finally, as part of the 1924 national delimitation policy—that is, the assignment of specific territories to particular ethnic groups or nations—Kyrgyzstan was designated an autonomous oblast within the greater Russian Republic (RSFSR). Meanwhile the Kazakhs found their homeland renamed the Kazakh Autonomous Republic, also administratively assigned to the RSFSR.

Limited political participation by a developing Kyrgyz intelligentsia was allowed, and some traditional social patterns returned. The Russian language, however, was made the official means of communication for administrative, governmental, and economic activities. Russians also held most positions of power in the political hierarchy of Kyrgyzstan. In 1926, Kyrgyzstan was promoted from "autonomous oblast" to "autonomous republic," but it remained within the Russian Republic.

The Rule of Stalin The Stalinist years brought renewed attempts to implement the Communist policy of collectivization, in which privately held lands were redistributed into large shared agricultural units run by elected or appointed officials. Collectivization elicited such strong opposition from the Kyrgyz peasant population that the Basmachi rebels increased their opposition efforts. The very idea of collectivization in a place where, for centuries, the inhabitants had held land in common on the basis of family and kinship ties seemed to serve no socialist purpose other than external control from Moscow. Indeed, Stalin's objective was to abolish the nomadic tradition in Kyrgyz life. As he ruthlessly attempted to eradicate this basic pattern of the Kyrgyz economy, Kyrgyz herders responded by taking their livestock far into the mountains, even into China. Nevertheless, by the middle of the 1930s, the Communists prevailed and the majority of Kyrgyz were resettled on collective farms.

During the 1930s, Stalin's intrusive policies not only sought to destroy the traditional pastoral way of life in Central Asia, but also to stamp out any Kyrgyz national movement. In this effort, Stalin eliminated the few independent Kyrgyz voices that had developed. The purges of the interwar period decimated the fledgling Kyrgyz native intelligentsia and any others who expressed ideas that could be construed as a threat to the new order. Not only high Party officials, including

three first secretaries of the Communist Party, but literary figures, writers, and poets, as well, were arrested and either sent to prison camps or executed. Ironically, in the midst of such horrors, Kyrgyzstan was elevated to full union republic status in 1936 under terms of the new Stalin constitution.

The advent of World War II once again brought mobilization orders for Central Asians. Well over a million were drafted. Little is known of their actual participation, but rumors have persisted that many deserted to the German side or worked with a group sympathetic to German war aims called the Turkestan National Committee.

Postwar Period The postwar period brought change to Kyrgyzstan. In 1950, Ishak Razzakov became first secretary of the Communist Party, replacing A. Rysmendiev who had served in this post during and after the war. The political relaxation that occurred after Stalin's death in 1953 included modest, if on the whole unsuccessful, attempts by the Kyrgyz to introduce cultural changes. These changes were largely undermined by local Russian bureaucrats who held the real power in Kyrgyzstan. One of the few new measures allowed was the teaching of Kyrgyz history in local schools. Razzakov, viewed perhaps as too supportive of these signs of Kyrgyz national life, was removed from office in 1961. Turdakun Usubaliev was chosen to replace him and occupied the main leadership post of the Party and government until 1985 when Mikhail Gorbachev oversaw the appointment of Absamat Masaliev as first secretary of the Communist Party of Soviet Kirgizia.

Kyrgyzstan: Contemporary Issues

Demographic and Economic Realities of Kyrgyzstan

After the establishment of the Soviet republics of Central Asia in 1936, ethnic Russians migrated to that region in unprecedented numbers. By a quarter-century later, in the 1960s, the Russian population in Soviet Kirgizia (Kyrgyzstan) had grown by 500 percent. More than a million Russians and Ukrainians, roughly one-quarter of the republic's total population, were living in Kyrgyzstan by the time of the 1979 census. The Russian migration into Kyrgyzstan did not affect all parts of the republic equally; rather, the urban centers,

particularly Frunze (Bishkek) and the surrounding area, became disproportionately Russified. From the 1930s on, Frunze became transformed into a predominantly Russian city.

As a consequence of the Russian urban settlement in Kyrgyzstan, much of the technical, industrial, and administrative leadership of the Kyrgyz republic became Russian. Within the capital city of Frunze, a Slavic elite (constituting, at its peak, more than two-thirds of the city's population) tended to perpetuate itself by dominating scientific and technical training institutes. Thus, even though ethnic Kyrgyz have, of late, been encouraged to prepare for jobs in the industrial sector, Kyrgyz students throughout the 1980s represented no more than one-fifth of those attending vocational-technical schools in the republic. This underrepresentation of Kyrgyz in the professions reflected the demographic realities of urban Kyrgyzstan. The Kyrgyz population in Frunze, despite its growth in absolute numbers, remained under 20 percent of the total city population throughout the 1980s. Part of the problem confronting the Kyrgyz urban population has been the lack of affordable housing.

The great majority of ethnic Kyrgyz have continued to reside outside their country's urban centers in the fertile valleys and more mountainous grazing regions of the republic. Although the cotton monoculture found in other Central Asian states has come to dominate the republic's valleys, there are many Kyrgyz who raise livestock, especially sheep, in the mountain foothills. Kyrgyz lands also contain considerable untapped mineral wealth in the less accessible mountainous regions. Together with Uzbekistan and Tajikistan, Kyrgyzstan shares a portion of the fertile Farghona Valley where rapid growth rates have brought the typical problems associated with rural overpopulation. For Kyrgyzstan, these problems include not just rural poverty and unemployment, but overgrazing and ever more intensive irrigation to accommodate the needs of cotton.

To address the problems of rural poverty and unemployment, Kyrgyzstan has embarked on the most ambitious program of economic restructuring anywhere in Central Asia. It was the first country in Central Asia to introduce its own national currency. The Kyrgyz som was launched in May 1993, backed by $62 million in credits from the International Monetary Fund. Inflation has been under control in Kyrgyzstan since the end of 1994, and the country is registering a positive growth in domestic production. Building upon its favorable image abroad, Kyrgyzstan has secured three times more investment and foreign aid per capita than any other republic of the former Soviet Union.

Still, the relative strength of the Kyrgyzstan economy has not been evenly felt. The contrast between the more impoverished rural Kyrgyz and the industrialized Russian elite of newly renamed Bishkek has not been lost upon contemporary Kyrgyz politicians, writers, and intellectuals. Dating from the greater openness or glasnost of the Gorbachev era, Kyrgyz writers began in the 1980s to address a number of national concerns relating to Russian cultural dominance in Bishkek.

Language Issue

Prominent among these national issues was that of school instruction in the Kyrgyz language. Chingiz Aitmatov, the internationally noted Kyrgyz writer who was elected chair of the Kyrgyz Union of Writers in 1986, launched a campaign for the establishment of urban Kyrgyz-language schools, particularly kindergartens. Despite the more than 100,000 Kyrgyz living in Bishkek, there was only one Kyrgyz-language high school (operating in three shifts) throughout the 1980s. In a debate enjoined against his Kyrgyz ideological opponent, Aaly Tokombaev (1904–1988), a staunch advocate of Russification, Aitmatov noted that not one kindergarten using Kyrgyz as the primary language of instruction was to be found in any of the larger urban centers, including Bishkek. Moreover, most Russian-language schools that formerly taught Kyrgyz had abandoned such instruction in the 1950s. So dominant had Russian become in Bishkek by the 1980s that most commentators noted two parallel problems of communication. Rural Kyrgyz lacked the knowledge of Russian necessary for succeeding in urban society, and urban Kyrgyz lacked a firm grasp of their own native language. Almost half of the Kyrgyz children in Bishkek were not studying their native language in the 1980s. The problem of Kyrgyz language instruction has begun to be addressed, and new Kyrgyz schools have been opened following the declaration of national independence in August 1991. Today, Kyrgyz is the official language of the republic, although Russian continues to be employed in some official government and trade matters.

Meanwhile, the democratizing leadership of Kyrgyzstan President Askar Akaev has exercised caution. The continuing importance of Russian and Ukrainian nationals for Kyrgyzstan's industrial and technical development has prompted him and other Kyrgyz leaders to cultivate the support of the Slavic population of Bishkek, who have been leaving Central Asia in record numbers. One example of this support for the local Russian population was President Akaev's 1991 veto of a potentially offensive article in the new land law. Akaev noted that the article in question stated, "the land is the property of the Kyrgyz people," and he asked that this law be amended to say that "the land is the property of Kyrgyz citizens and all other nationalities making up the republic's people" ("Kirgiz President Vetoes Land Law," *Report on the USSR* 3, no. 25, 12 June 1991, 34). It remains to be seen whether mandatory Kyrgyz language instruction in the schools can be instituted without a backlash of opposition from the country's urban Slavs.

Related to Kyrgyz language instruction is the concern voiced openly after 1985 for reform of the Kyrgyz language itself. Proponents of language reform argued that use of the Cyrillic (Russian) alphabet—a change introduced in 1940—violated traditional Kyrgyz sounds. One example was the use of the Cyrillic "k" to render both "k" and "q" sounds, which are distinct and different in traditional Kyrgyz. The elimination of such letters and sounds from the Kyrgyz language was unacceptable to those voicing concern for traditional Kyrgyz.

Although the adoption of the Cyrillic alphabet in 1940 may have made access to modern Russian easier for ethnic Kyrgyz, this benefit was at a cost. The use of a confining Cyrillic alphabet tended to obscure the fundamental similarities among the Turkic languages of Central Asia—Kazakh, Tatar, Uzbek, Kyrgyz, and others. Proponents of linguistic reform noted that it should not be necessary to translate Kazakh or Uzbek into Kyrgyz, yet the peculiarities of the new orthographic system exaggerated the differences between these Turkic languages, making them less accessible to one another in written form.

Environmental Concerns

Part of the rediscovery of Kyrgyz ethnic identity has also involved campaigns for the preservation of the fragile ecology of the republic. This concern for the Kyrgyz environment has been seen in the formation of, among other groups, the Ysyk-Köl Rescue Committee, a voluntary organization dedicated to the preservation of the largest inland body of fresh water in Kyrgyzstan. Attributing the deterioration and diversion of Kyrgyz water resources to the excessive demands of the cotton monoculture, the Rescue Committee has sought to rejuvenate the depleted Ysyk-Köl before it reaches the level of ecological disaster associated with the Aral Sea in Uzbekistan. One solution to the problem, proposed by the writer Chingiz Aitmatov, has been to divert mountain rivers so that they flow into Ysyk-Köl. As in other areas of water conservation, however, such a water diversion project would have major ramifications for downstream users, many of whom would be in Kazakhstan. As in other parts of Central Asia, the critical ecological issue of water conservation inevitably fuels economic, interethnic, and interstate conflicts.

National Origin

Alongside their campaigns for Kyrgyz language instruction and ecological awareness, the Kyrgyz intelligentsia of the 1980s reopened the thorny question of Kyrgyz national origins. According to the position set forth by Kyrgyz Communist Party First Secretary Turdakun Usubaliev, who held that post from 1961 to 1985, the Kyrgyz people have their origins in the Tian Shan mountain region of the current republic. Yet, such a view has tended to foreclose discussion of the much earlier and more prominent ancient Kyrgyz sites found further east and north in the Enisei River region. Kyrgyz epic poetry includes reference to this more easterly ethnogenesis, but Usubaliev placed restrictions upon publication of such epic poetry during his neo-Stalinist rule. For many Kyrgyz intellectuals, the ability to raise openly these broader questions of origin has become crucial for national self-understanding, as well as for wider communication with other Turkic peoples and ethnic Kyrgyz living outside Kyrgyzstan, including those in the Xinjiang province of China.

The focal point of this renewed identification with, and reinvention of, the Kyrgyz past has been the reissuance of new editions and translations of the great epic poem of Kyrgyzstan, *Manas*. The epic, consisting of some 250,000 verses (20 times longer than the *Odyssey* and *Iliad* combined), features the great warrior Manas. According to the epic, when Kyrgyz tribes some 1,000 years ago were caught in the great Eurasian steppe between rival Arab and Chinese powers, Manas succeeded in unifying these tribes and enabled them to establish a Muslim Kyrgyz state. The subsequent death of Manas in battle led to civil war and destruction of this unified state. The epic tale remains of central importance for access to early Kyrgyz culture. Prior to its initial publication in the nineteenth century, the epic was preserved by the so-called *Manaschis*, narrators who carried on and reworked the oral tradition. Today, as in the August 1995 events declared to mark the millennium of the epic, Manas is being effectively recast as an indigenous national hero for Kyrgyz seeking to build their own nation in the aftermath of Soviet rule.

Chingiz Aitmatov

The reopening of a Kyrgyz national agenda in the 1980s can be credited in great part to the remarkable leadership provided by the Kyrgyz intelligentsia. This intelligentsia, both in its ties with the past and in its prospects for the future, is epitomized by Chingiz Aitmatov, former chair of the Kyrgyz Union of Writers. Aitmatov is a writer of internationally recognized talent who is fully bilingual, writing in both Kyrgyz and Russian. Born in 1928 in a Kyrgyz mountain village, his early schooling was limited, even though he would later graduate from the Moscow Institute of Literature. At the age of 14, during World War II, he became a tax collector and secretary of the local village council. His first published article in 1952, "On the Terminology of the Kyrgyz Language," argued that the evolution of modern Kyrgyz had benefited by its borrowings from modern Russian.

Aitmatov's 1958 short story, "Jamilia," propelled him to international attention. It contained an explosive plot line depicting a young Kyrgyz woman rejecting the norms of her society by leaving her arranged marriage and running off with her true love. Aitmatov quickly advanced in the official Soviet intellectual establishment, serving on literary boards in Moscow and in the Kirgiz Soviet Socialist Republic. He became the head of the local cinematographers' union, and also served as correspondent for *Pravda* in Central Asia. His subsequent works of fiction, including the anti-Stalinist piece, *The Executioner's Block* (*Plakha*), and a novel set in Kazakhstan, *The Day Lasts More Than a Hundred Years*, reached wide audiences both inside the Soviet Union and beyond. Aitmatov's prose, which often depicts the values and traditions of his native Central Asia, has occasionally been compared to that of the Russian "village prose" writers who exhibit a nostalgia for traditional values and an environment free from the threat of an urban, industrial society.

Chingiz Aitmatov's leadership in Kyrgyz cultural issues of the 1980s was indicative of the wider importance of the intelligentsia in reshaping the Kyrgyz national agenda. Despite his prominent position in the official Soviet literary establishment, Aitmatov led the struggle for Kyrgyz instruction in schools, for language reform, and for the rediscovery of Kyrgyz historical memory, particularly in the matter of Kyrgyz ethnic origins. In the person of Aitmatov it is possible to note how the Soviet experience came both to mold the Kyrgyz intelligentsia, and at the same time to galvanize it in the 1980s against mindless Russification.

Ethnic Disturbances

While the reshaping of the Kyrgyz national agenda has been set against the context of Soviet Russian influence in the capital of Bishkek, the most serious outbreak of ethnic hostilities began not in the more Russified capital of the republic, but in the Farghona Valley, a region of contested Kyrgyz and Uzbek influence.

The worst outbreak occurred in the city of Osh in June 1990. The spark that ignited the violence appears to have been associated with the allocation to ethnic Kyrgyz of housing lots in the suburbs of Osh, a region dominated by Uzbeks. Thousands of Uzbeks gathered in the disputed region, along with hundreds of Kyrgyz. The dispute boiled over into the city of Osh itself, where the violence erupted. While the Uzbek population constitutes only about one-third of the Osh oblast, the city of Osh has a strong Uzbek majority. The violence in Osh also spread to other regions of Kyrgyzstan, with the ethnic Kyrgyz of Bishkek and elsewhere seeking to aid their fellow Kyrgyz nationals in Osh. In the end, over 230 were killed in the violence, with several hundred more listed as missing. Soviet Interior Ministry troops were dispatched to the region, and flights between the capital cities of Uzbekistan and Kyrgyzstan were temporarily suspended. What the Osh uprising demonstrated was the potential for out-of-control ethnic scapegoating and violence in the economically depressed areas of Central Asia. In the Osh oblast (that portion of the Farghona Valley located in Kyrgyzstan), more than 100,000 people were unemployed in 1990—figures that may well have worsened since then. Indeed, 60 percent of all unemployment in Kyrgyzstan was concentrated in this one region. The contending interests of divergent Turkic nations of the Farghona Valley ultimately meant that a conflict over economic resources—in this case, housing—could explode into a major interethnic calamity.

Prospects for Democracy in Kyrgyzstan

The events in Osh contributed to the strengthening of informal political groups already established in Kyrgyzstan. Most notable was the rise of an informal democratic opposition that labeled itself Kyrgyzstan (at a time when the Soviet republic was still called Kirgizia). Following the June 1990 violence in the Farghona Valley, representatives of the Kyrgyzstan group arranged for a joint meeting with their democratic counterparts in the Uzbek national front, Birlik. This meeting, held in Bishkek, sought to advance the common democratic goals of the two organizations, while at the same time helping to defuse interethnic Turkic confrontation. Adding his own voice to the call for ethnic peace was Chingiz Aitmatov who, in an appeal to the Kyrgyz and Uzbek nations, invoked the language of pan-Turkic identity:

> There is unemployment; there is an evil called monoculture; there is homelessness. But, we should never forget one thing: we are fraternal nations. Our roots are the same, they are joined in one Turkish family. . . . Now I am appealing to the Kyrgyz people not to show force toward our Uzbek brothers in the southern part of our republic. In fact, if a Kyrgyz raises his hand against the Uzbek people, he raises it against his

own people. ("Chingiz Aitmatov's Appeal to the Kirgiz and Uzbek Peoples," *Report on the USSR* 2, no. 24, 15 June 1990, 18–19)

The ruling Kyrgyz head of state and first secretary of the Kyrgyz Communist Party from 1985 to 1990, Absamat Masaliev, a lukewarm supporter of Gorbachev's perestroika who identified with more hard-line Moscow Communist Party leaders such as Egor Ligachev, steadfastly opposed the informal political movements. Well into 1990, despite the rising clamor of public demonstrations and hunger strikes, Masaliev forbade the public meetings of the democratic group called Kyrgyzstan. Still, the public outcry for alleviation of housing shortages, the prospects for wider ethnic violence, the mounting ecological concerns, and the rigidity of the Masaliev government fueled the movement for political democracy.

Facing ever greater public criticism of his rule, Masaliev, in what was clearly a major miscalculation, decided in October 1990 to create for himself a new executive presidency. Fully expecting to be confirmed in this position by the republic's legislative body, the Kirgiz Supreme Soviet, Masaliev received less than the required majority. In the next round of balloting, held on 27 October 1990, the liberal president of the Kirgiz Academy of Sciences, Askar Akaev, was elected with the support of a coalition of democratic forces in the Supreme Soviet.

Akaev proceeded to turn the office of the executive president into an active force for economic privatization and democratization, and Masaliev resigned from the chairmanship of the Supreme Soviet (remaining head of the republic's Communist Party). Although Akaev, a specialist in quantum optics, had become a Communist Party member in 1981, he quickly moved to establish his democratic credentials. He legalized the movement for democratic renewal, replaced the minister of the interior with a popular leader of that renewal movement, Felix Kulov, established a new cabinet of ministers free from Communist Party control, and advocated concrete measures for economic liberalization and privatization. Many came to see Askar Akaev as leader of a Kyrgyz island of democracy in a sea of authoritarian, dictatorial rulers in Central Asia.

Akaev was born in 1944 in the Kirgiz Soviet Republic. He graduated from the Leningrad Institute of Precision Mechanics and Optics. Returning to Frunze, he became a faculty member in the Polytechnic Institute, ultimately rising to a department head there. In 1981 he joined the Communist Party and served a year as head of the Central Committee's Department of Scientific and Educational Institutions. In 1989, after

two years as vice president, he was elected president of the Kirgiz Academy of Sciences.

The pace of change inaugurated by Akaev was a surprise to most outside observers. By February 1991, the Kyrgyz capital city of Frunze had been legally renamed Bishkek, the democratic movement known as Kyrgyzstan had held its first formal congress attended by 600 delegates, and efforts were underway to re-establish close ties with each of the neighboring Central Asian republics. This transformation of Kyrgyzstan, even before its formal declaration of independence in August 1991, has come to be called the Silk Revolution, a clear reference to the non-violent Czechoslovak Velvet Revolution of 1989. One mark of Akaev's commitment to democratization was his immediate call for the overthrow of those who plotted the Moscow coup in August 1991. Following the coup attempt, Akaev orchestrated a declaration of state independence by the country's Supreme Soviet, a declaration made on the 31st of August. State elections on October 12th, in which 90 percent of the electorate participated, yielded him a resounding 95 percent vote of confidence.

While Akaev is widely perceived to be the most effective democratic leader in the new politics of Central Asia, he is not without potential opponents. On one side are the forces of the old Communist order that continue to exercise a strong presence within the nomenklatura, the political appointees dating from before Akaev's tenure as president. On the other side are those nationalists, including some of the forces for democratic renewal, whose ethnic Kyrgyz agenda could pose threats to interethnic harmony.

Most recently, political opposition to Akaev has focused upon the president's support for a parliamentary decision to schedule early presidential elections in December 1995, one year ahead of schedule. The call for early presidential elections came on the heels of Akaev's September 1994 decision to dissolve the Kyrgyzstan parliament and call for new parliamentary elections. Although Akaev's ostensible reason for dissolving parliament was his charge that it was opposing the pace of reform needed for the advancement of the country, the subsequent parliamentary elections in the spring of 1995 were tarnished by procedural violations. Akaev's opponents have argued, not without some justification, that the early presidential elections also involved shortcuts around the democratic Kyrgyzstan constitution of 1993 that limit the president to two terms in office. Moreover, faced with having to secure valid petitions to run for the office, several of the potential opposition candidates were unable to qualify for the ballot.

Despite the claim of his opponents that Akaev is ruling by more authoritarian means, the Kyrgyz president has maintained his base of support, especially in the Farghona Valley where rioting occurred in 1990. In the December 1995 voting, Akaev received over 71 percent of the vote, with the former Communist Party First Secretary Absamat Masaliev receiving just over 24 percent. Akaev now works with a largely supportive bicameral parliament and a constitution that, as amended by referendum, gives increasingly wide latitude to his own executive authority.

The experiment of Kyrgyzstan in political democracy is being watched closely by Western powers and neighboring Asian states. United States secretaries of state James Baker and Warren Christopher have made visits to Kyrgyzstan the focus of their respective trips to Central Asia. In 1993, United States Vice President Al Gore called Kyrgyzstan the "bulwark of democracy in the region." Neighboring Turkic states, as well as Tajikistan and Iran, have established formal ties with Kyrgyzstan, as has the People's Republic of China. The problems of ethnic conflict and economic restructuring are daunting, however, no less so because of the continuing exodus of Slavic population from Bishkek.

TAJIKISTAN

Statistical Profile

Demography

Population: 5,786,000

Ethnic population

Tajik	64.9%
Uzbek	25.0%
Russian	3.5%
Other	6.6%

Major urban centers and populations

Dushanbe	602,000
Khujand (formerly Leninabad)	163,000
Khorugh	<100,000
Murgab	<100,000
Kŭlob	<100,000
Qŭrghonteppa (Kurgan-Tiube)	<100,000
Nurek	<100,000
Kalaikhum	<100,000

Historic religious traditions

Islam	90.8%
Christianity	9.0%

Languages: Tajik, Russian

Population by age

Age	Total	Males	Females
0–14	43.0%	21.8%	21.2%
15–64	52.5%	26.3%	26.2%
65 and over	4.5%	1.9%	2.6%

Male/Female ratio: 50% male/50% female

Rural/Urban population: 71.9% rural/28.1% urban

Annual population growth rate: 1.4%

Population density: 104.7 persons per sq mi

Government

Official name

Jumhurii Tojikistan (Republic of Tajikistan)

Capital: Dushanbe

Date of sovereignty/independence declaration
9 September 1991

Voting age: 18

Internal region	**Capital**
Badakhshoni Kŭhi (Gorno-Badakhshan)	Khorugh

Education

Literacy (age 15 and over who can read and write)

total population	98%
male	99%
female	97%

Level of education for persons over 15

completed higher education	7.5%
completed secondary education	55.1%
incomplete secondary education	21.1%

Number of higher education institutions: 10

Higher education enrollment: 68,800 students

Selected institutions of higher education and enrollment

Dushanbe

State University	10,000
Agricultural University	5,380

Socioeconomic Indicators

Annual birth rate: 33.1 births/1,000 population

Fertility rate: 4.5 children/woman

Infant mortality: 40.6 deaths/1,000 live births

Average life expectancy
69 years (male 66.1, female 72.1)

Annual death rate: 8.7 deaths/1,000 population

Average family size: 6.1

Annual consumption of electrical energy
2,800 kWh/person

Hospital beds per 10,000 persons: 105.8

Physical Features

Area: 55,251 sq mi

Land use
cultivated 6%
pasture 23%

Highest elevation
24,590 ft (Kommunizm Peak, in the Pamir Range)

Rainfall
up to 63 in./yr in the mountains, 6 in./yr elsewhere

Temperature

Winter	Summer
southeast, average	southeast, average
28°F–36°F	86°F
north, average –4°F	north, average 32°F
lowest, –81°F	highest, 118°F

Economic Production

Estimated per capita GNP: $350 (1994)

Agricultural output
cotton, livestock, grain, fruits, vegetables

Natural resources
hydroelectric power, petroleum, uranium, mercury, brown coal, lead, zinc, tungsten, tin, antimony

Industrial output
metallurgy, chemicals, fertilizers, cement, vegetable oil, machine tools, refrigerators, freezers

Currency
Tajik ruble or somon (introduced 1995)
1 ruble (or 1 somon) = 100 kopeks

Communications

Length of rail lines: 298 mi

Length of highways: 12,200 mi

Pipelines
natural gas ....250 mi

Telephones: 55 per 1,000 persons

Sources "Tadzhikskaia sovetskaia sotsialisticheskaia respublika" *Bol'shaia sovetskaia entsiklopediia* 25 (Moscow, 1977): 169–97; *Narodnoe khoziaistvo SSSR v 1990g.* (Moscow, 1991); *Naselenie SSSR* (Moscow, 1989); Matthew J. Sagers, "News Notes: Iron and Steel," *Soviet Geography* 30 (May 1989): 397–434; Lee Schwartz, "USSR Nationality Redistribution by Republic, 1979–1989: From Published Results of the 1989 All-Union Census," *Soviet Geography* 32 (April 1991): 209–48; *World of Learning*, 46th ed. (London, 1996), "Russia . . ." (National Geographic Society Map, 1993); *Europa World Yearbook, 1996* (London, 1996); *Demograficheskii ezhegodnik, 1995* (Moscow, 1995); "CIA World Factbook, 1995" (www.odci.gov/cia/publications/95fact/ti.html).

Tajikistan

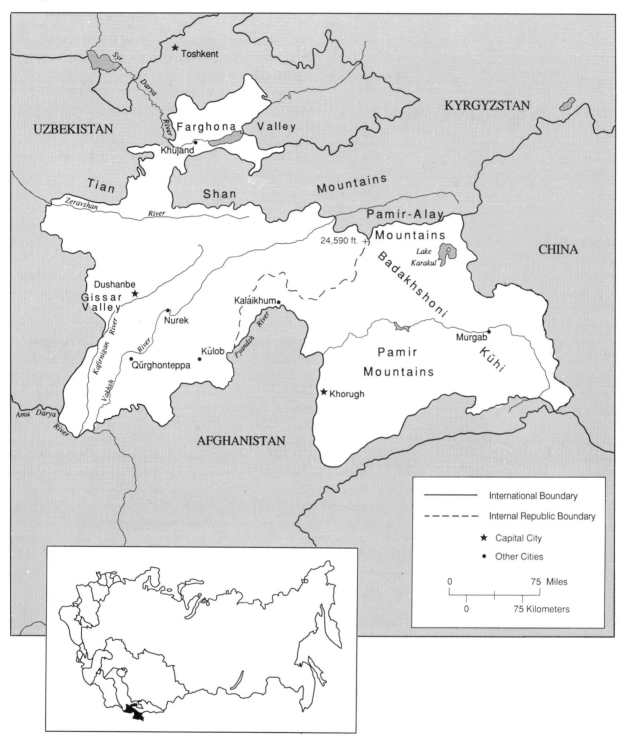

KYRGYZSTAN

UZBEKISTAN

★ Toshkent

Farghona Valley

Khujand

Tian Shan Mountains

Pamir-Alay

Zeravshan River

CHINA

Mountains

24,590 ft. +

Lake Karakul

Badakhshoni

Dushanbe ★

Gissar Valley

Kalaikhum

Nurek

River

Murgab

Kůhi

Kafirnigan River

Kůlob

Pyandzh River

Pamir Mountains

Qŭrghonteppa

Vakhsh

★ Khorugh

Amu Darya

River

AFGHANISTAN

International Boundary

Internal Republic Boundary

★ Capital City

● Other Cities

0   75 Miles

0   75 Kilometers

Tajikistan: History and Description

Physical Description

Borders Tajikistan, known for its rugged and beautiful mountainous terrain, is situated in the southeasternmost part of Central Asia. Bordered on the north and west by the former Soviet republics of Kyrgyzstan and Uzbekistan, the Tajiks share a southern frontier with Afghanistan and a disputed eastern boundary with China. Tajikistan has an extremely unusual northern border, in which a strip of its territory extends like a finger into Uzbekistan so as to incorporate part of the fertile Farghona (Fergana) Valley. The smallest of the Central Asian countries, Tajikistan (55,251 square miles) is approximately the size of Wisconsin.

Mountains The majestic high peaks of the Pamir Mountains, the "roof of the world," dominate the landscape of the eastern half of Tajikistan. The Pamirs boast the highest point not only in Tajikistan but in the whole of the former Soviet Union. This summit, Kommunizm Peak, stands 24,590 feet high. Other mountain systems, the Pamir-Alay, the Trans-Alay, and the Tian Shan, fan out into western Tajikistan. Over 90 percent of the country is mountainous, including the autonomous oblast of Badakhshoni Kŭhi.

Rivers Most of the rivers of Tajikistan feed into the drainage system of the Amu Darya, whose headwaters have their source in the Pamirs. The Amu Darya, one of two major rivers of Central Asia, flows westward through Tajikistan until it becomes the boundary between Uzbekistan and Turkmenistan, eventually emptying into the Aral Sea. The Syr Darya River, the other major Central Asian river, flows through the Farghona Valley in northern Tajikistan. The Zeravshan River follows a westward path through central Tajikistan.

Climate The climate of Tajikistan varies greatly. The alpine areas feature wintry temperatures and snow, while the river valleys can be either hot and desertlike or moderate and pleasant, depending on altitude and the shifting patterns of wind and weather.

Natural Resources Tajikistan contains rich stores of various minerals, as well as uranium and several other kinds of ore. It is an important exporter of cotton, grown mainly in the Farghona Valley but also in the Gissar Valley where the capital city Dushanbe is located. Grain and fruit are grown in the valleys, as well. Livestock, especially sheep and cattle, are raised on the country's hillsides. In Tajikistan, the yak is the traditional helper of the farmer or shepherd.

Ethnic and Historical Background

Tajiks, who may be the oldest inhabitants of Central Asia, are of Iranian ancestry. In contrast to most of the other peoples in the region, whose languages come from Turkic roots, spoken Tajik is close to modern Persian. Linguistically, Tajik belongs to the western Iranian group of Indo-European languages. Although several distinct dialects of Tajik exist, the variant spoken by the Tajiks of Samarqand and Bukhoro (both cities inside the borders of neighboring Uzbekistan) has provided the foundation for the modern Tajik literary language. Tajik was originally written in the Arabic alphabet, its first works dating from the great Arabic civilizations of Bukhoro (Bukhara) during the ninth and tenth centuries.

Tajiks customarily have been viewed as the settled or stationary people of Central Asia, in contrast to the nomadic or wandering groups. Archeological evidence shows that the ancestors of the Tajiks were farmers who inhabited the areas along the Amu Darya River valley, as well as valleys along the Zeravshan River and the Syr Darya in the Farghona Valley, since the first or second millennium B.C. By the time the Arabs conquered these regions in the seventh and eighth centuries A.D., the movement of Turkic-speaking nomads into the area had already begun to complicate the region's ethnic mixture.

The Samanid dynasty that arose in the ninth and tenth centuries, with Bukhoro as its capital, emerged as a great center of Arabic learning. The Tajiks are among the legitimate inheritors of this Arab civilization and literature, inasmuch as the development of the Tajik language dates from that time.

Later in the tenth and early eleventh centuries, as waves of Mongol invaders began to spread across Central Asia, the prevailing language of the ruling Turkic dynasties became Persian. By the fifteenth century, the settled peoples of Central Asia, while using both the Persian and Turkic languages, came to draw upon a similar cultural heritage. The distinction between specific Tajik or Uzbek nations appears to date from a later period. In fact, all settled people in the region were referred to by the term Sart, whether they spoke a Persian or Turkic dialect. The term Sart simply served to distinguish the town dwellers from the more nomadic, generally Turkic, peoples of the area. The bilingualism that developed during that period still prevails among some urban dwellers of present-day Tajikistan and Uzbekistan, leading occasionally to rival Tajik and Uzbek claims of ethnic domination in border areas.

From the Arab civilization, the future Tajiks also inherited the religion of Islam, the dominant religion of Central Asia. Despite their linguistic ties with modern Iran, the Muslim communities of Tajikistan are primarily Sunni, in contrast to the more fundamentalist Shi'ite Muslim presence in Iran. Regardless of the official state atheism of the Soviet period, virtually all Tajiks, and over 90 percent of the entire population of Tajikistan, have roots in Islamic tradition. The contemporary revival of Islam in Tajikistan is addressed later in this chapter.

Russian Conquest and Soviet Rule

Russian conquest of the area of Tajikistan dates from the nineteenth century. By 1867, Russian Turkestan, made up of most of the land eventually known as Central Asia, had been established. Many Tajik settlements, however, continued to find protection under the independent Muslim khanates that resisted the Russian advances. The khanate of Bukhara, for example, included Tajik centers within its domain during part of this time. By 1918, in the aftermath of the Bolshevik Revolution, the Red Army had gained control of most of what is now Tajikistan. The newly named Turkestan Republic, direct descendant of Russian Turkestan, was declared in April. Composed of Tajiks, Uzbeks, Kazakhs, and other primarily Muslim ethnic groups, it was organized as an autonomous republic within the larger Russian Republic. By the fall of 1920, in spite of occasional outbreaks by local armed Islamic rebel groups, or Basmachi, most remaining resistance to the Bolsheviks had been quelled, and the whole of Central Asia was brought together under Soviet domination.

In October 1924, Tajikistan was reorganized and designated an autonomous republic attached to Uzbekistan. Five years later, on the 5th of October, 1929, having received approval from Moscow, it was granted its own status as a full union republic and no longer lived under the shadow of the Uzbeks. The division and redistribution of Tajiks in this new republic was not ideal. Some Tajik settlements, both along the Uzbekistan-Tajikistan border and within the most important old historical centers such as Bukhoro, Samarqand, and Toshkent, remained in the hands of Uzbekistan. The population, however, was apparently pacified to the satisfaction of the authorities, although local resistance to the Sovietization of Tajikistan was not entirely stamped out until the late 1930s.

In spite of the national delimitation policy of the Russian authorities, a policy that assigned national groups to particular homelands, large groups of Tajiks still resided outside the borders of Tajikistan in other newly formed republics. Many Tajiks found themselves in Uzbekistan, a lesser number in Kyrgyzstan and in the other Central Asian republics. There were also more than a million Tajiks living outside the borders of the Soviet Union in Afghanistan, in China, and in the area that later became Pakistan.

Within Tajikistan itself, there remained many Uzbeks, Kyrgyz, Kazakhs, Turks, and other Muslims who ideally should have found themselves and their villages located inside the borders of their own newly established Central Asian republics. Alongside those peoples who had achieved their own republics, many other smaller ethnic groups remained in Tajikistan, such as the Pamiri people, the Mountain Tajiks, the Yagnobis, the Chagatais (Turkic), and the Harduris. Almost without exception these groups are Muslim but have a language or cultural tradition different from the Tajiks.

After being incorporated into the Soviet Union, the Tajiks were eventually encouraged to develop their own sense of nationhood, albeit without reference to religion. A sense of resentment toward Uzbek domination evolved as the Tajiks compared the privileges accorded Uzbeks in the cultural and economic sphere. As a part of this growing sense of Tajik nationhood, the Tajiks also came to appreciate the Persian roots of their language and the implications such a tradition implied in their relationship with Afghans and Iranians.

Soviet Leadership

In the 1920s, Soviet authorities encouraged native peoples to become active in the Communist Party in order to bring effective management and organization to the young republic. Initial directives from the government announced guidelines for the nationalization of natural resources, new water and land distribution programs, the emancipation of women, and free education for all citizens. These decrees, however, were not pursued until the rebellious Basmachi movement was wiped out. The pacification process became especially difficult because of the perceived threat both to Islam and to the traditional ways of life that the new decrees represented. Nevertheless, in spite of tremendous difficulties in communication between the Tajiks, who could not speak Russian, and the Russians, who were unable to express themselves in Tajik, local Tajiks eventually came to fill many local Party committees and other administrative posts.

The collectivization of agriculture was not achieved until the 1930s because of the violent objections of local Tajiks, many of whom now spoke from within the Communist Party itself. The disagreements on collectivization led to the purging of two local Party leaders, Nasratullah Maksum and Abdurakhim Khojibaev, both ethnic Tajiks. A series of purges then followed, the most extensive of which occurred in early 1934. As many as 10,000 victims may have perished during that time. The Party lay in ruins, decimated by the excesses of Stalin's paranoid policy. By 1937 a Russian, Dmitrii Protopopov, had been appointed first secretary, and many other Russians were brought in to staff lower level positions.

Tajikistan was then, and would be for many years, under more direct control from Moscow. Protopopov stayed on as first secretary until 1945. He was followed by a Stalinist Tajik, Bobojan Gafurov, who held the post from 1945 until 1956. The post-Stalinist era was not notable for outstanding reformers in the office of first secretary. Tursunbai Uljabaev, also a Tajik, was removed for corruption and abuse of power in 1961. Subsequent first secretaries, Jabar Rasulov and Rakhman Nabiev, retained the Tajik presence in the office, but did little to reform Party politics.

Tajikistan: Contemporary Issues

Standard of Living

Tajikistan is arguably the poorest country in Central Asia, and has the highest birth rate of any former Soviet republic. Since 1959, the population of Tajikistan has increased by more than three percent per year, a rate approximately three times higher than the previous Soviet average, and higher than that of most other developing nations of the world. Between 1959 and 1979, the population of Tajikistan increased by more than 100 percent. This rapid population increase has been reflected in chronic rural overpopulation and consequent high unemployment. Even before the destabilizing political events of the past decade, rural unemployment figures often exceeded 25 percent of the able-bodied work force.

To address the problems of rural overpopulation and poverty, directives were frequently sent from Moscow in the 1980s encouraging the development of labor resources in urban centers. Yet, as local Tajik leaders would occasionally lament, the absence of Soviet state investment in Tajikistan meant that migration to urban centers only had the effect of transferring rural poverty into urban poverty. Soviet state investment in Tajikistan ranked among the lowest per capita for any republic. One result was that, as of the 1989 census, two-thirds of the inhabitants of Tajikistan remained in small, underdeveloped rural villages.

Predictably, efforts to address this relative underdevelopment by antinatalist campaigns—Soviet-directed and Tajik-implemented governmental campaigns to persuade women to have fewer children—failed from the start. Such campaigns, occasionally launched also in Uzbekistan, were invariably seen as antinational drives directed against Asians by Moscow. The perception that these were selective, differentiated efforts aimed at Central Asia was fueled by the reality that in other parts of the Soviet Union, such as in European Russia, public policy occasionally was openly pronatalist.

Alongside the health and welfare needs of a poor population, one of the features of Tajikistan's poverty is its weak infrastructure. Because the country is dependent upon water from surrounding mountain streams, dams have been built for water storage. But some of these dams are of uncertain quality, having been constructed in an area split by seismic fault lines. In March 1987, a landslide set off by heavy rainfall in the Kŭlob region led to the collapse of a dam holding back 3 million cubic meters of water. The ensuing flood killed 36 people, leaving another 500 homeless. Such disasters have raised grave concerns about the status of other public works projects. The largest dam in all of Central Asia, the Nurek, lies just east of the capital, Dushanbe.

The Cotton Monoculture

By the 1980s, Tajikistan came to be the third largest cotton producing republic of the Soviet Union. Cotton production averaged over 900,000 tons annually. Although that was only about one-tenth of the total annual production of cotton (9 million tons) in the former Soviet Union, Tajik cotton is the more desirable long-staple variety. Given the limited amount of arable land in Tajikistan, the high production figures for cotton demonstrated that, as in the case of Uzbekistan (see pages 190–91), a cotton monoculture had developed, with marketing ties through Moscow. Tajikistan has become so dependent upon its cotton production that schoolchildren and urban workers have been routinely diverted into the fields to assist with harvests. The need for harvest labor, despite unemployment in rural Tajikistan, reflects the underproductivity and lack of technology in this predominantly rural country.

The clearest measure of the crisis facing Tajikistan in the 1990s is that cotton production has steadily dropped, plunging to less than 250,000 tons per year by 1995, one-fourth the previous Soviet-era production level. Similarly, industrial production dropped by more than 50 percent. Strapped by this drop in production, the Tajik government postponed the introduction of its own currency, the Tajik ruble or somon, until the end of 1995.

The collapse of the Tajik economy has been compounded by its dependence upon cotton monoculture. Efforts to diversify the economy have depended upon the development of urban manufacturing and the exploitation of the country's mineral reserves. As is the case elsewhere in Central Asia, Tajikistan has substantial mineral deposits, including uranium. In early 1992, U.S. Secretary of State James Baker visited Dushanbe, seeking assurances that Tajikistan would not provide weapons-grade uranium to any Asian neighbors who might be wanting to develop nuclear capability. Despite promises provided then to the secretary of state, Tajik leaders face the problem of how best to satisfy Western concerns with the need to generate economic growth, encourage foreign investment, and secure international markets.

Ecological and Environmental Issues

The question of water is for Tajikistan, as for other Central Asian countries, a critical issue. The heavy cultivation of water-intensive crops such as cotton only makes the problem of water shortage more acute. The occasionally conflicting interests of economic development and environmental concern have also been a part of the discussion over water in Tajikistan. In one of the first open debates of its kind over water usage, the informal Tajik group Ashkara (Openness) spearheaded opposition to state plans for the building of a large hydroelectric plant on the River Vakhsh. In a partial concession to environmental concerns, the state announced in 1989 that it would reduce the projected height of the dam by one-third.

Environmental issues have not only spawned conflict with industrial and economic development, environmental and energy concerns have also added to ethnic and regional rivalries in Central Asia. During the winters of 1990–91 and 1991–92, Tajikistan was forced to limit its central heating in major urban centers, often reducing dramatically the use of electricity in factories as well. In their explanation for the energy crises, Tajik officials blamed Uzbekistan for failing to provide power from its power stations. Such rivalries over energy have thus added fuel to environmental and ethnic conflicts.

Occasionally, environmental issues have required official resolution by the Uzbekistan and Tajikistan governments. In the case of a large Tajik aluminum plant near the Uzbek border, complaints by Uzbeks over water and air pollution led in 1991 to formal cooperative resolutions by the deputies of both the Tajik and Uzbek Supreme Soviets (their countries' parliamentary bodies). Under the joint resolutions, the Tajiks agreed to stop the operation of 100 electrolysis units at the plant during the summer of 1991, despite the fact that aluminum production figured significantly in the Tajik industrialization effort. Complicating this agreement has been Uzbekistan's demand for 30 million rubles in damages. Such ethnic rivalries make environmental problems all the more crisis prone and difficult to solve.

Ethnic Issues

Ethnic conflict, including the tensions between transplanted European Slavs and indigenous Islamic peoples, may be found within each of the Central Asian countries. In the case of Tajikistan, two unique features color the prospects for ethnic harmony. First, the majority Tajik nationality does not share with the rest of Central Asia a common Turkic language and ancestry. As noted earlier, spoken Tajik is a Persian (Iranian) language, markedly different from the Turkic languages spoken by most other people of Central Asia. The result is that, while the Tajiks are part of the common Islamic religious culture of Central Asia, they are less likely to be drawn into any pan-Turkic alliance or greater Turkic confederation, such as that of former Turkestan, that existed prior to the creation of separate Central Asian Soviet republics in the 1920s.

An equally important feature affecting ethnic and political conflict in Tajikistan is the reality that a disproportionately large part of the ethnically Tajik population resides outside the present Tajikistan borders. More than 900,000 Tajiks live in Uzbekistan, concentrated in the adjacent Bukhoro oblast, particularly in the ancient cities of Samarqand and Bukhoro. Similarly, more than 3,000,000 ethnic Tajiks reside in Afghanistan. As long as the political authority of the Soviet Union prevailed, the diffusion of Tajiks outside Tajikistan did not pose a significant problem. Official

Soviet Tajik ideology, as reflected in the publications of Bobojan Gafurov (1908–1977), Communist Party first secretary from 1946 to 1956 and subsequently director of the Academy of Sciences' Institute of Oriental Studies, held that the Russian annexation of Central Asia in the nineteenth century was a progressive development. Gafurov and official Soviet Tajik ideology advocated use of Russian by all Tajiks, including those Tajiks living in Afghanistan. This ideology had the effect of masking interethnic rivalry, while at the same time offering a defense for such actions as the Soviet intervention in Afghanistan in late 1979. As elsewhere, the passing of Soviet imperial power eliminated ideological defenses and reopened a series of old ethnic disputes for the Tajik people.

One such ethnic conflict is the Tajik dispute with the Uzbeks. Resting beneath the surface, the disagreement with Uzbekistan came to be openly articulated in 1988 when the secretary of the Tajik Writers' Union, Loiq Sherali, complained of Uzbek intellectual imperialism. Referring to Uzbek writings, Sherali noted the "national arrogance of several of our Turkic-speaking colleagues." (He is quoted in Annette Bohr, "Secretary of Tajik Writers' Union Voices Resentment," *Radio Liberty Research Bulletin*, 17 March 1988.) Sherali pointed out that Uzbek writers were trying to establish their own ethnic origins by creating an early national history based upon writers who, though they may have lived in Bukhoro, wrote in Persian (the case of Ibn Sina or Avicenna, 980–1031). Sherali complained similarly about Uzbek claims to what he said were "Persian-Turkic" poets from the eleventh to sixteenth centuries, who lived well beyond Uzbek borders in present-day Afghanistan.

While the ability to voice such resentments openly marked the early stages of intellectual glasnost in Tajikistan, the Soviet Tajik authorities were understandably wary of opening the door too wide. In January 1988, editor Khojaev of the Tajik-language Party newspaper, *Komsomoli Tochikiston*, was dismissed for publishing articles that, according to the charge, "wittingly or unwittingly aroused aspiration to national exclusivity and parochialism and undermined the basis of traditional friendship between the peoples of neighboring republics" (quoted in Bess Brown, "Limits to Glasnost in Tajikistan," *Radio Liberty Research Bulletin*, 11 April 1988). By August 1988, however, in a debate at the Supreme Soviet in Moscow on the Armenian-Azerbaijani conflict in Nagorno-Karabakh, Mikhail Gorbachev specifically referred to the conflicting Tajik-Uzbek claims, fearing a potential domino effect should property be allowed to be transferred from one republic to another. He was referring to the Tajik claim that 20 percent of the Tajik nation that resided in and around the historic city of Samarqand in Uzbekistan had been unfairly excised from the Tajik republic. In short, what was being challenged was the very drawing of Soviet-designed ethnic boundaries created in 1924. For Moscow, and for Moscow loyalists in Dushanbe, such challenges spelled danger.

In the case of the Tajik-Uzbek dispute, as in other such disputes throughout the former Soviet Union, the claims can go two ways. For just as the Tajiks can speak on behalf of their Tajik compatriots in Uzbekistan, the Uzbeks can cite the fact that more than one million Uzbeks live in Tajikistan. These disputes, which continue to produce intense interethnic friction, have since 1988 become the subject of occasional meetings between visiting delegations of Tajik and Uzbek leaders. The issue of the large Tajik aluminum plant near the Uzbekistan border discussed earlier became part of this simmering rivalry.

While Uzbek-Tajik interethnic tensions have been the source of long-term misunderstandings, it is only recently that observers have begun to focus upon the equally serious problem of *intra-ethnic* conflict. Magnified in the current civil war, this intra-ethnic conflict involves the divisions between the Pamiri peoples of eastern Tajikistan (Badakhshoni Kŭhi) and the western Tajik tribes surrounding Dushanbe. As in other cases of Soviet national delimitation policies, the Tajiks, as the titular nationality of the Soviet Socialist Republic of Tajikistan, gradually began to assimilate the Pamiri tribes of eastern Tajikistan, in what was called during the Soviet period the Gorno-Badakhshan Autonomous Oblast. Even though the Pamiri tribes were earlier considered to speak a separate east Iranian language similar but distinct from Tajik, they were in the process of becoming assimilated linguistically into Soviet Tajikistan. By the 1959 Soviet census, the Pamiri were no longer identified as a separate ethnic group, but rather included as Tajiks.

Still, the Pamiri, numbering 100,000 or more, are Shi'ite Muslims, unlike the more westerly Tajiks who are predominantly Sunni. It is that Shi'ite Muslim identification that links the Pamiri peoples of eastern Tajikistan with many of the Tajiks across the border in Afghanistan. In the civil war that now rages in Tajikistan, these ancient Islamic divisions have resurfaced with potential ramifications for the future of Tajikistan and all of Central Asia. For it is the Shi'ite Tajiks from Afghanistan, linked loosely with their Pamiri counterparts in southeastern Tajikistan, who most closely resemble traditional Muslim guerrilla warriors, or mujahedin, fighting the established authorities in Dushanbe as though they were engaged in a holy war or *jihad*. What the old authoritarian order of the Soviet Union had managed to hold together is now breaking apart amidst the violence of contemporary Tajikistan.

A final measure of how disruptive ethnic conflict can be for Tajikistan is the fate of the Russian and Ukrainian population, largely concentrated in the capital city Dushanbe. This transplanted European population has become increasingly uneasy, not because of overt ethnic hostility from the Tajiks—although such hostility has existed in all the newly independent Central Asian states—but rather because of fears that Tajikistan is destined to become an Islamic state. Although such fears may ultimately prove unfounded, the immediate result has been an unprecedented exodus of the Slavic and Jewish population from Dushanbe since 1990. Estimates are that more than half of the Russian population of Tajikistan has fled already in the 1990s. The human drama of this large refugee exodus, occurring in other parts of Central Asia as well, carries with it a substantial cost, for the Russian population in Tajikistan is disproportionately represented among the technical, medical, and civil service elite. These European Slavs of Tajikistan, like their counterparts in the other urban centers of Central Asia, are not easily replaced.

Islam in Tajikistan

The 1980s were marked by a resurgence of Islamic loyalties within the officially atheist Tajik Soviet Republic. The recovery of Islamic religious identity was not unique to Tajikistan. As elsewhere, traditional Moslem practices remained strongest in the rural, small-village setting. The somewhat more surprising presence of unofficial Islamic leadership in larger urban centers, however, posed special problems for the state authorities. In 1986, for example, the arrest of an unregistered mullah, Abdulla Saidov, in Qŭrghonteppa, a large city near the Afghan border, led to public demonstrations in which some local Communist Party members and intellectuals joined. The termination of Abdulla Saidov's activities as a mullah may have been related to mystical Wahhabi or other non-Sunni Muslim practices, or to his popularity and the size of his following, or to the strategic location of Qŭrghonteppa, near the Soviet-Afghan frontier, or perhaps to some combination of these factors. Nevertheless, the rally of the mullah's supporters seems to have taken the state authorities by surprise.

The spread of such popular religious sentiment, including the presence of Wahhabi and other unregistered clerical leaders, led to numerous state directives in 1987 and 1988 seeking to reenergize antireligious forces. Ironically, at a time when the early signs of glasnost in Moscow included friendly overtures toward the Russian Orthodox church, Tajik officials in Dushanbe, led by Communist Party First Secretary Kakhar Makhkamov, saw no conflict between support for Gorbachev's glasnost and an intensified crackdown upon unofficial and unauthorized Islamic movements.

By 1988, Tajik newspapers carried open reports of an unofficial, underground religious press in the republic. One such press, operating from the printshop of the Dushanbe Pedagogical Institute, had been turning out copies of an Islamic newspaper, *Islamskaia Pravda (Islamic Truth),* photocopies of speeches by Ayatollah Khomeini and Pakistan leader Mandudi, and republications of the works of a prominent theorist of Islamic revival, Jamal al-Din al-Afghani (see Bess Brown's report, "Description of Religious *Samizdat* in Tajikistan," *Radio Liberty Research Bulletin*, 23 May 1988).

By 1990, the Islamic Renaissance Party, an informal political group with alliances throughout the other Islamic republics of the former Soviet Union, was firmly established in Tajikistan, despite the efforts of governmental officials to ban it. In December 1990, the Tajik Supreme Soviet outlawed this Islamic party from Tajik territory and specifically forbade the establishment of informal parties of a religious nature. Kakhar Makhkamov, then the Tajik president, steadfastly sought to identify the Islamic Renaissance Party with extremist fundamentalists and Wahhabis. The Islamic Renaissance Party in Tajikistan, however, has tended, as elsewhere, to appeal to the intelligentsia, avoiding religious extremes and inclined, instead, to view Islam as an integral part of Tajik culture. Because of the appeal of democratic ideals to the Tajik intelligentsia, the Islamic Renaissance Party has also bridged what some see as potentially conflicting ideals of Islam and democracy. Unlike the pronounced anti-Western and antimodernist perspectives of Islamic fundamentalists and Wahhabis, especially in matters involving the rights of women, the Islamic Renaissance Party has tended to be more urban and moderate in its views. By openly charging that the Islamic Renaissance Party frightened the non-Tajik, Slavic population into leaving the republic, the Communist leadership may indirectly have advanced the process they sought to limit in their ban of this increasingly popular Islamic movement.

No event so clearly demonstrates the sensitivity of the recovery of Islamic identity as does the assassination in January 1996 of the Mufti Fatkhulla Sharifov, the spiritual leader of Tajik Muslims. He and all those in his household were killed on the first day of Ramadan, the Muslim holy month. Fatkhulla Sharifov, a pro-government loyalist, had been brought in by the Tajik authorities to replace Ali Akbar Turajonzoda, an opposition leader who was Sharifov's immediate predecessor. Responding to the assassination, Tajik President Imomali Rakhmonov sought to pin the blame on external Islamic fundamentalists. Yet, as Turajonzoda noted, Sharifov had been only partially trained in Islamic law. The positioning of all sides on the Sharifov murder, which has yet to be solved, reflects the degree to which Islamic identity remains politically charged in contemporary Tajikistan.

Political Unrest and Civil War

Since 1992, Tajikistan has been involved in an increasingly dangerous and violent civil war. That civil war has left more than 100,000 dead and hundreds of thousands homeless. Although the war reflects the pent-up tensions of deep-seated ethnic and religious conflicts, it also reveals the failure of Tajik political leadership to bridge the transition from Soviet republic to independent state. The central political dynamic in Tajikistan, as in other former Soviet republics, has been the destabilizing process of the challenge to old Soviet-style, Communist Party leadership. In Tajikistan this challenge has come from new informal political groups, as well as from a more militant opposition. The resulting political impasse unfortunately has dissolved into massive violence.

In the decade prior to civil war, political leadership in the Tajik Soviet Socialist Republic was dominated by two Communist Party first secretaries, Rakhman Nabiev (1982–85, 1991–92) and Kakhar Makhkamov (1985–91). While Makhkamov officially embraced the reformist, modernizing lead of Moscow's perestroika, he was unprepared to oversee the dissolution of Soviet power. Despite his occasional admonitions to the bureaucracy, including criticism of the performance of the Tajik KGB, Makhkamov became a dutiful leader in the wider Soviet bureaucracy and Communist Party. His efforts to maximize cotton production increasingly came to be viewed by Tajiks as part of the process of Soviet colonial exploitation, an exploitation made worse by the manner in which it tended to deform the Tajik economy.

February 1990 Riots In February 1990, the accelerating economic, ethnic, and religious conflicts within the republic triggered an outbreak of violence in Dushanbe that left more than 20 dead, hundreds wounded, and untold damage to housing and public buildings. The demonstrations apparently stemmed from rumors that Armenian refugees in Azerbaijan were being sent to Dushanbe and would be given housing priority. Because of the high demand for apartments in the capital and the reality that Armenians

actually were being sent to Tajikistan, there was some substance to the concerns of those protesting. Ultimately, the demonstrators became menacing, throwing rocks at policemen, engaging in looting and theft, and threatening non-Tajik citizens.

In violence reminiscent of Bloody Sunday in the Georgian capital of Tbilisi in the spring of 1989 (see pages 127–28), forces from Moscow were brought in to help quell the uprising, and order was restored—though only after tragic loss of life. In the Tajik case, the republican leadership specifically sought such assistance, fearing the demands of the protesters, who called for the resignation of all republican leaders and the redirection of profits secured from Tajik cotton production.

In retrospect, the events of February 1990 and the rise of informal political groups prior to, during, and after the uprising marked a turning point in the politics of Tajikistan. The February 1990 uprising galvanized the popularity of the republic's informal political opposition. Among the groups who played a role in the 1990 events were the Rastokhez (Renewal), a Tajik popular front group formed in the fall of 1989 with goals similar, if perhaps more modest, to those of the popular fronts in the Baltic and Ukraine. Leaders of Rastokhez were selected by the demonstrators outside Communist Party headquarters to negotiate the protesters' demands. When appeals for calm were ultimately made over television, Rastokhez representatives were among those appearing before viewers.

The riots of February 1990 also reflected the failure of the republican leadership to satisfy the basic social and economic needs of the population. Even official Communist Party representatives had to concede that as many as 70,000 inhabitants of Dushanbe were unemployed, and rural underemployment was potentially even more serious. Despite Makhkamov's promises for new public housing projects and better health care, his dominant message was that of the need to crack down on those opposition groups responsible for the February uprising. Part of the reason for Makhkamov's hard-line message was his concern for the mounting emigration of non-Tajiks from Tajikistan. Such out-migration, especially by ethnic Russians and Ukrainians (as noted above), had already been triggered by the 1989 law declaring Tajik the state language of the republic. But the February riots, and the efforts of some fundamentalist Islamic forces to capitalize upon such events for a more general antiforeigner appeal, sped the outflow of thousands of professionals, medical personnel, and skilled urban workers.

Makhkamov's political crackdown was curiously balanced by his openly avowed support for the liberal, reformist objectives of Boris Yeltsin in Moscow. On the 24th of August, 1990, the Supreme Soviet, backed by Makhkamov, declared the republican sovereignty of Tajikistan. So as not to escalate further the emigration of non-Tajiks, the sovereignty declaration specifically identified all ethnic groups as having equal standing in Tajikistan.

For the opposition, the period following the February events was marked by increased, open political organization. In August 1990, the Democratic Party of Tajikistan, a party of liberal intellectuals, held its initial congress. Moreover, even though the Rastokhez and Islamic Renaissance parties were forbidden to organize in Tajikistan, informal public support for these groups grew.

Moscow Coup The opposition between informal political groups and the Makhkamov government came to a showdown in the immediate aftermath of the abortive coup d'état in Moscow in August 1991. The effort by hard-line Communist officials to depose Mikhail Gorbachev produced ripple effects throughout all of the Soviet republics. In the case of Tajikistan, these effects were made even more dramatic by Makhkamov's apparent support for the coup plotters, offered in the early hours of the Moscow crisis. Despite Makhkamov's subsequent ban upon Communist Party operations in the government, the Tajik Supreme Soviet faced demands from demonstrators for the resignation of the republic's leadership. On the 31st of August, 1991, the Supreme Soviet accepted the resignation of Makhkamov. Following a month of bitter conflict between the government and opposition forces, elections were called for November 1991, and all parties were allowed open participation in the process. The Tajik Supreme Soviet declared the formal independence of Tajikistan on the 9th of September, 1991.

The November 1991 elections brought little resolution to the political situation in Tajikistan. According to the official election returns, monitored by outside observers, the chair of the Tajik Supreme Soviet and former Communist Party first secretary, Rakhman Nabiev, received 58 percent of the votes cast. Davlat Khudonazarov, chair of the local cinematography workers' union and candidate of both the Democratic and Islamic parties, received only slightly more than 25 percent of the vote. More than 80 percent of the electorate voted. The results marked a surprising recovery by the Tajik Communist Party, which had renamed itself the Tajik Socialist Party. Charges of election fraud, however, haunted the victors. Khudonazarov accused the republic's leadership of falsifying the results and offered photographic evidence to back up his charge of election irregularities.

Civil War In May 1992, President Rakhman Nabiev sought to co-opt the support of regional and nationalist parties by assigning one-third of the ministerial posts to their representatives. This Government of National Reconciliation was quickly challenged by Nabiev's own conservative supporters from the region around Kŭlob. Amidst mutual recriminations, the conservative anti-Islamic loyalists from Dushanbe and the Kŭlob region began to arm themselves, as did their anti-Communist coalition opponents.

The civil war that followed can be compared to some of the worst fighting in former Yugoslavia (Bosnia-Herzegovina) during the same time period. Supporters of the old Communist regime claimed that the oppositionist democratic and Islamic coalition—including strong support from the Pamiri region of Badakhshoni Kŭhi—was being armed by the Afghan resistance. Both sides claimed that the other was benefitting from materiel provided by the Russian 201st Motorized Rifle Division located on the outskirts of Dushanbe and at the Tajik-Afghan border. As many as 70,000 were killed in the sporadic fighting, and hundreds of thousands more became wartime refugees. The cost to the Tajik economy was devastating. European Slavs left Dushanbe in numbers that have yet to be fully calculated, while Tajik oppositionists fled by the thousands across the Afghan border.

In September 1992, midway through the fighting, President Nabiev, who would die of natural causes in 1993, was forced by the opposition to resign. The resignation of Nabiev left unclear who was in control of the Tajik government. The democratic and Islamic parties, despite their growing influence, never assumed full authority. In October, pro-Communist forces loyal to the old regime temporarily seized parts of Dushanbe, but Russian forces deployed in the capital initially kept these Communist loyalists from retaking the government by force. By November, however, the pro-Communist forces operating from their base of strength near Kŭlob retook Dushanbe and secured the resignation of the interim government.

In reestablishing the old regime, the Tajik Supreme Soviet, a parliamentary body dominated by former Communists, played the central role. It abolished the office of the presidency and granted executive powers to the chairman of the Supreme Soviet, Imomali Rakhmonov. In the months that followed in 1993, the new conservative pro-Communist Tajik government launched a crackdown on nationalist, democratic, and Islamic parties, outlawing virtually all such opposition and replacing media and other institutional leaders deemed sympathetic to the anti-Communist forces.

Amid ongoing civil war in the countryside, the Rakhmonov regime has put its authoritarian stamp upon Dushanbe and the Tajik regions to the north in the Farghona Valley. Beyond Dushanbe, especially to the east and south in Badakhshoni Kŭhi and along the Afghan border, antigovernment Islamic guerrilla forces remain in control. In the spring of 1996, the leader of the United Tajik Opposition, Said Abdullo Nuri, proclaimed in a broadcast on the Voice of Free Tajikistan in northern Afghanistan that 70 percent of Tajikistan was under the control of the mujahedin, or Islamic guerrilla fighters. The same deeply engrained religious, ethnic, and regional divisions in Tajik society that set the nation's civil war into motion are contributing to the volatility of contemporary Tajik politics.

In offsetting these regional divisions, the conservative Tajik government has sought to label all outposts of resistance as dangerous pockets of Islamic fundamentalism, a charge that is exaggerated. In the crackdown on opposition groups, the Islamic Renaissance Party and the democratic Rastokhez movement have been outlawed, along with all other informal parties that operated more-or-less openly between 1991 and 1992. Concerned about the spread of Islamic fundamentalism in Central Asia and the cross-border "interference" of ethnic elements from Afghanistan, the Russian Federation has provided important military support to the Rakhmonov government—as many as 25,000 soldiers from the Russian 201st Motorized Rifle Division have been serving in Dushanbe and along the Afghan border. Neighboring countries in Central Asia, reluctant to let the civil war undermine the authority of a Rakhmonov government that is not altogether unlike other authoritarian regimes seeking political stability in the region, have also weighed in with military support for the Tajik government.

Nevertheless, the effort to brand all opponents of the Tajik government as Islamic fundamentalists has begun to lose its effect. Russian President Boris Yeltsin, disappointed with the slow pace of peace negotiations that had begun in 1994 among rival Tajik factions, called for a withdrawal of Russian forces to begin in mid-1996. His argument, which carried increasing force at home, was that the factional fighting in Tajikistan was not worth the loss of one additional Russian soldier. With violence again on the rise in Tajikistan in 1996, and the militarily weak Rakhmonov regime facing an ever-wider constellation of opposi-

tion forces, Russian and Central Asian allies must balance their alarm over the gains of revisionist forces in Tajikistan against the reality that outside powers may have little capacity to alter the outcome of this most tragic upheaval in Central Asia.

In a sign of the more general war weariness after four years of civil war, the Rakhmonov government and rebel forces, the latter represented by Islamic opposition leader Said Abdulla Nuri, signed formal agreements in Moscow in December 1996 pledging a new national reconciliation commission and a permanent peace settlement by July 1997. Whether this latest peace effort represents a real end to the bloody fighting or another tactical interlude remains to be seen, especially in light of the January 1997 rebel capture of United Nations hostages.

International Alliances

The events in Tajikistan, as elsewhere in Central Asia, are not occurring in an international vacuum. While the United States has set up an ambassadorial staff in Dushanbe and U.S. secretaries of state have visited the capital, other regional powers have also courted the Tajik government. The Iranian government has established a presence in Tajikistan, even though the fundamentalism of Iranian Shi'ite leaders has been rejected by officials in Dushanbe. Turkey, commonly viewed as a modern secular state that seeks to separate religion and politics, has been a potential model for Tajik leaders. Like its Turkic neighbors, the Rakhmonov government has also established formal diplomatic relations with Turkey.

Finally, Tajikistan's continuing market ties to Russia, especially in the export of raw cotton, remain part of the much wider economic linkage of Dushanbe to Moscow. For war-torn Tajikistan, as for the rest of Central Asia, the international repercussions of the collapse of the Soviet Union continue to be played out amidst the ethnic and regional rivalries of this poorest of the former Soviet republics. Given such rivalries, the continued presence of Russian troops both in Dushanbe and at critical international borders offers potential stability, even as it serves to remind Tajikistan of the continuity that has existed before and after Soviet rule.

TURKMENISTAN

Statistical Profile

Demography

Population: 4,450,000

Ethnic population

Turkmen 73.3%
Russian 9.8%
Uzbek 9.0%
Kazakh 2.0%
Other 5.9%

Major urban centers and populations

Ashgabat 517,000
Chärjew 164,000
Dashhowuz (Tashauz) 114,000
Gyzylarbat (Kyzyl-Arvat) .... <100,000
Mary 94,000
Nebitdag 89,000
Krasnovodsk 55,000

Historic religious traditions

Islam 87%
Christianity 11%

Languages: Turkmen, Russian, Uzbek

Population by age

Age	Total	Males	Females
0–14	39.8%	20.2%	19.6%
15–64	56.1%	27.7%	28.4%
65 and over	4.2%	1.6%	2.6%

Male/Female ratio: 49.5% male/50.5% female

Rural/Urban population
54.9% rural/45.1% urban

Annual population growth rate: 2.0%

Population density: 23.6 persons per sq mi

Government

Official name: Turkmenistan

Capital: Ashgabat

Date of sovereignty/independence declaration
27 October 1991

Voting age: 18

Education

Literacy (age 15 and over who can read and write)

total population 98%
male 99%
female 97%

Level of education for persons over 15

completed higher education 8.3%
completed secondary education 56.8%
incomplete secondary education 21.3%

Number of higher education institutions: 9

Higher education enrollment: 38,900 students

Selected institutions of higher education (and enrollment)

Ashgabat
Gorkii State University 11,000

Socioeconomic Indicators

Annual birth rate: 32.0 births/1,000 population

Fertility rate: 3.7 children/woman

Infant mortality: 46.4 deaths/1,000 live births

Average life expectancy
65.4 years (male 61.9, female 69)

Annual death rate: 7.9 deaths/1,000 population

Average family size: 5.6

Annual consumption of electrical energy
2,600 kWh/person

Hospital beds per 10,000 persons: 111.0

Physical Features

Area: 188,455 sq mi

Land use
cultivated 2%
pasture (including some desert lands) 70%

Highest elevation
10,299 ft (Kugitangtau Peak, in the Gissar Range)

Rainfall
4 in./yr; more than 16 in./yr in the mountains

Temperature

Winter	**Summer**
northwest, average 23°F	northwest, average 82°F
south, average 39°F	south, average 90°F
lowest, –26°F	highest, 122°F

Economic Production

Estimated per capita GNP: $1,380 (1992)

Agricultural output: cotton, grapes, livestock

Natural resources
petroleum, natural gas, coal, sulfur, salt

Industrial output
natural gas, petroleum products, textiles, carpets

Currency
manat (introduced November 1993)
1 manat = 100 tenge

Communications

Length of rail lines: 1,325 mi

Length of highways: 11,438 mi

Pipelines
crude oil .... 156 mi
natural gas .... 2,750 mi

Telephones: 75 per 1,000 persons

Sources "Turkmenskaia sovetskaia sotsialisticheskaia respublika" *Bol'shaia sovetskaia entsiklopediia* 26 (Moscow, 1977): 341–67; *Narodnoe khoziaistvo SSSR v 1990g.* (Moscow, 1991); *Naselenie SSSR* (Moscow, 1989); Matthew J. Sagers, "News Notes: Iron and Steel," *Soviet Geography* 30 (May 1989): 397–434; Lee Schwartz, "USSR Nationality Redistribution by Republic, 1979–1989: From Published Results of the 1989 All-Union Census," *Soviet Geography* 32 (April 1991): 209–48; *World of Learning*, 46th ed. (London, 1996); "Russia . . ." (National Geographic Society Map, 1993); *Demograficheskii ezhegodnik, 1995* (Moscow, 1995); *Europa World Yearbook, 1996* (London, 1996); "CIA World Factbook, 1995" (www.odci.gov/cia/publications/95fact/tx.html).

Turkmenistan

KAZAKHSTAN

UZBEKISTAN

Garabogazköl Aylagy

Dashhowuz
Khiva

Kara

Krasnovodsk

Kum

Cheleken
Nebitdag

Gyzylarbat

Desert

Amu

Chärjew

Darya

Caspian Sea

Sumbar *River*

Kopet Mountains

Ashgabat

Tedzhen

Mary

Kara *Kum* *Canal*

Kerki

10,299 ft. +

River

River

Murgab

River

IRAN

Paropamiz

Mountains

AFGHANISTAN

	International Boundary
	Canal
★	Capital City
●	Other Cities

0   200 Miles

0   200 Kilometers

Turkmenistan: History and Description

Physical Description

Borders Turkmenistan, fourth largest of the former Soviet republics, is located in the southwestern part of Central Asia. Somewhat larger than the state of California, Turkmenistan (188,455 square miles) is bordered on the north and northeast by the newly independent states of Kazakhstan and Uzbekistan, and on the south and southwest by the Islamic states of Iran and Afghanistan. Turkmenistan's western border follows the long coastline of the Caspian Sea, stretching over 300 miles in length. The territory of Turkmenistan includes the unrelentingly arid expanse of desert known as the Kara Kum, one of the largest sand deserts in the world. Covering between 80 and 90 percent of the country, the extensive Kara Kum has long been a barrier to nomadic Turkmen tribes inhabiting the major oases on the periphery of this inhospitable terrain. Two low mountain ranges in the south, the Kopet and the Paropamiz, enrich the otherwise bleak landscape of Turkmenistan.

Rivers One of the driest regions in Central Asia, Turkmenistan boasts one major river, the Amu Darya. For much of its course, however, this river is on the Turkmenistan-Uzbekistan border in the northeastern part of the country. Originating to the east, in the mountains of Tajikistan, the Amu Darya travels across Turkmenistan in a northwesterly direction for over 600 miles. The vitally important Kara Kum Canal, built after World War II, diverts water from the Amu Darya to other parts of Turkmenistan as the canal proceeds 500 miles to the west, reaching beyond the capital, Ashgabat (Ashkhabad). Other rivers, in particular the Murgab, Tedzhen, and a few smaller streams, flow into Turkmenistan from the mountainous borderlands shared with Iran and Afghanistan, often forming oases before evaporating on the desert floor. Thus, the sources of fresh water needed for the survival of Turkmen agriculture originate outside the country's borders.

Cities Few large cities are found in Turkmenistan, and most towns are either related closely to existing river oases or situated near the Caspian Sea. The country's capital and most populous city, Ashgabat, was established by Russians as the fortification of Poltoratsk toward the end of the nineteenth century during tsarist colonial expansion into Central Asia. Ashgabat suffered a devastating earthquake in 1948, but it has since been mainly rebuilt. Chärjew (Chardzhou), the second largest Turkmen city, is found on the Amu Darya river near the Uzbek border. Krasnovodsk, the chief port, lies on the eastern shore of the Caspian Sea on the industrialized Mangyshlak Peninsula.

Climate The extremely arid climatic conditions of Turkmenistan are reflected in long, hot summers and brief winters. Farming is done in irrigated areas along the country's few rivers. The major crop is cotton, as it is throughout Central Asia. Turkmenistan is second only to Uzbekistan in the amount of cotton produced in the region. Fruits and vegetables are also grown, particularly grapes and grains. Turkmenistan is rich in several natural resources, most notably oil and gas, as well as sulfur and potassium. Extensive oil deposits are found on the Caspian peninsula of Cheleken near Krasnovodsk and inland a bit near the town of Nebitdag. Reserves of natural gas and mineral deposits exist in the area of Chärjew. Thanks to the riches of the Caspian Sea, Turkmenistan has developed a fishing industry. In addition, animal husbandry (mainly goats and Karakul sheep) and sericulture (silk-worm cultivation) occupy the Turkmen tribes. Traditionally, Turkmenistan has also been one of the centers of the centuries-old, oriental rug-weaving industry.

Ethnic and Historical Background

The Turkmen people in the twentieth century tend to identify themselves primarily as members of a particular clan or tribe. According to Alexandre Bennigsen and S. Enders Wimbush (*Muslims of the Soviet Empire: A Guide*, London: C. Hurst and Co., 1985, 98), Turkmen may be grouped into 7 large and 24 small tribes. The seven major tribes are the Tekke in the central part of the country, the Ersary in the southeast, the Yomud in the west, the Goeklen in the southwest, the Salor in the east, the Saryk in the south, and the Chowdor in the north.

The Turkmen language belongs to the southwestern subgroup of Turkic languages and, therefore, is more closely related to the language spoken by Azerbaijanis than to the languages spoken by other Central Asian peoples. A twentieth-century Turkmen literary language, based on the Tekke and Yomud dialects and written in a modified Cyrillic alphabet, was developed during the Soviet period. Works written in this new language, however, have yet to develop the authority still accorded classical eighteenth-century lyrics, verse, and other poetry. These earlier writings employed a compound Turkic (Chagatai) literary model and used the Arabic script.

Turkmen constitute the vast majority of the population of their country. Many Turkmen, however, are found elsewhere in Central Asia and the Middle East. Over 100,000 reside in other parts of the former Soviet Union, primarily in neighboring republics, and one million or more live in Iran, Afghanistan, Iraq, and Turkey. Other national groups residing in Turkmenistan include Russians (in urban centers) and Uzbeks (in the northeast), as well as lesser numbers of Kazakhs and Tatars.

The origin of the Turkmen tribes dates from a period as early as the eighth century when Turkic peoples were migrating from the east into Central Asia. Some of these peoples belonged to tribes that later came to form the Ottoman and Seljuk Turks, founders of important Middle Eastern empires. These semi-nomadic early Turkic tribes eventually absorbed some of the more sedentary Iranian and other peoples already inhabiting the region. By the tenth century, Turkish documents first mention a people called Turkmen.

As a result of the Arab invasion of Central Asia in the tenth century, Turkmen tribes accepted Islam as their religion. Later, in the eleventh century, Turkmen leaders founded the Seljuk Empire at Merv, the oasis called Mary in contemporary Turkmenistan. During the Mongol invasions of the thirteenth century and in subsequent years, control of the territory constituting modern Turkmenistan passed to various regional khanates. Turkmen tribes survived this period primarily through military alliances with contemporary Muslim rulers such as the emirs of Bukhoro (Bukhara) or the khans of Khiva or Kokand (Qŭqon).

Russian Conquest

By the time of the final Russian advance into Central Asia in the second half of the nineteenth century, the Turkmen peoples still functioned politically and economically in tribes, with individual Turkmen tribal units offering their military services to one or another warring Central Asian khanate. Although the Russians had tried as early as 1717 to mount a military expedition against the Khivan Khanate, it was not until 1881, in the massacre of Turkmen at the fort of Geok-Tepe, near Ashgabat, that tsarist forces succeeded in conquering the last of the Central Asian lands not yet under their control. The greatest resistance the Russians encountered in their military advance into Central Asia proved to be that of the fierce Turkmen forces. By 1885, however, all of Central Asia was finally controlled by Russians. Russian General Skobelev established

Turkmenistan as the Transcaspian oblast, and the territory was thereafter ruled as a military colony.

Turkmen tribes continued their seminomadic existence well into the twentieth century, although some had previously settled in the oases and were devoting themselves to agriculture. Segregation by family, clan, and tribe, as well as the perpetuation of separate spoken dialects, worked against any unified effort to counter the Russian presence. Colonial policies inevitably brought some modern innovations to this outlying region of the empire. A railroad was built from Krasnovodsk on the Caspian Sea eastward to Ashgabat and then across the desert to Mary and on to Bukhoro. Turkmen, however, enjoyed little or no participation under the colonial system, and many suffered the loss of valuable pastureland to incoming settlers from Russia.

The major crisis in Central Asia during World War I was the revolt of 1916, in which native peoples rose up against a Russian order to conscript Central Asians for noncombatant duties. Although it is uncertain whether or not the response of Turkmen tribes to this directive constituted a true expression of nationalism or rather a more diffuse anti-Russian movement, the Turkmen during this period and in the subsequent Russian Revolution managed to regain control of their territory. Under the leadership of Junayd Khan, a respected Turkmen tribal elder, Turkmen military forces reversed the Bolshevik takeover of Ashgabat and later took command of the khanate of Khiva. By 1918 they had even achieved a short-lived independence separate from Bolshevik-controlled Turkestan. This relatively brief period ended in 1920 when Red Army forces defeated Junayd Khan and his fellow Turkmen holding Khiva. These Turkmen then joined the Basmachi (anti-Soviet) guerrilla movement, widespread in Central Asia throughout the 1920s, and fought against the Soviet consolidation of power well into the 1930s.

Soviet Rule

In October 1924, Stalin created the union republic of Turkmenistan, carved out of existing Turkmen tribal landholdings and parts of the old khanates of Khiva and Bukhara. Turkmenistan was designated one of five tribal/ethnic groups meeting the criteria for nationhood devised by Soviet historians and ethnographers. Thus, Turkmenistan formally became a part of the USSR.

In spite of this formal incorporation into the Soviet Union, Turkmen tribes continued to resist the implementation of Soviet policies throughout the 1920s and into the 1930s. Although external controls were relaxed for a time, in an attempt to gain greater cooperation from the indigenous peoples, Turkmen tribes fought the collectivization directive of 1929 that attempted to force the traditionally nomadic Turkmen to settle permanently in one place in order to pursue cooperative agricultural activities.

Turkmen leaders did not escape the purges that swept through Russia and the other Soviet republics in the 1930s. Denounced as nationalists, high leaders of the Turkmen Communist Party, such as Gaigisiz Aitakov (Turkmen premier) and Nedirbai Atabaev (president of the Turkmen Supreme Soviet), were tried on charges of sympathizing with opposition elements within the intelligentsia, then were executed. Lesser leaders suffered similar accusations and were also purged in 1937–38. After World War II, this pattern continued as intellectuals, writers, and others became victims.

After Stalin's death in 1953, during the regime of Nikita Khrushchev, Turkmen leaders continued to press for greater native control of political and economic affairs in Turkmenistan. Suhan Babaev, first secretary of the Turkmen Communist Party, was ousted in 1958 for proposing that only Turkmen should fill important Party leadership posts in Turkmenistan. Yet, the subsequent first secretaries all were drawn from Turkmen leadership. The successor to Babaev, Juma Karaev, lived only two years after his appointment and was succeeded by Balysh Ovezov in 1960. In 1969, during the tenure of Soviet leader Leonid Brezhnev—a period marked by cynicism and rampant corruption in the Turkmen Republic—Ovezov was removed and replaced by Mukhamednazar Gapurov. With the advent of Mikhail Gorbachev and his reform-minded policies of perestroika in 1985, a new group of political appointees came to head Communist Party leadership positions at both the republic and oblast levels. The job of first secretary of the Turkmen Soviet Republic went to Saparmurad Niyazov, a Communist Party functionary having important ties within both the republic and Moscow.

Turkmenistan: Contemporary Issues

Economic Dependence and Independence

During the Soviet period, the Turkmen Soviet Socialist Republic developed, not unlike other Central Asian republics, a pattern of colonial economic dependence upon the Moscow center. Encouraged to produce ever greater quantities of cotton, Turkmenistan came to participate in the wider development of the cotton monoculture in Central Asia. As elsewhere, the demand for increased cotton production in Turkmenistan led to extravagant misuse of scarce water resources. Graft and corruption became routine as unrealistic projections of cotton yields led to falsely inflated production figures. By 1985, the year of the onset of Gorbachev's reforms, Moscow authorities openly challenged the weak performance of Turkmenistan agriculture, complaining that the republic's economy required far greater discipline and modernization. In all, labor productivity in agriculture was lower in 1985 than it had been in 1970—despite considerable state investment in the agricultural sector. By the 1980s, Turkmenistan had become dependent upon Moscow for many basic food commodities, including meat, eggs, and other protein. Unable to feed itself, the republic had become, in the view of the Moscow center, an economic liability.

The subsequent resignation of the Turkmen Communist Party First Secretary Gapurov, and his replacement by Saparmurad Niyazov, were seen as indications that Moscow sought to reverse this pattern of agricultural weakness. Muscovite sincerity, however, was undermined by a continued insistence on unrealistically high cotton production figures. Nevertheless, in the years since 1985, the replacement of all oblast-level first secretaries, along with the minister of agriculture, not only began to address the problems of corruption inherited from the Brezhnev era, but paved the way for more open-ended discussions regarding the future of Turkmen agriculture.

At the end of the Soviet era, Turkmenistan remained impoverished and backward. The republic has the highest infant mortality rate of any former Soviet republic, its badly polluted streams and canals yield the most unreliable drinking water of any Central Asian state, and the problem of rural unemployment is a chronic source of social instability.

Most observers of Central Asia, however, are quick to point out that, with the exception of Kazakhstan, no state in the region faces brighter prospects for economic independence and development. How is it that such an encouraging picture can emerge out of such relative poverty and economic dependence? The answer is found in the abundant oil and natural gas reserves of Turkmenistan. While cotton production will continue to secure export earnings for the newly independent republic, the greatest source of foreign currency for domestic development undoubtedly depends on the country's export of natural gas. The Turkmen political leadership recognizes the importance of these natural resources and has already entered into bilateral agreements to secure full international market value for its oil and gas exports. Indicative of this was Turkmenistan's decision to withhold gas exports to Ukraine in 1991–92 until the Ukrainians, like the Russians, agreed to pay full market value. In 1992, Turkmenistan also began to seek international partners to develop a pipeline to carry gas to Turkey and, ultimately, to western Europe. As a result, there exists alongside the grating poverty of Turkmenistan realistic hope for increased international trade earnings and expanded domestic food production. This juxtaposition of grating poverty and potential oil wealth has observers concluding that Niyazov would like to preside over a new Middle East "sheikdom swimming in money" (Lowell Bezanis, "Joining Forces with Iran and Russia," *Transition* 1, no. 14, 11 August 1995, 72–73).

The hopes for Turkmen economic development ought not to be confused with developments in the equally complicated sphere of privatization and economic restructuring. Here, Turkmen political leadership has shown reluctance to divest itself of long-standing governmental subsidization and control of the domestic economy. In November 1993, the government freed prices and issued its new state currency, the manat, even as it sought to manipulate exchange rates and prohibit the circulation of foreign currencies. Modern capitalism in the form of international investment and selective market pricing has been encouraged, but the economy is still being controlled by an entrenched system of favorites whose tenure often predates the advent of reform in the 1980s.

Ecological Issues

The most serious long-term domestic problem threatening the economic development and health of Turkmenistan is the Soviet legacy of disregard for land and water resources. The Soviet-engineered attempt to maximize short-run agricultural production at the expense of these limited land and water resources has left a series of environmental problems that now beg to be addressed. Two issues—the Kara Kum Canal diversion of the Amu Darya River for the purpose of irrigating cotton fields, and the draining of the Garabogazköl Aylagy (Kara Bogaz Gulf) on the

Caspian Sea—pose ecological problems of potentially disastrous proportions.

Kara Kum Canal Construction of the Kara Kum Canal, begun in 1954, has been hailed in rather utopian terms as the greatest blessing ever bestowed upon the Turkmen people. Stretching from the city of Kerki in the east, where waters of the Amu Darya River are diverted into the canal, to the capital of Ashgabat and beyond in the west, the Kara Kum waterway is a massive project intended to turn arid desert lands into a fertile agricultural plain. In conception, the project compares to the U.S. diversion of the Colorado River in the celebrated Central Arizona Project.

While the Kara Kum has, indeed, provided the basis for increased agricultural and cotton production, the problems associated with its construction are now being revealed. Diverting approximately 25 percent of the Amu Darya River at Kerki, the Kara Kum Canal has become the single greatest factor depleting the flow of the Amu Darya into the Aral Sea (see pages 190–91). Reduced now to a mere one-third of its original volume, the depleted Aral Sea has become the greatest natural disaster of Central Asia. Winds crossing its dried sea bed carry salts and chemicals across the agricultural fields of Central Asia threatening, ironically, the very fields that are irrigated by waters that used to flow into the Aral.

Moreover, to save costs in the construction of the Kara Kum, the canal was not lined with concrete. Thus, much of the water passing through the canal seeps into the ground and is lost. The consequent rise of ground water levels along the canal, and the absence of proper drainage, has meant that adjacent lands have experienced considerable soil salinization. By the 1980s, more than half of the lands within the Kara Kum canal zone were considered heavily salted and thus unsuited for agriculture (see Annette Bohr, "Turkmenistan under Perestroika," *Report on the USSR*, 23 March 1990, 24–25).

Kara Bogaz Gulf Due to the scope of the Aral Sea disaster, observers of Central Asia have sometimes lost sight of another major ecological problem looming in Turkmenistan—namely, the elimination of the Kara Bogaz Gulf (Garabogazköl Aylagy) on the Caspian Sea. In 1980, the inlet to the gulf was dammed in order to maintain high water levels in the Caspian Sea. Construction of the dam was premised upon the fear that the Garabogazköl Aylagy was draining the Caspian Sea, a premise that has now been entirely discredited.

Rather, in the years since 1977, the Caspian Sea has been rising steadily by an average of 14 centimeters per year. The damming of the Garabogazköl Aylagy has no doubt contributed significantly to that rise by halting drainage of the Caspian Sea into the Kara Bogaz Gulf. As a consequence, thousands of square miles of Caspian coastal territory have been lost to the rising sea waters. Entire coastal villages in Kazakhstan have been lost. On the western coast, the capital of the Russian autonomous republic of Dagestan, Makhachkala, could well be taken over by the rising waters. The Caspian Sea also now poses a threat to coastal oil-drilling sites in Azerbaijan.

Originally, the plans for the dam included the provision of a lock that would allow for replenishment of the Kara Bogaz. Another cost-saving measure was introduced, however, and the lock was not built. As a result, the Kara Bogaz is drying up. The creation of this evaporating salt lake not only undermines the productive capacity of the large Karabogazsulfat chemical plant—the Kara Bogaz having been an invaluable source of rare chemicals—but the dry bed of the Kara Bogaz Gulf now also threatens the surrounding agricultural regions. Just as the drying Aral Sea bed has proved to be the source of unhealthy saline and chemical winds blowing over agricultural terrain farther east, so also the wind-blown salts of the Kara Bogaz Gulf threaten the grain-growing lands of the southwestern region of the Russian Federation. Turkmen opposition to the damming of the Kara Bogaz Gulf has been made known by prominent leaders of the republic's Academy of Sciences, but to date, the effort to reverse the harmful effects created by the dam have produced sparring between rival bureaucratic agencies rather than any resolution of the problem. While the issue raises larger questions of competing sovereign claims to the Caspian Sea, Turkmen authorities will ultimately need to decide whether further construction or destruction of the Kara Bogaz dam best serves the interests of Turkmen economic and ecological well-being.

Political Democratization?

In spite of some initial public participation in political life in the 1980s, Turkmenistan has remained among the former Soviet republics least affected by the process of democratization. Public life remains largely controlled by political appointees, such as those of the nomenklatura or Party-appointed elite who were elevated under Soviet and Communist Party influence. In a slight modification of that system of political favoritism, there have been notable efforts by the Turkmen president in the 1990s to revive and manipulate old clan and tribal divisions by appointing regional or oblast administrative heads from the predominant clan of a given region—for example, a Tekke in Mary,

and a Yomud in Dashhowuz. Similarly, government ministerial appointments have come to be dominated by old clan leaders—most notably the Tekke throughout the security and police apparatus.

At the head of this political system stands Saparmurad Niyazov, president of Turkmenistan. Niyazov came to office through prominent appointments in the Turkmen Soviet government and Communist Party. An electrical engineer by training, Niyazov held minor Party posts in the early 1980s before rising to republican and central Moscow recognition while first secretary of the Ashkhabad (Ashgabat) City Party Committee. In March 1985, Niyazov was appointed chairman of the Council of Ministers of Turkmenistan. In the traditional Soviet division between government and Party positions, the Council of Ministers' chairmanship constituted the leading post in the Turkmen Soviet Republic's government. Nine months after being appointed to head the Council of Ministers, in December 1985, Niyazov was chosen, at the age of 46, to head the Communist Party of Turkmenistan, the highest office in the republic.

In the ensuing years, Niyazov has remained the only Central Asian head of state to survive the entire Gorbachev period and retain full power into the post-Soviet era. Niyazov has done so while giving lip service to formal elections, popular referenda, and public participation, albeit within a highly controlled political process. Typical of Niyazov's style is his handling of the issue of Turkmenistan independence in the wake of the abortive August 1991 Moscow coup d'état. While all the other republics were declaring their independence, Niyazov appealed to popular support for such a declaration, setting a national referendum for October 1991. After a campaign in which Niyazov strictly controlled the media urging support for the initiative, more than 94 percent of the electorate voted for Turkmenistan independence. Although the referendum gave the appearance of democratic participation in the public life of the country, the reality was rather one of a carefully controlled political environment.

Similarly, Niyazov appealed for people's support when he became in 1992 the first president of a former Soviet republic to submit himself to popular ballot. The result of the June 1992 election, the first held under the new Turkmenistan constitution, was an overwhelming Niyazov victory. He received more than 99 percent of the vote. Although the election was probably meant to demonstrate to the world the process of democratization at work in Turkmenistan, Niyazov's election had been guaranteed by the fact that no opposition party was permitted to qualify for the ballot. In response to complaints that the Turkmenistan government has not gone far enough in the protection of civil and human rights within its newly independent state, Niyazov is quick to point out that the most important prerequisite for building a modern democratic, secular state is political stability. His repression of informal political organizations seeking recognition as legitimate parties appears to conform to this concern for political stability.

For their part, the Turkmen intelligentsia seems more concerned to advance national goals, including the Turkmen language, than to seek direct political representation. In the meantime, Niyazov has engineered a measure of personal authority in the new republic unparalleled in other Central Asian states. In the weeks leading up to the June 1992 presidential elections, a virtual cult of personality was developed around Niyazov. (For an analysis of how that cult has been extended, at the expense of basic human rights, see the analysis of Helsinki Watch representative Jeri Laber, "The Dictatorship Returns," *New York Review of Books*, 15 July 1993, 42–44.) Despite his autocratic ways, it is probable that, except for the occasional stirring of the small Turkmen intelligentsia, Niyazov also retains popular support. His vision of a stable, secular Turkmen state that welcomes foreign investment seems to accord for now with the wishes of much of the Turkmen population, which desires, more than anything else, improved economic performance. As for the substantial Russian population, comprising nearly half of the population of Ashgabat, it, too, has been reassured that Niyazov will not stand for any interethnic strife that would dampen prospects for international investment.

Niyazov's commitment to interethnic peace may also be motivated by a concern for the maintenance of stability within the predominantly Turkmen nation. For, lurking below the surface are not only potential conflicts between national groups, but also conflicts between traditional Turkmen tribes—conflicts that could undercut the legitimacy of the secularized Turkmen political bureaucracy. Despite these hidden sources of discontent, the only significant instability faced by the Niyazov government since 1985 was the May 1989 riots in Ashgabat and Nebitdag. Those riots appear now to have been launched by young people suffering from chronic unemployment.

In July 1995 there was a recurrence of demonstrations in Ashgabat when 1,000 protesters, mostly Turkmen, marched in the streets to complain of shortages of bread, water, electricity, and other basic needs. The Niyazov response was to brand the demonstrators as drug addicts. That charge, while it was almost surely contrived, may have resonated with a public that has witnessed an astounding rise in drug use. Indicative of how dramatic this rise has been was Niyazov's televised announcement that people would only be arrested for possession if they were found to have more than five grams of opium on them—no small amount. Drugs arriving from Iran and Afghanistan are readily available on the streets of Ashgabat, prompting one Niyazov critic to say that "the entire nation has turned to smoking opium instead of drinking vodka because opium is cheaper" (Avdy Kuliev, quoted in "There is Only One Way Out—By Getting Rid of This Leader and This Government," *Transition* 2, no. 10, 17 May 1996, 37). Niyazov's response has been to fill to overflowing Turkmenistan's notorious prison system and to strengthen further his internal security apparatus. For now, despite the unanswered shortages in housing, basic foods, and health care, Niyazov's authoritarian leadership has made Turkmenistan the most politically stable state in Central Asia.

International Geopolitical Issues

As might be expected by its commitment to expanded foreign trade and Western investment, the Niyazov government has been particularly careful in developing its relations with the West. It has sought ties with Europe and the United States. Frequently meeting with Western economic and business leaders, the Niyazov government has also solicited membership in the Conference on Security and Cooperation in Europe and in the International Monetary Fund.

These overtures to the West have not, however, been at the expense of Turkmenistan's ties with its neighbors. Bordering the nations of Iran and Afghanistan on its southern frontier, Turkmenistan has also moved to secure its future relations with the Islamic states of the Middle East. On these matters, the Niyazov government has already sent unmistakable signals. Turkmenistan has actively pursued cordial ties with Iran, seeking to secure support for needed oil and gas pipelines through Iran and Turkey to the West. Niyazov's own visit to Iran in 1994 and the launching of pipeline construction have, nevertheless, yielded little progress for Turkmenistan because of the lack of credit from Western companies frightened of doing business with Iran.

On other international fronts, the Niyazov government has been notably cautious in dealing with Turkey and the other Turkic governments of Central Asia. Preferring to craft bilateral agreements with individual states, Niyazov has shied away from participation in any pan-Turkic bloc. His early state visit to Turkey and the rapid establishment of diplomatic relations with the Turkish government have not been followed by progress in establishing the desired gas pipeline through that country.

Within the republics of the former Soviet Union, Turkmenistan has played a rather ambivalent role in the fragile informal alliance known as the Commonwealth of Independent States (CIS). Initially hosting a meeting of Central Asian states that requested inclusion in the Commonwealth, Turkmenistan has at the same time demonstrated a reluctance to give too much authority to the new body. Instead, Niyazov has come to rely increasingly upon improving bilateral relations with the Russian Federation. Sensing the improved relationship between Russia and Iran and the importance of working with Russia for alternative pipeline construction through the Russian Federation, Niyazov has entered into broad ranging negotiations with the Russian Federation. These talks have yielded, among other agreements, a pact for Russian training of Turkmenistan military forces. Similarly, Niyazov has secured bilateral talks to resolve the trade impasse with Ukraine over purchase of Turkmen natural gas. This bilateral approach has also distinguished Turkmenistan's position in talks with the other Central Asian states of the former Soviet Union.

The Turkmen Cultural Inheritance

Islam Overwhelmingly Islamic by religious tradition, Turkmen Muslims come largely out of the Sunni branch of Islam. In this respect, despite Iranian radio and other religious propaganda efforts, Turkmen religious traditions differ from those of predominantly Shi'ite Islam in Iran. Islam in Turkmenistan has shown little inclination to follow the more fundamentalist strains of Islam that are popular in Iran and other parts of the Middle East. Not only does fundamentalism not seem to be attracting broad numbers of Islamic faithful in Turkmenistan, or other parts of Central Asia, but most Turkmen follow their own brand of vernacular Islam. Recently, efforts have been made to publish a parallel text edition of the Koran in Arabic and modern Turkmen. The revival of Islam in Turkmenistan has increasingly taken the form of the reopening of mosques and religious institutions closed during the Stalinist and Khrushchev eras.

Turkmen Language The recovery of Turkmen cultural identity has also been associated with the issue of the Turkmen language. The native intelligentsia has sought to strengthen language instruction in Turkmen in the schools. The Slavic population of Ashgabat is increasingly being encouraged to develop second-language ability in Turkmen. Adding to the difficulty of recovering the Turkmen literary tradition is the fact that few members of the Turkmen intelligentsia are able to decipher early Turkmen manuscripts that were written in the Arabic script. Curiously, the large number of Turkmen living in Afghanistan and Iran have sought to reestablish ties with Turkmenistan, but the strength of this cultural connection is limited by the inability of fellow nationals on each side of the international border to read the other's script. Although there has been some encouragement for the study of Arabic, as elsewhere in Central Asia, the Turkmen language in Turkmenistan is likely to continue to be written using Cyrillic script for the foreseeable future, even though a transition toward use of Latin and Arabic scripts is already visible.

Turkmen History Perhaps most interesting in the recovery of Turkmen cultural identity is the renewal of interest in national Turkmen history. At the end of the 1980s, it became possible for Turkmen writers to question openly the established Soviet version of the incorporation of Turkmen territory into nineteenth-century Russia. This view held that the Turkmen lands were voluntarily joined to the Russian Empire in the latter half of the nineteenth century. Such a reading of history was particularly offensive to national traditions because the Turkmen were notable for putting up the most sustained and effective resistance to Russian imperial advance of any people in Central Asia. In the most memorable of these nineteenth-century resistance efforts, Turkmen defended the fortress of Geok-Tepe in 1881 against overwhelming military odds. In the end, almost 15,000 Turkmen were killed in the battle. Later, the surviving Turkmen soldiers were also killed by Russian forces. That it is once again possible to write and speak openly about the revered memory of the battle of Geok-Tepe is a mark of the reawakening of Turkmen cultural and historical consciousness.

Whether this emergent Turkmen consciousness will lead to yet further economic, political, and diplomatic separation from Moscow remains unclear. For now, the most important agenda facing Turkmenistan is the use of its relatively abundant natural resources to reverse the destabilizing patterns of high unemployment, high infant mortality, and a declining standard of living.

UZBEKISTAN

Statistical Profile

Demography

Population: 22,562,000

Ethnic population

Uzbek	71.4%
Russian	8.3%
Tajik	4.7%
Kazakh	4.1%
Tatar	2.4%
Karakalpak	2.1%
Korean	0.9%
Kyrgyz	0.9%
Ukrainian	0.8%
Turkmen	0.6%
Turkish	0.5%
Jewish	0.3%
Other	3.0%

Major urban centers and populations

Toshkent	2,094,000
Samarqand	370,000
Namangan	312,000
Andijon	297,000
Bukhoro (Bukhara)	228,000
Farghona	198,000
Qŭqon (Kokand)	176,000
Nukus	175,000
Qarshi	163,000
Urganch	129,000
Margilan	125,000
Jizzakh	108,000

Historic religious traditions

Islam	88%
Christianity	9%

Languages: Uzbek, Russian, Tajik

Population by age

Age	Total	Males	Females
0–14	39.9%	20.2%	19.7%
15–64	55.5%	27.7%	27.8%
65 and over	4.6%	1.8%	2.8%

Male/Female ratio: 49.7% male/50.3% female

Rural/Urban population
61.3% rural/38.7% urban

Annual population growth rate: 1.7%

Population density: 130.6 persons per sq mi

Government

Official name
Uzbekiston Respublikasi
(Republic of Uzbekistan)

Capital: Toshkent

Date of sovereignty/independence declaration
31 August 1991

Voting age: 18

Internal republic	Capital
Karakalpakstan	Nukus

Education

Literacy (age 15 and over who can read and write)

total population	97%
male	98%
female	96%

Level of education for persons over 15

completed higher education	9.2%
completed secondary education	57.7%
incomplete secondary education	19.8%

Number of higher education institutions: 46

Higher education enrollment: 321,700 students

Selected institutions of higher education (and enrollment)

Toshkent

State Technical University	20,000
State University	19,300
Institute of Railway Engineers	12,000

State Economics University 11,000
Electrotechnical University of
    Communications 5,100
Samarqand
    State University 16,000
    Samarqand Cooperative Institute 7,000
Nukus
    State University 7,000

Socioeconomic Indicators

Annual birth rate: 33.3 births/1,000 population

Fertility rate: 3.7 children/woman

Infant mortality: 28.2 deaths/1,000 live births

Average life expectancy
69.5 years (males 66.2, females 72.6)

Annual death rate: 6.6 deaths/1,000 population

Average family size: 5.5

Annual consumption of electrical energy
2,130 kWh/person

Hospital beds per 10,000 persons: 123.7

Physical Features

Area: 172,741 sq mi

Land use
cultivated 10%
pasture 48%

Highest elevation: 12,507 ft (in the Gissar Range)

Rainfall
3 in./yr in the plains and foothills
up to 39 in./yr in the mountains

Temperature

Winter	**Summer**
average 18°F	north, average 79°F
lowest, −35°F	south, average 86°F
	highest, 108°F

Economic Production

Estimated per capita GNP: $950 (1994)

Agricultural output
cotton, vegetables, fruits, grain, livestock

Natural resources
petroleum, natural gas, coal, gold, uranium, silver, copper, lead, zinc, tungsten, molybdenum

Industrial output
textiles, food processing, machinery, metallurgy

Currency: sum (introduced July 1994)
1 sum = 100 teen

Communications

Length of rail lines: 2,163 mi

Length of highways: 41,875 mi

Pipelines
crude oil .... 156 mi
natural gas .... 506 mi

Telephones: 63 per 1,000 persons

Sources "Uzbekskaia sovetskaia sotsialisticheskaia respublika" *Bol'shaia sovetskaia entsiklopediia* (Moscow, 1977); *Narodnoe khoziaistvo SSSR v 1990g.* (Moscow, 1991); *Naselenie SSSR* (Moscow, 1989); Matthew J. Sagers, "News Notes: Iron and Steel," *Soviet Geography* 30 (May 1989): 397–434; Lee Schwartz, "USSR Nationality Redistribution by Republic, 1979–1989: From Published Results of the 1989 All-Union Census," *Soviet Geography* 32 (April 1991): 209–48; *World of Learning*, 46th ed. (London, 1996); "Russia . . ." (National Geographic Society Map, 1993); *Europa World Yearbook, 1996* (London, 1996); *Demograficheskii ezhegodnik, 1995* (Moscow, 1995); "CIA World Factbook, 1995" (www.odci.gov/cia/publications/95fact/uz.html).

Uzbekistan

KAZAKHSTAN

Aral
Sea

Karakalpakstan

Kyzyl

Kum

Desert

★ Nukus

Lowland

Farghona
Valley

Tian Shan
Mountains

• Urganch

★ Toshkent

Namangan •

Andijon •

• Khiva

Qŭqon •

Margilan •

Farghona •

Kuvasai •

TURKMENISTAN

Zeravshan

Guliston •

KYRGYZSTAN

Jizzakh •

Bukhoro •

River

Samarqand •

Turkestan Range

• Qarshi

TAJIKISTAN

12,507 ft. +

Termiz •

Amu Darya River

Turan

AFGHANISTAN

	International Boundary
- - -	Internal Republic Boundary
★	Capital City
•	Other Cities

0   200 Miles

0   200 Kilometers

Uzbekistan: History and Description

Physical Description

Borders Surrounded by the four other newly independent states of Central Asia, Uzbekistan is situated in the middle of this historically Islamic region. Kazakhstan is located to the north and west, Turkmenistan is to the south, and Kyrgyzstan and Tajikistan lie to the east. On its eastern border, Uzbekistan shares with Kyrgyzstan and Tajikistan the rich agricultural Farghona (Fergana) Valley. A short border is shared with Afghanistan at the extreme southern Uzbekistan frontier. Uzbekistan also includes the autonomous republic of Karakalpakstan. The desert lands of Karakalpakstan are in the western part of the republic, a region that encompasses the southern half of the Aral Sea.

Cities Three large cities, each located within an oblast of the same name, constitute the most heavily populated areas of Uzbekistan. By far, the largest of these cities is the capital Toshkent (Tashkent), followed by Samarqand, and then Farghona (Fergana). These three settlements have all developed along and around ancient river valleys and oases in which early civilizations flourished. The capital, Toshkent, was rocked by earthquakes in 1966 and has been substantially rebuilt. The importance of water for urban development in Central Asia is reflected in the location of the other large cities in Uzbekistan—Bukhoro (Bukhara), Qŭqon (Kokand), Andijon (Andizhan), Namangan, Qarshi, Nukus, Urganch, Termiz, Jizzakh (Dzhizak), and Guliston.

Topography and Climate Most of the territory of Uzbekistan is situated between the Syr Darya and the Amu Darya rivers. These rivers originate in the mountain streams east of Uzbekistan and then flow in a northwesterly direction to the Aral Sea. The Syr Darya, the Amu Darya, and the Zeravshan cut through an area of flat plains known as the Turan Lowland. To the east of this dry plain rise the mountains of Tian Shan and the Turkestan Range. The plains region typically receives little rainfall, with the long, hot summer months followed by mild winters. Uzbekistan also contains one truly arid region called the Kyzyl Kum Desert.

Ethnic and Historical Background

The history of Central Asia is, in part, a history of small tribal groups of Turkic-speaking settlers and nomads. Archeological investigations of these peoples, among whom are the forebears of modern Uzbeks, place them in the area of contemporary Uzbekistan as early as the twelfth century. However, the idea that these tribes form, in effect, a single Uzbek nation is a relatively recent concept, with Uzbek nationalism dating only from the twentieth century, particularly the Soviet period.

The Uzbeks are the most populous of the Turkic, Islamic peoples of Central Asia. The nation was formed over many centuries, during which a relatively settled Iranian (Tajik) population shared the region with a more nomadic group of Turkic tribes. The language that came to predominate was Turkic. There are at least three identifiable subgroups of modern Uzbeks: Kypchak, Turki, and Sart. The largest Uzbek subgroup is the Sarts. Culturally similar to the Tajiks, the Sarts have been the most settled and least nomadic. Uzbeks of Sart descent are not separated by tribal divisions. The Turki are tribes residing primarily in the region of the Farghona Valley and Samarqand. The Kypchak are the once nomadic group that formed a link between other Uzbeks and the Kazakhs to the north. The Kypchak have maintained their tribal identity, even though they have become largely assimilated into the modern Uzbek nation of the twentieth century. In the autonomous republic of Karakalpakstan, the Karakalpak people are being assimilated into the dominant Uzbek culture, despite the fact that they are ethnically closer to the Kazakh population north of the Aral Sea.

Tamarlane Politically, Uzbeks share the sense of a glorious past dating from the great triumphs of the fourteenth-century Islamic Mongol leader Tamarlane (Timur). During the great civilization of fifteenth-century Central Asia, a descendant of Tamarlane known as Ulug Beg emerged as the ruler of an area centered around Samarqand. Ulug Beg's state, although it did not survive after his death in 1449, was an important link with the great imperial tradition of Tamarlane and the conquests of the Golden Horde. As the historian Edward Allworth notes in his recent history of the Uzbeks, the Uzbeks today find the origins of their history in that great age of Tamarlane (Timur) and the successor states of the region (Edward Allworth, *The Modern Uzbeks from the Fourteenth Century to the Present: A Cultural History*, Stanford, CA: Hoover Institution, 1990). In the sixteenth century, the term Uzbek or "Ozbek" came to be adopted by the successor nomadic, Turkic-speaking tribes. These tribes settled in and around the same region of Samarqand where Ulug Beg had earlier ruled.

Period of Decline This Muslim civilization began to decline in the seventeenth and eighteenth centuries because of the bypassing of ancient trade routes that had earlier crossed the arid, desert-like lands of Central Asia. Upon the demise of the Turkic khanates of the seventeenth and eighteenth centuries, there arose first the Khiva Khanate, later the Bukhara Khanate, and finally in the early nineteenth century, the Kokand Khanate. As political power in the region devolved to the khans controlling these oasis areas, foreign trade was expanded to include also the Russian Empire.

The Russian Conquest

Russian expansion and conquest of the Uzbek region began in 1865 with the surrender of Toshkent to tsarist military forces. This surrender was quickly followed by the defeat of Bukhara in 1868, Khiva in 1873, Kokand in 1876, and all other smaller tribes within the next decade. By 1900, Russian colonial influence in local affairs had come to dominate. Growth in the marketing and trading of cotton boomed, aided by the many miles of newly built railroad lines. Russian, Ukrainian, and Belarusian immigrants streamed in, despite their uncertain welcome.

World War I The events of the First World War, and the tsarist need in 1916 for additional workers to assist the Russian armed forces, brought a request from Petrograd for a military draft of the native peasantry. A violent and widespread uprising resulted as a protest against this call-up of the local citizenry. The revolt failed, however. Within a year, the course of revolutionary events in Russia radically altered the relationship between the imperial center and the local Uzbek nationals.

Russian Revolution and Civil War In November of 1917, after the Bolshevik Revolution, a new Soviet order was heralded in Toshkent. After what appeared to be a passive acceptance of the situation by local residents, the course of events changed. Incidents related both to Bolshevik interference in Muslim religious affairs, as well as to requisitions of food, triggered resistance efforts, some of which focused on demands for local autonomy. A loosely organized group led by conservative Muslim forces called the Basmachi (Qorbashi) emerged as an anti-Communist force and began what was essentially a guerrilla struggle against the Bolsheviks. When the Red Army forces began to secure the upper hand in the Russian Civil War, Bolshevik efforts came to be directed also against the Basmachi insurgents, with the end result that Soviet power was secured also in the old Russian colonial regions of Central Asia.

In incorporating the republic of Uzbekistan into the Soviet Union, Lenin's followers were guided, in part, by his so-called nationalities policy. Based on the idea that native cultures could actually be encouraged to develop along their natural path, the assumption of Leninist "national self-determination" was that ethnic identity need not conflict with socialist forms of economic and governmental life—forms that were to be largely directed from the center of government, in Moscow. In Central Asia, this doctrine of national self-determination came to mean the radical breakup of the region into "ethnic" republics. Thus, in 1924 the area known as Russian Turkestan was formally dissolved, and in its place new Soviet republics were established, based upon ethnicity. From the perspective of Moscow, one important advantage of the nationalities policy was that it effectively undermined local sentiments that supported a union of Uzbek peoples with other Turkic-speaking groups outside the republic. The division of what had been Turkestan effectively elevated certain groups, such as the Uzbeks, to the status of privileged nations, while at the same time establishing boundaries that foreclosed pan-Turkic or pan-Islamic unity in Central Asia. It was a twentieth-century case of "divide and conquer." For the first time in the modern period, Uzbek tribal subgroups that had shared a common history beginning in the fourteenth century were effectively being forged into a common "privileged" nation. This served the political and economic interests of Moscow, even as it could be justified on the grounds of "national self-determination."

The Uzbek Soviet Socialist Republic (UzSSR)

The Uzbek Soviet Socialist Republic (UzSSR) was officially incorporated into the Soviet Union in May of 1925, following the successful consolidation of Soviet power in the northern and middle part of Central Asia. The administrative organization of the territory underwent certain changes during the years after it joined the union. For instance, in 1929 the Autonomous Republic of Tajikistan was separated from Uzbekistan, and in 1930 the Uzbek capital was changed from Samarqand to Toshkent.

Following the 1925 establishment of the Uzbek republic, there was a period of economic growth and industrialization in Uzbekistan. Economic policies, launched from the Moscow center and implemented by increasing numbers of Russians migrating into the country's urban centers, set ambitious goals for increasing cotton production. Ultimately, the economic plan for the Uzbek republic was to increase cotton production enough to make the Soviet Union independent from foreign cotton imports. This long-term plan was to establish a precedent for Moscow-centered economic planning and political management within the new republic. Moreover, in implementing new land and industrialization policies, the organs of central planning inevitably forced changes in traditional Islamic ways of life. For example, Islamic women, often accustomed to the veil, were drafted into the work force.

Collectivization of Agriculture In agriculture, the process of collectivization transformed traditional Uzbek village society. Soviet-installed managers, including Russified Uzbek "water lords" who controlled the irrigation system, represented a modern, transformed version of the old authoritarian order that had prevailed in Central Asia from the medieval period. Nevertheless, the land and water reforms of the late 1920s, which provided plots for landless peasants, did achieve the desired result of increased cotton production. Within a decade of the establishment of the Uzbek republic, over 90 percent of cotton growing was collectivized and production had virtually doubled. By the mid-1930s, the Stalinist regime came to pursue a modest retreat in socioeconomic areas and was far more careful and conservative in handling the economy than it was in dealing with political leadership.

Accompanying production successes in cotton, as well as in silk and citrus growing, were increases in electrical production, textile manufacturing, and petroleum output. The educational system—although a focal point of conflicting Russian and Uzbek interests—was enlarged and illiteracy was reduced. Similarly, general health care was expanded to reach people not previously served by the medical profession.

Political Leadership Under Stalin, the responsibility for governing the Uzbek republic lay both with native Communist leaders and with Russian bureaucrats imported from Moscow. The first secretary of the Uzbek Communist Party has consistently been Uzbek. Holding that office from 1925 until his removal in 1937 was Akmal Ikramov. Charged with harboring nationalist tendencies, Ikramov was tried, found guilty of treason, and shot in 1938. Ikramov had arisen out of the generation of Islamic modernizers or Jadids, many of whom initially sided with the new Bolshevik government. His death was a part of the more general bloodbath associated with Stalin's great purge of Party leaders in the last half of the 1930s.

The purge of Uzbek Communist Party leadership from 1937 to 1938 opened the door for a new generation of Party elite bred in a more harshly Stalinist mold. Usman Iusupov, Uzbek Party first secretary from 1937 to 1950, fit squarely into such a pattern, as did his close associate, Abdujabbar Abdurakhmanov. In 1950, Iusupov and Abdurakhmanov took higher Party positions in Moscow. Following a period of transition and de-Stalinization in Uzbek Party politics in the 1950s, Sharaf Rashidov assumed the post of first secretary in 1959. He held that position until 1983, a period during which Uzbek politics became re-Stalinized. Rashidov was later implicated in the corruption of the notorious "Cotton Affair" described later.

After Rashidov's passing, the mantle of the new anticorruption leadership fell to Inamzhon Usmankhojaev and Rafik Nishanov. The problem with the anticorruption campaign was that it provoked agitation over the ongoing interference of Moscow in Uzbek politics. When Nishanov left for Moscow in 1989, his successor and present-day ruler of Uzbekistan, Islam Karimov, studiously sought to disassociate himself from center-dominated politics, calling for Uzbek sovereignty and locally based decision making. Nevertheless, despite Karimov's outward new style, he has been trained within the same Communist Party echelons that have produced all Uzbek political leaders from the death of Akmal Ikramov to the present.

Uzbekistan: Contemporary Issues

Reinterpreting the Past

Uzbek history is today being rewritten in two remarkable ways. First, the account of Russian territorial conquest is being significantly revised. Second, the very identity of the Uzbek nation is being subjected to re-

examination. No topic in modern Uzbek history has been so politically sensitive as that of the Russian imperial conquest of Central Asia. Throughout the Soviet period, it was assumed that Russian territorial acquisitions in these lands were "progressive" acts, in which local peoples were liberated from the tyrannical hold of ruthless and inefficient feudal khans. In the Stalinist period, such acquisitions were even characterized as the "voluntary" ceding of territory by the indigenous population. In the current interpretation of Central Asian history, the Russian conquest is revealed as a period of opposition by local people and leaders to the Russian military advance. Typical of this historical revision is the work of Uzbek historian Hamid Ziyaev. Writing in the Uzbek monthly, *Sharq Yulduzi,* Ziyaev cites the manifesto of a mid-nineteenth-century emir enjoining his troops to fight against Russian conquering forces:

> Faithful Muslim subjects! . . . We are the descendants of Timur [Tamerlane], we shall demonstrate how to recapture our land. Muslims! I hope that you will show the infidels how valiantly the Muslim people fight for our religion and our land. The people are expecting victory from you—let them say after the battle that you defended religion and the homeland, and rid our land of the infidels. (Internally quoted in James Critchlow, "Central Asia: The Russian Conquest Revisited," *Report on the USSR*, 8 March 1991, 17)

Identifying the Uzbeks as the heirs of Tamerlane, such reinventions of the Russian conquest draw openly upon the authority of once discredited, elite emirs in order to castigate the imperial Russian "infidel."

As significant as the reexamination of the Russian conquest may be for Uzbek nationalism, potentially even more far-reaching is the questioning by some Uzbek intelligentsia of the very identity of Uzbekistan. Within the pages of Uzbek literary periodicals, there have been proposals for a return to the use of the pre-1917 terminology of "Turkestan" or "Turan." Behind such proposals is the growing realization that the peoples of Central Asia have tended not to identify so much with the nation, but rather with their tribal or local affiliation, or with their unity as Muslims. Proposals for a return to "Turkestan" reflect questions that people were not allowed to raise during the establishment of the Uzbek Soviet Socialist Republic in 1925. Where does the Uzbek "nation" fit in this picture? James Critchlow begs the question in his article, "Will Soviet Central Asia Become a Greater Uzbekistan?" (*Report on the USSR*, 14 September 1990, 17–19). Uzbek political elites were among the biggest "winners" in the Soviet national delimitation policy of the 1920s, which granted union republic status to Uzbekistan at the expense of other tribes and nations that the Soviets decided to subordinate to Uzbek authority. This has led to an understandable continuity between Uzbek political leadership of the Soviet period and that of the newly independent state of Uzbekistan. Still, while there are many Uzbek na-

tionals who have benefited from political and economic structures established over the course of 65 years in Soviet Uzbekistan, the future of the Uzbek nation now rests upon how conflicting visions of nation, tribe, and religious community will be sorted out in the post-Soviet era.

Cotton Monoculture

One legacy of the Soviet period is an Uzbek economy dominated by rural poverty and a disproportionate dependence on cotton. The rural cotton regions west of Toshkent and in the Farghona Valley have the highest birth rates, largest average family size, and greatest level of unemployment, not only within the republic of Uzbekistan itself, but within all of Central Asia. While the range of economic problems confronting modern Uzbekistan is daunting by any standard, what makes the newly independent republic particularly vulnerable is its single-crop economy—the so-called cotton monoculture. The cotton monoculture entailed a set of colonial economic relationships in which the growth of a single cash crop in Uzbekistan became the basis for a Russian textile industry that developed far from the source of the fiber. As late as 1990, central state planning structures in Moscow called for still further increases in cotton production in Uzbekistan, with an eye toward yields exceeding a phenomenal five million tons a year in the arid lands of Uzbekistan and Turkmenistan.

Cotton and the Environment: The Aral Sea Disaster

The establishment of the cotton monoculture by Moscow was made possible by massive irrigation projects that drew upon the Amu Darya and Syr Darya rivers. These two river systems, the Syr Darya draining largely through Kazakhstan and the Amu Darya forming the border between Turkmenistan and Uzbekistan, travel through Central Asia from the eastern mountainous regions near China before feeding into the Aral Sea. Yet, the Aral Sea, once the world's fourth-largest inland body of water, has become so depleted by the reduced flow of the Amu Darya and Syr Darya that it now holds less than one-third of its original volume of water. Only a small portion of the water used for irrigation is returned to the rivers after leaching the cotton fields in the agricultural oblasts of Uzbekistan, Turkmenistan, and Kazakhstan. Not only does this mean a diminished water supply for the Aral Sea, but the river water that ultimately reaches the sea is a sludge severely polluted by pesticides, defoliants, and fertilizers. Despite the precautions posted against use of Aral Sea water, people of the region continue to bathe their children in it, and to use it for drinking, cooking, and washing clothes. The long-term impact of this Aral Sea disaster upon the ground water in the area has only begun to be calculated.

The problem of the Aral Sea has received international attention as a serious environmental and health issue. Of the 1.25 million people living in Karakalpakstan, immediately adjacent to the Aral Sea, approximately two-thirds are suffering from hepatitis, typhoid, or cancer of the esophagus (see the investigative article by William S. Ellis, "The Aral: A Soviet Sea Lies Dying," *National Geographic*, February 1990, 73–93). Infant mortality in Karakalpakstan is estimated at 111 deaths for every 1,000 live births. For comparison, the 1987 rate for the former Soviet Union was 25.4 deaths per 1,000 live births, and the rate for the entire Uzbek republic was 45.9 deaths per 1,000 live births. Of every 100 children in Karakalpakstan, 83 suffer from some type of serious health ailment.

Not only those in the immediate vicinity of the Aral Sea have been affected. Millions of tons of dust from the dried Aral Sea bed are blown by prevailing winds over Central Asia's most fertile crops, depositing a contaminated, chemical-laden cover as far away as the Farghona Valley. One measure of the potency of such winds is to be found in the high salt content of local precipitation.

Political Corruption and the Cotton Affair

The development of the cotton monoculture and its attendant environmental problems have not happened without the support of local Uzbek leadership. From the late 1970s to the mid-1980s, the central Soviet authorities paid out to Uzbekistan officials more than a billion rubles for cotton that was never received. The padding of cotton-production figures and related charges of corruption came to be associated with the rule of Sharaf Rashidov, Uzbek Communist Party general secretary, and head of the republic for 25 years until his demise in 1983. The corruption of the Rashidov years and the false figures for cotton production, what came to be known as the Cotton Affair, were the focus of a public campaign against corruption in 1986 when Soviet Communist Party General Secretary Mikhail Gorbachev, together with conservative Party stalwart Egor Ligachev, launched a crackdown in Uzbekistan. In the ensuing months, tens of thousands of Uzbekistan Communist Party members were purged, some 3,000 police officers were fired,

and the long-time Uzbek Communist leader who profited from the cotton diversions, Rashidov himself, was widely discredited.

The Cotton Affair, like other scandals in Soviet life, quickly came to assume a symbolic importance beyond the surface claims of corruption. The temporary prosecutors sent down from Moscow in the late 1980s brought an ominous air of fear to the republic's Uzbek officials. As Western observer James Critchlow puts it, "No grievance is more sensitive than the widespread feeling among Uzbeks that corruption and 'the cotton affair' were used by Moscow as pretext to prosecute on ethnic grounds" ("Further Repercussions of the Uzbek Affair," *Report on the USSR*, 24 April 1990, 21).

The Restructuring of Uzbek Politics

The Uzbek reaction to the crackdown following the Cotton Affair reflects the degree to which the process of political restructuring launched by Moscow also opened the way for the development of informal and independent groups in Uzbek politics. The most important milestone in this process was the establishment of the Uzbek popular front organization known as Birlik (meaning Unity, or The Unity Movement for the Preservation of Uzbekistan's Natural, Material, and Spiritual Riches). Begun as a working group in November 1988 by Uzbek intellectuals in Toshkent, Birlik held its first, unsanctioned public demonstration in March 1989, drawing over 12,000 people. The demonstrators, among their other demands, appealed to the republic's Congress of Agricultural Workers for a reduction in cotton production and an end to the wasteful cotton monoculture of Uzbekistan. Later, following the May 1989 founding congress of Birlik, the movement denounced a republican draft language law of October 1989, demanding that instead of bilingualism—a euphemism for continued precedence and parallel use of Russian in Uzbekistan official life—Uzbek be designated the republic's language of interethnic communication as well as its state language. The rapid spread of Birlik's popularity could be gauged by the October 1989 demonstration held in Toshkent that gave voice to Uzbek feelings on the language question. Over 50,000 people attended, according to official estimates, and 100 Birlik leaders were temporarily arrested. By the end of 1989, the Birlik movement at its second congress extended its scope, opening its membership ranks to non-Uzbek Central Asian groups, and even encouraging Birlik chapters outside Uzbekistan.

Birlik is by no means the only independent public voice that has been raised. Initially a moderate wing of the Birlik movement, Erk (Freedom), became the first Uzbek opposition group to be registered as an official party in September 1991. The Erk Party, which claims its strength among the Uzbek intelligentsia, offers as its stated goals the drive for human rights, the national revival of Uzbekistan, and complete independence.

The Communist Party of Uzbekistan, having broken with Moscow, renamed itself the People's Democratic Party of Uzbekistan. Its leader, Islam Karimov, has indicated that the new party rejects any notion of a state religion, but it claims to welcome the revival of spiritual and cultural traditions and is also committed to the development of a sovereign and independent Uzbekistan. The renamed Communist Party has lodged within itself some opposition elements. Indeed, President Karimov's decision to call presidential elections for December 1991 was a result of open and unprecedented criticism directed at his leadership from within the Uzbek parliament, the Supreme Soviet.

In the years since Karimov's election as president, the drive for centralized authority and political stability has taken place at the expense of political democratization and human rights. Karimov has banned the Erk Party and arrested many of its leaders. Abdurrakhim Pulatov, a professor of physics in the Uzbek Academy of Sciences who helped found the Birlik movement in 1988, was forced into exile in Turkey in 1993 after facing intensified harassment. The pattern of accelerating repression was confirmed in 1994 in the attempts by the Uzbek National Security Committee, successor to the Uzbek KGB, to kidnap Uzbek political opposition leaders abroad, while some of them were participating in a human rights conference in Kazakhstan. Meanwhile, the Uzbek news media have become vehicles for government propaganda, and journalists have been subject to police surveillance. There are no independent newspapers registered in Uzbekistan (see Roger D. Kangas, "Uzbek Media Remain Restricted and Devoid of Criticism," *Transition* 1, no. 18, 6 October 1995, 76–77).

In December 1994, elections were held for the new parliamentary Supreme Assembly (Olii Majlis). Yet, in the absence of all but a cultivated "opposition" of local business interests (the Fatherland Progress, or Vatan Tarakkieti), Karimov's People's Democratic Party gained over 200 of the 250 seats. Opposition candidates from the Erk Party and other dissenting groups were banned from the ballot. In 1995, Karimov sought and secured referendum support to extend his presidency to the year 2000.

Despite these signs of authoritarian rule, Islam Karimov enjoys a goodly measure of support from an electorate that appears to accept the need for govern-

mental guarantee of political stability. In a 1994 poll conducted in Uzbekistan, over 75 percent of the population said that the government should be able to ban publication of "ideas too dangerous for society" (see Roger D. Kangas, "Uzbek Media Remain Restricted and Devoid of Criticism," *Transition*). Karimov has endorsed the "Uzbekization" of public life, granting a measure of public endorsement to the recovery of religious and ethnic identity. But, this bow to religious and ethnic identification has not been accompanied by freedom of religion or speech. Groups that once thrived under Gorbachev's glasnost of the 1980s have been largely silenced or confined to the underground in the 1990s.

The Voice of Islam

In Uzbekistan, as elsewhere in Central Asia, Islam is the dominant religion of the native Turkic population. In the 1980s, alongside other groups expressing political opposition, there arose the resurgent voice of Islam. For most of the Soviet period, Islamic religious leadership was organized according to four spiritual jurisdictions closely overseen by Soviet authorities. Independent-minded Islamic reformist, or Jadid, leadership was undermined by the end of the 1920s. Mystical Sufi movements remained alive in the rich Islamic religious life of small tribal groupings. But, officially recognized Islamic leadership came under control of Soviet-authorized Muslim spiritual jurisdictions. One of the spiritual jurisdictions set up by Moscow was centered in Toshkent. There, the chairman of the Muslim Religious Board for Central Asia and Kazakhstan (MRBCAK) served both as the Islamic mufti for Central Asia and as the recognized voice of Islam for Soviet authorities. In February 1989, the long-time MRBCAK chair, Shamsutdinkan Babakhan, was removed from his office after a three-hour demonstration led by a group calling itself Islam and Democracy. Complaining that Babakhan drank, womanized, knew not a chapter of the Koran, and, in general, served the interests of the KGB, the protesters were able to secure a commitment for Babakhan's removal. The 1989 demonstration by Islamic believers in Toshkent was undoubtedly part of an effort by religious nationalist reformers bent on cleansing the officially registered Islamic clerical ranks of charlatans.

The resurgent public voice of Islam in Central Asia assumed several different tones in the months following the removal of Babakhan. Within the Uzbek intelligentsia, a reformist tradition built upon the pre-revolutionary Jadid movement has sought to link traditional Islamic culture with more secular and democratizing goals. For the intelligentsia, the recovery of Turkic and

Islamic identities is often compatible with a commitment to human rights and democratic political ideals. Not lost upon the political authorities—who fear such linkage of Islam with reformist politics—was the discovery that among the 400 arrested in Toshkent at the January 1991 Central Asian Congress of the Islamic Renaissance Party was Abdurrakhim Pulatov, co-chair of the Birlik movement. This overlap of Islamic identification with democratic opposition reflects, in part, the recovery of Jadidist intelligentsia traditions of the late nineteenth and early twentieth centuries.

It is not only the Islamic nationalist reformers who have led the opposition to "official" Islam. The distrust of state-designated, registered Islamic clergy by most Muslim believers has resulted in a parallel Islam led by unregistered mullahs. This parallel Islam is strongest in the subnational tribes of rural Uzbekistan and is most often associated with conservative Sufi mystical movements.

A third faction in the current recovery of Islam in Uzbekistan is found in the Wahhabi movement. The Wahhabis have long been a part of Islamic life in Central Asia, but because of their conservative insistence upon "pure" Islam (including such practices as the exclusion of women from public life) they have little common ground with modernizers in the tradition of the Jadids. At the same time, the Wahhabis adhere to a strict interpretation of the Koran and reject Sufi and other mystical Islamic practices. There has been some speculation that the mid-1989 riots in the Farghona Valley (described in the next section) were led, in part, by supporters of the Wahhabi movement (see James Critchlow, "Islam in Fergana Valley: The Wahhabi 'Threat,'" *Report on the USSR*, 8 December 1989, 13–17).

The Fergana Valley Riots and Interethnic Conflict in Uzbekistan

While the 1980s may have ushered in new political and religious voices in Uzbek public life, that openness also occasioned the outbreak of public riots directed against non-Uzbek national minorities. The most serious of these outbreaks occurred in June 1989 in the Farghona Valley, the easternmost region of Uzbekistan. As many as 100 were killed in the violence, most of them minority Meskhetians—Georgian-speaking peoples of the Islamic faith. The event that triggered the outbreak apparently occurred in the town of Kuvasai, 15 kilometers southeast of the city of Farghona. An incident between a Meskhetian and an Uzbek vendor in the local market led to wider conflict. When a large number of Meskhetians subse-

quently gathered in the area, violence erupted, with the first loss of life occurring at the end of May 1989. By early June, the violence had spread to several other cities, including the regional capital of Farghona, where armed Uzbek youth set fire to Meskhetian homes. The rapid spread of violence suggested that plans may have been underway for some time to launch a symbolic strike against targeted minorities, and the Meskhetians may have constituted a safer target than the larger Slavic population of urban Toshkent. Ultimately, central Soviet Interior Ministry troops had to be dispatched to quell the Uzbek rioters, who chanted such slogans as "Uzbekistan for the Uzbeks." Before the tumult subsided, 11,000 of the 60,000 Meskhetians in Uzbekistan were evacuated to makeshift refugee camps in the Russian republic.

There are several explanations for this outbreak in the Farghona Valley. First of all, it is the most densely populated region in all of Uzbekistan, with over 280 residents per square kilometer (for comparison, the average overall population density for the former Soviet Union was approximately 13 residents per square kilometer). The population of the Farghona oblast increased by 27 percent between 1979 and 1989, whereas that of the former Soviet Union grew by only a little over 9 percent.

The largely rural Uzbek native population, which more than doubled in size between 1959 and 1979, is faced with chronic rural overpopulation and underemployment. Most industry, on the other hand, is concentrated in Toshkent where the Slavic population is greatest. Of the estimated 22,000 Uzbek youth coming onto the job market in the Farghona oblast each year, 1 in 5 cannot find employment. From the perspective of the Uzbeks, the trouble has been that non-Uzbek nationals—Meskhetians, Crimean Tatars, Jews, Russians, and Germans—live better than do the native Uzbeks in their own republic. This perception also applies to the Meskhetians, who were transferred to Central Asia by Stalin in 1944. Of the estimated 400,000 Meskhetians living in lands of the former Soviet Union, only a few reside in Georgia. Others are found in Azerbaijan, Uzbekistan, and Kazakhstan. While some Georgians equate a Muslim with a Turk and reject the "Georgianness" of the Meskhetians, their language and former homeland have been historically connected to the present-day republic of Georgia.

The Farghona Valley violence, as well as the wider ethnic hatreds, have fed upon chronic Uzbek unemployment, rural poverty, high birth rates and infant mortality, and the accumulation of environmental and health problems associated with cotton monoculture. These deeper problems, however, do not justify the spread of ethnic violence. Conscious of that, the Birlik movement, despite its nationalist message, has carefully sought to disassociate itself from the Farghona Valley events.

The Language Question

Symbolic of the gradual Russification of Uzbekistan during the Soviet period was the shifting fate of the language question. When the Uzbek republic was established in 1925, modern Uzbek used a modified Arabic alphabet. Although only 3.7 percent of Uzbeks could read and write—a reflection of the difficulty of mastering the Arabic orthography—some Uzbeks concerned with increasing literacy joined in 1926 with Soviet calls for latinization of the Uzbek alphabet. Edward Allworth has noted that no nation employing the complicated Arabic alphabet, with the possible exception of Lebanon, has achieved more than 68 percent literacy (see Allworth, *Uzbek Literary Politics*, The Hague: Mouton, 1964). The drive for increased literacy came to be equated with use of the New Unified Turkic Alphabet, and ultimately with the conversion to the Latin alphabet in 1930 (its use actually began in 1928).

Adoption of a Western alphabet constituted a radical reform that had far-ranging implications for Uzbek culture and tradition. With the elimination of the Arabic script, the Koran and other traditional works became practically inaccessible until after World War II when new editions of the old works began to be prepared in the new script.

By 1940, Stalin had imposed another orthographic reform—this time the use of the Cyrillic script. As early as the 1880s, Russian missionaries had experimented with the use of Cyrillic in rendering the Uzbek alphabet, but the formal orthographic change of 1940 facilitated the teaching of Russian to Uzbeks and the more rapid introduction of Russian vocabulary. It also had the effect of undermining a generation of Uzbek national writers, for whom the Cyrillic script was largely foreign. In language, as in politics and economics, the Soviet period marked the victory of the Moscow center in Uzbek public life.

Behind the passions and programs of the Uzbek nationalist agenda, the language question has remained the most important and symbolic issue for the Uzbek intelligentsia. Today, the language question is being addressed both in national legislation and in the daily lives of Uzbek citizens. A new piece of legislation entitled "Law of the Uzbek Soviet Socialist Republic on Languages" was proposed in 1989. That law called for continued bilingual use of Uzbek and Russian as official languages of the republic. But for most Uzbek intellectuals, the proposed use of the old term "bilingualism" was thoroughly repugnant. For these Uzbek nationals, bilingualism had become a code word under which Uzbeks were expected to become bilingual, but Russians were not. Not only did Birlik enjoin the issue, but a groundswell of complaints cited the fact that Uzbek schools taught far more Russian than Russian schools did Uzbek. What Birlik's national agenda called for was a language law that would formally declare Uzbek the state language.

Although Uzbek has now become the state language of Uzbekistan, the power of Uzbek nationalism has begun to make itself felt in other language-related matters. Lectures at Uzbek universities are now increasingly delivered in Uzbek, not Russian. The Toshkent Pedagogical Institute has been pressured to train more and better teachers of Uzbek, including instructors in Old Uzbek (with Arabic script). Even local residents born in Central Asia of Slavic parentage have begun to feel the pressure to develop skills in modern Uzbek.

Further complicating the language question is the unresolved issue of the orthography or script to be used for modern Uzbek. For many of the Uzbek intelligentsia, the return to Arabic script has become an important part of the national agenda. In mid-1989, the Uzbek literary newspaper, *Ozbekistan adabiyati va san"ati*, began a special section devoted to teaching the Arabic alphabet. Uzbek primary schools are now also obliged to introduce the Arabic script. For the intelligentsia, the recovery of the Arabic orthography is essential for the renewal of literary traditions that predate the Soviet period when the Cyrillic or modern Russian script was introduced. Whether, and for how long, the Cyrillic script will continue to be used for modern Uzbek will be one of the barometers for judging the advance of Uzbek cultural nationalism.

Open-Ended Questions

The dawn of political independence in Uzbekistan leaves in its wake a series of unresolved, open-ended questions. The establishment of political independence has not been accompanied by democratization. Uzbek political leaders continue to impose limits upon the growth of informal public voices such as Birlik, Erk, and the Islamic Renaissance Party. The drive to diversify Uzbekistan's economy and to find new markets for cotton continues to confront a nation bearing the legacy of a cotton monoculture closely tied to Russian markets. Nevertheless, the process of economic restructuring and privatization is advancing slowly. The Uzbek currency introduced in July 1994, the sum, is among the more stable of Central Asian currencies.

The loyalties of Uzbek Muslims are being torn between the more secular, modernizing Islamic tradition of the Jadid movement on the one hand, and the localized, mystical sects of Islam on the other. Alongside pan-Turkic movements, these religious claims upon the Uzbeks have become a part of the unofficial debate over Uzbek national identity in the post-Soviet era. As leaders of this debate, Uzbek intelligentsia face the question of whether loyalty should continue to be given to the modern, secular Uzbek nation or should be broadened to include wider regional, pan-Islamic, and pan-Turkic allegiances.

Meanwhile, the problems of public health in Uzbekistan plague the newly independent state. If Uzbek birth rates continue to rise (with population increases three or four times the average for the former Soviet Union), and with infant mortality rates the highest of all former Soviet republics, the stability of Uzbek politics will inevitably be affected. The growing ranks of the unemployed only add to this picture of potential disruption. Such political instability carries with it in Uzbekistan the prospect that ethnic minorities may become the scapegoats for declining living standards. That, in turn, can only hasten the departure of Russians from the great urban centers of Uzbekistan. As elsewhere in Central Asia, Russians and other urban Slavs of Uzbekistan remain important for economic development, but they harbor fears of regional ethnic violence.

The seemingly inevitable disappearance of the Aral Sea and accompanying desertification in Central Asia symbolize the wider environmental crisis of the region. No country of Central Asia, least of all Uzbekistan, has the resources to address the Aral Sea problem alone. There have been efforts to bring the Central Asian states together on the Aral Sea issue, most recently in Nukus (Karakalpakstan) in 1995. Yet, in the absence of international financial support, it is difficult to contemplate the dismantling of the cotton monoculture, the construction of water purification systems and sewage treatment plants, and the other measures that would reverse the effects of the post–World War II Soviet command economy in Uzbekistan. As a result, the prognosis for the environment and public health in Uzbekistan remains grim.

AFTERWORD

More than five years have passed since the abortive August 1991 coup d'état, an event that led directly to the collapse of the Soviet Union at the end of that year. The underlying sources of Soviet disintegration lay not, however, in the immediate politics of 1991, even though the events in Moscow may have hastened the timing of that collapse. Rather, the deeper causes behind the fall of the Soviet Union were to be found in those ethnic and cultural forces that, having survived Russification and Soviet centralization, found renewed strength in the drive for national and religious freedom. This drive for independence dominated the political debate of the 1980s and continues to do so in the 1990s. Out of the struggle for renewed national and cultural freedom have emerged the newly independent states bearing the names of the former Soviet republics.

Since 1991, however, the euphoria of national independence has given way to a more sober assessment of the painful costs of economic and political change. In moving toward market-driven economies, the new states of Eurasia have encountered dramatic losses in production, heightened rates of inflation, and rising unemployment. Even in the emerging arena of private economic life—a sector that is now responsible for over half the gross domestic product of some of the newly independent states—the haunting specter of corruption crushes the idealism of would-be reformers. The problem of corruption has not only led to recurrent assassinations, but has also been manifest in the demands of local mafias for ever larger "insurance payments" in return for protection from criminal violence. Reverting to patterns that used to be associated with underdeveloped economies, the newly independent states of Eurasia have seen a dramatic widening of the gap between a very small, wealthy elite and a mass society with limited buying power and curtailed social services. The curtailment of such services, the weakening of the safety net for the unemployed, and the diminishing value of pensions for the elderly all reflect, in turn, the increasing difficulty faced by the newly independent states in developing dependable systems of tax revenue.

These sobering economic realities are now paralleled by a political malaise that undermines the confidence of citizens in public officials. Initial conflicts between elected parliaments and executive leadership have invariably been resolved in favor of authoritarian executive leadership. The increased powers granted to the Russian presidency in the 1993 Russian constitution reflect the same general pattern that has taken hold in most of the newly independent states. Behind the wall of reinforced executive authority there remains the hidden power of the old nomenklatura. This bureaucratic security-minded elite has invariably weathered changes in government by maintaining the personal ties that continue to dominate political life in the newly independent states. Political patronage continues to thrive in Eurasia.

Looming over the politics of transition are also the grim results of ecological and human degradation—a degradation bred by generations of disrespect for the environment. In the Soviet period, human and natural resources were often squandered in the name of arbitrary and ill-considered short-term production goals. The deadly devastation caused by the depletion of the Aral Sea, the chemical pollution in the Altai, and the nuclear catastrophe of Chernobyl are now being visited upon the first generation of post-Soviet Eurasian nationals. Wrenching decisions confront policymakers as they weigh the desperate energy needs of Ukraine and Armenia, for example, against the human dangers of reopened nuclear generating stations, such as those at Chernobyl (Ukraine) and Medzamor (Armenia).

Meanwhile, the renewal of ethnic and religious identities, so important in the initial drive for independence from the Soviet Union, has also reawakened dormant cultural and tribal loyalties within many of the newly independent states. The conflict between new state authority and the secessionist aims of national and tribal groups has resulted in the single greatest source of bloodshed in post-Soviet Eurasia. Nowhere has this conflict been so graphic as in the breakaway Republic of Checheniia (Chechnya), a war-torn north Caucasian region where Chechen rebels successfully held out against Russian military forces until a truce and withdrawal of Russian forces was negotiated in 1996. Yet, for every Chechen rebel who has caught the attention of international news media, there are hundreds more—the Abkhazians of Georgia, the Pamiri rebels of Tajikistan, and the Russian holdouts in Trans-Dniester Moldova—who seek at virtually any cost to challenge existing international borders in the name of ethnic justice. The politics of cultural and ethnic awakening remains among the most unsettling dimensions of the new Eurasia.

One of the greatest ironies of the transition underway in modern Eurasia is that the most articulate advocates of freedom in the former Soviet Union, the intelligentsia, must now be counted among the greatest losers in the process. To be sure, many of the intelligentsia remain committed to the process of political and economic transformation. But, the institutions where many of them worked—including some of the greatest universities and scientific institutes of the twentieth century—now face closure amidst wholesale cutbacks in state funding. The resulting brain drain from the former Soviet Union is palpable. Indeed, severe funding losses at critical institutes, such as those conducting research in nuclear energy and environmental safety, have raised fears about the possible diversion of human and technological resources to rogue international powers. More encouraging is the fact that, despite prohibitive costs, a new post-Soviet generation of talented young scholars is increasingly well linked to the computerized information networks provided by electronic mail and the Internet.

With some notable exceptions, the internationalization of information *within* Eurasia has not been matched by international support *for* Eurasia. The sustained level of international commitment extended to western Europe following World War II stands in stark contrast to the more limited efforts underway in post-Soviet Eurasia. Indeed, the proposed expansion of the NATO defense alliance to include Poland, Hungary, and the Czech Republic has been widely interpreted in Russia and throughout Eurasia as an effort to exclude and thereby isolate the newly independent states of the former Soviet Union. To be sure, Western lending agencies, such as the International Monetary Fund,

have played a vital role in assisting the new Eurasian governments toward more stable currencies, but the absence of large-scale international investment has hampered recovery efforts. The new Eurasian states contain a wealth of human and natural resources, but the development of those resources has been stalled by legal barriers and political uncertainties in the newly independent states. Often the efforts of non-governmental agencies (NGOs) and foundations have been as important in the development of Eurasia as the aid of foreign governments. The work of the American Bar Association's Central East European Legal Initiative (CEELI) has yielded slow, but steady, advances in legal reform within a few of the Eurasian states. Similarly, the Soros Foundation has sought to close the gap left by the loss of governmental support for vital scientific and scholarly institutions in Eurasia.

While internationally funded development can play a modest role in the economic and political restructuring of Eurasia, the most important forces of renewal are internal to the region. Among these can be counted the efforts at regional cooperation between the newly independent states. Joint Russian-Ukrainian agreements over the Black Sea Fleet and collaborative meetings between Central Asian heads of state, however tentative, are important signs of post-Soviet cooperation. Such cooperation, while it risks being viewed as a return to Soviet-style integration, can also be seen as a pragmatic accommodation to concrete issues, such as environmental protection and natural resource marketing. To export its oil to international markets, Kazakhstan, in cooperation with both American and Russian companies, is building a new pipeline through the territory of other former Soviet republics. Belarusian appeals for economic reintegration with Russia, while they reflect in part the misplaced nostalgia of President Lukashenka for a now distant Soviet past, also must be understood as the natural expression of concern from a Belarusian state that cannot be expected to meet alone the extraordinary expense of the Chernobyl clean-up.

Thus, amid the grim forebodings of economic deprivation, ethnic conflict, and old-fashioned political patronage, the newly independent states of Eurasia prepare to meet the twenty-first century, unwilling to return to the regimented centralization of a Soviet past, but unlikely to survive without the international collaboration of their former Soviet counterparts.

GLOSSARY

Adat. Customary law, as opposed to religious law *(sharia),* followed in Muslim societies. So vital were the norms of *adat* in Islamic Central Asia that, for example, the Bolshevik government, after incorporating Turkestan, developed a dual system of courts whereby justice was administered to Muslims in accordance with local customary law so long as it did not violate the laws of the Soviet government. *Adat,* or customary law, addressed a wide range of issues, including those related to ownership of land. *See* **Sharia**.

All-Union Congress of People's Deputies. Legislative body elected in March 1989 by the citizens of the 15 union republics of the USSR. This Congress, often referred to as the Soviet Parliament, should not be confused with the Russian Parliament chosen from the Russian Congress of People's Deputies, which was elected in 1990 by the citizens of the Russian Republic (RSFSR). The All-Union Congress of People's Deputies ceased to exist after the collapse of the Soviet Union.

Autocephalous. Independently ruled or, literally, self-headed. A term used to describe the autonomous administrative status of a church body or institution that is not subordinate to higher ecclesiastical authority.

Autonomous regions. Ethnically based territorial units designated as national homelands for non-Russians inhabiting lands within the Soviet Union. "Autonomous republics" ranked just below union republics in importance, followed by "autonomous oblast" and "autonomous okrug" units. Many autonomous regions within the former Russian Soviet Federated Socialist Republic have declared their own sovereignty within the new Russian Federation. *See* **Union Republic, National Delimitation Policy, Oblast,** and **Okrug.**

BAM (Baikal-Amur Mainline). Controversial rail line constructed in the 1970s and 1980s in Eastern Siberia and the Russian Far East. The railway runs from Bratsk near the Lena River to Komsomolsk on the Amur River. Extending over 2,000 miles through permafrost and 7 mountain ranges, the line is intended for transport of the rich natural resources being extracted from the region.

Basmachi. Muslim anti-Bolshevik guerrilla movement widespread in Central Asia from 1918 to the 1920s. The Basmachi (Qorbashi) fought for national independence, but by the late 1920s the Red Army had forced almost all remaining Basmachi to flee to Afghanistan.

Bolsheviks. A wing of the Marxist Russian Social Democratic Workers' Party (RSDRP) led by the Russian revolutionary Vladimir I. Lenin. Lenin and his Bolshevik followers seized power in the October Bolshevik Revolution of 1917. *See* **Mensheviks, Russian Revolution,** and **Russian Social Democratic Workers' Party.**

Central Committee of the Communist Party of the Soviet Union (CCCPSU). The ongoing assembly that officially oversaw Communist Party affairs in the Soviet Union between official Party congresses. Composed of 426 members, the body normally met twice a year, and formal decrees of the Party were issued in its name. In practice, although the Politburo and Party Secretariat officially reported to the Central Committee, policymaking in the Communist Party of the Soviet Union invariably fell to the much smaller Politburo. *See* **Politburo.**

Civic Union. A Russian political coalition formed in 1992 to advance the interests of an industrial lobby composed largely of managers of state-run enterprises. Although its political message has at times been blurred, it initially opposed the radical restructuring of the Russian economic system sought initially by Russian Federation President Boris Yeltsin.

Cold War. An ideological conflict between communism and democracy that strained relations between the Soviet Union and the West, particularly the United States. While the conflict polarized the world on the basis of rival systems or ideas, it also came to have practical impact upon the international and domestic policies of the Soviet Union and the United States, contributing in particular to the development of the nuclear arms race. Although there remain problems in Cold War demobilization, most observers see the collapse of the Soviet Union at the end of 1991 as marking the end of the Cold War.

Collectivization. Stalinist agricultural policy launched in the late 1920s in which peasant-held land was nationalized by force and administered by state agents. Peasants who had previously operated out of their own villages were resettled onto large, shared, communal farms and directed to work cooperatively, pooling their labor and resources. *See* **Kulaks**.

Commonwealth of Independent States (CIS). A loose confederation of former Soviet republics established in December 1991 to coordinate interrepublican policies, especially military and economic affairs. The CIS now includes all former Soviet republics, except for the Baltic states (Estonia, Latvia, and Lithuania).

Communist Party. Successor to the pre-1917 Bolshevik wing of the Russian Social Democratic Workers' Party, the Communist Party became the highest ruling authority in the Soviet Union. Through its administrative secretariat, its Central Committee, and its Politburo, the Communist Party controlled appointment to government offices and guided all major policy decisions. While the government of the Soviet Union functioned through bureaucratic ministries and a Council of Ministers, the Communist Party subordinated the governmental machinery to itself. Just as the first secretary headed the Communist Party in each republic, so also the general secretary of the Community Party of the Soviet Union (CPSU) was the leading figure in the overall ruling structure of the Soviet Union. *See* **Russian Social Democratic Workers' Party (RSDRP), Bolsheviks, Politburo, Central Committee of the Communist Party of the Soviet Union (CCCPSU), First Secretary (of the Communist Party),** and **General Secretary.**

Confessions. Christian church divisions often marked by differences in such things as liturgical practice and the celibacy or non-celibacy of priests. In this sense, it is possible to speak of the Eastern Orthodox "confession" as distinct from that of Latin-rite Christianity, also called Roman Catholicism.

Congress of People's Deputies. *See* **Russian Congress of People's Deputies.**

Cossacks. Eastern Slavs of Ukraine, who sought to retain a measure of governmental autonomy (under the office of the *hetman*) until absorption by the Muscovite and Russian empires in the seventeenth and eighteenth centuries. Bohdan Khmelnytsky, hetman of the Dnieper or Zaporizhzhian Cossacks in the middle of the seventeenth century, launched the most renowned Cossack drive for autonomy from the Polish-Lithuanian Commonwealth. *See* **Great Russians, Slav,** and **Little Russians.**

Cotton monoculture. Soviet centralized agricultural policy in which the state committed a region, notably Central Asia, to a single-crop economy—cotton. Continuous increases in cotton production, to be centrally marketed through Moscow, were expected under this policy.

Czar, Czarist. *See* **Tsar, Tsarist.**

Democratic Russia. A broad political coalition in Russia (1990–91) committed to democratic reform. Democratic Russia, whose editorial views were often reflected in the Moscow newspaper *Nezavisimaia Gazeta (The Independent Newspaper),* had its base of support among the Russian liberal intelligentsia, although it also received support from some Communist Party reformers.

Duma. Following the 1905 Revolution in Russia, four successive State Dumas were elected beginning in 1906, thereby creating prior to the 1917 Russian Revolution a parliamentary institution with limited powers. Under the terms of the new 1993 Russian constitution, the elected lower chamber of the Russian Parliament has again come to be called the "Duma," and serves as the official legislative body of the Russian Federation. The Duma is frequently referred to simply as the Russian Parliament, since the other chamber, composed of regional representatives, does not have comparable legislative authority. *See* **Russian Congress of People's Deputies** and **Supreme Soviet.**

Eastern-rite Christianity. Christian churches historically tied to Byzantium or the Greek East. Although the schism between the churches of East and West left the Eastern Orthodox Church separated from the Latin-rite or Roman Catholic West, the sixteenth- and seventeenth-century union of some Eastern-rite dioceses with their Roman Catholic counterparts led to the formation of a Uniate or Greek Catholic Church with ties to Rome. Both the Greek Catholic Church (including the Ukrainian Catholic Church) and the Eastern Orthodox Church follow the Eastern rite. *See* **Greek Catholic Church** and **Uniates.**

Eurasia. Broad landmass of Europe and Asia stretching from the East European Plain in the west to the Pacific Ocean in the east.

Exarchate. Administrative term used in Eastern Orthodox Christianity to indicate a particularly important diocese that is subordinate directly to a patriarch and often tied to a historically important region (e.g., the Exarchate of Minsk and Belarus).

First Secretary (of the Communist Party). Highest leader in a Communist Party organization. Used in particular to denote the highest Communist Party/governmental figure of each of the former union republics of the Soviet Union. *See* **General Secretary.**

Five Year Plan. Basic organizing principle of centralized planning within the Soviet Union; used to guide state investment, economic growth, and development. The first Soviet Five Year Plan covered the period from 1928 through 1932.

General Secretary. Title accorded the First Secretary of the Communist Party of the Soviet Union. *See* **First Secretary.**

Glasnost. Derived from the Russian term for "voice" *(golos),* this policy of openness and freedom of expression was introduced by Mikhail Gorbachev in the 1980s as part of his attempt to reform the Communist system from within.

Golden Horde. Often equated with Mongol rule in East Slavic lands from the thirteenth to the fifteenth centuries and beyond, the Golden Horde led by Genghis Khan and his warriors conquered the Kievan Rus grand princedom in the middle of the thirteenth century. The Mongols imposed a loose tribute-collecting system of authority that allowed the Slavic population to retain its identity while still being subordinated to Mongol political and economic control. The geographical and eth-nic origins of the Golden Horde are found among the Turkic and Mongol population of Central Asia.

Great Russians. Historic term used for a major subgroup of the Eastern Slavs inhabiting the lands around Moscow. Other Eastern Slavic peoples include the Belarusians, Rusyns, and Ukrainians. The Great Russians (or, simply, Russians) became the dominant ethnic and linguistic power behind the successive Muscovite, Russian, and Soviet empires. *See* **Slav, Cossacks,** and **Little Russians.**

Greek Catholic Church. An Eastern-rite Catholic Church that recognizes the authority of the Roman Catholic hierarchy, including the papacy, but retains a married clergy and follows the Eastern Orthodox liturgical calendar. Greek Catholics, many of whom live in Belarus and Ukraine, are also known as Uniates. *See* **Eastern-rite Christianity** and **Uniates.**

Gulag. Russian acronym for "Chief Administration of Corrective Labor Camps." A vast system of work camps and prisons located primarily in Siberia and the Russian Far East. Although the gulag swelled to an almost unimaginable size, housing millions of victims of Soviet repression, it had its precedent during the tsarist period when Siberia was used as a place of exile for political prisoners.

Jadids. Muslim reformers in the Russian Empire of the late nineteenth and early twentieth centuries who sought accommodation with the modern, secular world while holding onto their Islamic identity.

Kievan Rus. According to historical chronicles of the period, the political unification of East Slavic tribes dates to the middle of the ninth century (A.D.), when these tribes were gathered under the authority of the Grand Prince of Kiev. The resulting grand princedom—with its geopolitical center on the Dnieper River in Kiev, its own law code and monetary system, and its newly adopted Christian religion (from the end of the tenth century)—is generally referred to as Kievan Rus. For 400 years, before it was conquered by the Golden Horde in the middle of the thirteenth century, the grand princedom of Kiev, or Kievan Rus, continued to rule over a vast stretch of territory, including most lands from the Baltic to the Black seas and east to the Ural Mountains.

KGB (Komitet gosudarstvennoi bezopasnosti). Now officialy renamed the Federal Security Service (FSB), the KGB (Committee of State Security) formerly served as the police surveillance arm of the ruling Communist Party. The KGB had its own monitors at every level of Soviet government activity and in each of the former union republics. Its network of informers numbered in the hundreds of thousands. There has been talk of using the offices of the former KGB for attacking problems of corruption in contemporary post-Soviet society. Although many of the KGB's former secrets are currently being reported in the Russian press, most KGB archives remain closed to the public and little information is available about their contents. *See* **NKVD.**

Khanate. A Muslim "principality" in those Eurasian lands formerly occupied by the Mongol Empire, particularly in Central Asia, based on the political power of a local ruler (khan). In the course of its defeat of the Mongol Tatars, the Russian Empire gradually absorbed the Muslim khanates.

Kulaks. A class of independent freeholding peasants destroyed during the Soviet drive to collectivize agriculture in the late 1920s and 1930s. As many as one million kulaks and their families died as they were deported to the labor camps of the gulag. *See* **Collectivization** and **Gulag.**

Little Russians. Historic term used by the Muscovite and Russian Empires to designate the Eastern Slavs of Ukraine. Today, the term "Ukrainian" is the proper designation, and "Little Russian" is obsolete. *See* **Slavs, Cossacks,** and **Great Russians.**

Mensheviks. Despite the Russian term, which refers to the minority (*menshe* meaning lesser), the Mensheviks were the larger of the two factions of the Marxist Russian Social Democratic Workers' Party (RSDRP), the other faction being the Bolsheviks. Mensheviks supported the development of a mass workers' party, breaking with Bolshevik leader V. I. Lenin in 1902 over the direction and organization of party authority and discipline. *See* **Bolsheviks** and **Russian Social Democratic Workers' Party.**

Muscovy, Muscovite. During the period of Mongol rule, following conquest of Kievan Rus by the Golden Horde, the city of Moscow (in Russian, Moskva), founded in the twelfth century on the Moskva River, became a military, political, and religious center within the east Slavic world. By the end of the fifteenth century, the grand prince of Moscow (the tsar of Muscovy) had defeated the Mongols in battle, securing thereby the political and economic independence of Muscovy, and the ascendancy of Moscow over other Slavic river cities of the Volga River basin. The resulting grand princely or tsarist state is referred to as Muscovy, or Muscovite Russia. Peter the Great (1672–1725) transformed Muscovite military, political, and social institutions. The resulting new European state structure, with its capital in St. Petersburg, came to be identified as the Russian Empire (Rossiiskaia imperiia), as distinct from Muscovy.

National Delimitation Policy. Soviet policy dating from the 1920s that assigned a specific territory to one dominant ethnic group or nation. Drawn from the Leninist doctrine of "national self-determination," this policy offered the promise that native cultures could develop toward full ethnic identity. In practice, regions were broken along ethnic lines in such a way that non-Russian groups remained divided and dependent upon central Soviet authority. *See* **Autonomous regions.**

Near Abroad. Coined by Russians to refer to those non-Russian union republics of the former Soviet Union severed from the Russian Federation in 1991, the "near abroad" is most often used to identify the post-Soviet demographic reality wherein ethnic Russian population is now subordinate to the non-Russian titular nationalities of newly independent post-Soviet states. In the view of Russian nationalists, these ethnic Russians of the "near abroad" are hostage to alien rule.

NKVD. Earlier name for the KGB, dating from 1934. The term KGB came to be applied only in 1954. *See* **KGB.**

Nomadism. Ancient practice of tribal groups moving from place to place for their livelihood, according to the season. Nomads often traveled in patterns suited to the needs of their herds. Soviet policies in the Siberian north and in Central Asia attempted to crush such seasonal nomadism by enforcing fixed settlement patterns.

Nomenklatura. The established bureaucratic apparatus of government officials who owed their position and status to Communist Party appointment during the Soviet period. Its members remain as a legacy of the Communist system in all of the newly independent states, and they still exercise great influence over military and economic policies, and the press.

Oblast. An administrative region of the former Soviet Union (and successor states), comparable to, but often far larger than, the American county. An "autonomous oblast," however, was the homeland for a particular ethnic group. Many autonomous oblasts have declared themselves independent republics following the collapse of the USSR. *See* **Autonomous regions** and **National Delimitation Policy.**

Okrug. A small administrative subdivision of the Soviet Union. An "autonomous okrug," however, was a homeland for a small tribe or people with a population insufficient to qualify for any higher status. *See* **Autonomous regions** and **National Delimitation Policy.**

Pale of Settlement. Territory west of the Dnieper River (part of present-day Belarus, Lithuania, Poland, and Ukraine) in which most East European Jews lived and in which the Russian tsarist government sought to confine Jewish settlement. Many of the Jews who perished in the Holocaust of World War II came from this region. *See* **Pogroms.**

Peoples of the North. Small indigenous tribes inhabiting the Arctic area.

Perestroika. Broadly used term to denote Mikhail Gorbachev's policies in the 1980s for the restructuring and revitalization of Soviet society through limited political and economic reform.

Permafrost. A type of Arctic soil in which the underlying layer is permanently frozen. Permafrost is found in northern Siberia and the Russian Far East, primarily above the 64th parallel. *See* **Tundra**.

Plenum. A full meeting (assembly) of all the members of a governing body, usually with reference to the Central Committee of the Communist Party of the Soviet Union. *See* **Central Committee of the Communist Party of the Soviet Union.**

Pogroms. Acts of racist violence visited against Jewish persons and property, sometimes resulting in deaths and the forced flight of residents. This persecution of Russian Jews came to be particularly felt within the Pale of Settlement in the decades prior to World War I (e.g., the Kishinev pogrom of 1902, or the Odessa pogrom of 1905). *See* **Pale of Settlement** and **Russification.**

Politburo. The highest and most powerful group of policymakers in the Soviet Union, chosen from the membership of the Central Committee of the Communist Party. *See* **Central Committee of the Communist Party of the Soviet Union.**

Purges. A series of persecutions and trials resulting in exile or execution of Soviet citizens, both Communist Party members and others, who were accused of anti-socialist, anti-Soviet behavior by Josef Stalin and his aides. The massive Communist Party purge of 1937–38 is sometimes referred to as the Great Purge.

Red Army. The Soviet armed forces established by Vladimir Lenin under the initial leadership of Leon Trotsky in the aftermath of the 1917 Russian Revolution.

RSFSR (Russian Soviet Federated Socialist Republic). Official name of the Russian Republic during the Soviet period, renamed the Russian Federation in 1991.

Ruble zone. Those Eurasian regions and states of the former Soviet Union that continued to use the old Russian currency for monetary transactions in the early 1990s. Today the ruble zone is confined to the Russian Federation.

Russian Civil War. Lengthy struggle following the Russian Revolution of October 1917 between the new Bolshevik Red Army and the loosely organized anti-Communist White Army led by forces loyal to the Russian tsar. The battles spread throughout Russian lands to Siberia and the Far East and down to Central Asia. In spite of international assistance from Western powers, the Whites lost the war and many fled abroad to Manchuria and to Western Europe.

Russian Congress of People's Deputies. Elected in 1990, this was the highest legislative body of the Russian Republic and its successor Russian Federation prior to the new 1993 Russian constitution. Because the allocation of seats in the Russian Congress of People's Deputies was not strictly by popular ballot, the Congress reflected the disproportionate power of Communist Party and other institutional representatives of the former Soviet Union. The standing Russian Parliament, or Russian Supreme Soviet, was chosen from the ranks of this Russian Congress of People's Deputies. In between sessions of the Congress, the Russian Supreme Soviet served as a standing Parliament. The Russian Congress of People's Deputies should not be confused with the All-Union Congress of People's Deputies, which passed out of existence with the collapse of the Soviet Union. The Russian Congress of People's Deputies, as well as the Supreme Soviet, has been superceded by the parliamentary duma created under the 1993 constitution. *See* **Duma, Supreme Soviet** and **All-Union Congress of People's Deputies.**

Russian Revolution. The Russian Revolution of 1917 was actually two revolutions, the first occurring in March with the overthrow of the tsar and the coming to power of a "Provisional Government." The second revolution took place in October when the Bolshevik faction of the Russian Social Democratic Workers' Party, under the leadership of Vladimir Lenin, seized control of the government. These revolutions, commonly linked as the Russian Revolution of 1917, should not be confused with the Russian Revolution of 1905 which resulted in the creation of Russia's first popularly elected parliament.

Russian Social Democratic Workers' Party (RSDRP). Early Marxist political party, formally founded in 1898, from which there emerged the revolutionary leadership of the Bolsheviks and Mensheviks. *See* **Bolsheviks** and **Mensheviks.**

Russification. Dating particularly to the last quarter of the nineteenth century, there were sustained efforts in the Russian Empire, occasionally with use of force, to assimilate non-Russian population. This Russification included language-restrictive measures in such places as Baltic, Polish, and Ukrainian territories, wherein Russian was mandated as the sole language of instruction in non-Russian schools and universities. It also included greatly reinforced efforts to convert non-Orthodox believers to Eastern Orthodox Christianity. The encouragement of Russian settlement and migration into non-Russian areas, a policy continued in the Soviet era, was also a part of this wider effort. In its most abhorrent form, Russification involved officially condoned acts of mass violence against minority Jewish residents of the Pale of Settlement, resulting in death or forcible eviction of Jews from long-standing urban and rural settlements. Russification has invariably been a nativist reaction to the multi-ethnic realities of Eurasia. *See* **Pogroms.**

Shamanism. Ancient form of religious practice common among indigenous peoples of Siberia. It features a spiritual helper or shaman who mediates between the visible and spiritual worlds. Shamans heal the sick, communicate between the living and the dead, and carry out traditional tribal ceremonies.

Sharia. Islamic religious law based on the Koran. *See* **Adat.**

Shi'ite Muslims. Followers of a form of Islam practiced in some parts of the Caucasus region and Central Asia, especially Tajikistan. Commonly associated with the type of Islam practiced in contemporary Iran, this branch of Islam takes its name from the movement that rejected the first three caliphs, and regarded Ali and his descendants as the legitimate successors to Mohammed. *See* **Sufism, Sunni Muslims,** and **Wahhabis.**

Slav. An Indo-European language grouping with origins on the great East European Plain, the Slavs are divided into at least three major linguistic subgroups—South Slavs (including the people of former Yugoslavia and the Bulgarians), West Slavs (including Poles, Czechs, and Slovaks), and East Slavs (including Russians, Belarusians, and Ukrainians). The Soviet Union and its historical antecedents, the Kievan, Muscovite, and Russian states, incorporated virtually all East Slavic lands. Within the East Slavic language subgroup, the Russian language gained special empire-wide standing because of its association with the center of political and bureaucratic authority.

Soviet. The word *sovet* in Russian means "council." The term first took on its twentieth-century political meaning during the 1905 Russian Revolution when "councils of workers' deputies" (the Soviets) organized the events leading to a general strike in St. Petersburg in October of that year. Claiming the inheritance of these workers' councils, and calling in its propaganda for "all power to the Soviets," the Bolshevik government employed the term Soviet as an integral part of the new state's name, the Union of Soviet Socialist Republics. The term Soviet also came to be used loosely as an adjective referring to the Soviet Union.

Steppe. Vegetation zone characterized by thick grasses, few trees, and rich soil. The great European steppe stretches through the heartland of modern Ukraine from the Carpathian mountains in the west to the Ural foothills in the east.

Sufism. A mystical Islamic order. The largely underground, parallel clergy of the Sufi brotherhoods offered a form of dissent to the officially recognized Islamic spiritual jurisdictions of the Soviet Union. Sufism originated in the ninth century as an anti-clerical movement whose leaders acquired great power. In the modern period, Sufism was occasionally used as a movement against Russian authority in Central Asia. Sufism requires strict obedience to the will of God as interpreted by Sufi leaders. *See* **Shi'ite Muslims, Sunni Muslims,** and **Wahhabis.**

Sunni Muslims. Followers of a form of Islamic belief prevalent throughout Central Asia, with the exception of portions of Tajikistan. Normally associated with the more moderate contemporary wing of Islam, the term takes its origin from that branch of Islam that accepts the first four caliphs as the rightful successors of the prophet Mohammed. *See* **Shi'ite Muslims, Sufism,** and **Wahhabis.**

Supreme Soviet. A term denoting the elected parliamentary or legislative body of Soviet republics and, often, their newly independent Eurasian successors (e.g., the Belarusian Supreme Soviet). The Russian Supreme Soviet was not elected directly, but was a regular standing parliament drawn from the elected Russian Congress of People's Deputies. It ceased to exist following the December 1993 election and the implementation of a new Russian constitution. *See* **Russian Congress of People's Deputies.**

Taiga. Russia's coniferous forest zone covering vast areas of Siberia.

Titular nationality. The name of the ethnic group after which a territorial entity (republic, oblast, or okrug) is named. *See* **Autonomous regions.**

Tsar, Tsarist. First associated with the name for the Russian grand prince of Moscow, the term "tsar" was drawn from the imperial Roman title, "caesar." Meant to reflect the quasi-religious, as well as obvious political, authority of the head of state, the term was used throughout the period of the Muscovite and Russian empires to refer to the Russian ruler or monarch. From the time of Peter the Great, the Russian head of state was also referred to as "emperor." The spelling of "tsar," rather than "czar," reflects prevailing Library of Congress transliteration rules.

Tundra. Fragile, treeless, permafrost zone found in the Arctic regions of northern Russia and Siberia.

Turkestan. A historical term referring to the Muslim lands of Central Asia that were annexed into the Russian Empire during the nineteenth century. Initially combined by the Bolshevik government into a single Republic of Turkestan, the area was subdivided in 1936 into the Kazakh, Kirgiz, Tajik, Turkmen, and Uzbek union republics. These union republics today form the newly independent states of Kazakhstan, Kyrgyzstan, Tajikistan, Turkmenistan, and Uzbekistan.

Uniates. Name used interchangeably with Greek Catholics. *See* **Eastern-rite Christianity** and **Greek Catholic Church.**

Union republic. One of the 15 constituent republics of the former Union of Soviet Socialist Republics (USSR).

Virgin Lands. Nikita Khrushchev's land-use program of the 1950s that sought intensive cultivation of wheat on millions of hectares in northern Kazakhstan and southern Siberia. Widespread and recurring droughts in this dry region discredited the project.

Wahhabis. The Islamic sect founded by Abdul Wahhab (1703–1792), whose followers are found in isolated regions of Central Asia. Known for their strict observance of the Koran, the Wahhabis insist upon the use of the veil for women. They have resisted both modernist and mystical interpretations of the Koran. *See* **Shi'ite Muslims, Sufism,** and **Sunni Muslims.**

INDEX